MUSIC AND THE POLITICS OF CULTURE

Music and the Politics of Culture

edited by Christopher Norris

LAWRENCE & WISHART
LONDON

Lawrence & Wishart Limited
144a Old South Lambeth Road
London SW8 1XX

First published 1989

2319/4

ML
3800
m87

Photoset in North Wales by
Derek Doyle & Associates, Mold, Clwyd
Printed in Great Britain
by Billing and Sons, Worcester

Contents

Christopher Norris

Introduction

Philosophers and purists may reject the idea that music possesses any kind of 'extra-musical' significance, any meaning beyond what is objectively *there* in the notes, the form or the structural relations that a competent listener should be able to grasp. This position has indeed found some notable advocates, from Hanslick to Stravinsky and a whole modern school of formalist critics and aestheticians. All the same it is a decidedly counter-intuitive argument, maintained against the vast majority of those – composers, performers and listeners alike – whose experience tells them otherwise. In fact it is a doctrine mostly subscribed to by conservative thinkers who want to drive a wedge between musical understanding and the wider context of worldly and socio-political concerns.

Stravinsky's *Poetics Of Music* is probably the single most extreme modern statement of a radically formalist position that attempts to expunge all traces of music's involvement with a world outside its own self-enclosed, ontologically privileged domain.[1] And as W H Auden came to regret his own youthful left-wing sympathies, so his poems increasingly aspired to the condition of music, an art of purely formal techniques and devices, one whose very nature saved it from the messy business of political commitment. 'For poetry makes nothing happen: it survives/In the valley of its saying where executives/Would never want to tamper'.[2] Music holds out the seductive ideal of a language purged of all merely temporal concerns, a language that could best live up to its own responsibilities by rejecting every claim upon the artist's political conscience. 'Only your art is pure

7

contraption', as Auden wrote in a poem addressed to the composer – Britten or Stravinsky perhaps, but implicitly any such artist whose good luck it was not to get involved, like Auden himself, in political affairs which then returned to haunt his older, wiser self. Music thus becomes the last refuge of authentic values in an age given over to the clash of competing ideologies.

The same impulse is at work in those varieties of formalist aesthetic that deny music any power to express 'extra-musical' meanings and values. One major source of such thinking is the long tradition, going back at least to Pythagoras, which assimilates music to the laws of mathematical harmony and proportion, a realm of pure knowledge ideally untouched by mere vicissitudes of time and place. Such ideas have always served as a useful means of blocking or deflecting any treatment of music in its social and political context. Thus, according to Susan McClary in a recent essay,

> from early times up to and including the present, there has been a strain of Western culture that accounts for music in non-social, implicitly metaphysical terms. But parallel with that strain is another which regards music as essentially a human, socially grounded, socially alterable construct. Most polemical battles in the history of music theory and criticism involve the irreconcilable confrontation of these two positions.[3]

Formalist thinking continues to exert a strong hold over experts and lay listeners alike because (as McClary argues) it is able to provide two different kinds of ideological reassurance. On the one hand it confirms the privileged role of those who can grasp such recondite ideas, explaining music from a standpoint outside all contingent historical interests. On the other it offers a comforting sense of mystery to those (mere amateurs or non-initiates) who know very well how music can influence their deepest feelings and convictions, but who don't want to think that such effects can be obtained through any kind of conscious or social-manipulative grasp.

> Neither priest nor consumer really wants to break that spell ...
> For if one recognises the power of music to manipulate through
> unknown means, one at least wants to believe that human hands
> are not working the controls. [And] if one is working the
> controls, one most understandably wants to deny responsibility,
> to displace it elsewhere.[4]

Thus formalism can be seen to represent in its purest, most
seductive yet coercive form that version of aesthetic
ideology that polices the boundary between experience and
knowledge, art for the consumer and art as a realm of
specialised understanding inaccessible to all but the expert.

> Both musician and layperson collude in this mystification, both
> resist establishing connections between the outside, social world
> and the mysterious inner world of music.[5]

The essays that follow all start out from an opposite
conviction. That is to say, they make a point of putting music
firmly back into its socio-political context, resisting any form
of that mystified appeal to its supposedly metaphysical,
transcendent or timeless character. Nevertheless, the
'politics of music' is a phrase capable of many interpretations, as this volume demonstrates clearly enough. It can
mean any one or any combination of the following, very
roughly schematised approaches. There is a politics of
musical production and reception, an account of the ways in
which music has been composed, performed and understood
under changing social and historical conditions. At its best
such writing negotiates the passage between several
disciplines without losing sight of their distinctive methods
and imperatives. It brings together the skills of the musical
critic with those of the cultural historian, the sociologist and
(in some cases) the student of comparative anthropology. Its
aim may be to reconstruct the values and assumptions of
some earlier epoch, as in the wide-ranging chapter by
Wilfrid Mellers on Purcell and the politics of the English
Restoration period. Or again, the critic may focus – like
Alan Durant – on contemporary modes of musical
production, on the different forms that music takes
according to its role in promoting or challenging our

normative habits of response. Ken Hirschkop raises similar questions in an essay that asks what use might be found within musical criticism for those ideas about language, ideology and discourse developed by the Soviet cultural theorist, Mikhail Bakhtin. For Bakhtin, literary history was a kind of running battle between on the one hand those 'high' traditional forms (like epic or lyric poetry) which sought to impose a single, monological voice of authority, and on the other those 'low' genres (like the novel) which sustained an open-ended dialogue or polyphony of social codes, and could thus have a powerful subversive effect upon the ruling ideology of their day.[6] Hirschkop suggests that this idea can be extended to the history of musical styles and conventions, where a kind of 'dialogism' (Bakhtin's term) often works to unsettle the established relationship between high and low genres.

To conceive of music in these terms – as a field of competing social forces, rather than a self-enclosed organic evolution of forms – might open it up to the kind of transformative understanding that would break with classical models and precedents. Among those models is the idea of musical history as a kind of unfolding destiny in sound, a process that involves the increasingly dynamic use and exploitation of tonal resources implicit in the nature of all musical experience. And this in turn gives rise to a series of questions addressed by the essays in this volume. Is tonality indeed a 'natural' resource, a constitutive aspect of music's expressive power, and one that moreover has some deep affiliation with the character of human creativity? Deryck Cooke argued as much in his classic study *The Language Of Music*, a book whose claims are here examined in an essay by the composer and critic David Matthews.[7] The main problem with such arguments is their tendency to imply that music reaches its peak of achievement only within a certain, distinctly European tradition, and then only in works that manifest the kind of intensive thematic and tonal development that lends itself to precisely this approach. And the treatment of tonality as a musical touchstone goes along with a range of associated values, notably those of organic form, of the 'classical style' and the sonata-principle as that which reconciles opposing forces through a kind of dialectical process whereby conflicts are resolved through the integrating power of long-term tonal development. The decidedly Hegelian cast of these ideas is no coincidence, given the fact that they emerged among German theorists, critics and philosophers in the period of late-romantic aesthetic speculation. In effect, they provide a set of legitimising values and grounds for precisely that kind of music wherein German romanticism found its elective homeground.

One idea especially – that of organic form – became the very hallmark of aesthetic theory in the wake of German romanticism.[8] And it is a concept that has persisted down to the present day, in alliance with a version of musical history that foregrounds those composers, from Bach to Beethoven, Brahms, Wagner and beyond, whose music can be heard as a progressive working-through of the dynamic possibilities inherent in the nature of tonality. The essays in this volume go various ways around to question the values, aesthetic and historical, bound up with this way of thinking. Some contributors – Lionel Pike among them – continue to work on the premise that music is indeed a 'language of the emotions', and tonality the single most basic resource that enables such emotions to find an adequate thematic and structural form. But it is also very clear from his detailed analysis of Robert Simpson's Tenth Quartet that Pike sees tonality, not as a 'natural' language imposing its own quasi-organic laws of development, but more in terms of its capacity to change our conventional habits of perception. Thus he finds it altogether appropriate, in a work dedicated to the ideal of peace, that Simpson should explore regions of harmonic and tonal contrast that don't so much exploit the more aggressive, dramatic or conflictual aspects of sonata-form development. Pike's essay stands as a striking example of how close analysis can always go along with a keen sense of the social meanings that inform every aspect of musical language and style.

Other contributors examine the ways in which music has been enlisted in the service of ideological values or political creeds. This process takes one particular form in the kind of

pervasive mythology built up around figures like Elgar and
Delius, composers whose music is felt to represent some
quality of 'Englishness' that defies analysis but somehow
informs every note of their work. Meirion Hughes's essay
shows how Elgar himself came to live out this mythology in
his social and professional career; how his music not only
'reflected the mood of its time' but served to articulate its
conflicts and tensions, along with the deeply felt need for
some assertion of national and class identity against those
threatening forces of upheaval. And in the case of Delius, as
Robert Stradling argues, we can see how that same ideology
of 'Englishness' lays claim to a composer whose music, on
the face of it, resists assimilation to any one national school.
In short, there was an effort – at whatever 'unconscious'
level – to ignore the cosmopolitan sources and influences so
clearly at work in Delius's music, and to annex that music to
an English tradition which alone held the key to its elusive
innermost character.

The approach here adopted by Stradling and Hughes has
been developed mainly by literary theorists and workers in
the field of cultural studies. Their interest has focused
primarily on topics like the 'rise of English studies' and the
way that canonical readings feed back into the sense of a
unified cultural tradition, a sense informed by those same
(often tacit) values and assumptions that define what shall
count as truly great works of literature.[9] In music likewise,
the process often works to exclude or discount any challenge
to received ways of thinking, especially where this challenge
is mounted in overtly political terms. Thus Paul Harrington
reminds us that composers like Holst and Vaughan Williams
– the second generation of the so-called 'English
renaissance' – were in fact strongly socialist in political
leaning, a point that is very often lost to view through the
general concern to establish their credentials as authentically
native figures. And so there develops that powerful
mythology of Englishness, a sense of deep-laid cultural
character and destiny somehow manifest in musical form. As
always, the result of this hegemonic drive is to repress or to
marginalise any sense of the conflicts, the divided loyalties
and class-affiliations that affect a composer's work. Thus

music becomes a most effective means of preserving tradition – one particular tradition – against any threat from social forces beyond its power to contain or control. And the same kinds of pressure may be brought to bear on contemporary music by subjecting it to misconceived styles of performance that manage to efface its more challenging or 'difficult' aspects.

One exemplary case of such treatment was the 1985 West German première of Alexander Goehr's opera *Behold the Sun*. This work grew out of Goehr's fascination with the history of utopian and millenarian thought, in particular the 16th century Anabaptist rising at Münster, an episode that ran the all-too-familiar course from noble beginnings to an upshot that mixed high tragedy with brutal farce. The opera has a quite extraordinary depth and range of dramatic statement and bears impressive witness to Goehr's powers as an analyst of present-day cultural politics, as well as the problems that face any serious composer who attempts to take account of them in musical terms. It draws on a great variety of sources, some of them historical (like Norman Cohn's *The Pursuit of the Millenium*), others deriving from the long tradition of utopian-speculative thought whose modern summa is Ernst Bloch's great work *The Principle of Hope*. It manages to express both the deep disenchantment that comes of so many promising revolutions betrayed, sidetracked, turned into a grim parody of their own aspirations, and a sense of the abiding utopian impulse that somehow survives these temporal setbacks. Together with his Reith lectures of 1988 it shows Goehr as one of the few modern composers who have (in Nietzsche's words) suffered the destiny of music in our time like an 'open wound', as matter for intensely serious thought at both a creative and an intellectual level. But the première of the opera captured little of this, as Nicholas Williams recounts in his chronicle of the events surrounding that ill-starred performance. The work was subject to cuts, revisions and gratuitous changes of emphasis whose effect – whether deliberate or not – was to muffle its political point and reduce it to a sequence of set-piece operatic scenes. One need not be a victim of left paranoia or hooked on conspiracy theories to perceive something deeply symptomatic in this whole unfortunate episode.

There are similar lessons to be drawn from the way that Shostakovich's music has been pressed into service at the bidding of cold-war ideological aims and imperatives.[10] Anything that sounds, to the innocent ear, like straightforward Socialist Optimism can always be treated as an episode of forced rejoicing crude enough to deceive the idiot Party watchdogs but grasped straight away by sharp-eared Western critics. This technique had already been developed to a high point of subtlety before it found triumphant confirmation in the Shostakovich 'memoirs', purportedly transcribed from conversation and faithfully edited by the émigré Soviet musicologist, Solomon Volkov.[11] The result – among record reviewers especially – has been to canonise those performances that lay the greatest stress on elements of irony, covert double-meaning, cryptic ambiguity or whatever, and to treat as merely naive or superficial any reading that fails to register such sentiments. Quite simply, if the music is to prove its moral worth then it *must* exhibit, at every point, a muttering undertow of suppressed ironic comment. The logic of this position is nicely revealed in one critic's remark (concerning a record of the Fifth Symphony) that 'the triumph of the coda seems hollow, its exultation bitterly false – and the symphony gains in stature thereby'.[12] And of course the same logic works to opposite effect in the case of those performances that fail to uncover such a complicating sub-text and treat the music as a hard-won affirmation of socialist hopes and ideals. That Shostakovich himself once took such a view is of course beside the point now that we *know* (thanks to Volkov) that everything he said and wrote during his lifetime was a double-edged message to posterity. It has long been a favourite ploy among literary critics to domesticate otherwise disturbing or subversive texts by discovering subtle ironies at work, thus allowing them to 'mean' more or less whatever the critic would wish to read into them. The same trick of thought is often applied – albeit in a less self-conscious or systematic fashion – by Western commentators on Shostakovich. Malcolm Barry's essay here sets out both to redress the historical record and to grasp what is at stake when music is subjected to such pressures of political and ideological circumstance.

Claire Polin explores some current varieties of alternative (counter-hegemonic) music in her essay on 'The Politics of Minimalism'. Here also there is a challenge to those ruling ideas that have shaped our sense both of musical history (as a sequence of progressively evolving masterworks) and of musical form (as the inward, 'organic' process by which those works achieve such pre-eminent status). Polin doesn't draw any specific implications for a feminist musical aesthetics. But her claims might well be extended to suggest that the very marginality of woman's role in a male-dominated order gives her a particularly keen sense of whatever may disturb or disrupt that order. As John Shepherd writes in a recent essay on 'Music and Male Hegemony':

> Music reminds men of the fragile and atrophied nature of their control over the world. The male fear of women is mirrored in the threat posed by uncontrollable musical experience to the 'moral fibre' of the rationalistic scribe-state ... [and so] the answer has been to isolate those components, pitch and rhythm, which can be objectified and frozen through a 'fully analytic' notation ... This parallels the way in which a material and notational control is exercised over processes fundamental to the creation of people and the reproduction of culture in general.[13]

Shepherd's argument, very briefly, is that the division of experience enforced by these gender-roles is reproduced in music as the split between notated and non-notatable elements, and that the latter – principally qualities of timbre and other such 'subjective' nuances – can none the less achieve a degree of liberation from the forces of social control. Thus

> the existence of music, like the existence of women, is potentially threatening to men to the extent that it (sonically) insists on the social relatedness of human worlds and as a consequence implicitly demands that individuals respond.[14]

This connects on the one hand with what Polin has to say about the more progressive aspects of minimalist art, and on the other with Shepherd's explicit challenge to the male-dominated values and prerogatives of present-day musical culture.

One could, however, take a very different view of the whole minimalist phenomenon, one that would treat it (in Adorno's terms) as the furthest point yet reached in that trend toward 'regressive' or stultified habits of response engendered by the modern culture-industry.[15] Minimalism would then represent a facile escape-route from the problems and complexities of authentic musical experience into a realm of naive, uncritical pleasure that merely reproduces the dominant patterns of present-day cultural consumption. And indeed, as Claire Polin herself concedes, there is an aspect of the minimalist enterprise that does give grounds for such a negative assessment. Its proponents may claim that this music achieves a decisive break with the forms and conventions of Western (post-classical) tradition; that it offers an alternative, participatory mode of musical experience where old distinctions at last fall away, not only between composer, performer and audience but also at the level of harmonic structure and development. Minimalism could then be seen, along with other forms of 'postmodern' art, as an overcoming of the conflicts and antinomies that characterised all forms of cultural expression under the sway of a dominant (bourgeois-capitalist) system of social relations. But one could just as well pursue Adorno's diagnosis to exactly the opposite conclusion: that the minimalist aesthetic is one more instance of a massively generalised cultural regression, a part of the process whereby music is deprived of its genuine critical edge and listening reduced to a species of mindless, preconditioned stimulus-response. Thus art is transformed 'into a lubricant for the system, ... into untruth, or into goods for the culture-industry calculated for the consumer'.[16]

For Adorno, the last hope of resisting such pressures was by way of a rigorous immanent critique, an account of how music might yet express the truths of present-day existence, but express them in exactly that indigent, distorted form that would bring out the extent of our alienated condition. And the only works that Adorno found adequate to this purpose were those, like Schoenberg's, which effectively revoked the promise of an earlier, affirmative music; which showed how that promise had been falsified in the event, so that only a kind of inhuman concentration on matters of style and technique could express the full truth of this predicament. 'These works are magnificent in their failure ... It is not the composer who fails in the work; history, rather, denies the work in itself.'[17] Any music that failed to address this situation – that avoided the passage through a radical critique of the classical style and its humanist values – could only be treated as an adjunct to the process of cultural commodification. If Adorno found symptoms of exactly this vicious pandering to fashion in Stravinsky's neo-classical style, one can imagine how the present-day minimalist productions would have served to confirm his gloomiest forecasts.

Alastair Williams takes this as one of his starting-points for an exploration of the ways in which contemporary music is seeking a path beyond the stark alternatives posed by Adorno's diagnosis. In Ligeti he finds the most striking example of a music that has indeed carried through such a process of self-imposed immanent critique, but which yet succeeds in emerging with a sense of renewed creative possibility. Williams has some pertinent things to say about the connection between Adorno's 'negative dialectics' and the current mode of deconstructionist philosophy and literary theory. Both are too easily misconstrued as expressions of a last-ditch nihilist outlook, closing off all prospects of a meaningful encounter with past and present cultural forms. I take up a related line of argument in my essay on Ernst Bloch, the Marxist utopian and visionary thinker for whom music figured allegorically as a source of redemptive hopes and aspirations. In particular, my essay questions the idea of Bloch and Adorno as antagonistic thinkers, the one staking everything on a secular eschatology, a vision of redeemed future promise, the other relentlessly subjecting such claims to the rigours of negative critique. As in Williams's argument this simplified opposition is rejected, and I locate some of those moments in Bloch where utopian thinking holds out against the lures of false or premature hope; also, conversely, those passages where Adorno asserts that neither music nor philosophy can carry on without at least some residual faith in better things to come.

The reader will have gathered by now that the essays in this volume are united by no single creed, ideology or line of approach. But they do converge on the point addressed very briefly in this last paragraph: that in the end it is mistaken to draw a sharp line between 'negative' and 'positive' approaches, modes of understanding that seek to demystify received ideas about music, and those that hold out some ultimate faith in music's power to transcend such limiting perspectives. Above all, they are agreed in rejecting that form of still potent aesthetic ideology which insists that music and politics just don't mix, or that any attempt to treat music in political terms is at best a mere footnote to the history of transient tastes and ideas.

> The *quid pro quo* of progress and reaction makes orientation in contemporary art almost as difficult as in politics, and furthermore paralyses production itself, where anyone who clings to extreme intentions is made to feel like a backwoodsman, while the conformist no longer lingers bashfully ... but hurtles forward, rocket-powered, into the pluperfect.[18]

Adorno's words find ample confirmation in the current state of musical criticism, theory and aesthetics. These essays represent at least a common desire to clear away some of the sources of confusion.

Notes

[1] Igor Stravinsky, *Poetics of Music*, (trans Arthur Knodel and Ingolf Dahl), Harvard University Press, 1947.

[2] W H Auden, 'In Memory of W B Yeats', in *Selected Poems*, Faber 1979, p 82.

[3] Susan McClary, 'The Blasphemy of Talking Politics during Bach Year', in Richard Leppert and Susan McClary (eds), *Music And*

Society: the politics of composition, performance and reception, Cambridge University Press 1987, pp 13-62; 15.

[4] *Ibid*, p 17.

[5] *Ibid*, p 17.

[6] See for instance Mikhail Bakhtin, *The Dialogic Imagination,* Michael Holquist (ed), University of Texas Press 1981.

[7] Deryck Cooke, *The Language Of Music,* Oxford University Press, 1962.

[8] For a brief account of this metaphor and its genealogy, see G S Rousseau, *Organic Form: an ideology in literature,* Routledge and Kegan Paul, 1973.

[9] See especially Peter Widdowson (ed), *Re-Reading English,* Methuen 1981, and Chris Baldick, *The Social Mission Of English Criticism,* Clarendon Press, 1983.

[10] On this topic, see Christopher Norris (ed), *Shostakovich: the man and his music,* Lawrence & Wishart, 1982.

[11] Solomon Volkov, *Testimony: the memoirs of Shostakovich,* Hamish Hamilton, 1979.

[12] See the present author's letter, 'Ambiguous Shostakovich', in *Gramophone,* February 1983, p. 892. The issue was taken up by several correspondents and has since then rumbled on, as a muted but audible subtext, in various reviews of Shostakovich recordings.

[13] John Shepherd, 'Music and Male Hegemony', in Leppert and McClary (eds), *Music And Society,* op cit, pp 151-72; 158.

[14] *Ibid*, p 158.

[15] See especially T W Adorno, *Philosophy Of Modern Music* (trans. Anne G Mitchell and Wesley V Blomster), Sheed and Ward, 1973 and *Aesthetic Theory* (trans. C Lenhardt), Routledge and Kegan Paul 1984. The best introductory study is Martin Jay, *Adorno,* Fontana, 1984.

[16] T W Adorno, 'Culture And Administration', *Telos,* No 37 (1978), p 101.

[17] Adorno, *Philosophy Of Modern Music, op cit,* p 99.

[18] Adorno, *Minima Moralia* (trans. E F N Jephcott), New Left Books 1974, p 219.

Wilfrid Mellers

The Heroism of Henry Purcell: Music and politics in Restoration England

In 1710 Roger North, antiquarian and music historian, published an account of English music as it had evolved during his lifetime. Throughout the turbulent 17th century the tradition of string consort music had provided a precarious lifeline; and of this tradition perhaps the most distinguished, and certainly the longest lived, representative was John Jenkins, who began his career as a servant of the first Elizabeth, and ended it at the court of Charles II. North, with benevolent condescension, complains that Jenkins's music, though more 'airy' (he meant tuneful) than some, was still not airy enough:

> He was a great Reformer of Musick in his Time, for he got ye better of ye dulnesse of ye old Fancyes, and introduced a Pleasing Aire in everything he composed ... But to do right in showing what was Amisse in ye manner of Mr Jenkins, It was wholly devoid of Fire and Fury, such as the Italian Musick affects, in their Stabbs and Stoccatas, which Defect is only excusable on ye Humour of ye Times, which These will not bear.

Indeed they could not, for the Restoration was not a restoration of old values. Politically, the brilliant Earl of Halifax summed matters up when he wrote in his wry prose: 'When people contend for Liberty, they seldom get anything by their Victory but new Masters'. Culturally, Bishop Spratt, in his history of the Royal Society, founded in 1667 as the artifactor of the scientifically orientated future, remarked that 'if our Church should be Enemy to Commerce, intelligence, discovery, Navigation, and any sort of Mechanicks, how could it be fit for the present Genius of the nation?' Of course it couldn't; the pristine world of the early Caroline court, obliterated by the War, was not recoverable.

Neither Court nor Country won the War. If anyone did, it was the City, since with the growth of scientific enquiry, England was becoming 'a nation of shopkeepers'. The shift towards commerce was naturally associated with the rapid growth of London, the capital city to which at least eight thousand people a year gravitated, whether driven by poverty or lured by the prospect of material gain. Though Britain still had an agrarian economy – as late as 1688 80 per cent of the five and a half million inhabitants of England and Wales were still dependent on the land – the winds of change were blowing ever more briskly. From 1660 onwards even the gentry expected to spend a few weeks each year in London; for the increasingly potent middle classes the centrality of the capital, given relatively easier communications, could promote greatly enlarged earnings for the clever or lucky few. The expanding export and import trade – bartering wool, traditional source of English wealth, for the exotic resources contingent on institutions such as the East India Company – was fashioning an acquisitive society in many ways comparable with our own. The seeds of Britain's might as an industrial nation were sown; Christopher Hill tells us that as early as 1640 it was already producing three times as much coal as the rest of Europe put together. Thirty years later mercantile adventure (and sometimes misadventure) had become unstoppable.

Exceptional fortunes were made, and since status is manifest in styles of living, this directly affected the arts. Artists themselves became commodities – social acquisitions to the new (even more than the old) rich. Both private individuals and public institutions such as the universities and the Inns of Court were now more active than the

Church, the traditional patron, as promoters of the arts. 'Conspicuous consumption' by businessmen, attorneys, and doctors, as well as minor gentry, fostered the building of the City churches and civic halls, and encouraged pageantry and artistic ostentation at 'shows' for Lord Mayors. Book publication expanded by way of subscription lists; new theatres were erected and old ones enlarged. Public concerts – as distinct from performances at home, Court or in Church – first occurred in 1677-78, financed significantly, by Thomas Britton, a small-coals merchant of Clerkenwell. Concerts in taverns and coffee-houses mushroomed in their wake, affording a means whereby middle class merchants and small gentry could emulate the nobility.

The traditional centres of church music, the Chapel Royal and Westminster Abbey, declined in importance, though they still served as nursing-ground for a Blow and Purcell. At the time of the accession of Charles II they had been stimulated by the French and Italian theatrical fashions which the King relished; but they lapsed back into conservative inertia when such music found its natural home in the burgeoning theatres themselves: into which the mainstream of music was now directed. At a fashionable commercial level theatre meant plays enlivened with incidental music, and 'operas' which were closer to what we call musicals than to 'grand' opera. At a lower, still commercial, level theatre meant music for chatting, eating, drinking and dancing to in coffee-houses and public places where one-time rural folk tunes could be metrically marshalled and tonally tidied to make jolly ballads. Some of these 'Pleasant new Playhouse Tunes' were eventually collected in Playford's immensely successful *English Dancing Master* of 1690. 'Lillibulero', originally a rural folk song, became an urban political pop song because its melody was instantly memorable and readily adaptable to doggerel. Pop songs – as compared with real folk songs – then as now called for a measure of theatrical projection, even if at a low level. In all areas the number of professional performers, both musical and theatrical, strikingly increased. This was only to be expected, since music and drama were now commodities that needed to be exhibited in order to be sold.

Although this brought profit – not merely in a pecuniary scnsc – as well as loss, it also encouraged the moral values, or non-values, of the smart alec. John Locke, whose lucid prose was so well-honed a tool for the propagation of the new scientifically rational philosophy, deprecated the study of music – 'often in such odd company' – by the young on the grounds that it wasted time better spent on the acquisition of useful knowledge. We may detect here the first stirring of an attitude that, a century later, will prompt Dr Burney to define music as 'an Innocent Luxury, unnecessary indeed to our Existence, but a great Improvement and Gratification of the sense of Hearing'. This changing approach to music has a parallel in the field of religion. John Aubrey reported that 'old wives' tales, spooks and phantoms' vanished when the wars brought 'liberty of Conscience and of Inquisition'; now 'even children fear no such things'. Magic was still toyed with, but gamesomely. When an astrologer offered his services to Charles II, the Merry Monarch took him to Newmarket to spot the winners.

It is not therefore surprising that although Charles II wanted to emulate the absolutist glories of the Sun King across the Channel, and sent his artists to study in France, they were for the most part unable to inform grandiosity of manner with grandeur of spirit. Both the moral core and the sense of stylisation were lacking; when Dryden, superb as satirist and as re-creative translator, assayed the Heroic as tragic dramatist, it was with disillusioned wishful thinking rather than conviction. The conflict between the veracities of private passion and the necessities of public duty – the heart of Corneille and Racine – was abandoned. What mattered was the display of simulated emotions exhibited by characters faced with synthetic moral choices. A tragedy of simulation and dissimulation is a contradiction in terms. Since comedy could, and did, flourish on deceit, it worked more effectively in the Restoration theatre – though, apart from Congreve, none of the dramatists achieved, or even attempted, anything like Molière's comedy of manners *and* morals.

The spirit of the age is illuminated in this passage in Congreve's *Love for love*, (1695) wherein Valentine feigns madness:

It's a Question that would puzzle the Arithmetician, if you
should ask him whether the Bible saves more Souls in
Westminster-Abby, or damns more in *Westminster-Hall*; for my
part, I am *Truth*, and cannot tell: I have very few Acquaintance.
   Pray what will be done at Court?
Scandal will tell you; I am *Truth*, I never come there.
   In the City?
Oh, Prayers will be said in empty Churches, at the usual Hours.
Yet you will see such zealous Faces behind *Counters*, as if
Religion were to be Sold in every *Shop*. Oh, things will go
methodically in the City, the Clocks will strike Twelve at Noon,
and the Horn'd Herd Buzz in the Exchange at Two. Wives and
Husbands will drive distinct *Trades*, and Care and Pleasure
separately occupy the Family. Coffee-Houses will be full of
Smoak and Stratagem.

Charles II was himself an arch-representative of Congreve's
'Way of the World' Some of the musical consequences of
this are evident when, in *Love for love*, the servant Jeremy,
asked whether he likes music, replies 'Yes, I have a
reasonable good Ear, Sir, as to Jiggs and Country Dances;
and the Like; I don't much matter your *Solo's* and *Sonata's*,
they give me the Spleen'. That expression of the Plain Man's
taste accords with that of the monarch himself. Roger North
tells us that whereas Charles I and Cromwell alike loved
music, Charles II had an 'utter Detestation' of fancies, and

> never could endure any Musick that he could not Act by
> keeping the time, which made the common Andante or els the
> Step Tripla ye only musicall styles at Court in his time. And
> after ye manner of France he sett up a Band of 24 Violons to
> play at his Dinners, which disbanded all ye old English Musick
> at once. He was a lover of *slight songs*, and endured ye
> accompanying very well, providing he could beat the time.
> Once he was invited by Sir J.W. to hear some English musick,
> who was not a little rediculed for his paines, and as to Skill he
> used to despise it & say Have I not Eares, to Judge as well as
> anyone?

The sardonic Halifax documented the Character of this
King who Knew What He Liked when he wrote:

> The Familiarity of his Wit must needs have the Effect of *lessening* the Distance fit to be kept to him ... Formality is sufficiently revenged upon the World for being so unreasonably laughed at; it is destroyed, it is true, but it hath the spiteful Satisfaction of seeing everything destroyed with it. Where Wit will run continually the Spring is apt to fail; so that it groweth Vulgar, and the more it is practised, the more it is debased.

That sounds – since 'L'Etat c'est Moi' – like a portrait of the society as well as of the King. Of course the shift from old world to new is not all loss. Although North's reference to the 'common Andante' and the 'Step Tripla' is disparaging, that technical development had a positive aspect, reflecting the (necessary) triumph of the humanist's 'corporeal' metre at the expense of the Churchman's 'spiritual' rhythm. Charles II's passion for the new (Italian and especially French) music was genuinely modern and, in its fashionable terms, modernistically genuine. But it surrendered too much. The equilibrium between positive and negative forces which characterises the mind of *England* in the closing decades of the century is most deeply revealed where one might most expect to find it – in the work of the Restoration composer most conspicuously endowed with genius. Although Henry Purcell was in the vanguard of Progress, his greatness lies in the fact that his music reveals realities that his age (and Charles II as its representative) preferred to ignore or evade.

Born in 1659, on the eve of the Restoration, Purcell produced at the age of twenty a series of works written as exercises in an archaic style, that of the string fancy which, as we've noted, had been a lifeline throughout those war-ravaged years. Like those of Gibbons, Ferrabosco and Jenkins, Purcell's fancies start as instrumentalised fugato. Indeed the last of them, the five-part fantasia 'on one note', is a swan-song of the old convention; the technique of the *In Nomine*, in turn derived from the medieval *cantus firmus*, is carried to its ultimate: the 'firm song' has become one continuous note. At the same time the augmented intervals and cumulating false relations in this piece – and still more in the fourth four-part fancy in C minor – anticipate the more melancholic passages in Purcell's operas; and although the rhythmic independence of the parts is a legacy from vocal polyphony, the physical animation of the quick sections resembles Purcell's later dance music for the Restoration theatre.

For, despite his roots in England's past, Purcell was a passionate modernist. Our music, he believed,

> is yet in its Nonage, a forward Child, which gives Hope of what it may be hereafter in England, when the Masters of it shall find more Encouragement. 'Tis now learning Italian, which is its best Master, and studying a little of the French Air, to give it more of Gayety and Fashion. Thus being further from the Sun, we are of later Growth than our Neighbour Countries, and must be content to shake off our Barbarity by degrees.

Purcell was quick to follow these precepts, for he soon embarked on the composition of trio sonatas for two violins and continuo, on the model of 'famed Corelli', who had codified the formula into a microcosm of the techniques of Italian baroque opera. 'English' false relations and sobbing appoggiaturas imbue Purcell's trio sonatas with an ardour earthier than that of Italian Corelli or French Couperin; in apparent paradox, the modernity of the music springs from its being, as Roger North put it, 'Clogg'd with somewhat of an English Vein'. Although Purcell is indeed heroic, his heroism, being that of a man of the English Restoration, is invaded by a touch of brash animality and sexual swagger.

This one can detect even in his treatment of the *notes inégales* which English music borrowed from French. In France unequal durations were not written out because they were too subtle for notation. The English version, with sharply pointed dots, is more frequently notated and sounds more aggressive – the plain man's conscious assertion of superiority; whereas Couperin simply knew he was superior. Purcell's two-part counterpoint, in the violin parts of his sonatas, maintains the 'thew and sinew' of English string polyphony; the dance music prances in physical gestures; and he offers his own very English version of the rhetoric of the Italian voice, riddled with Roger North's 'Stabbs and Stoccatas'.

An opera, or at least a theatre, composer was thus already latent in Purcell's early instrumental works. Theatrical ambition had no doubt been fuelled by his acquaintance with the stage music of his immediate predecessors, notably Matthew Locke (1621-1677) and his own teacher John Blow (1649-1708). Locke had started out as an ecclesiastical musician at Exeter Cathedral. At Exeter he met Charles I's French Catholic wife Henrietta Maria, seeking a haven of quiet with her son, later to be Charles II. Under Henrietta Maria's protection Locke eventually went to the Low Countries, became a Catholic, and returned to England in anticipation of Charles's restoration. Henceforth he was a prevailingly secular musician to a secular age. In 1653 he produced a harbinger of the Royal Restoration in the form of a masque concocted to a book by James Shirley, with musical assistance from Orlando Gibbons's second son Christopher. This piece, *Cupid and Death*, modifies masque convention in a significant way: for although resolutely monarchical even during the Interregnum, its manner is, at least until its apotheosis, not Grand but Low – closer to pantomime and music-hall than to opera.

The story, adapted from Aesop, offers a pawky commentary on the obsessive seventeenth century theme of sex and death, love and war. The protagonists, lodging at the same inn, have their bows and arrows exchanged by a mischievous Chamberlain, a representatively 'political' modern man who narcissistically thinks he can play ducks and drakes with Nature. The interchange of weapons between two forces often considered near-identical results in a series of japes congenial to smart alecs; senior citizens gallumphing in caprine cavortings and military heroes dissolving in sensual or sentimental embrace were then, as now, good for an easy guffaw. Until the apotheosis the only serious singing role is that of Nature, who passionately protests, in lyrical and often powerful arioso, against the threat she's exposed to by man's smartness and cynicism. Her ecological eloquence rouses the chorus – us the People – to poignantly harmonic lament at their (our) irresponsible destructiveness. Even Death has had enough, and shoots the Chamberlain, who had started all the trouble. The effect of the shooting is not, of course, to kill the Chamberlain, but to make him fall in love with two court apes who happened to be in his company. In playing tricks with nature, love and death, man has reduced himself to ape-like stature. Inversion reaches its nadir when the Chamberlain – having had his ape-wives ravished from him by a brutish Satyr as the antimasque comes to claim its own – attempts to hang himself. The antimasque has become the heart of the matter, pathetic as well as grotesque.

That the piece seems short-winded is part of the point: it flicks through a cinematic sequence of not very closely connected 'clips' because modern life is itself 'one damn thing after another'. Throughout, the lively, often piquantly chromatic, irregularly rhythmed dance music says what there is to say on behalf of the New Age, which comes into its own when godly Mercury descends as *deus ex machina*. Mercury saves the Chamberlain from suicide, banishes the antimasque, restores Love and Death to their proper selves and, in dialogue, regenerates Nature. He, mightier even than she, will soon tidy up the mess left by both War and Protectorate; and by the time of the repeat performance in 1659 the identification of this Mercury with Charles II has becomes the immediately practical, realistic point, without losing its philosophical implications. Just as the communal music of choric lament is truly pathetic, even incipiently tragic, so Charles-Mercury is a figure larger than life, a god as well as a man. His arioso is long, grand, even more ornately spacious than Nature's; and although he admits that even he cannot bring back to life the arbitrarily slain lovers, who are victims of that arbitrary war, he can inspire music wherein the Renaissance dream of an Arcadian paradise on earth, refashioned in the most modish French style, can seem momentarily to have come true. This is both a vision of the Elysian Fields and prophecy about the New Society. 'If this place be not heaven', sing the chorus, 'one thought can make it, And Gods by their own Wonder led mistake it'. This 'mistaking Earth for Heav'n' (Dryden's phrase) is, interestingly enough, in A major, traditionally a key of youth, newness and what we would call wish-fulfilment.

Whereas Locke was a man of the theatre John Blow was an Establishment figure associated with both the Chapel Royal and Westminster Abbey. Nonetheless he owes his place in history to the fact that, making a 'masque for the King's Entertainment', he unwittingly effected the crucial transition from masque into opera. Two thirds of his *Venus and Adonis* celebrate the Arcadian revels of lovers who, in those presumptive Elysian Fields, pretend they 'haven't a care in the world'. What brings them to *life* is again, in English paradox, the fact of *death*: for only when Adonis has been slain by the boar – who may be his own 'blind' lust – does Venus apprehend the reality of love. *Cupid and Death*, shuffling around this knowledge, had defused it in satire; Blow, when his Venus sings 'Alas, Death's sleep thou art too young to take', attains tragic awareness. Her ululations – Lombard sobs that become almost screams – are emotional torment that finds relief in physical gesture without ceasing to be music. She is really heart broken – by what she had intended to be a frivol. Her mental state is marvellously reflected in the string postlude, with its hesitant, limping rhythm, like a bird with a broken wing.

Blow's *Venus and Adonis*, produced in 1683, must have been in Purcell's mind when in 1689 he received an invitation to make a theatre piece for his friend Josias Priest's school for young ladies. He cannot have realised how significant an event this was to prove: whereas Blow's *Venus* was conceived as a masque and turned into an opera fortuitously, *Dido and Aeneas* was designed by Nahum Tate as a spoken heroic tragedy which, musicked by Purcell, became more not less dramatic, since the music revealed the true passions behind the rhetorical facade. *Dido* is Purcell's only real opera on the traditional heroic theme of the clash between public and private morality. That it is not a grandiloquent court ritual but a miniature affair lasting about an hour, intended for performance by adolescent girls, is not the frustration it might seem: for the intimate scale of the piece is the condition of its truth. *Because* Purcell lived in a community unable to encompass the Heroic as exemplified in Louis XIV's France, he was able to invert conventional values and to equate Dido's instinctive nature – her 'love' – with her heroism – whereas patriarchal Aeneas's 'Empire' is a deceit. He has a 'poor' part, with no aria, not because he was a man smuggled into a girls' school but because, in the conception of Tate and Purcell, he is a poor thing; and Dido discovers, in the savagely farcical scene in which she upbraids him as a 'Deceitful Crocodile', that it is more heroic to be a woman than a queen. After idiotic shilly-shallying, Aeneas stomps off to a tatty Empire, while Dido remains to greet solitude and death. Significantly, the only important characters apart from Dido are Belinda, a 'common' serving girl who is close enough to her mistress lightly to emulate her heroic music; and the Sorceress, who darkly emulates Dido's kind of arioso because she is the alter ego of Dido herself. In this sense Dido has both masque and antimasque within her, as to a degree we all have. The real negation within her psyche reveals the antimasque, naturalistically presented on stage, for the sham it is.

All this is anticipated and encapsulated in the overture, which sets Dido's private heroism in the context of unheroic public life. The opening slow (pavane-derived) section is Dido-music, its grandeur contained in the arching sweep of the melody and the gravity of the rhythm, its personal passion in the dissonantly sobbing and sighing harmony. The quick section embodies the public world, as in Lullian convention, only instead of being a triple-rhythmed, graciously fugued round-dance, it is now in duple time, fast and perfunctory. Though still conventionally in fugato, it is now low in manner; later we'll recognise it as a communal get-together of those middle class Restoration gossips and harridans whom Tate and Purcell call witches, and of those sailors who, like imperious Aeneas, take a 'boozy short leave of their Nymphs on the shore, while never intended to visit them more'. The evil of both witches and sailors is their triviality, which would destroy Dido because it fears her truth. In more than one sense they are *common* men and women: the bingo-playing multitude, the instant tycoons, the wide boys and social climbers who, in Restoration Britain as in ours, had come to represent the public world.

The tragic grandeur of *Dido and Aeneas* is thus not in the

public music but in the creation, in arioso, of Dido's ongoing psychological life. In her two arias, in the first and third acts, each on a ground bass, her passion itself becomes ceremonial, the ostinato pattern standing both for the social Law, against which she rebels, and Fate, which she has no choice but to accept. Her sublime final lament is a chaconne – a triple-rhythmed marriage dance which still graced the weddings of important persons. Dido, having renounced Aeneas and a Congrevean Way of the World incommensurate with her truth, commits herself to marriage with Death, though it is unclear whether she stabs herself or dies of a broken heart – a seventeenth century malady discussed in Burton's *Anatomy of Melancholy*. During her lament the chromatic ground promotes dissonances that sob and throb through the string texture, while her vocal line stabs and jabs as it rises in proud arches, culminating in a sustained high G on the words 'Remember me'. She asks us to remember her in so far as she is humanity's scapegoat; but to 'forget my pain' because that has been not only suffered but transcended. Purgation is aurally incarnate when, as Dido dies, the bass's chromatic descent spreads through the string orchestra. Her world dissolves with her, leading into a final chorus in which Cupids – at once plump fruits of sexual love and cherubic angels of the old world – chant over her an archaic 'canon four in one'. In thus honouring private experience and spiritual values at the expense of the public life, *Dido and Aeneas* discovers the heroism inherent in every man, *and especially woman*, in proportion to his or her imaginative capacity. So the opera is prophetically both democratic and feminist, and could have occurred only in a society that had *failed* to attain its patriarchally autocratic ideal.[1] This is the ultimate link between the seventeenth century and us, the implications of which are still being hammered out. The pain is not abated, though we cannot manage the heroism.

One's first instinct is to say that *Dido* is a flash in the pan, a creation of genius greater than the Restoration warranted. And it is true that the superficiality of the Restoration comedy of (mostly bad) manners as compared with Molière's, and the pasteboard heroics of the attempts of

Dryden, let alone Shadwell, to emulate Racine, have a still crasser complement in the Restoration's refurbishing of old plays by out-of-date dramatists like Shakespeare. *King Lear* with a happy-ever-after ending seems to us to betray the phonyness of the Restoration vision of the Good Life, while Purcell's *The Fairy Queen* has rather less relation to Shakespeare's *A Midsummer Night's Dream* than has a twentieth century movie musical to 'the book of the film'. Of course Purcell contributes, at the height of his powers, in 1692, some magnificent and some deeply expressive music; but this doesn't alter the fact that *The Fairy Queen* is a series of 'shows' introduced, for commercial appeal rather than as ritual ceremony, into a spoken play. Moreover, the commercial dimension wasn't even successful. The profligately expensive masques of the first Caroline period were at least paid for out of the royal coffers, being a monarch-glorifying rite of humanism as well as an entertainment. *The Fairy Queen* cost more than £3000 – an enormous sum in contemporary terms – yet failed to please the 'public' enough to make money for its sponsors.[2]

On reflection, however, such an account of Restoration musical-theatrical enterprise seems over simple. Purcell's fairy queen may be a candy floss figure compared with his Carthaginian one, but what she stands for is not all loss. The lack of a central purpose, allied to the fecundity of Purcell's invention, becomes almost a virtue; certainly, if we are ever to create a musical-theatrical convention as adequate to democracy as opera seria was to aristocratic autocracy, we will have to reckon with Purcell's flexibility. Even Shadwell's 1695 rehash of Dryden and Davenant's rehash of Shakespeare's *The Tempest*, grotesquely though it distorts Shakespeare's human and metaphysical intentions, prompts Purcell to music which, in melodic span and harmonic momentum, foreshadows the 'reasonable' control of wayward Nature typical of English Augustanism. The fully fledged da capo aria 'Halcyon days' suggests that at the time of his premature death Purcell was about to effect an intrinsically and historically crucial synthesis of Shakespearean prodigality with Handelian order.

Further evidence of this is offered by a comparison of two

of Purcell's St Cecilian Odes, one composed in 1683 near the beginning of his career, the other in 1692, towards its end. Odes to St Cecilia, patron saint of music, were fashionable in Restoration England, many poets from laureate Dryden downwards turning them out for musicking by soli, chorus and orchestra, at monarch-and-state glorifying festivities. Dryden's two St Cecilian odes, in classical baroque stanzas with intricate rhyming schemes to display man's triumphant artifice, are fine examples of public rhetorical poetry. They present Cecilia as a female Orpheus whose music effects and affects the order implicit not in an abstract godhead, but in the mechanical view of Nature. Music is the force whereby the 'jarring Atoms' cohere to make the Newtonian universe. Her order is a social analogy, for the fluctuating tensions of harmony must bow to the public ceremony of dance and to a scheme of tonality linked to dance metres. But music's function is orphic too, since a properly ordered whole promotes the fullest expression of the parts. Thus music is to be valued also for its direct effect on human conduct. The trumpet's loud clangour excites us to arms, the warbling flute makes us more amorous, the skittish violin more frisky, and so on. Indeed, the universal order is dedicated to the fulfilment of man's sensual nature. Though 'from Harmony, from Heav'nly Harmony, this Universal Frame began', it runs through 'all the Compass of the Notes' in order that the Diapason may 'close full in MAN'. Milton, in *At a Solemn Musick*, had deplored the loss of the Perfect Diapason that symbolised man's oneness with God. For Dryden the octave is synonymous with Man himself, the apex of creation. If Paradise has been Lost, the sacrifice is justified, since Man has been Found.

Purcell's 1683 ode, *Welcome to all the Pleasures*, has a text by a versifier who follows Dryden's prescription. Ostensibly it celebrates the hedonist's paradise – those endless sensual gratifications which, since sexual orgasm may be construed as a dying, seem to be independent of Time. Yet the music qualifies the buoyant message, since it is scored for slight forces – solo voices which combine to make a small chorus, with strings and continuo, like a secular verse anthem – and opens with a French overture that, in linear and harmonic density, sounds like operatic *tragedy*. The climax of the work is a heart-rending tenor aria that yearns, through gently painful upward appoggiaturas, for Eden, inviting love-as-music to become an 'innocent fire' that will 'temper the heat of desire'; while the final chorus – in E major, traditionally the key of heaven – seems to refer to a world beyond the hedonist's here and now, since it dissipates into thin air. For Purcell, the hedonist's sensual paradise is far from a Vanbrugh-like 'huge Leap of Littleness' (Pope's phrase), being as insubstantial as a masque decor, or a dream. Although the architecture of Vanbrugh's Castle Howard induces theatrical surprise and illusion, it cannot be said to hint at a spiritual heaven: as do the inconclusions of Purcell's *Dido and Aeneas* and *Welcome to all the Pleasures*.

By the time of the bigger, more fully scored St Cecilian Ode of 1692 (also to a Drydenesque hack text), Purcell's humanistic New World has garnered substance. Here the overture and dances are more sustained in their handling of 'architectural' tonality, which underlines the relation between musical and political organisation. The basic key relationships of tonic, dominant, subdominant and relative are enriched with sequential modulations; the halves of binary form answer one another like mirrors. Fugato has become a principle of unity defined by and *fitting into* the harmonic and tonal scheme, thereby demonstrating how the public weal must be the arbiter of individual destiny. The Restoration had been driven by what Hobbes called 'the perpetual and restless desire of power after power, that ceaseth only in death'. In personal terms this was the force behind Restoration sexuality; its public manifestation is in political organisation. In Purcell's late ode (though not in the earlier one), energy and order are interlaced much as they are in Dryden's tense equilibrium between colloquial speech rhythms and the metrical beat of his heroic couplet and elaborate stanzaic forms. The musical 'bar' (a prison) and the poetic 'beat' (a martial dominance) join forces to promulgate an irresistible order.

Even so, Purcell's greatness still lies in the fact that his musical planned society allows scope for the personal life – in, say, the languishing chromatics and appoggiaturas in the middle section of the Symphony. This personal element existing within the public Whole corresponds to the emanations of the private life in recitative and arioso which for Purcell, as for his Dido, is man's unaccommodated condition. The Ode's alto arioso "Tis Nature's voice' – originally sung 'with incredible graces by Mr Purcell' – begins with Nature's acoustic fact of the triad, which flowers, through sobbing suspensions and illustrative roulades, into a consummation of personal feeling. Like Dido's arioso the piece creates, before our ears and eyes, the heart of human nature, as distinct from the Nature from which we come; and to which we return when, in the monumental, near-Handelian chorus 'Soul of the World', the 'jarring Atoms' of Newtonian physics are marshalled by man's will and intellect. Man has learned, through the two falls of Satan and of Eve, to *impose* order on time and space; and although Purcell did not live to fashion a classical heroic opera, he magnificently deploys in this Ode all the techniques that will typify opera seria as practised by Handel. Handel himself later set Dryden's original St Cecilian ode in a manner indebted to Purcell, but more classically, even complacently, assured.

It is not surprising that the music of Purcell's last few years – 1692-95 – should reflect the more moderate mood and manners of the Bloodless Revolution of 1688. Constitutional monarchs still needed, or at least enjoyed, glorification. If Charles I believed unequivocally in his Divine Right and Charles II thought his Human Right sufficed so long as there was enough of it, William was depicted routing the Catholicism of James II, in the guise of Hercules the Protestant Conqueror. And William and Mary favoured a theatrical-operatic style of architecture, even in churches. French elegance and Italian opulence are tempered by Dutch sobriety, but one can say as much, to a lesser degree, of the architecture of Charles I's and Charles II's time. Petworth Chapel had a family pew designed as theatre box, with drawable curtains that showed off, rather than concealed, the noble occupants. Theatricalism promotes surprise and illusion, while the family aspect suggests domesticity. Post-second-Revolution architecture often compromises between the baroque and the decorum of the classically styled Meeting Place, which can be related, after the ostentation of Charles II, to the Puritan strain within Protestantism. Purcell himself created the noblest musical synonym for this architectural style, in the Funeral Music he wrote for the royal obsequies in 1695 – which proved to be the last year of his life as well as of Queen Mary's. It is significant that this music should be, as so often with Purcell, both retrospective and progressive – especially in the weirdly but *starkly* chromatic 'Thou knowest, O Lord'. Listening to this grand yet oddly savage elegy not merely for Queen Mary, but on the vanity of human wishes, one may well think that Purcell could not have grown into a high classical Augustan. Perhaps he died at the right, if chronologically premature, moment; like his Dido, he had to expire because the 'world' wasn't ripe for his kind of heroism.

In this context it may be pertinent that 'the last song Mr Purcell set, in his sickness' should have been a Mad Song – contributed to his incidental music for D'Urfey's typically cynical burlesque of Cervantes' *Don Quixote*, a tale itself turning on madness and illusion. D'Urfey's sexy Altisidora, as predatory as a Restoration buck, attempts to seduce the Don from his idealistic addiction to his Eternal Beloved, acting out, through her arioso-scena 'In rosy bowers', all the degrees of seventeenth century madness, specified in the score as Sullenly Mad, Mirthfully Mad, Mellancholly Mad, Fantastically Mad, to the ultimate Stark Mad, which alone can match her desperation. Technically, she alternates between arioso and dance-formalised airs, though the latter don't last long since dance's social discipline is inadequate to deal with such 'outrageous' sexual passion. That it is sexual is patent in the invocation to the God of Love and attendant Cupids, the 'rosy bowers' being incarnate in undulating chromatics, the Cupids in tripping arabesques. She is using music to 'win dear Strephon whom my Soul enjoys', and the sexual metaphor is more to the point than the reference to her soul. When she passes from Sullen into Mirthful Madness she briefly frisks in a gavotte, tripping 'like any fairy'. She's indulging in a hopeful game, but is deflated by Mellancholly Madness, leading to 'Death, cold Despair, and fateful Pain', audible in sobbing appoggiaturas low in register, and in Lombard syncopations that act out mental agony in body-gestures. 'Tempests' of passion whirl in scales, only to be effaced when her pulse slows to a dismal thumping, emulated in a Dead March in B flat minor – a fifth lower, even, than 'infernal' F minor!

That Altisidora's madness is feigned doesn't make it less frenzied, nor even less crazy in its implications. She's frantic because for her, even more than for the protagonists in *Cupid and Death*, life is without rhyme or reason because without religious sanction or social precedent. This bears on the fact that even Purcell – not merely the hack composers of his age – tends to be a bit short-winded. His prodigal invention compensates for his movements' brevity; they're soon spent unless bouyed on the Law of a ground bass, which implies habituation, whether to social convention or to the necessities of fate. In 'In rosy bowers' Purcell 'compensates' by making the last, stark-maddest section the most sustained. Having made the sex-death paradox of the frying-freezing lover basic to everything we do or fail to do, he survives by finding life *within* lunacy: an anticipation of the normalcy-lunacy inversion of our century's R D Laing. After the wildest bit of arioso ('No, no, no, I'll straight run mad'), Purcell's final section becomes almost an aria, in stable C major, very fast, but metrically regular, and with ordered sequences moving through the conventional classical baroque tonal relationships. The 'Way of the World' being itself crazy, there may be salvation in the fact that the Sauvage Man is come again, metamorphosed into a sexually predatory woman: a maenad or Bacchic Terrible Mother, inverting the 'normal' male image in the same way as Dido, as Heroine, had ousted the macho Restoration Hero. Altisidora is the dark Sorceress within Dido herself, now taking the centre of the stage.[3]

This is an apex to the lunacy that goes back to the beginning of the century and earlier. In the early years melancholy and malcontent were more than a fashion, and in Purcell's time, at the dawn of the Age of Reason, a remarkable number of talented men went crazy, the Earl of Rochester being merely the wildest and woolliest.[4] Although there is a streak of fearful farce in 'In rosy bowers', as there is in most lunacy, the effect of Purcell's music is far from the parody D'Urfey intended. It may be hyperbole when Altisidora yells that her torments are such that she is prepared to die 'a thousand deaths', since one death would, after all, suffice. Remembering the seventeenth century pun on the literal and sexual meanings of dying, however, we may take this as her madness's ultimate desperation: her lust for life is so scaredly and scarily frantic because it must be so irremediably coupled with death – a husband whom she, unlike Dido, is unwilling to accept. We in the twentieth century, likewise obsessed with sex and death as we confront *our* scientific (electronic) revolution, must find Purcell's encapsulation of his and our predicament even more forceful, and no less bewildering.

Neurasthenia is not, of course, the immediate impression given by the art of Purcell's age. It was a period of material prosperity, which nurtured a vigorous crop of native talents to sing and dance in its praise, and was rich enough to buy more from foreign parts, especially France, Germany and Italy. But they all celebrated the resplendent facade; whereas Purcell's genius saw behind it. Without being in the least priggish about his jaunty age – he was a master of the low musics from beer-garden caper to bawdy-house catch in which it revelled – he foresaw, having created his Dido, an alternative destiny, more hopeful, though undeniably tragic. His own strength and exuberance he discovered in a Dido-like acceptance, not evasion, of 'the pain of consciousness'; and in this there is no peer composer to warrant comparison with him. Nor is there a worthy literary parallel, for Dryden as public poet and Congreve as socially satirical dramatist lack the tragic sense and the spiritual dimension that in Purcell were allied to, though not a product of, the long tradition of Anglican vocal polyphony and domestic consort music for strings.

Perhaps the only valid comparison with Purcell is offered by Sir Christopher Wren, whose greatness is classical and baroque in a way as odd as Purcell's. The Great Fire was an end that might also have been a beginning. Dryden in *A Secular Masque* – the title may mean that although all masques are secular this one, at this moment in history, is acutely so – wrote off the Restoration with the words:

> The Wars brought nothing about;
> The Lovers are all untrue.
> 'Tis well an Old Age is out,
> And time to begin a new.

The poem was published in 1700, the year of Dryden's death, and of the turn into the new century. When Wren rebuilt London after the Fire he fused the High Baroque flamboyance of Vanbrugh with the 'practical' Augustan classicism of Hawkesmoor and Talman, restraining grandeur of ambition by that awareness of democratic realities which led him to remark that 'in our Reformed Religion it would seem vain to make a Parish Church larger, than that all who are present can both hear and see'. This complements Purcell's synthesis of grandeur of spirit with respect for practical necessities in the making of music for any occasion. Both Wren and Purcell achieved a British compromise between Court and Country, Church and Parliament, Religion and Science. Wren lived to make that compromise the basis for a great ongoing tradition of British architecture, which Purcell failed to establish for music. Even so, the compromise that Purcell effected is still the key to our future, should we have one. Non racist, non sexist democracy, though an unrealisable ideal, remains the best we have.

Notes

[1] The uniqueness of Purcell's Dido lies in her being a female Hero to a male hero who is a non-value and inoperative; whereas the Aeneas of Purcell's source, Virgil, is of course one of the most illustrious heroes ever, torn by an equally weighted conflict between two positives, Love and Duty. When classical dramatists have a tragic heroine as central figure they usually give her a touch of the sorceress and Terrible Mother. This is true of Racine's Phèdre, and more obviously of Lully's Armide, not to mention Circe. Purcell's Dido has a sorceress within her, as noted, but this only makes her a more 'real' heroine, not one less 'good'. Operatic tragic heroines who may be accepted at face value, as complements to male

heroes, begin to appear with democratic Enlightenment: perhaps incipiently in Rameau, certainly in Gluck's Eurydice and Iphigenia – though not his Armide, who is a more psychologically probing descendent of Lully's.

It may be worth noting that there is a superficial, sociological manifestation of the feminism which Purcell's Dido profoundly reveals in the fact that during his time women began to compete with men as poets, dramatists and novelists, if not as composers. Female poets and composers had flourished sporadically in the closed circles of Renaissance courts; professional singing actresses like Mrs Bracegirdle were, however, a new phenomenon: as was a figure such as Mrs Aphra Behn, who not only competed with men as dramatist and novelist in a commercial world, but did so with conspicuous success.

[2] The economic motive for the introduction of 'shows' is pointed by Pierre Motteux's apology for his play *Beauty in distress*: which lacks 'all the Things that now recommend a Play most to the Liking of the Many. For it has no Singing, no Dancing, no Mixture of Comedy, no Change of Scene, no Rich Dresses, no Show, no Rants, no Similes, no Battle, no Killing on the Stage, no Ghost, no Prodigy'.

[3] The virginally radiant Emma Kirkby's singing of Altisidora's Song is very curious in effect, even a shade kinky. Dido's part was of course written for a school-girl, and although a school-girl cannot be ripe for heroism, a certain pathos may spring from an adolescent performance, if deeply felt. Altisidora, however, would have been sung in the professional theatre by a professional singing actress such as the aptly named Mrs Bracegirdle referred to above. She earned fame as the first Millament, whom she played with appropriate vivacity. She was also a trained singer capable of negotiating the demanding vocal music that Purcell contributed to a revised, quasi-operatic production of *The Indian Queen*, a vastly complicated verse-tragedy by Dryden and Sir Robert Howard, on the fashionable theme of tensions between the civilised and the savage life, with some ambivalence as to which is which. On the evidence of a startling contemporary engraving, she seems to have played the title role, Zempoalla, very much a Heroine-Villainess and pagan sorceress. Purcell died before he could complete the music, which was finished off by Daniel Purcell, and presented in 1695. At that date Mrs Bracegirdle's voice wouldn't have resembled Jessye Norman's; but neither would it have sounded like Emma Kirkby.

[4] This phenomenon continued during the high Augustan age. Such apostles of Reason, Truth and Nature as Pope, Johnson, Gray and Cowper, though not clinically certifiable, displayed symptoms that modern science would diagnose as neurotic. Some remarkable poets who were their near-contemporaries, notably Smart and Clare, ended in lunatic asylums. Romantically 'mad' Blake was in an eighteenth century tradition.

Meirion Hughes

'The Duc D'Elgar': Making a Composer Gentleman

Elgar is, outwardly, a retired army officer of the conventional Victorian type. He prides himself on his conventional appearance. I have often heard him use the phrase 'a Great Gentleman'. It is his sublimity of encomium – his encomiastic apex. No doubt he sublimates *himself* as a G.G. – the Duc D'Elgar.[1]

In the spring of 1922, Siegfried Sassoon encountered Sir Edward Elgar, grand old man of English Music and patriarch of the nation's musical Renaissance. He was forcibly struck by the composer's overt social presence, an obsession with class. On one level his observations might reflect nothing more than a hardy perennial of gossip, apparently trivial and ephemeral. On another, however, they are profound evidence of a politics articulated by class, and of the cultural tensions implicit in English social relationships. The career of Edward Elgar is a study in the hidden strength of such considerations, and the power they exerted upon his creative mentality. Sassoon, only half-knowingly, perhaps, had hit upon one of the most significant and still unacknowledged keys to Elgar's complexities.

From his earliest years, Elgar was subjected to the powerful ideological input of the English class system. He

41

was born into a lower middle-class family. His father was a piano-tuner and shopkeeper by trade, and his mother was a farmer's daughter; as a family they embraced the *status quo* and revered the monarchy as a matter of course. Elgar left school at fifteen and since – for financial reasons – there was no question of his going on to study music, he began a brief traineeship in a lawyer's office. In his 20s and 30s (until long after his marriage) he made a living as a freelance teacher of violin and piano and as a part-time orchestral player. The nearest Elgar got to the security of a musical post was as musical factotum at the Worcester Asylum, a position which he held for seven years.[2]

Elgar's marriage changed everything. It is *the* crucial event in understanding the transition from Ted Elgar of No 10 High Street to Sassoon's 'Duc d'Elgar' of 1922. Until 1889 – the year of his marriage – Elgar's compositional efforts were confined to songs, short occasional pieces and several unfinished scores. His only published work consisted of a handful of commercial salon pieces and precisely three short choral works. In stark contrast to the struggling musician, his wife, Caroline Alice, was, by birth, upper-class. Her father, Sir Henry Gee Roberts, had been a distinguished general who had served the Empire in India. Her mother's family, the Raikes, were long-established Gloucestershire gentry. Both Caroline Alice's parents were dead when her marriage to Elgar took place. Her remaining family regarded it as a catastrophe, and viewed Elgar himself as an upstart opportunist – to the extent that one of the bride's aunts cut her off from a promised legacy. For them, Elgar's being a shopkeeper's son was a fault dimensionally compounded by his Roman Catholicism.

Elgar's marriage marked a clear determination to detach himself from the class from which he had sprung. Under his wife's guidance Elgar set out to become a 'gentleman'. To this end, Elgar changed his appearance and bearing, adopting what could be termed a military cut; his dress became self-consciously immaculate and his Worcestershire accent appropriately modified to fit the new self-image. Many different witnesses attest to this process. Mary Alder, a pupil from the early 1890s recalled him always 'dressed in ...

plus-fours and gaiters' – when giving violin lessons.[3]

Rosa Burley, who knew Elgar well, observed of him in 1891;

> He had at this time, and indeed never wholly lost, a marked Worcester accent and was not then a young man of any particular distinction, yet he had a habit of speaking of Malvern in the condescending manner of a country gentleman condemned to live in a suburb ...[4]

Miss Burley attests that Elgar 'condemned' *Cavalleria Rusticana* not on musical grounds, but 'because the characters of the opera were persons in low life;[5] and that Elgar, when playing at the Three Choirs Festival, 'always tried to avoid carrying a violin case about with him for fear of looking like a musician'.[6] Arnold Bax, visiting Elgar unannounced in August 1901, remarked that Elgar was 'dressed in rough tweeds and riding boots, his appearance was ... that of a retired army officer turned gentleman farmer'.[7] His life-style also altered with marriage, with constant visiting, mainly of his wife's friends and acquaintances. A pattern of annual holidays in Germany was established in the 1890s. There can be little doubt that Caroline Alice's influence was decisive in this process. She certainly wanted to move her husband up-market, for her own sake as well as for his. Moreover, what is more remarkable – though hardly a coincidence – is that Elgar's career as a serious composer dates from this transformation. It is certainly true that the possession of gentility was the *sine qua non* of professionalism and success in the world of the Arts, but Elgar's transformation was pronounced – even bizarre and disturbing, as many friends and acquaintances attested. In effect (it may be argued) the artist could fully emerge *only* with emancipation from his social class. Caroline Alice did far more for her husband than line his paper and set out his desk – the conventional view of her role, as accepted by his biographers and by the millions who have seen the memorable but misleading portrayal in Ken Russell's celebrated television study.

At a personal level, at least, Elgar did not cut himself off from his family, and occasionally even served behind the

counter at No 10 High Street, Worcester, until well into
the 1890s. Without a doubt, Elgar's background continued
to be an embarrassment to his wife. Her attitude can be
gauged from a letter of 1900 to the journalist F G Edwards,
who was planning an early notice of the composer: 'as E has
nothing to do with the business in Worcester would you
please leave out details which do not affect him and with
which he has nothing to do – his interests being quite
unconnected with business ...'[8] Mrs Elgar obviously felt that
since the facts could not be changed then they might at least
be edited.

It is surely more than coincidence that Elgar's marriage
was also followed by the almost immediate composition of
his first large-scale orchestral work *Froissart*. At once the
significance of much of Elgar's subject matter is striking, for
this Concert Overture begins a long sequence of works
related to the themes of chivalric or noble heroism. For the
rest of his compositional life, he was regularly to draw upon
such concepts, which are both profoundly meaningful in his
aesthetic make-up and are a useful guide to his psychological
make-up. In these works, the composer pictured a pantheon
of heroes, all of whom in some way reflects aspects of
gentility, thus providing us with a subjective definition of
Elgar's own. Somehow he clearly needed to express his
fascination with the theme of noble chivalry as a condition of
being, and found his inspiration for this in an encounter, of a
type thoroughly characteristic in men of his generation, with
Romantic literature in the sentimental Gothic tradition. He
drew promiscuously on images of nobility – above all the
'lordly hero' – from a wide range of reading, from Tennyson
to popular fiction. He sought to emulate these ideals, even
where they were they were widely contrasting and even
contradictory. Contemporary tropes of gentlemanliness
were plundered by Elgar, with a bias towards those
packaged in the stereotype of the solid squire and
empire-builder, with its agenda of cigars, dogs, fishing, and
horsc-racing, cricket and a dislike of football. He never
ceased to aspire to membership of the imperial class to
which his wife's family had belonged.

With *Froissart* he quarried his material indirectly from Sir

Walter Scott's novel *Old Mortality*, which nevertheless authentically conveys the qualities extolled by the medieval chronicler, of loyalty to kingship and women, pure religion and a code of courage. These were virtues seminal to the concepts of gentility and knighthood which dominated the composer's imagination. After *Froissart* he passed on to a type of choral symphony, a setting of Longfellow's *The Black Knight* (1893), and the two cantatas *King Olaf*, (text also by Longfellow, 1896), and *Caractacus* (1898) all of which treated these knightly ideas. He never quite abandoned this imaginary landscape in which he felt so secure, and in later life explored it anew with his Symphonic Study *Falstaff* (1913) – that bittersweet mixture of scepticism and nostalgia – and the theatre scores to *King Arthur* (1923), and *Beau Brummel* (1928). Even this last work depicts 'a gentleman who is ready to sacrifice his life, his career, his friendship with the Prince Regent, to save a woman's honour'.[9]

Meanwhile, Elgar's transformation into 'gentleman and composer' was most eloquently delineated in the *Enigma Variations* of 1898-99. This symbiotic relationship between the sociological and the spiritual can be observed especially in his choice of the 'friends pictured within'. Elgar himself made no secret of the fact that his work was full of secrets. Over what has long been, all unchallenged, the best-known of all English musical works, he delighted in title and form, often returning to muse publicly about its genuinely private aspects. Of the twelve friends who comprise the variations, six were close gentry acquaintances of Caroline Alice from before her marriage: Richard Townshend (Var.3), a Cambridge scholar and master of the Redmarley estate; William Baker (Var.4), Old Etonian, barrister and squire of Hasfield Court; Isobel Fitton (Var.6); Winifred Norbury (Var.8); Dora Penny (Var.10), daughter of the Rector of Wolverhampton and related to the Baker family; and Lady Mary Lygon (Var.13), sister of Earl Beauchamp and Woman of the Bedchamber to the (later) Queen Mary.

Four of the remaining friends were upper middle-class: Hew Steuart-Powell (Var.2); Richard Arnold (Var.5), the poet's son; Troyte Griffith (Var.7), an architect whose

father was a master at Harrow; and Basil Nevinson
(Var.12), a 'London gentleman' and member of the
Conservative Club in the capital. Augustus Jaeger (Var.9)
and Dr George Sinclair (Var.11) were professional 'friends':
the former the cosmopolitan editor of *The Musical Times*
and music-reader at the publishing house Novello's, the
latter the organist at Hereford Cathedral. Caroline Alice
herself provided Variation I, while Elgar portrays himself in
the last – in the guise of his wife's pet name, 'E D U'. The
gentlemanly *persona* is given full rein here – bluff, confident,
even defiant, with its *largamente* and *grandioso* markings.
This assertive coda, like the work as a whole, represents
emphatically, and with documentary precision, the identity
of musical with social aspiration examined in this chapter.
One of the secrets of *Enigma* is that in its fusion of elements
it was, in every way, its author's calling-card and new
pedigree. Thus was established the political trajectory of
Elgar's career.

The fame which the *Variations* brought him after 1899
gave Elgar both the incentive (and to some extent the
means) to support his search for an elevated status. It must
be remembered that it was the music of 1899-1902 that
'made' Elgar: in addition to the *Variations*, there were
Cockaigne and *Pomp and Circumstance No 1*, with its 'Land
of Hope and Glory' setting. In all these compositions we
observe the extent to which gentlemanliness was a way of
life for Elgar. *Nobilmente* (noble, lofty and exalted) became
the hallmark of the Elgarian musical style; an *expressive*
marking – the technical term is beautifully ambiguous –
which he uses repeatedly, even obsessively. Elgar first used
the marking *nobilmente* in his orchestration of the *National
Anthem* which was especially commissioned for the
coronation of Edward VII in 1902. Moreover, the notion
was embedded in the tempi, the dynamics and the
instrumentation; it inheres in the very fabric of many of his
compositions. As a result, he began to collect the emblems
which attested to his transmogrification. Honorary doc-
torates came from Cambridge (1900) and Durham (1904).
The Athenaeum opened its doors, and above all, a
knighthood (1904) crowned a remarkable five-year period.

In every sense, Elgar had arrived. An acquaintance of King Edward's, cynosure of society, he had by 1908 moulded himself into the proudest and most perfect symbol of Great Britain's world-historical apogee. Inextricably linked with all this was the fact that he was by now the composer of a hugely successful symphony – the first recognised English essay in that most indispensable of forms, which was pronounced a masterpiece by Richter, the greatest living *German* conductor. Elgar had become the 'Nelson' of English music – an image which was enthusiastically endorsed by the popular press. The *Daily Mail* reported of the premiere of the *Violin Concerto* in November 1910 that Elgar was 'a tall, military figure, baton in hand ...', and that the concerto was received 'With rapturous applause such as might have greeted the victor of Trafalgar ...[10]

No sooner had his long campaign ended in victory than it suddenly seemed insubstantial, and perhaps hardly worth the effort. As we shall see, as early as 1906 Elgar felt his hard-won gentility and all that it meant to him to be under threat from the pressure of the masses – as represented by the Liberal landslide in the General Election of that year. Elgar's obsession at the height of his reputation with *nobilità* and honours *per se* can be gauged from a letter to Troyte Griffith reporting on the ceremony in 1911 at which the composer was awarded the Order of Merit: 'I wish you wd. write to the Worcester paper & say a little what the Order of M really is! ... At the Investiture Sir G Trevelyan & I were marshalled next to G.C.B. & *before* G.C.M.G. (which is Ld. Beauchamp's highest distinction!) ...'[11] By the 1920s, Elgar's carefully nurtured image, so appropriate for the age of power, imperialism and the Great War, was a ghastly liability. His character as well as his music came under the brutal scrutiny of the post-war generation whose values were distinctly altered. He had come to embody the comfortable hypocrisies of pre-war England. Most of all he was identified with the pernicious 'old lie' of patriotism. Cecil Gray in *A Survey of Contemporary Music* (1924) accused Elgar of 'self-righteous, complacent Pharasaical gentlemanliness'.[12] He also asserted that 'Imperialism' was a 'contaminating influence over his whole work'.[13] Elgar was for that generation a caricature – 'a personification of Colonel Bogey'.[14]

In this very period, however, Sir Edward had set his sights firmly upon a peerage, to *nobilita* in the most literal sense, 'Duc d'Elgar' in reality. As early as 1923, he thought that he deserved a peerage.[15] Perhaps the radical decline in critical esteem influenced the fact that not until 1931 was he awarded such a title, and even then merely a baronetcy (First Baron Broadheath) as a personal honour from King George V. Elgar valued it highly – but it was deemed to be technically outside the peerage, despite its hereditary character. Moreover, it was ironic that the honours system in the 1920s had hit an all-time low with Lloyd George's ruthless misuse.[16]

Despite Elgar's pretensions, and because of them, the shadow cast over his life by the shop at No 10 High Street was a long one. The accusation of 'vulgarity' haunted him constantly – both in his life and in his art. The composer's class and provincial origins in themselves made him almost literally 'vulgar' (that is, 'of the masses'). Not surprisingly, 'vulgarity' was a charge often levelled at his music too – in that his work was too brash, tasteless and too populist to be taken seriously. In 1931 E J Dent – Stanford's successor as Professor of Music at Cambridge – noted that:

> He was a violin player by profession ... He was, moreover, a Catholic, and a self-taught man ... For English ears Elgar's music is too emotional and not quite free from vulgarity.[17]

These words amounted to an indictment of Elgar as an *arriviste*, who had somehow made it from the asylum band to the green room, false gentleman, and since Catholic, false Englishman.

Twenty years before Dent's brutal onslaught marred the composer's old age, the critic Francis Toye had written an article entitled 'Velgarity' in *Vanity Fair*, in the immediate aftermath of the triumphant premiere of the *Violin Concerto*. Toye claimed that

> he [Elgar] is likely to be overwhelmed by the torrents of snobbery, advertisement, and flattery ... 'master and hero' though he may be, the time is not yet come for his deification ...

the cause of Elgar is best served by a total abstention from 'velgarity'.[18]

There can be no doubt that the composer was inwardly conscious of and sensitive upon this issue. Indeed, it is of some interest to note that already the composer had actually anticipated, and sought publicly to answer, this charge – in 1905, in his first lecture as Peyton Professor of Music at Birmingham University.

> Vulgarity [he asserted] often goes with inventiveness and it can take the initiative ... the commonplace mind can never be anything but commonplace, ... no polish of a University, can eradicate the stain.[19]

It was a distressing aspect of Elgar's social aspirations that he and his family could never afford the unremitting financial demands of their upward mobility. Elgar had no private income, no salaried post (except for the professorial tenure at Birmingham, 1905-1908) and no pension that he could rely on – he was, in economic terms, a professional musician throughout this life.[20] Money – or rather the lack of it – was a recurrent embarrassment even though from the earliest years of the marriage Elgar always travelled first class and Caroline Alice retained at least two maids. To give only a few examples of financial strain: in 1890 Caroline Alice had to sell her pearls; in 1900, friends had to help to pay for the Cambridge doctoral robes; and as late as 1912 wealthy friends had to club together to furnish Elgar's grand new Hampstead house. Generally speaking, Elgar regarded the USA as a prime source of lucrative engagements, exhibiting the double standards about Americans and their culture familiar to both his era and ours. During one tour he admitted that 'my feelings are dead against coming here again but my pocket gapes aloud.'[21] In practice, even foreign travel, outwardly a sufficient symbol of success, was no luxury but, quite on the contrary, a means of *reducing* expenditure. Trips to Italy, for example, were designed 'to economise "in the South" '.[22] Even so the going was often difficult. In April 1908 Elgar wrote to Jaeger

I cannot afford to get a *quiet* studio where I might have worked
and my whole winter has been wasted for the want of a few
more pounds ...[23]

Being a gentleman did not come cheaply in Edwardian
society. Elgar's financial difficulties to some extent
continued into the 1920s and 1930s, despite a legacy from his
friend and patron Frank Schuster; at the end of his life a
large house and a staff of four maintained his social
credentials.

As is implied above, and indeed is implicit in the politics
of Elgar's day, his social 'desertion' must be seen in tandem
with his simultaneous religious 'apostasy'. Elgar was brought
up to be a staunch Catholic, within a small community of
believers in Worcester. The second half of the 19th century
saw a dramatic upswing in the fortunes of Catholicism in
England; numbers were swelled by a steady stream of
(largely middle-class) converts from Anglicanism, as well as
by a considerable influx of poor immigrant Irish. This
advance however was achieved only in the teeth of
Protestant hostility – both Anglican and Nonconformist;
new fears about Irish immigration and Fenianism were
added to old prejudices, going back to the Reformation, of
Catholic 'disloyalty' and 'subversion'.

Elgar's faith was bound to separate him from the
mainstream of English society, since Catholics had limited
access to civil careers and the professions and no access at all
to political office. Rosa Burley reports a conversation with
the composer about the religious discrimination to which he
had been subjected:

> He told me of post after post, which would have been open to
> him but for the prejudice against his religion, of golden
> opportunities snatched from his grasp by inferior men of more
> acceptable views.[24]

The religious context of his music also created serious
difficulties. For example, the text of *Gerontius* had to be
'de-Romanised' for performance at the Three Choirs Festival
of 1902, in the wake of objections from the Worcester clergy.

From the mid-1900s onwards, Sir Edward gradually lapsed
from his Catholic faith. After the family had moved to
Hereford in 1904 Elgar's attendance at Mass fell away

over the years – although he kept up appearances during Festival weeks. Paradoxically enough, Lady Elgar, who had converted to Catholicism almost as an index of her total commitment to her husband and his career, remained in the Church until her death. It goes without saying that all of the composer's friends acquired in London life – a life which he ritually embraced and celebrated with the brilliantly worldly overture *Cockaigne* – were either formal Anglicans or various varieties of indifferent hedonists. His Catholicism was ungentlemanly and (by ubiquitous implication) unpatriotic; and his parade of religious belief was grossly unfashionable in the post-Victorian permissiveness of Edwardian Britain.

As belief faltered, so did the confident hold upon his subject matter that had inspired and purified a work like *Gerontius*. The enormous problems he had in finishing (or not finishing, as it turned out) his enormously ambitious choral tryptych on the New Testament are evocative. His embarrassing failure to complete the second oratorio – *The Kingdom* – in 1906, almost certainly stemmed from a spiritual as well as an artistic crisis. In 1918, when Laurence Binyon proposed that Elgar should set a 'peace ode' to music, the idea was rejected, since (as the latter put it) God seemed 'cruelly obtuse to the individual sorrow and sacrifice – a cruelty I resent bitterly and disappointedly'.[25] In his final illness, Elgar talked of burial without religious ceremony, or even – an act anathema to any Catholic in those times – of cremation. On his deathbed, he refused to see a priest, and last rites were administered only once he had lost consciousness. In the last few months of his life Elgar confided in his doctor that he had no faith in life after death: 'I believe there is nothing but complete oblivion.'[26]

It was in 1914 that this prolonged process reached a culmination and perhaps a resolution. As a result of a direct and flattering approach, Elgar put his signature to the famous Ulster Petition as one of 'twenty distinguished men' who supported Carson and the Protestants against the Liberal Government's Bill of Home Rule for Ireland. Without question, for any Catholic, this was an issue of considerable delicacy. Of course, it would be misleading to suggest that all English Catholics necessarily felt a commitment to the Bill – many Conservatives, even by this time some MPs, were Catholics. Elgar himself had no connections with Irish Catholicism and had always been true-blue Tory. But all the same, the capture of Elgar's name (one of only two Catholics on the list) was a veritable scoop by the radical Unionists. The composer had gone somewhat further than simply to declare that his religion was unimportant to his basic political philosophy. He had publicly disavowed any political role for Catholicism. In the long run, it was an act that perhaps did Roman Catholicism in this country more good than harm. But from the point of view of the composer's own soul, it could be seen as the last utterance in a Petrine Denial, in which Elgar pragmatically reconciled himself to a Godless world.

The signatories to the Ulster petition – clearly if not explicitly – embraced anti-Parliamentary activity, a denial of constitutional law, and desertion of loyalty to King and Country, should the Home Rule Bill pass the Lords and receive the Royal Assent. Each specifically declared 'that if the Bill is passed, I shall hold myself justified in taking or supporting any action that may be effective to prevent it being put into operation'.[27] In signing it, Elgar placed his friends, his clique, his party – things which all met in the notion of his adopted *class* – before all other considerations. There could hardly be a better talisman of the central importance of *nobilita* to his life and music. For the purposes of this essay, only on a secondary level does it also serve to underline the ideological importance of Elgar to the forces of Conservatism – the name of whose fallen leader, Arthur Balfour, appeared alongside his at the foot of the fateful document.

Elgar followed his family in being a firm Tory from his youth. In the General Election of January 1906, after almost twenty years of continuous Conservative rule, the Liberals had stormed back into power on a radical platform, having successfully soft-pedalled the Home Rule issue during their campaign. The election result shocked Elgar; in his judgement the Liberals threatened the very foundations of the social order upon which his status and gentility depended. On January 20 he wrote to his (Liberal) friend Frank Schuster:

> Having turned out the Hotel Cecil and having installed the
> *waiters* in place of the gentlemen, you will probably have to
> drop music and musicians to seem respectable among the
> governing body.[28]

Not only were the Liberals vulgarians (he proposed) but they
also lacked an appreciation of music. After some months of
Lloyd George rampant, the Elgars were clearly becoming
desperate at the turn of political events. Emigration to
America seemed to offer a solution: 'I sail on April 6 and shall
make arrangements to live in the USA: this country is no
longer possible for *respectable* people.'[29] It is clear from many
letters however, that Elgar detested the USA and only put up
with touring there for financial reasons.

By May 1906 the family had resolved to weather the new
political climate – not with passive acceptance, but apparently
by Sir Edward's going into party politics himself. The circumstances surrounding Elgar's flirtation with the idea of a
political career are intriguing. The Worcester Conservative
Association underwent a crisis in the months which followed
the 1906 Election. No sooner had the constituency dutifully
returned a new Tory member (a certain G H Williamson)
than allegation of corruption filled the air. By May, it seemed
likely that Williamson would be unseated and a by-election
called. Elgar, who was living in Hereford at the time, thought
that he might be able to help the Worcester Tories in their
hour of need. In a letter to a friend he speculated:

> Do they want a Unionist Candidate ... If they have no man
> ready in case of an election, do you think they wd. have me? ...
> I should like it but I am not sure how the land lies.[30]

What better step on the road to *nobilità* could Elgar possibly
take? Life as the Tory member for Worcester would have
gone well with his knighthood, and ensured a rapid
acceleration in the process of his ennoblement. Disappoint-
ingly, however, there is no evidence that Elgar approached
the constituency party directly. Williamson was eventually
unseated on petition of corruption (in 1908) and a new Tory
member was elected at a by-election.[31]

During the 1920s, and up to his death in 1934, Elgar

remained a staunch Conservative, but did not enter the arena of active politics. Lady Elgar's opinion on the rail strike of 1919 gives some indication of the political tenor of the Elgar household in the later years. 'Traitors, they ought to be shot – worse than the worst enemies ...'[32] Given his attitude to the Liberal platforms of the 1900s, there can be little room for doubt of Elgar's feelings towards the Labour Party; when he discovered that the first Labour premier, Ramsay Macdonald, had been admitted to the membership of The Athenaeum – in 1924 – he threatened to withhold his subscription 'until I am assured that the club is free from persons such as no gentleman can associate with'.[33] When the club confirmed Macdonald's membership under Rule XII, which admitted for example 'royal princes' and 'cabinet ministers', Elgar resigned.[34]

It may be argued that Elgar's search for nobility conformed to a pattern of sociological metamorphosis which can be observed in the historical development of the three-way relationship between art, politics and society. Since the late 18th century artists had often sought to rise above the status of artisan, to distinguish genius from mere skill, and to attain the worldly status which reflected both the spiritual greatness and political uses of their product; this usually involved attempting to free themselves from the shackles of patronage. Elgar however, oddly, seems to reverse this phenomenon. Far from wishing to escape from the vestments of the flunkey, which marked the composer out in the palace as occupying a status something between that of the head footman and the majordomo, Elgar actually craved a place at court and the uniform which proclaimed it. He was so naively delighted with his courtier's finery that he often wore it on public occasions which were deemed by others to be inappropriate.[35]

The pinnacle of Elgar's achievement, announcing his establishment as one of the greatest living Englishmen, was his relationship with the Royal Household. He became, in all except the most formal sense, court composer to the dynasty of Saxe-Coburg (from 1914, Windsor). Long before his actual appointment to the office in the 1920s, he was in all save mere technicality, Master of the King's Music. His career and his artistic success were undeniably dependent to a great extent on this supreme connection. Like many great composers who were also canny businessmen, Elgar understood the need for the attention and patronage of the court. He was perhaps the last composer (even the last major artist) to associate his work so explicitly with a ruling house. Again it illustrates his conservative and 'Romantic' character, his profound aspiration to 'belong' and to be at one with his time and place. This ineluctable yearning he expressed through his use of the term 'bard' to identify his vocation, as if summoning up a misty anthropology of tribe and culture, such as are celebrated in one of his earliest successes, *Caractacus*.

However, Elgar started to compose Royal Music partly by chance. It was at the instigation of Novello's (his publishers) that he composed two works – the *Imperial March* and *The Banner of St George* for Queen Victoria's Diamond Jubilee celebrations in 1897. Elgar approached these pieces as a Tory monarchist and as an artist who was prepared to participate in a state event and reflect a national mood. They both proved immediately popular when premiered in London in May 1897, the March in particular being widely played during the festivities. This success was quickly capitalised upon by the production of another patriotic work in 1898 – the cantata *Caractacus*, already mentioned. Although this work is ostensibly about the defeat of Ancient Britons at the hands of the Romans, it enthusiastically anticipates Britain's future imperial glory:

> The clang of arms is over,
> Abide in peace and brood
> On glorious ages coming,
> And Kings of British blood.

When Elgar's attention was drawn to the crude patriotism of the cantata, he replied self-consciously:

> I knew you would laugh at my librettist's patriotism (and mine) – never mind: England for the English is all I say – hands off! there's nothing apologetic about me.[36]

The triumphant premiere of *Caractacus*, at the Leeds
Festival in October 1898, was arguably the turning-point in
Elgar's career. As *The Court Journal* remarked: 'Mr.
Elgar has not inaptly been dubbed "the Rudyard Kipling of the
musicians" '[37] Perhaps most significantly of all, Queen
Victoria accepted the dedication of *Caractacus* – this
magnificent boon being secured by Sir Walter Parratt,
Master of the Queen's Music who had become Elgar's
champion at court. The fusion of patriotism with royalty and
empire was in the making, and Elgar, in the same way as
millions of his countrymen, on a level which was at once
representative and yet sublimely transfigured, had become a
'soldier of the Queen'.

Around this time, the composer was steadily building up
his ideas and resources for the composition of a major
extended orchestral work. He was particularly attracted to
the idea of a symphony on the subject of General Gordon.
Elgar, as a Catholic, had a special interest in the 'Gordon'
story, because of the bizarre coincidence that the General
had spent time during his final months in Khartoum
annotating a text of Cardinal Newman's poem *The Dream of
Gerontius*. Since Gordon's death in 1885, Catholics in
England had been quite taken with the speculation that the
greatest hero and martyr of the empire might have become
one of the Church's most illustrious converts. Elgar was
aware of the enormous public interest which had grown
around the Gordon myth, and this would have helped to
popularise the symphony. Novello's however, gave him no
encouragement with the project, with the result that the
'Kipling' of music quickly began to chafe in his new role: 'I
tell you I am sick of it all: why can't I be encouraged to do
decent stuff and not be hounded into triviality ...'[38]
Nevertheless, during 1899-1902, Elgar did produce things
that he really wanted to write; the *Enigma Variations*
brought most success at home and *The Dream of Gerontius*
quickly achieved recognition abroad – if not in England.

Elgar's role as a royal composer was affirmed and
enhanced when, following Queen Victoria's death in
January 1901, Parratt approached him suggesting that he set
a Coronation Ode by Benson to 'immortal music'[39].

Following a further initiative by Henry Higgins – the Chairman of the Covent Garden Opera Syndicate and perhaps more influential in such matters with the new King than Parratt – Elgar agreed to the project. It was to become his most important work as royal composer. From its inception it had the royal seal of approval, and was scheduled to be premiered at a State Concert at Covent Garden in honour of that event, and in the presence of Edward VII. Meanwhile, in association with these august events, Elgar made a new and sumptuous orchestration of the *National Anthem*.

The *Coronation Ode* is a predictable affirmation of monarchical and imperialist values, although the British traumas in the Boer War overshadowed the whole work. Of the seven sequences, two (No 5 and No 6) are unambiguous prayers for peace:

> Peace, gentle peace, who smiling through thy tears,
> Returnest when the sounds of war are dumb ...
> When comest thou Our brethren long for thee.

The Ode ends, however, on the triumphalist note of the *Land of Hope and Glory* setting. It was at Elgar's request that Benson wrote fresh lines to fit the trio tune of his new *Pomp and Circumstance March No 1* – already a huge popular hit. The King accepted the dedication of the Ode in May 1902, a few weeks before the concert. As things turned out the king's appendectomy led to the postponement of the coronation and the cancellation of the State Concert, and Elgar failed to receive his widely-expected knighthood in the Coronation Honours List. In fact, the *Coronation Ode* was not given in the King's presence until June 1903 – when Elgar met Edward VII and the Prince of Wales for the first time. Like so many others, he warmed to the king on a personal level, and the character of the new monarch seemed in every way to confirm and massage his absolutely identification with the Edwardian *status quo*.

In addition to national prominence, however, Elgar had by now secured an international reputation; for the first time since Purcell, an English composer had projected himself to the front rank of the music of his day. Elgar had become the 'flagship' of English music, as potent an emblem of British greatness and security as the greatest battleship of the Royal Navy. It must be remembered that throughout the 19th century European music had been dominated by Germans; for many people, Elgar was taking the Germans on at what they culturally did best, and that at a time of increasing tension in Anglo-German relations, when it was most important for the national psyche. Even the new German musical *Held*, Richard Strauss himself, like many of his countrymen, had acknowledged Elgar's genius. Perhaps by now every acknowledged artist was a kind of hero, in the dramatic sense, but Elgar was so in the popular patriotic sense as well. The public could experience through him a higher, almost spiritual, dimension of pride and communion. As one reviewer expressed it

> the huge audience ... called and recalled the man who had achieved a triumph not only for himself but for England, and hailed him with wonder and submission as master and hero.[40]

Because he was the first independent English figure in creative music, his style became (almost by default) somehow a peculiarly *English* voice. The fact that he seemed so typical of his people, that he served the Crown, and that he sang of the nation in harmony with Hardy and Kipling, all sanctified this process. The time had thrown up the man.

But history rarely works entirely in these providential ways. Although Elgar's emergence may have been in different ways influenced by accidental contingencies, it was also consciously shaped by human agency. Above all was the mundane and uncertain process of accumulating patronage, which was indispensable to Elgar's success. As we have seen, Sir Walter Parratt was vital in establishing his position as composer to the Royal Family. Parratt (1841-1924) was primarily an organist, and had become Master of the Queen's Music in 1893 – a post which he held until his death.[41] He advanced Elgar's career at court in several ways. He set out to acquaint the Queen and her circle with Elgar's music, mostly in the form of short occasional pieces for private concerts. 'I hope that you are aware that I use your music constantly and the Queen likes it', he reported cheerfully in July 1889.[42] In May 1899, Parratt summoned Elgar to Windsor Castle by telegram to conduct a specially-commissioned part-song at a concert given under the Queen's window. The song was one of a compilation by distinguished artists, performed in honour of the Queen's birthday. It was the closest that Elgar ever got to the person of Queen Victoria, but as a consolation Parratt introduced Elgar to other members of the Royal Family. Later that year the older musician organised a concert at the Royal Albert Institute at Windsor, at which Elgar conducted no fewer than eleven of his own works, in the presence of Princess Christian, the queen's third daughter. In addition, Parratt acted as 'go-between' on the matter of royal dedications that Elgar wanted to make. His first success with *Caractacus* – 'I will certainly bring the matter before the Queen's notice. It will certainly not be my fault if your request is not granted'[43] – was followed by others. Finally Sir Walter Parratt also encouraged Elgar to write official music for the court; as we have seen it was Parratt who came up with the idea of setting Benson's *Coronation Ode*.

The reasons for Parratt's patronage are not difficult to find: that he was a genuine and enthusiastic advocate of Elgar's music there can be no doubt, but self-interest also played a part. Parratt was so inadequate as a composer that Elgar's cooperation as a surrogate must have been a godsend to him. Elgar acknowledged Parratt's help and encouragement in the dedication to him of the *Five Part-Songs* (1903). But the connection faded after 1903, as Elgar relied less on Parratt and more on other links with the Court. There can be little doubt that the post of Master of the King's Music declined in reputation as a result of Sir Walter's long and undistinguished tenure, and it was largely owing to Elgar's personal intervention at court (together with the offer to take on the job) that the post was maintained in being after 1924.

Elgar's greatest lay patron was unquestionably Leo (Frank) Schuster (1840-1927). Schuster was a member of a large expatriate German-Jewish family with extensive banking interests. As such, he moved in some of the most exalted circles in the land – he was acquainted with members of the royal family, mixed freely with elements of the aristocracy and prominent politicians, and had access to a wide spectrum of people in the musical world, both in England and abroad. Schuster first met Elgar in 1899 and was immediately impressed, so much so that he had installed a specially commissioned bust of the composer in his music-room by the end of the year.

For the rest of his life, Schuster provided assistance of all kinds to the composer and ultimately left him a substantial legacy. Here too, however, the connection was most effective during 1901-1904, when it was important in associating Elgar's music with the court. The *Coronation Ode* may have been Parratt's idea, but it was Schuster's efforts that transformed an 'idea' into the reality of a State Concert at Covent Garden with the King's patronage. Elgar asked Schuster's opinion about setting Benson's Ode and was encouraged to write the music with the promise:

> I shall do what I can to further your interests ... It can only be done by talking – and when I run against the right person – as I hope to do – I shall talk no end![44]

The 'right person' was Henry Higgins, to whom Elgar was introduced by Schuster later that year (1902) at the Leeds Festival. The outcome was the Royal Commission for the Ode and the abortive 'gala concert'.

The King atoned for the disappointment of 1902 by attending the London premiere of the *Coronation Ode* in 1903 – although he seems to have fallen asleep during the performance! But at any rate, within a relatively short space of time, the bitter frustration of 1902 was swallowed up in a resounding and unique success. In 1904, Schuster re-activated the Higgins connection with an idea for a three-day festival at Covent Garden, entirely devoted to Elgar's music – an unprecedented event for an English composer. The negotiations were finalised in November 1903: Elgar's music would have the prestige of the Opera House, coupled with the sympathetic artistry of Richter and Halle forces. Schuster stood as financial guarantor for the festival. Hoping to secure royal patronage for the event, Elgar's wife approached Schuster:

> That wd. really be a great point for it, how should he be asked? ... – but the Festival is altogether so wonderful (thanks to you) to think of that nothing seems impossible.[45]

In the event, in March 1904, the King attended on two evenings, the Queen on all three. The *Sunday Times* reported on the 'Elgar Festival' that 'in its locale and patronage [it] is an indication that our upper-classes are no longer disdainful of any movement in native music'.[46] Schuster can be seen to be a powerful force in Elgar's emergence as a national figure: in an age when connections counted for so much, especially to a man of Elgar's origins, Schuster supplied them in abundance.[47] His gratitude to his greatest admirer was swiftly manifested in the dedication of the Concert Overture *In the South*, first performed at the 1904 Elgar Festival.

Once the firm connection with Edward VII had been forged, the composer began to enjoy the personal attention of the King. A few weeks after their first meeting, Parratt reported delightedly: 'The King has taken a great fancy to you.'[48] Whilst Prince of Wales, the new monarch had long since become the centre of public interest, which increased in the decades of his mother's seclusion and old-age. Moreover, his circle had always been self-consciously different from that of the Victorian court. In particular, the King had nurtured (often controversial) links and friend-ships among the capitalist elite, foremost among whom were Jewish financiers. Many of these men were descendants or connections of the distinguished *Hofjuden* (Court Jew) families which had been influential in several European monarchies since the 17th century. Edward VII's friends – J B Priestley's 'Jewish plutocrats' – included Baron Hirsch, Sir Ernest Cassel, the Rothschilds, a nucleus which expanded to include the Speyers and Schusters. It was one of the few characteristics of 'King Teddy' which tended to diminish affection for him, both amongst the upper classes and the masses.

Moreover, the King – an 'arch-vulgarian' according to

Henry James – was not a music lover in any true sense. His approach to the arts 'was that of a *bon vivant* seeking distraction rather than an aesthete seeking enlightenment'.[49] Nevertheless, he certainly helped to create an atmosphere in which the arts generally had a greater opportunity to flourish; and he and Queen Alexandra seem genuinely to have liked Elgar's music. The latter's appreciation of this can be seen in the dedication of the *Second Symphony* to the King – a decision made two months before the King's sudden death in May 1910, 'so that dear kind man will have my best music'.[50] The king developed what was called a *Beamtendel* (roughly translated from the German as a 'nobility of officialdom') which he patronised and encouraged. It was a concept derived from the Viennese Habsburg Court of the Metternich era, since similarly this group consisted not only of state officials and administrators, but also of top professionals and artists, and included Sir Edward Elgar. In this way the composer and his royal namesake met socially on several occasions during 1903-1910.

Elgar did not establish the same rapport with George V that he had enjoyed with Edward VII. In fact Elgar had a low opinion of the king and queen, which occasionally surfaced in private company. Siegfried Sassoon noted one 'petulant tirade' in 1922 when Elgar said:

> We all know that the King and Queen are incapable of appreciating anything artistic ... I've been a monkey-on-a-stick for you people long enough. *Now I'm getting off the stick.*[51]

Two years earlier Elgar had refused to take part in the ceremony to unveil the new Cenotaph, the much-admired Lutyens monument, which he thought 'vulgar and commonplace to the last degree'.[52] In April 1924, during his campaign to save the Mastership of the King's Music, Elgar asserted that: 'everything seems so hopelessly and irredeemably *vulgar* at court'.[53]

Nevertheless, from the outset of the new Georgian reign his role as 'unofficial laureate' was recognised in the commission for the music for the coronation of 1911. This time there was to be little new music, Elgar being required to rework the 1902 Ode in collaboration with Benson. Alterations to the music were limited to a sequence for the new Queen, an Offertory and a March. Moreover, Elgar – now responding like most such appointees – clearly found the work burdensome and unprofitable:

> I have had really no time for anything except 'official' (more or less) work: now the 'tumult and the shouting dies' and the net gain is little.[54]

Perhaps surprisingly – and certainly to Lady Elgar's intense disappointment – Elgar refused the invitation to attend the Coronation.[55] Elgar quickly realised that George V really had no authentic interest in himself or his music – indeed in *any* music. The King was later to confess (to Sir Thomas Beecham) that his favourite opera was *La Boheme*, because it was shorter than most things he was obliged to sit through.

Nevertheless, royal commissions kept coming Sir Edward's way during the new reign. There were three aspects to Elgar's 'royal' music: there were occasional pieces, written specifically for court ceremonial and royal display; there were compositions for a royal anniversary or with some other Royal event in mind; finally, there was music dedicated to the sovereign. George V patronised Elgar's hard work in the national cause during the Great War. However, not until 1924 was Elgar's long connection with the Court formalised by his appointment to the Mastership of the King's Music. This post had been long scheduled to lapse, but Elgar urged the court authorities to retain it:

> its suppression would have a very bad effect abroad – where the effacement of the last shred of connection of the Court with the Art would not be understood.[56]

Elgar offered himself for the post out of a sincere concern for its demise, but his hopes of a peerage at this time probably played a part too.

Elgar wrote but a handful of works in the official capacity he had at last achieved. Just before his appointment he had written the *Pageant of Empire* music and the *Empire March* for the opening ceremony of the 1924 British Empire Exhibition at Wembley. In 1929, he wrote a carol (*Good Morrow*) on the King's 'happy recovery' from illness. In 1931, the delightful *Nursery Suite* was written and dedicated to the Duchess of York and her two daughters and in 1932 Elgar wrote an Ode for the unveiling ceremony of a memorial to Queen Alexandra.

In return for service to the Court and to the musical life of the nation generally, Elgar could (and did) expect official recognition. During the reign of Edward VII, Elgar received only one official honour – his knighthood (1904), the award of which was clearly linked to the coronation music and the Elgar Festival at Covent Garden. During the next reign however, Elgar was to receive a further four honours – all of which were in the *personal* gift of the monarch. The Order of Merit – founded by Edward VII in 1902 as royal recognition of a number of the very brightest national luminaries – paradoxically only came his way after the old king's passing, in the Coronation Honours list of 1911. This was the most prestigious honour he was to receive. The OM is limited to twenty-four individuals at any one time who have distinguished themselves in art, literature, science or war – and is a personal award of the sovereign. Elgar had to wait until 1928 for further official recognition, which came in the form of knighthood of the Royal Victorian Order (KCVO), created by Queen Victoria specifically for those men who had rendered personal service to the sovereign or members of the Royal Family. Elgar was not impressed: 'H.M. has offered me the wretched KCVO(!!!) which awful thing I must accept! Alas!'.[57] In June 1931, he was much more pleased to accept the baronetcy already noted – 'though fit of hereditary status yet somehow not quite fit to sit in the House of Lords'.[58] In June 1933, Elgar received a GCVO (the first division of the Royal Victorian Order), an honour which placed him alongside the Lord Chamberlain as a servant of the royal household. These later honours were ordained not so much because of continued musical output as in recognition of Elgar's past service and his position as Master of the King's Music.

By the late 1920s, however, there was a significant revival

of Elgar's music, linked with his 70th and 75th birthdays. In his last years, he basked in the sunshine of an Indian Summer of popular affection, represented by increased financial security and the munificent patronage of the new era of the great communications industries. Monarchy and banker were replaced by international business (The Gramophone Company) and the public corporation (The British Broadcasting Corporation).

The centrality of Elgar to the musical history and culture of modern Britain has arguably encouraged the suppression or distortion of significant elements in the interpretation of his life and work. His biography and artistic status have generated a nationalist myth, an image which has successfully resisted overthrow. After the vicissitudes of critical estimation accorded him in early and mid-career, in old age a shining exemplar was definitively constructed. This happened particularly as a result of the celebrations surrounding his later anniversaries, which made him a national institution, 'our Shakespeare of music' as Lady Stuart of Wortley revealingly described him.[59] This mainstream view was enshrined in a spate of biographies in the period 1927-36. This orthodoxy has, it is true, undergone an important modification at the hands of Michael Kennedy. Whilst Kennedy's partly alternative treatment tends to confirm a version of Elgar, which crept in after the Great War, as a bard of the English countryside, he undermines the notion of Elgar as an uncomplicated imperialist and patriot – a notion which helps to make the image so imposing and solid. Kennedy's Elgar is a prophet of decline, composer of the 'funeral march of a civilisation', a man who was contemptuous of jingoism and whose very patriotism was subject to bitter disillusion.[60] This interpretation itself, however, has recently been frontally challenged by a reading which seeks to re-establish the artist as the echt-representative of Edwardian Imperialism. There seems no room for doubt that Elgar was, quite willingly and consciously, both a 'cultural warrior' and a political figurehead.[61]

Although by no means removed from the debate, this essay has sought a different angle of approach. It demonstrates that Elgar's life and music were rooted in late-Victorian values and the politics of class. He was an artist morbidly concerned with appearances and status, so much so it seems that his art was incapable of expression until 'released' from the prison of his lower middle-class status. The key agencies of this liberation were his marriage and his achieving of vital establishment patronage. These factors would not be so important in understanding his contribution were it not for the fact that the music itself, in so much of its subjectivity and subject-matter springs directly from these profound preoccupations. Indeed, his work could not have been conceived and cannot be fully understood without reference to this fundamental context of its creation.

I wish to thank Dr Robert Stradling for all encouragement and help in the writing of this essay. I would also like to thank the Trustees of the Elgar Birthplace Trust, Mr James Bennett (the Curator at the Birthplace) and Mr Peter King, Librarian at Uxbridge College.

Notes

[1] *Siegfried Sassoon, Diaries 1920-22*, R Hart-Davies (ed), Faber and Faber 1981, p 124.
[2] In a letter to the journalist H G Edwards (19 September 1900), Elgar commented: 'as to the whole "shop" episode – I don't care a d–n! I know it has ruined me and made life impossible until I what you call made a name – I only know I was kept out of everything decent "'cos his father keeps a shop" ...', British Library, Edwards Papers vol vi (Egerton 3090) p 39.
[3] Mary Alder (BBC interview in 1973) quoted in Jerrold Northrop Moore, *Edward Elgar: A Creative Life*, Oxford University Press 1984, p 172.
[4] Rosa C Burley and F C Carruthers, *Edward Elgar: The Record of a Friendship*, Barrie and Jenkins 1972, pp 25-26.
[5] *Ibid*, p 25.
[6] *Ibid*, p 36.
[7] Arnold Bax, *Farewell My Youth*, Longmans, Green and Co 1943, p 30.
[8] Alice Elgar to F G Edwards, 18 September 1900, *Edwards Papers* vol vi, pp 35-38.
[9] *Birmingham Post*, 5 November 1928.

[10] *Daily Mail*, 11 November 1910.

[11] Elgar to Troyte Griffith in July 1911, quoted by M Kennedy, *Portrait of Elgar*, Oxford University Press 1982, p 182.

[12] Cecil Gray, *A Survey of Contemporary Music*, Oxford University Press 1924, p 92.

[13] *Ibid*, p 81.

[14] Osbert Sitwell, *Laughter in the Next Room*, Macmillan 1975, p 196.

[15] Elgar to Lady Alice Stuart of Wortley, 12 September 1923, (Elgar Birthplace Trust).

[16] See M de-la-Noy, *The Honours System*, Allison and Busby 1985, p 102. Between Jan 1921 – June 1922, Lloyd George sold 74 baronetcies at about £40,000 each, peerages went for £100,000.

[17] B Maine, *Elgar, His Life and Works*, Bell 1933 (reprinted Cedric Chivers, Bath 1973), pp 277-278.

[18] *Vanity Fair*, 16 November 1910.

[19] Edward Elgar (ed P M Young), *A Future for English Music and Other Lectures*, Dobson 1968, pp 47 and 49.

[20] Lady Elgar had an annual private income of £300.

[21] Letter from Elgar to Novellos, his publishers, 29 June 1905; quoted in Northrop Moore *op cit*, p 463.

[22] Elgar to Jaeger, 25 October 1907 (Hereford and Worcester Record Office, Elgar Papers, 705:445:8781).

[23] Elgar to Jaeger, 26 April, 1908 (HWRO: 705:445:8784).

[24] Burley, *op cit*, p 26.

[25] Quoted in Kennedy, *op cit*, p 277.

[26] Quoted in Northrop Moore, *op cit*, p 818.

[27] Letter to *The Times*, 3 March 1914.

[28] Elgar to Frank Schuster, 20 January 1906, (HWRO: 705:445:7008).

[29] Elgar to Troyte Griffith, 17 March 1906, (HWRO: 705:445:7276).

[30] Quoted in Northrop Moore, *op cit*, p 499.

[31] *A History of the Worcester Conservative Association* (Worcester Conservative Association, 1978) p 34. The notion of becoming an MP obviously attracted Elgar greatly. When the Oxford musician Ernest Walker visited him in July 1907, the subject of politics cropped up: 'Elgar said that if he had been able to live a completely independent life he would have liked to be an MP. Innocently Walker asked for which Party: "Consaervative of course" Elgar snapped out.' M Deneker, *Ernest Walker*, Oxford University Press 1951, p 110.

[32] Quoted in P M Young, *Alice Elgar, The Enigma of a Victorian Lady*, Dobson 1978.

[33] Draft letter from Elgar to The Athenaeum, 11 December 1924, (HWRO: 705:445:5045).

[34] Elgar to The Athenaeum, 13 December 1924. (HWRO: 705:445:5046). He confirmed this decision two weeks later to the club, saying that it was 'no longer an honour to belong to The Athenaeum'. (HWRO: 705:445:5049).

[35] By the 1920s the Three Choirs Festival had become the focal-point of Elgar's calendar: 'Wearing the robes of his doctorate or Court dress with orders, he was a magnificent and striking figure except to those who found

his delight in dressing up merely a pompous affectation. Even so admiring a friend as Schuster, ... called him "the pouter pigeon".' Kennedy, *op cit*, pp 304-305.

[36] Elgar to Jaeger, 12 July 1898, (HWRO: 705:445:8313).

[37] *The Court Journal*, 8 October 1898.

[38] Elgar to Jaeger, 20 October 1898 (Elgar Birthplace Trust).

[39] Parratt to Elgar, 12 March 1901, on the premiere of the Violin Concerto. (HWRO: 705:445:1969).

[40] *Daily Mail*, 11 November 1910.

[41] It is almost certain that Parratt first met Elgar at the Worcester Three Choirs Festival of 1896.

[42] Parratt to Elgar, 20 July 1898 (HWRO: 705:445:1970).

[43] *Ibid*.

[44] Schuster to Elgar, 28 March 1901 (HWRO: 705:445:6966).

[45] Lady Elgar to Schuster, 7 January 1904, quoted in Northrop Moore, *op cit*, p 426.

[46] The *Sunday Times*, 13 March 1904.

[47] In October 1902 Schuster also introduced Elgar to the Duke of Norfolk and to Mrs Charles Stuart-Wortley (wife of Sheffield Tory MP and daughter of the painter Millais). The result of their joint endeavour was the first London performance of *Gerontius* at Westminster Cathedral (June 1903).

[48] Parratt to Elgar, 16 August 1903 (HWRO: 705:445:1957).

[49] Gordon Brooke-Shepherd, *Uncle of Europe*, Collins 1975, p 230.

[50] Quoted in Northrop Moore, *op cit*, p 574.

[51] *Siegfried Sassoon Diaries 1920-22, op cit*, p 169, entry for 8 June 1922.

[52] Elgar to Lady Stuart of Wortley, 22 January 1920 (HWRO: 705:445:7687).

[53] Elgar to Lady Stuart of Wortley, 16 April 1924 (Elgar Birthplace Trust).

[54] Elgar to Canon Gorton, 16 July 1911, quoted in Kennedy *op cit*, p 240.

[55] Rosa Burley suggests that Elgar's boycott of the Coronation was due to the fact that so little new music was commissioned for the event, she also speculates that Elgar regarded the fee as inadequate (Rosa Burley, *op cit*, p 189).

[56] Elgar to Lady Stuart of Wortley, 16 April 1924 (Elgar Birthplace Trust).

[57] Elgar to Lady Stuart of Wortley, 24 December 1927, quoted in Kennedy, *op cit* p 182.

[58] De-la-Noy, *op cit*, p 60.

[59] Lady Stuart of Wortley to Carice Elgar, February 1934, quoted Kennedy, *op cit* p 330.

[60] Kennedy, *op cit*, p 186. See also (eg) Maine: J F Porte, *Elgar and His Music*, Pitman and Sons 1933; F H Shera, *Elgar, Instrumental Works*, Oxford University Press 1931; W H Reed, *Elgar As I Knew Him*, Gollancz 1936.

[61] This argument finds support in a lecture 'Elgar, Kipling and Edwardian Imperialism', given by J Richards to the Conference 'Music and Politics' (University of Lancaster, 1987). I am grateful to Dr Richards for permission to use a typescript of this lecture.

Robert Stradling

On Shearing the Black Sheep in Spring: The Repatriation of Frederick Delius

Marcia Funebre

On 24 May 1935, the body of Frederick Delius was re-interred in England, having been transported for the purpose from his home in the French village of Grez-sur-Loing, where he had died almost a year earlier. The organisers of this event had decided that the churchyard of St Peter's in Limpsfield, a parish on the Kentish borders of Surrey, was an appropriate site for his sepulchre. From time immemorial, this settlement has been amongst the lushest corners of our land, in terms of its fertility, and amongst the richest, as regards its denizens. With their customarily abundant degree of theological accommodation, the Anglican authorities permitted the burial of this volubly committed atheist in consecrated earth.

Although no formal service was held, a few pieces of music by Delius were played inside the church, and Sir Thomas Beecham gave a funeral oration at the graveside.[1] 'We are here today', he began, 'to bid farewell for ever to Frederick Delius, a great Englishman and a famous man.' On the face of things, suitable words, innocently enough expressed. But the speaker went on immediately to add the apparently gratuitous remark (as if in parenthesis): 'You will have read that it was his wish to be buried in the soil of his native country'. Suddenly the sunny late spring day has a cloud; the broad consoling harmony of the elegy is interrupted by a sour jangle. Anxious to reassure his hearers that the music and its performance was sound, the text free of inner contradictions, Sir Thomas quickly continued. Here is the whole of the subsequent paragraph of his speech.

> I think it may be said that nowhere in the breadth of this land could a fairer spot be found than this to satisfy his wish, nor a more auspicious occasion than this beautiful day.

Beecham knew well enough that the problematic of his position could hardly be wished away as simply as this. Indeed, he had decided to confront it head on, and in so doing to wish it away in a more emphatic and definitive manner. So he continued thus:

> It may have struck some of you as requiring a little explanation as to why Frederick Delius, who left these shores as a very young man, a wanderer and almost an exile, has returned to them finally only yesterday ... I think I am able to give you the explanation.

With the exception only of some conventional phrases in praise of the dead hero's character and the qualities of his music, Beecham went on to devote the whole of his discourse to this 'explanation'. He claimed that the absence of Delius from England had been motivated by a generalised wanderlust rather than by any fundamental incompatibility. Moreover, the composer was so moved by the spirit of self-sacrifice and moral idealism which his countrymen displayed during the First World War that he felt himself drawn back to them. At the same time, his music – 'extraordinarily redolent of the soil of this country and characteristic of the finer elements of the national spirit' – was discovered by his compatriots. These powerful and complementary processes, like some elemental phenomenon, together developed towards the great Festival of the music of Delius held in London in 1929, an event 'without parallel in the musical history of this country'. Here the identity of artist with nation was fused, as in the funeral rites at Limpsfield it was later to be sealed for ever. In what may be regarded as a classic example of the self-fulfilling prophecy, Beecham declared

> I am proud to say that the greatest respect and understanding of his works proceed from the people of this land, that it grows daily, and it shows no sign of diminishing – and so far as it is possible to foresee, if there is any music that will remain honoured and immortal in the memory of the people of any one country, it is the music of this composer.

Beecham was already by this time the main advocate and exponent of Delius. It was an association which the composer had recognised, and which latterly came to be appreciated far beyond the confines of the musical world. Interviewed on BBC television a few years before his death, the conductor asserted (however) that 'Delius and I were at opposite ends of the pole in terms of character, interests and attitudes ... apart from his music we had nothing in common whatever'.[2] On the face of things this also was an odd remark for Beecham to make. Indeed the claim is palpably open to question in one significant respect. Beecham's family background was strikingly akin to that of Delius, for both were rooted in manufacturing industry and in the north of England. Finer details apart, ultimately it cannot be denied that the career of Delius as an artist was made possible by the business success of his progenitors. This was famously the case with Beecham, whose inherited financial resources were devoted to the musical arts and specifically used to advance the cause of his favoured composer.

Both men, it may be surmised, saw the vocation of High Art and its spiritual concerns as providing an escape from the world of their fathers and an atonement for its sins. Both despised the materialism of their economic origins, and aspired to a purer life of aristocratic refinement and creative achievement.[3] It was no accident that Beecham actually referred to Arnold, Carlyle and Ruskin in his speech at Limpsfield, when describing the reaction of Delius to Victorian capitalism.

England at that time seemed to be a country given up to the

worship of commercial prosperity and little else besides. It ...
revolted the finer spirits of that time, and in certain cases drove
them out ... Delius was born in a part of the world which was
particularly odious to him ... It was the arid, hard business
North.

This, it seems, was the 'explanation' of why the composer
decided to lay his bones in the succulent land of Surrey – an
area he had never lived in, and had not even visited for any
length of time – rather than the sterile terrain of Bradford.

Despite his eloquence, one or two of Sir Thomas's
auditors at Limpsfield remained somewhat sceptical of this
'explanation' and the whole business of 'repatriation'.
Indeed, later in life, Beecham himself disavowed much of
his earlier rhetoric, notably that which concerned the alleged
'English' characteristic and personality of the composer.
These salutary pains of hindsight came about as a result of
reading the many letters and other original documents of
Delius which his widow Jelka had left to Beecham's care.
Here Sir Thomas discovered – to his chagrin – that he and
his friendship had been no more sacred to the man than
anybody or anything else. All the same, on the issue of the
reburial itself, he remained unrepentant. As far as Beecham
was concerned, when he had explained something, it stayed
explained.

> A good deal of useless and slightly indecorous comment was
> made ... about his choice of burial place. I am able to assert that
> there was never the slightest uncertainty upon this point, and
> that he passed on his wishes to those nearest to him and in his
> confidence with characteristic lucidity of utterance. His last
> home was to be a quiet country churchyard in a south of
> England village. I can understand that to some persons this
> decision seemed at the time to be unaccountable ... [but] it was
> bordering closely upon insensibility to argue about it.[4]

Danse Macabre

One who is about to embark upon an act of unsanctioned
exhumation would be wise to anticipate the gravedigger's
curse. In this frame of mind, we must agree with Sir Thomas
about the composer's expression of his burial wishes;

moreover, nothing that he said at the graveside (or subsequently published) contains what may be regarded, in any ordinary sense of the term, as a falsehood. It is the sub-textual signification of his speech, with its eternal proclamation concerning his subject's place in musical history and in national culture, which is the main area of investigation here. What happened at Limpsfield was not predetermined by destiny, nor ordained by nature, and never decreed by the spontaneous overflow of popular feeling. On the most mundane level, of course, the ceremony, like any other, had been arranged by the friends and family of the deceased. But this was no ordinary burial; it rather resembled the 'bringing back home' of a wartime national hero from some corner of a foreign field. Those actively involved in it were strongly – even ruthlessly – dedicated to the advance of the artistic reputation of Delius. I make no suggestion of a conspiracy to ignore or subvert the composer's wishes. What was done took place very largely according to his desires, or at least with his grudging permission.

To deconstruct the presentation of Delius as an 'English Composer' we must begin with this act of literal (if posthumous) repatriation. This last word is deliberately chosen for its overtones of 'naturalisation' and 'nationalisation'. The point of my essay is not *directly* to address the issue of what constitutes an 'English' or any other variety of 'national' composer, nor does it seek to provide a conclusion about the status of Delius in this respect. These complex and fascinating issues are marginal herein to an examination of how our present perception of the composer took shape, how it was projected as a permanent image onto the screen of our national consciousness. My own opinions concerning the aesthetic arguments are present only as an adjunct to this historical analysis.

The State Funeral of Frederick Delius – for such it was despite the absence of crowned heads and crowded streets – was the last in a sequence of acts representing cultural rites of passage. By them, the composer, or rather his *persona*, was carefully reshaped into a form acceptable to the British public, or at any rate (in the first instance) the

musically-subscribing part of it. The original raw material –
and the abjectival element in the metaphor is deliberate –
was highly intractable. The task of cosmetic morphology was
undertaken only with great difficulty, and fell short of
complete accomplishment. These, however, are some of the
reasons which make it an excellent case study in cultural
assimilation and national recuperation.

Strictly speaking, Delius had no need of naturalisation.
He was as English as John Bull, as British as Britannia,
having been born in Bradford of officially naturalised
German parents who came over in the 1850s and remained
settled here until their deaths. This large and busy family of
Teutonic tykes endowed their fourth son with certain
attributes. He was brought up bilingually in German and
English. As fitted the former rather than the latter ambience
– to all educated Germans, England was *das land ohne
musik* – he imbibed at home a love of music. His lasting
regional affiliations were located only in an interest in
cricket, which he played as a young man.[5] In every other
respect he turned his back firmly, and at the first available
opportunity, on his nurture environment. So far as this
ambitious and gifted young man was concerned, England,
Yorkshire, Bradford, family and home and all, were nothing
more than the neutral vessel which had carried his star to
earth. Even in the catalogues of Artists' Lives, those
endless, yellowing pages, forever foxed by the spots of
selfish individualism, the biography of Delius is an
outstanding record of utterly self-willed monomania. He was
a man careless of authority, duty, and responsibility;
untrammelled by consideration and social conscience to a
degree which is almost breathtaking when his historical
circumstances and social background are considered. With
the possible exception of his contemporary, Scriabin, no
major composer was so indifferent to conventional morality.
He was a living (and livid) rejection of Victorian values, to
an extent which would have given even Lytton Strachey
pause for thought.

The degree of the alienation of Delius from his origins
may already be apprehended. It brings us nearer to
understanding the remarkable exercise involved in placing

him, diametrically opposed as he was to the mores of all political states and social majorities – and *above all* to British exemplars – into any kind of fixed and positive relationship with 'This England'. Yet the feat was achieved, and history was made, to be incapable of unmaking, even by the historian. For all its modest obscurity, the simple headstone at Limpsfield, with its advertisement of the remains of Frederick Albert Theodore Delius – who had been christened merely but evocatively as Fritz – is a national shrine, a cultural mausoleum. It is also a site of ideological struggle. It stands as a document, a conscious artifact of the campaign to install Delius as a tableau in our national pageant. It helped to make this rabidly anti-English and even anti-social personality a part of the fabric of English society.

Allegro Risoluto

For good or ill, Delius is today widely regarded as an English Composer. It follows by definition that his creative legacy is seen as sufficiently meeting criteria laid down for the award of that distinction. Beecham's vision is now reified ideal: popular, critical and scholarly sources provide a consensus view of Delius as an integral part of the English Heritage, and a major figure in the British Musical Renaissance. His music is regularly performed, broadcast and recorded in this country. Since 1929, there have been two further festivals devoted entirely to his work – in London in 1946, again under the aegis of Sir Thomas Beecham, and the centenary concerts at Bradford in 1962. There exists a Delius Trust, formed to conserve, edit and publish his scores and his literary memorabilia, as well as to patronise and promote performance; and a Delius Society which provides a forum and a lobby for his admirers amongst the music-loving public at large. In 1984 he was widely commemorated, alongside Elgar and Holst, in many performances which recollected the milestone in English musical history represented by the year 1934. Subsequently, he was present in a limited series of stamps issued by the Post Office and dedicated to British Composers. His preferment above Vaughan Williams on this occasion may be regarded as a special triumph, for reasons which will later become evident.[6] At any rate, it may be asserted that Delius is an established member of the group of four modern composers – namely, those mentioned in this paragraph – who shine in the galaxy with a brightness dimensionally more intense than that of other, lesser, luminaries.

Available statistics suggest that the 'popularity rating' of Delius, as reflected in performances broadcast on BBC Radio 3, is about 50 per cent of that of Elgar.[7] This might not seem impressive, until one considers the much higher profile always given to the latter, whose sounder set of 'national' qualifications can hardly be subject for debate. At present, in an average year, Delius receives 97 airings in this medium compared to Elgar's 192 and Holst's 66. Of course, Elgar's rating effectively places him in the same league as Schumann, Mendelssohn and Richard Strauss – that is to say, on a par with all but the very greatest. Nevertheless, for his part, Delius has achieved the status of a 'Great Composer' – at least in this country. These data are complemented by the level of scholarly interest. In Foreman's basic source dissertation, Delius registers 40 pages of bibliographical information compared to 46 for Elgar and 23 for Holst.[8]

Indeed, though difficult to credit from statements made by Delius himself, English critics had greeted his music with warmth from the very beginning. In the aftermath of his first London concert in 1899, the press notices were mostly favourable. Even the *Musical Times* recognised his talent, complaining only (if significantly) that his work seemed excessively gloomy; he needed to 'cheer up and be like M Glazunov'. Memory of the occasion was not obliterated by the triumphant first performance of the *Enigma Variations* which, in what might have been a fatal contingency, took place only a few weeks later, launching the overdue fame of Elgar. In fact *The Gazette* linked their names together as 'Two Promising Young Men'. Four years later one critic (perhaps aware of what was happening in Germany) in effect supported the claim of Delius *against that of Elgar* as 'the biggest composer we have produced for many a long day'. This was a maverick view, given the fact that Delius and his music had been absent from London in the interim. Furthermore, it was accompanied by the incongruous and ominous caveat that 'he can scarcely be claimed for England'.[9]

On the whole, a marked indifference to our subject predominated in Britain for twenty years, during which his music received little more than occasional obeisance from the masters of English taste and opinion. One widely-distributed reference work allowed him only a one-line mention *in the appendix* of a new edition, which appeared shortly after the end of the First World War. It referred sniffily to the fact that 'F Delius, of German parentage, is highly esteemed by many'.[10] On the other hand, some converts were made who proved crucial to later developments. The youngest and most strident of these was the teenage ex-Etonian Philip Heseltine, who became a humble acolyte of Delius. However, it is worthy of mention at this stage that when Joseph Holbrooke, at the beginning of the Great War, 'published a series of extraordinary articles on British Music versus German Music', and Heseltine entered the lists, he did so not because he wished to claim Delius for the national cause, nor to whitewash his 'Prussian' connections, but rather in order to cite his hero 'as a cosmopolitan composer who had no need to stress his nationality to push his music'.[11]

Heseltine adhered consistently to this line when, nearly a decade later, he came to publish the first full-length study of Delius in the English language. Although he did not overlook the need to stress certain important links between the composer and his native background, this theme was by no means given a central place. In fact, somewhat surprisingly for such a notorious iconoclast, Heseltine's reaction to several of the composer's more 'heretical' works was one of orthodox bemusement and disapproval. This was to adopt an attitude utterly characteristic of the type of 'English' critic which he and his mentor privately took delight in excoriating. Such are the casualties of war.[12]

Any further equivocation inside the ranks was avoided by the recruitment to them of an even doughtier campaigner.

This was Cecil Gray, Heseltine's contemporary and associate in polemic, who included a long chapter on Delius in his first major book. The treatment represented nothing less than a deliberate attempt to replace Elgar with Delius as the echt-English composer. The attack was subtle and effective in method:

> They are both profoundly English; and while Delius reveals a strikingly close affinity to the Elizabethans as well as to the poets of the romantic movement, Elgar is more representative of the England of today, or, more accurately, of yesterday.

Gray's eulogy contained several of the ideas which were to become seminal in all pro-Delius discourse. Two of them are present already in the brief quotation just made: that Delius' music was somehow genealogically related to that of the only previous great age of English Music three centuries earlier, and that it was poetic in essence – an analogy intended very much to bring lyrical, rather than epic, poetry to mind. The writer proceeded to develop these claims and to add others.

> Sweetness and sensuousness is perhaps the most noteworthy characteristic of English art. The purist who would condemn it in the music of Delius is at the same time condemning Dowland and Purcell ... It is the very quintessence of the English spirit in art ... [Delius stands for] the reconciliation of qualities generally conceived of as opposites: the union of the two different fundamental aspects of the national mind – the Anglo-Saxon and the Celtic.

Any historical approach to this text would be bound to reveal the broadly political nature of Gray's attack. He laid great stress on the tranquillity and repose induced by a hearing of Delius' music, by implication contrasting it with the more martial strains of Elgar. In the aftermath of an awful war, and near the beginning of the first great movement of middle-class pacifism which was part of the reaction to it, this was a timely move. Yet simultaneously, Gray insinuated the idea that whereas Elgar was too *specifically* English, Delius better represented the 'union' of the four countries – despite the quietly impressive fact that 'he has never claimed to be a nationalist composer'. Gray's seductive style and intellectual weight, allied to a flair for subjective value-judgement, were quickly to make him one of the most distinguished critics of an age, innocent of musicology, which placed a premium on such qualities. His championship gave a decisive impetus to the Delius cause. Gray spoke for a generation which was almost guiltily turning its back on the jingoistic imperialism with which Sir Edward Elgar was ineradicably associated. His parthian shot was suitably audacious:

> Delius is first and foremost a creative artist for whom music is the means of expression of spiritual realities. Elgar, on the contrary, is primarily a craftsman ...[13]

Proselytising for Delius meanwhile continued in the pages of *The Sackbut*, a magazine produced by Heseltine and Gray, devoted to debunking stuffy old attitudes in musical life and advancing trendy new ones. Beecham chimed in with two newspaper articles. One appeared in the *Evening Standard* in 1927; the second, timed to coincide with the Delius Festival of 1929, was carried by the *Daily Mail*, and bore the suggestive title 'The Composer who stands for England'. One of England's most prominent artistic figures – whose depreciation of Elgar was to become an open secret – was promoting the cause of a rival in the most public medium then available, the popular press.[14]

1929 was also the year in which most western governments signed the Kellogg-Briand pact, 'renouncing war as an instrument of national policy'. Support for disarmament and the League of Nations was still on the increase, and in the year before the death of Delius, pacifism registered one of its most spectacular triumphs with the resolution of the Oxford Union that 'This House will not fight for King and Country'. In such a political atmosphere even some of the 'heretical' characteristics of Delius now began to count in his favour. By a strange osmosis he acquired the (posthumous) reputation of an existentialist rebel, even of a Leftist.[15] It may be argued that every British institution needs its resident nonconformist, its token dissident, the better to define normative identities. The British Musical Renaissance is no exception. Indeed, one suspects that Beecham was instinctively conscious of this paradox when writing his funeral oration.

Subtly connected with this was the idea which now moved to the forefront of Delius propaganda. It presented his art as having the English countryside at the nucleus of its inspiration. Green thoughts, after all, unite the protester with the patriot in their green shade. This trope proved the most successful of all those mobilised in the campaign, to the extent that it became in time an almost unquestioned assumption of Delius criticism. It plugged the composer into a whole programme of positive and affirmative evaluation of 'English' culture and identity which had been gathering strength for a generation. Pro-Delius writing now deployed an emotive vocabulary in which words like 'soil', 'nature', 'national', 'folk', 'landscape', were of key significance. Both Heseltine and Gray had already drawn attention to the use by Delius of old English tunes, the latter praising his 'natural and inherent penchant for folk-song modalities'.[16] As we have seen, Beecham had linked music and 'soil', during a ritual in which the man who had produced the former was buried – in a sense *buried himself* – in the latter. The seed thus planted grew into a mighty tree. No less a savant than Constant Lambert agreed that 'Elgar and Delius have in their widely different ways, written music that is essentially English in feeling.' Some years later, Eric Blom concurred with Gray that '[Delius's] work is the ideal counterpart of English lyric poetry'.[17] Most luxuriant in the imagery of its own growth was the postwar study by Arthur Hutchings whose general conclusion about his subject ran as follows:

> He sings of the transitory beauty of summer, the English summer that we still know ... If the time comes when hills, woods, lanes and hedgerows are utterly spoiled ... the loveliness we once knew may be captured only as an emotional experience in the poetry of Keats and the music of Fred Delius.

The argument proceeds to cite examples, with the aid of a prose style inscribed with all the perfervid emotions of the war for national survival during which it was written. The response to Delius has become an instinctual part of what Fitzgerald called 'a century of middle class love'.[18]

> *Brigg Fair* and *On Hearing the First Cuckoo in Spring* ... evoke the spirit of our English countryside ... with Delius we feel as we do when reading Jefferies or Hardy, English writers who identify our thoughts ... unmistakably the beloved skyline of our English fields, woods, rivers, hills, dawns and sunsets ... the casual listener is at one in feeling with his countryside and countryman.

Delius is here a sacralised talisman, a totem whose big magic fuses us into oneness with our culture and nation. Not surprisingly, the points of technical analysis which the author adduces in support of this thesis are selective and invariably subjective/impressionistic in character. In place of any genuine dialectic, the reader's consciousness is besieged by an armoury of imagery, insisting with a primitive sub-Lawrentian beat upon its own liturgical truth. Listening to Delius is an Act of Faith. Hutchings produced the first study of Delius which might be regarded as *fully professional* in the modern sense; in that it was produced by a full-time university academic. Ironically, his faith permits him blatantly to set aside the overwhelming evidence of explicitly non-English origin surrounding certain works. He says, for example, about *In a Summer Garden*, that 'the original garden was in France, but every sight, sound, and odour, implicit in this music that defies analysis, is part of our English inheritance. The lazy Loing is taken as some native Avon, Ouse or Medway'. Yet Hutchings could hardly have been ignorant of the fact that this work was written with the composer's own garden at Grez quite concretely in mind, that the river whose movement is summoned up was specifically the Loing, and that it was dedicated to his Danish-German wife.[19]

The discourse of a picture-postcard England, which came to dominate the self-image of the nation as a strategy of the later stages of heavy industrialisation, and was later rooted in position by the Great War, was by no means restricted to those of a conservative inclination.[20] Some surprising gardeners took up the tools of William Morris and helped to shape the utopian landscape. For example, near the beginning of *The History of Mr Polly* we find the following passage:

> There is no countryside like the English countryside for those who have learned to love it; its firm yet gentle line of hill and dale ... its deer parks and downland, its castles and stately houses, its hamlets and old churches, its farms and ricks and great barns and ancient trees, its pools and ponds and shining threads of rivers, its flower-starred hedgerows, its orchards and woodland patches, its village greens and kindly inns. Other countrysides have their pleasant aspects, but none such variety ... as our mother England does.[21]

The elements of this English Idyll are so functional and pervasive that still only slowly – if indeed at all – are they seeping out of our mentality. Even in the contemporary Britain of canned satire and scholarly scepticism, the Merrie Olde England of multitudinous cliche remains in many ways part of the collective psyche, and provides a major role in – what in this case seems a perfectly apt phrase – our invisible earnings. (What was invented partly to compensate for and even to disguise industrial progress, has become perhaps our greatest industry, that is, the subject of tourism.)

Since Hutchings, it has proved difficult for commentators to treat of the 'natural' element in the music of Delius independently of the 'national'. To Christopher Palmer, for example, Delius was a member of an influential school of 'nature-mystics' which inhabited the musical world of his time. In spite of his own thesis, Palmer is obliged to admit that

> nature-mystics could not have existed in music before the rise of nationalism, and consequent reappraisal of folksong, because the far-reaching changes ... brought in its wake were endemic in musical representation of the folksong milieu, i.e. nature, the countryside.

Not surprisingly, despite his confident statement that 'I have no intention whatever of allowing myself to be caught in the particularly thorny thicket of Delius's Englishness', he lapses only ten pages later into the claim that 'Bax and

Delius were the two supreme poets of the English revival'. Later still he is positively enmeshed by the thorny thicket, and writhing only worsens his predicament:

> Delius is certainly not 'English' like Vaughan Williams, whose music can be truly appreciated only in terms of the English scene. The English take [the latter] to their hearts because they sense that the English woods, fields and streams which went into its making also went into the making of part of themselves.[22]

The final bars in this movement belong to perhaps the most persuasive of postwar Delius advocates, Deryck Cooke. Not a man to swallow myths, and keenly aware of the conditioning of our perception created by historical contexts, Cooke peremptorily dismissed any meaningful identification of Delius with a national background. Nonetheless, perhaps in the last analysis susceptible like other mortals to the elemental lure, he surmised that at least Delius 'may have invented the English pastoral style'.[23]

Scherzo – Con Malizia

Of course not everything in the garden was lovely, and from its very genesis serpents crawled in the undergrowth. According to Heseltine, *The Times* opposed Delius bitterly in the early years. The well-disposed Robin Legge in the *Daily Telegraph* was more than cancelled out by the attitude – at best lukewarm – of Ernest Newman, whose voice from the columns of the *Manchester Guardian* was sweetest to the ears of the British musical public. After the Great War, Newman continued to champion Elgar, passing over Sir Edward's unlikely protagonist in total silence. Although he was to make diplomatic overtures to Grez following the success of *Hassan* in the West End, Newman remained unconvinced over the basic issues propounded by Delius supporters. In what was probably a jibe at Newman's expense, Constant Lambert later recalled:

> It was once said of Delius that he divided English critics into two camps, those who did not know his music disputing the opinions of those who did.[24]

The attitude of Ralph Vaughan Williams was even more forthright. The younger composer's attempt to pay court to the elder in 1907 was treated with ill-disguised indifference, and thereafter he became an inveterate enemy.[25] In the wake of the Delius Festival, Vaughan Williams contributed a foreword to Sir Henry Hadow's *English Music* – published in the Longman series *The English Heritage* – in which he directly challenged Gray and Beecham. Employing a phraseology chillingly evocative of its time, he claimed that the great native composers could only be produced by 'blood and soil'. Elgar was repeatedly referred to as the real precursor of Englishness, whilst Delius was implicitly excluded by the ineluctable rules of nature and culture.

> Cosmopolitanism in art means loss of vitality. It is the stream pressing against its narrow banks which will turn the mill wheel. In every nation except ours the power of nationalism in art is recognised. It is the very advocacy of a colourless cosmopolitanism which makes one occasionally despair of England as a musical nation.

This seemingly unexceptionable utterance was in fact an anti-Delius manifesto taken from a cue in Hadow's text. Delius' work was here described as 'a tributary which for most of its course has run through alien regions'. The thin praise allotted to it carried a deadly rider.

> Many of its most pictorial pages are suggested by English scenes and English landscapes ... Yet his distinctive qualities are not those of our national art ... A far more central and representative figure is Vaughan Williams.[26]

Heseltine's description of Delius as a 'cosmopolitan' was now turned to the disadvantage of the cause. Indeed, the word had acquired fresh and disturbing overtones since the use of it by the composer's disciple. In the 1930s, if not before, it had become a synonym for 'Jew' in many European languages. Delius himself was so little known in England that even his supporters were often uncertain as to his precise origins. Writing in 1924 (for example), Cecil Gray had presumed him to be of Dutch extraction. In an irony which is at once amusing and sinister, this mordant anti-semite was at times regarded as Jewish, a notion that his aloof and defensive lifestyle did nothing to counter.[27] How widespread it was, and the effect it had on the standing of Delius in this country, can only be matter for speculation. At any rate, use of the word 'cosmopolitan' remained (until Palmer's study) a token of disfavour amongst the critics. 'Delius was a cosmopolitan in culture, withdrawn and solitary in his music'; 'nothing in common with any English tradition ... an isolated cosmopolitan'.[28]

Meanwhile in 1937, the posthumous reputation and stature of Delius were examined in the pages of the celebrated Cambridge quarterly *Scrutiny*. This was the equivalent of being considered for entry into the Pantheon of Authentic English Artists, in the (notional) musical section of 'The Great Tradition' invented by its founder, F R Leavis. The journal's music editor, Wilfrid Mellers, found the application of Delius deficient in certain key areas. True, he had been a supporter of D H Lawrence against the persecution of the English bourgeois establishment; this was a definite plus. In itself the music was found to be distinctive and valuable. But its character

> has nothing to do with any sense of nationality or community. I know that distinguished critics have seen in Delius's music some profoundly English quality (something connected with 'worship of Nature') but ... there is nothing English about the music of Delius.

One of the strongest points against him was the alleged 'Death Tendency' of his work, coupled with its clear lack of a positivist or humanist basis. This vitiated any claim to true Englishness.[29]

The *Scrutiny* article had been occasioned by a review of a well-known book about Delius by his amanuensis, Eric Fenby. As Mellers rightly remarked, for all his devotion to the music, and his intimacy with the man, Fenby was extremely loath to consider Delius as a national figure. On the contrary, the young Yorkshireman believed that the music of Delius – for all its worldly beauties – reflected a spiritual wasteland, a desolate impasse, sans hope, sans

God, sans all the solid and consoling English virtues. Awkwardly for the 'Delius Cause', Fenby was appalled at most of the composer's 'extra-musical' ideas and ultimately repelled by his personality. He challenged the High Priests of Delius, Gray and Beecham, at the outset of his published memoir, in stating his belief that it was *Elgar*'s music which conveyed 'the mood of blessed felicity, by which I mean an active and loving rest in God'. Fenby expressed the feeling that Elgar's works were indelibly associated with England, sustaining him in his most depressed moments amidst the alien flora of Grez.[30] Even before the death of Delius, Fenby had written privately to Elgar:

> Although ... I have been acting as hands and eyes to your contemporary Frederick Delius ... nobody could possibly have a greater love and admiration for your music and for yourself than I ... I know of no other modern music which brings Heaven to Earth and sings so much of true goodness and the joy of healthy living ... it never failed to bring England to France.[31]

Several aspects of Fenby's approach amounted to a self-inflicted wound for the Delius campaign. Even more telling, however, is the fact that Beecham himself ultimately came closer to Fenby's point of view. In his full-length study of Delius (1959) he treated most of the composer's opinions to liberal doses of sarcasm. Although he made no explicit retractions, many of his earlier claims were undermined in the process. Indeed, Sir Thomas's personal disappointment led him too far, even into a denial of the English associations of a work like *Brigg Fair*.[32]

Little wonder, therefore, that the question continues to divide English critics. At his centenary mark of 1962, Delius had not achieved the recognition of a place in Dent's definitive *Master Musicians* series.[33] Though Cooke, with great analytical skill and formidable dialectic, established his objective claim to universal greatness, he nonetheless acknowledged that Delius was 'a stateless artist' who had 'an entirely un-English attitude to life'. Other experts remained unconvinced on one or both of these issues. Only a year after the centenary, John Warrack ignored Delius entirely in an article on the English Musical Renaissance. There are still musicians and music-lovers everywhere who (it has been neatly put) 'can hardly bear to sit in the room while a Delius work is being played'. Sympathy and antipathy on the subject spring from sources which are unusually deep.[34]

These subterranean contradictions and ambiguities help to explain why Delius, although recognised as a composer of stature only in this country, is even here very far from being *fully* accepted. Excepting only a short (but significant) period after the Second World War, there has never been a fashionable 'craze' for Delius. The mass-appeal which Heseltine foresaw never materialised, and as many have noted, appreciation has been both muted and (as it were) private; something shared between a minority of consenting adults, rather than capable of filling a public arena. For example, Ken Russell's film *A Song of Summer*, based upon Fenby (1968), though no less accomplished than his earlier promotion of Elgar, did not inspire a repeat of the popular enthusiasm which greeted the latter.

When the Delius repertoire of our orchestras is examined, it is found to contain a mere handful of his works. This consists of the tone-poems which supposedly contain 'English' elements, which if added together occupy hardly more concert-space than one of Elgar's symphonies. These pieces were all written within a relatively short span of a composing life which – with one lengthy interruption – stretched over some 45 years. The major choral and vocal works with orchestra, representing a far more significant area of Delius's overall achievement, are comparatively rarely heard. The six operas are almost wholly ignored, several of them having recently been recorded for the first time, whilst most still await a full professional premiere on the stage. His four concertos are luxury items. The average (or unmotivated) reader is constantly presented with a kind of expurgated, and thus sanitised version of the full text. Despite the greatly increased numbers of performances in the year 1984, these boundaries were still, on the whole, faithfully respected.[35]

Rondo Alla Tedesca

Delius has thus achieved a secure immortality, but one which is oddly circumscribed as to its social conditions, and limited to the English-speaking world. Without his contemporary English supporters, a smallish group of subsequent English advocates, and a fairly select English audience, so far from being a 'great universal', Delius would at best be a minor cult figure, and at worst have been completely forgotten. He has become marooned within the very culture he despised, a victim of his own *dictum* that 'British Music as a rule won't stand crossing the Channel'.[36] This sentence was pronounced with all his customary arrogance at the height of his own success – a success which was based in Germany.

Since for over half a century Delius has been virtually unknown on the continent, it is difficult to realise that for more than ten years his music had a huge following in Germany. The flow of the mighty river of *Appalachia* and the tide of *Sea Drift* swept irresistibly across the Fatherland. Delius enjoyed the attention of some of the foremost German impresarios, executants and critics of the day. And what a day it was! Any musician could almost afford failure elsewhere so long as he was successful in the Reich. In this pre-war decade, when competition in the concert-halls and opera-pits was as sharply contested as the international power-struggle, and Europe crowded with an *embarras de richesse* of composing talent never seen before nor since, Delius carved out a niche which at one time threatened to rival that of the Crown Prince, Richard Strauss.[37]

After 1900, nearly all his premieres took place in Germany, and by 1906 he had gained his first publishing contract with the new Berlin firm of Harmonie. Most of his closest advisers were German, and when the financial rewards of success began to accrue, he duly invested them in German Stock.[38] Although the Great War was to annihilate these savings, it failed to asphixiate interest in the music, which revived in the early Weimar period. Not until the mid-1920s, with the rise of the new generation, did Delius suffer eclipse – a fate he shared with other late-Romantic figures, and which even cast its shadow upon the brilliant orb of Strauss. In contrast to that of its own sons, however, decline of Delius in Germany proved both absolute and definitive. Its completeness may be gauged from the almost non-existent relationship of a modern German virtuoso like Dietrich Fischer-Dieskau to a composer who left almost as much gratifying music for the lyric baritone as Strauss did for the soprano. Apart from one hardly successful encounter, early in his uniquely long career, the singer who has mastered and recorded virtually everything else of any distinction written for his range, has never performed Delius.[39]

Elgar's recognition in this country had come about in part because of success in Germany, and Delius naturally expected similar developments in his favour. For close on a century, England had been an exclusive musical colony of the Austro-German schools, which for a further century before that had shared its exploitation more or less equally with the Italians. Of course, a growing sense of cultural competition was woven into the darkening web of Anglo-German national rivalry. But even the jealousy and fear which marked the latter seems in no way to have diminished the English welcome for German music. Indeed, according to one authority, many indigenous talents actually operated under what may perhaps be called Teutonic *noms de guerre* in order to assist their careers – like the conductor Basil Cameron, who around 1908 adopted the singularly unfortunate professional name of Hindenburg.[40] The celebrated composer of Merrie England chose to use only his middle name of German as a providential alternative to his somewhat embarrassing surname which happened to be *Jones*. In 1903, by what seems a perverse act of contrary motion, Delius dropped his first name of Fritz in favour of the English Frederick, calculating (perhaps) that the latter was still German enough, and that his surname catered perfectly for all eventualities of prejudice. Four years later he visited England for professional reasons for the first time since 1899, hoping to build a following around Henry Wood's successful premiere of his *Piano Concerto*.

Delius himself appreciated that 'national music' offered

peculiar advantages to any composer. The only music other than his own which he genuinely loved was that of Edvard Grieg, a composer whose greatness was everywhere acknowledged as stemming from his Norwegian roots. Grieg had once written to Delius, 'it is my fervent wish that you will one day receive in your own country the recognition you deserve'.[41] The latter's own early work experimented with various 'ethnic' styles, the best of which were associated with Florida or with Norway itself. It is certain that such experiences had entirely effaced any residual feeling for his birthplace long before 1907. In Bradford for his father's funeral in 1901 he could hardly contain his contempt for the people he met – those, presumably, who had come to record respect and offer sympathy. ('I really could see those sort of people wiped out by thousands with the greatest equanimity'.) When he arrived for the 1907 expedition, he wrote to Jelka merely that 'London is a splendid field [for success]'.[42]

Nevertheless, he was able quickly to produce a work aimed at the English market, and which drew not only upon distant experience but upon an almost uncanny divination of what was happening in English composition. The result was *Brigg Fair – An English Rhapsody*, which marked a sudden and otherwise unaccountable departure of style towards a less difficult language more acceptable to British tastes. Delius maintained this mode more or less consistently until 1914, culminating in a work which is in many ways an English Pastoral symphony – the *North Country Sketches* – and could slip into it almost on demand in later life.[43]

Delius stayed in England for nearly a year, but apart from a successful performance of *Appalachia* which inspired several of those individuals (including Beecham) who were to become his English adherents, the response was disappointing. He was offered no impressive positions or contracts. The 'English Music' lobby seemed to want rather to yoke him to the wagon of the common cause than to perform, applaud and reward Delius himself. They had badly misjudged the man – and tried to use him too blatantly. By now, Delius was well into middle age, and was undergoing the secondary stages of the syphilis he had contracted from a Parisian prostitute some years earlier. Not surprisingly, the negative aspects of his personality worsened, and he departed in disgust. No doubt Granville Bantock was closely echoing the composer's own recriminations when he tried to reassure him that 'you will get your recognition here in spite of time-servers and double-dealers.'[44]

Although he returned for the odd commission, Delius from now on generally held himself aloof in Grez. Apparently secure in his German popularity, he allowed free rein to his antipathy to all things English. This tendency was especially marked in the correspondence with Heseltine, which began in 1911. His first informal missive of the series was wholly characteristic, in this respect as in most others.

England and America have, I believe, the monopoly of hypocrites ... I cannot stand the moral atmosphere of England.[45]

In the spring of 1914, his prestige in Germany reached its apogee with performances of *A Mass of Life* at Wiesbaden, *Two Orchestral Pieces* at Frankfurt-am-Main, and *Songs of Sunset* at Elberfeld – all within a few weeks.[46] The outbreak of war was a tremendous blow to his fortunes and prospects just when (at the belated age of 52) they seemed on the point of apotheosis.

In one sense, at least, he reacted appropriately: 'I hate and loathe this German militarism and autocracy and I hope it may be crushed for ever'. But despite the shelter he received in England, the national struggle evoked no trace of positive emotional response. 'I can get up no enthusiasm for the war', he told his young admirer. Soon afterwards he was fiercely urging Heseltine to use a writing opportunity to 'attack the whole idea of English composers, etc.', adding his conviction that 'there is no real English music'.[47] Now domiciled at a property (loaned by Beecham) in Watford, his presence helped bring about a spate of performances in 1914-15. But Delius remained immune to the passions of nationalism, to a degree which, in almost anybody else, might be worthy of admiration. For example, in the autumn of 1916, when the orgiastic butchery of the Somme and Verdun was spending itself in mutual exhaustion, he was capable of cool and prophetic detachment:

> The war will have changed much ... many will have realised the *rot* that has been going on and the hollowness of patriotism and jingoism and all the other isms.[48]

As soon as it became possible, Delius had escaped from England to neutral Norway. 'Here we are in this glorious country', he told Heseltine; 'since I left England my spirits have been gradually rising [and] Watford is like an unpleasant dream to me now'.[49] Moreover, as soon after the Armistice as was practically possible, the Deliuses returned to Germany, where a surprisingly warm reception awaited them. The composer's anxiety to revisit the Fatherland may not (however) have been purely a result of musical considerations. Frankfurt, where he spent a good deal of time in 1920-23, was the world centre for the treatment of syphilis, location of the research clinic directed by the founder of modern chemotherapy, Paul Ehrlich. By presumably restricting his access to Ehrlich's wonder-drug Salvarsan (Preparation 606), the war had precipitated the worst stages of Delius' illness. Its later years therefore saw a serious deterioration in his condition, which now proved irreversible, and by 1922 he had become the near-sightless paraplegic familiar in his pictures. Upon the hapless Heseltine, who was kept entirely in the dark as to the gravity, and (of course) the nature of the affliction, Delius vented all his spleen.[50]

Spleen was something which Frederick Delius possessed in Baudelairian abundance. He struck out in venomous hatred at every custom, belief and institution which he associated with England, in a display which makes the later excesses of Angry Young Men seem mild. Space forbids a thorough illustration of the promiscuous barrage which

Delius unleashed against 'Englishness' – both in writing to Heseltine and other correspondents, and in conversation with many an English visitor to Grez. It can be demonstrated by reference to many extant sources, that he bitterly disparaged the very coin of cliche about 'Old Roast Beef Yorkshire Pudding England', which (even as he wrote) was pouring bright new from the mint of cultural usage, and was later to be rolled out in his support.[51] Moreover, if the condition (and conditions) of music in England were his main targets, he frequently explained and supported his opinions by reference to the background of religious, social and explicitly political factors. He derived his attitudes on all these things – music included – directly from Friedrich Nietzsche.

Despite recent signs of his cautious rehabilitation in certain scholarly quarters, Nietzsche has been the anathematised philosopher of our century, the thoroughly modern Machiavel. The capitalist West and the communist East have been united in distaste for the writings believed to have underpinned two catastrophic German bids for world power. Now Delius was a Nietzschean thinker through and through, an intellectual thrall of the German philosopher who – by the 1920s – was identified by the English middle class (rightly) as a natural enemy, and (wrongly) as the veritable prophet of Prussianism. As far as his English reputation was concerned, Delius could hardly have selected a worse model than the man whom he recommended to all his friends and visitors as 'the most significant thinker of modern times'.[52] From Nietzsche he repeated – often in parrotted or paraphrased terms – the opinions that 'Christianity is Paralysis'; that patriotism (*vaterlanderei*) is despicable; that democracy produces only slavery and socialism merely another form of despotism. If this were not unusual enough for an alleged 'English' artist, Delius made clear that he agreed with Nietzsche not only on these evils in general, but on their particularly evil dominance in England.[53]

1916 was the supreme year of sacrifice, which witnessed the most resounding clash of the *kulturschlacht* between Germany and its enemies. During this of all years, Delius

brought to fruition the most thoroughly Nietzschean of all
his works, a description from which I do not exclude *A Mass
of Life*. Unlike the latter, the text of the *Requiem* was not
taken directly from Nietzsche, but rather from Judaeo-
Christian scripture, glossed and interlarded with words of
the composer's own devising. All the more telling,
therefore, is the fact that both text and music – insofar as
they may be validly distinguished for the present purposes –
were a vicious rejection of English standards of principle and
taste. It was almost as if Delius intended to encase these
sentiments eternally in a major work, so belligerent was the
insulting defiance he hurled at Britain.[54] In 1919, he scoffed
to Heseltine,

> British Music has had more than a fair chance and has been
> performed much too much ... I don't claim to be a British
> composer;

pointedly adding a year later that 'they are playing again a
good deal of my music in Germany'.[55]

On visits to London he exhorted Heseltine to devote *The
Sackbut* to a crusade against the principle and practice of
'English Music'. Included in his dismissive comments were
not only individual composers and their methods, but the
whole apparatus of British musical life, from standards of
performance to education and the curriculum.[56] From his
bottomless interior well of vitriol he spattered even those
disposed to be helpful. When the appearance of Heseltine's
and Gray's books failed to produce results commensurate
with the hopes raised by the popular success of *Hassan*, he
reverted to listing the places in Germany where he was still
obtaining performances.[57] In fact, his fame in that country
was ebbing rapidly. By the time of his death, German
musicians were oblivious to Delius. In a truly farcical
incident, Erich Kleiber gave an impromptu obituary, having
been informed of what he evidently understood to be the
passing of *Sibelius*.

> I am particularly touched by this news for just as I received it on
> the telephone I was studying the very beautiful Fourth
> Symphony of Delius. I have been studying all his works lately

because I am hoping to make him better known in Germany, but this symphony is perhaps his most mystical work ...[58]

Da Capo e affetuoso

For all his outward bluster, therefore, Delius became inwardly concerned that his music might never obtain a purchase in the country where it had the greatest potential. The choice between immortality in England or no immortality at all was being posed. His response was nothing if not resourceful. In 1919, he gave a long press interview in which his tone was constructive and polite – if not exactly modest – on the future of English Music (no apostrophes now called for).[59] Meanwhile, his defiance had ever stronger hints of envy and chagrin.

> They gave a concert of English Music in Paris last April and took care to leave my name out of the programme – why? The real *Britishers* were all there; this is all very amusing of course [...]
>
> Strangeways sent me his magazine for January with a long dissertation on Vaughan Williams, the *Great English Genius*!!!
>
> The article on Elgar by Shaw in *Music and Letters* is worthy of the Pink 'Un or *The Tatler* [...]
>
> What an article on VW – God! it exposes the author to ridicule.[60]

In 1920, Delius recommended that *The Sackbut* carry a feature series on

> 'We should like to know' – Let us say as an example – 'We should like to know why none of the works of Delius were included in the programmes of the so-called British Music Festival'.[61]

He now began to affect a pose of English nostalgia, so patently false and exaggerated, it suggests that, since he had perforce to adapt and compromise, he had decided at least to enjoy the act. He responded to a prompt from Heseltine:

> What you say about the Celtic element in my music is perfectly true. I have a latent streak somewhere deep down in my being which flames up every now and again – probably atavistic from my Northern forbears.[62]

This deliberate mocking of a friend and disciple was of a piece with the way in which he treated the old Yorkshire 'connections' which now made welcome overtures to him. Their envoy was his sister Clare, whom (save for one unsuccessful wartime reunion) he had not seen for some twenty years. He invited Clare to Grez, putting on for her benefit a touching performance of fond remembrance for the Dales and Moors, the Bradford companions of his youth, and local delicacies like Wensleydale cheese. Doubtless to his delight, she was completely taken in.[63] He treated several reporters, and even the civic dignitaries of Bradford (who journeyed to Grez to present him with the Freedom of the Borough) to an even more ridiculous routine. None of his visitors registered any awareness that they were being simultaneously exploited and insulted. 'Oh! for the honesty of the brothel', Delius had expostulated during one of his blasts against English moral hypocrisy. But he himself could not be an honest whore, needing to deck his compromises out as an elaborate private joke.[64]

For some time, the recipe appeared to have little effect. In despair, Jelka told Heseltine in 1926, 'they give mighty little of his music in England now ... it seems all to be the Elgar clique'.[65] But already the situation was changing dramatically. The Bradford honour was only one of a series, which began suddenly in 1923 with the award of the Gold Medal of the Royal Philharmonic Society, the offer of an honorary degree by Oxford, and (early in 1929) his creation as Companion of Honour by George V. By Jelka's own admission, even the last of these evoked none of the normal (or required) sentiments in her husband's breast. But by now the arrangements for the all-important festival were in hand, and anxious not to rock the boat, Delius wryly recited the appropriate litany of modest gratitude.[66] The same consideration inspired him to register a complaint (via Jelka):

I was so annoyed at all the stupid things Newman told us last night ... on the wireless ... He said that *Delius was really not English at all but quite international*. Morever he said that in *Sea Drift* for example, as in other works, he composed the words in

German, thinking of probably German performances. Not a word of truth in that ... What could be more English in feeling than *Brigg Fair, North Country* in fact most of his works? Fred's idiom's English ... these Music Critics do all they can to hinder the listener from understanding Delius.[67]

Newman's move could hardly have been better timed to outflank the pro-Delius campaign, at the moment when his music was beginning to be heard on the BBC and was reaching the recording studio. The worry revived that perhaps Delius would after all remain, (to use his own words), 'the officially not understood original genius'.[68] Every effort was put into making the Queen's Hall Festival that autumn a definitive success. To accompany the unprecedented number and scale of the concerts went a publicity bandwagon which included press stories, interviews, commissioned portraits, and finally the dramatic and agonised journey of the crippled genius to attend the occasion. When it was all over, Heseltine called on the poet Bruce Blunt to celebrate the scene.

> From the peopled hall
> Call upon call of praise and love
> To the ringing roof ascends.
> Under a lighted dome
> The wanderer comes home:
> His country makes amends.[69]

Delius always regarded himself as an entirely autarkic entity – in his music as in his life he refused to acknowledge debts, thus avoiding any admission of weakness or inferiority. He built his *Heldenleben* upon the pedal point of his declaration of independence from his parents, and later was known to have exhibited a fierce unconcern for the favour of the great and the good. Any patronage – including the financial support he received from his uncle and his wife – had to be on his own terms. Nietzsche taught him that the Higher Man had to reject the claims of persons or institutions, established moral codes and ideas, and the fear of Death and God, in order to enrich and lead the lower. Much evidence suggests that Delius was convinced he belonged to an elite corps of what might be termed the *artistocracy*, neo-Waldensian priests or *iluminados* incapable of error.[70]

In some ways the 19th century cult of The Great Artist reached its culmination in Nietzsche. Yet at the same time, we can trace in his writings the origins of a diametrically contrary discourse, which was to lead to modern movements of cultural introspection and critical self-awareness, above all, perhaps, the poststructuralist discipline of deconstruction. An ideological Janus, Nietzsche stands on the bridge between two centuries. He points out how myths and cultures, morals and customs are created by men in response to the circumstances of power and survival, and have no abstract validity. Though Delius believed his art to be *true* rather than merely *useful*, he may nonetheless have been subliminally aware of the need to be born again in England, the more urgently as he began (as it were) to die elsewhere. To this extent, he himself was the author of the process already described, by which his music was grafted onto the British curriculum.

In like manner, supporters of Delius were motivated by an awareness – limited and opaque but nonetheless powerful – that cultural laws existed under which certain artists were accepted and sanctified by a society, whilst others were marginalised or even excluded. The first quarter of the present century witnessed the operation of such social mechanisms on a wider and more obtrusive scale than ever before, because of their explicit expropriation by and on behalf of the state.[71] Sensitive minds like Heseltine, Gray, and Beecham perceived that the monumental masonry of immortality had been levered inexorably into place in the case of Elgar, and was probably on the move for Vaughan Williams and Holst too. The amount of space left in the Pantheon was limited. Moreover, his advocates suspected that they lacked many of the resources from which a convincing mausoleum could be constructed on behalf of Delius. Their reaction was to manipulate their client's image almost with the expertise of modern public relations firms. Some characteristics were suppressed, others stressed; yet others were altered subtly by a kind of cosmetic surgery, the better to be advanced as qualifications frankly *different* from those of some established rivals in the market, but equally British and attractive. Delius was processed and packaged like a new cheese, based perhaps on sturdy Yorkshire Wensleydale, but with some milder, softer, slightly Gallic elements, a sort of musical Lymeswold. Thus the 'Impressionism' of his music was turned to good use as a testament to his abiding feeling for the English landscape, and his relationship to Nietzsche was 'explained' as wholly non-political, an admiration limited to the artistic and poetic feeling of the philosopher.[72]

As his mundane being suffered the final phase of its death-agony during the five years after the festival, Delius the immortal was therefore undergoing taxidermy, preparatory to being presented to the nation. However, the embalmers knew that all their unguents would be wasted if the corporeal remains were left abandoned in France. Everything depended on a final physical repatriation. The candidate collaborated, and during his last year of life informed various visitors of his desire for burial in an English country churchyard. In the months after his death, through the agency of the eminent musical family of Harrison, the arrangements were made in the latter's home parish of Limpsfield, and carried through in the way already described.[73]

Beecham himself was later to admit that the act of transubstantiation at which he officiated did not go unopposed by certain sincere believers. Amongst these were Delius's amanuensis, Fenby, and his sister, Clare. The latter refused to accept that Delius had ever countenanced burial anywhere but in Bradford or its environs, and took severe umbrage at Beecham's unsympathetic remarks about the North. It ought to be taken into account that she felt cheated of the vicarious fame she would have enjoyed had her brother been brought in eternal triumph back to his birthplace.[74] But it is difficult to dismiss her account of attempts to preclude the writing and to prevent the publication of her own book on Delius, made by the 'official' Delius interest; attempts which (she claims) were accompanied by threats and the offer of bribes. Nothing could more dramatically demonstrate the intensity of the emotional and political commitments involved.[75]

Fenby's opposition was of a different, but equally damaging kind. In the first place, he rejected the notion that any aspect (real or imagined) of Delius' connection with Britain was essential to his art. Even more to the point, Fenby from the first, and *even before he had actually come face to face with Delius*, reacted with an almost animal instinct against what he stood for. He felt that he had entered a spiritual world alien and even hostile to his own. Of central significance here is Fenby's description of his first arrival at the house in Grez.

> Mrs. Delius said, 'This is the room where Delius has written all his finest music' ... Immediately I felt the atmosphere was somewhat sinister, and I was curiously ill at ease. To the very end of my days in Grez I never fully overcame that unpleasant feeling in the music room. Sometimes, when I have been hundreds of miles away, I have suddenly remembered it and shuddered. *I cannot understand it at all*.[76]

On more than one homecoming from Grez, Fenby turned to Sir Edward Elgar as to a priest in the confessional; 'we are of the same faith so I greet you without embarrassment'. He was full of misgivings, so powerful that they amounted to a sense of penitential guilt, which only contact with the Catholic custodian of the grail of English music could absolve.[77] The young man's remorse was a reaction produced by the cultural antibodies analysed in this essay. Both these, and the immunising serum designed by the early apostles of Delius, will always be present in the biochemistry of any judgement made about his music. Dr Fenby, who contributed so much to appreciation of the latter, was in 1935 still only vaguely aware of the forces working around him. When Delius's coffin was loaded into the hearse for transport to England, he

> could not help remarking how wrong Delius had been when he had chosen to be buried in England. He belonged to Grez and only to Grez. My friends agreed with me ... I will not write of the funeral service ... For me it was all wrong ... [Delius] had blundered.[78]

Fenby knew instinctively that in some way he needed to exorcise Delius from his life. 'Let us give the [artistic] creator homage ... but let us not make a God of him', was a cry from the soul which, by a kind of contextual inversion, permits a diabolical interpretation. Only half-consciously, perhaps, Dr Fenby put his finger on it. 'I have known Pan', he claimed years later (*a propos* of the pagan fantasy *An Arabeske*), 'in the person of Frederick Delius'.[79]

I wish to thank Terry Hawkes for his incisive observations on a draft version of this chapter, and Meirion Hughes for several helpful suggestions.

Notes

[1] The text of Beecham's speech used here is that printed on the sleeve of the Delius centenary disc ALP 1889. A slightly condensed version, also differing in some trivial phraseology, appears in Clare Delius, *Frederick Delius: Memories of my Brother*, Nicholson and Watson 1935, pp 276-77.

[2] Original BBC TV interview with Edmund Tracey 1959, re-broadcast on Radio 3, 27.1.86.

[3] A sociological syndrome identified and exemplified in M Wiener's celebrated *English Culture and the Decline of the Industrial Spirit, 1850-1980*, Penguin 1985.

[4] Sir T Beecham, *Frederick Delius*, Severn House 1959, p 212.

[5] L Carley and R Threlfall, *Delius: A Life in Pictures*, Oxford University Press 1977, p 6. Yet Neville Cardus, who included Delius in his *A Composer's Eleven* (1958), somehow failed to notice this unique qualification! The Carley-Threlfall study noted above provides what is probably the most useful and vivid source of biographical information.

[6] The Delius stamp was valued at 31p – not far below Elgar who registered 34p. The others so honoured were Handel (17p), and Holst (22p).

[7] The following calculations are based on data for transmissions in 1981-84 inclusive provided by Jill Mintz of BBC Radio 3's music staff (August, 1985). I am very much indebted to her for some painstaking work on this subject.

[8] Calculated from data to be found in L Foreman, *The British Musical Renaissance – A Guide to Research*, 3 vols, London 1972.

[9] P Heseltine, *Frederick Delius*, Bodley Head 1923, pp 44-9; C Delius *op cit*, pp 122-25; *Music Teacher*, December 1950, p 563; Carley and Threlfall, *op cit* p 42.

[10] H Davy, *History of English Music*, Curwen 1921, p 486.

[11] F Tomlinson, *Warlock and Delius*, Thames 1976, p 19.

[12] See, e g, Heseltine, *op cit* p 115-6, where he makes a thoroughly 'conventional' attack on the *Requiem*.

[13] C Gray, *A Survey of Contemporary Music*, Oxford University Press 1924, pp. 58-77 and 90-92.

[14] 'Delius, the Neglected Genius', *Evening Standard* 13.1.27. 'The Composer who stands for England', *Daily Mail* 11.10.29.

[15] Gray, Heseltine and other Delius supporters were themselves political radicals with Labourite sympathies. Gray often excoriated the English musical establishment in explicitly social terms. In his Warlock memoir (see below, n.36) he carefully censored several of Delius's anti-democratic and anti-socialist diatribes.

[16] Heseltine, *op cit*, pp 76-7; Gray, *op cit*, p 75.

[17] C Lambert, *Music Ho!*, London 1934, p 124; E Blom, *Music in England*, Faber 1942, p 200.

[18] In *Tender is the Night*.

[19] A Hutchings, *Delius*, Macmillan 1948, pp 81-3 and 153-54.

[20] The sedulous nurturing of the 'English Garden' mythology, and the creation of the 'Southern Metaphor', by cultural formations in this country are carefully chronicled by Wiener (*op cit*, pp 42-64 and 72-80). See also A Howkins, 'The Discovery of Rural England', in R Colls and P Dodd, *Englishness: Politics and Culture 1880-1920*, Croom Helm 1986, pp 62-88.

[21] H G Wells, *History of Mr Polly*, p 1.

[22] C Palmer, *Delius – Portrait of a Cosmopolitan*, Duckworth 1976, pp 143-53 and 190.

[23] D Cooke, 'Delius – A Centenary Revaluation', *The Listener* 25.1.62., pp 195-96, reprinted in *Vindications: Essays on Romantic Music*, Faber 1982, pp 116-22.

[24] Heseltine, *op cit* p 114: E Newman, *A Musical Motley*, Bodley Head 1919, pp 314-15; Lambert, *op cit*, p 88.

[25] Carley and Threlfall, *op cit*, p 61; Palmer, *op cit*, p 147.

[26] Sir H Hadow, *English Music*, Longman 1931, pp XI-XII and 165-67. Gray's direct counterblast to these views can be found in his *Predicaments, or Music and the Future*, OUP 1936, p 125.

[27] Gray, *A Survey of Contemporary Music, op cit*, p 75; C Delius, *op cit*, p 17.

[28] W McNaught, *A Short Account of Music and Musicians*, Novello 1938, pp 34-5; G Abraham *et al* (eds), *The New Oxford History of Music Vol X*, 1974, p 39.

[29] W Mellers, 'Delius and Peter Warlock', *Scrutiny*, March 1937, pp 384-97.

[30] E Fenby, *Delius as I knew Him*, Bell 1937, pp 4, 162 and 170.

[31] Fenby to Elgar, 28.11.1932. Worcestershire Record Office 705:405:1068. (I owe this reference to Meirion Hughes.)

[32] Beecham, *op cit*, pp 166 and 183-85.

[33] One eventually appeared in 1972 (by A Jefferson).

[34] Cooke, *op cit*, p 196; J Warrack 'Elgar and After', *The Listener*, 26.12.63. p 1084; P Gammond and B James, *Music on Record*, 2 vols

Hutchinson, 1962, Vol I, p 108.

[35] It is instructive to compare the definitive list of works with the discography, and also with the performances scheduled for 1984, in the folder *Delius, 1862-1934; compiled by The Delius Trust to mark the 50th anniversary of his death.* (I am most grateful to Mr Martin Williams, the Trust's Secretary, for sending me a copy of this useful reference work.)

[36] Delius to Heseltine, 24.9.12. British Library, Additional Ms. 52547, pp 31-5. (A small selection from this correspondence appeared in C Gray, *Peter Warlock: A Memoir of Philip Heseltine*, Cape 1934.)

[37] Carley and Threlfall, *op cit*, pp 47-53; Palmer, *op cit*, pp 93-5. Delius' publishers, Harmonie of Berlin, issued the first study of his music in 1907 (by Max Chop).

[38] Beecham, *op cit*, pp 135 and 189-90.

[39] Cardus, (*op cit*, p 230) mentions a poorly received performance of *A Mass of Life* in London with Fischer-Dieskau, c.1955.

[40] E D Mackerness, *A Social History of English Music*, RKP 1964, pp 207-08 and 220.

[41] Quoted by Carley and Threlfall, *op cit*, p 17.

[42] L Carley (ed), *Delius: A Life in Letters 1862-1908*, Scolar 1983, pp 195 and 284.

[43] There is, to my mind, no disputing the radical change in style and approach in 1907. Delius moved suddenly from a sensuously chromatic harmonic idiom to one based on a sweet and lyrical diatonic flow. Abandoning the musical equivalent of free verse, he adopted more classical, or at least more clearly structured forms – from the chaconne/passacaglia of *Brigg Fair* to the quasi-symphonic outlines of the *North Country Sketches*. For the duration, he gave up his penchant for large-scale works based on 'advanced' or 'exotic' texts, and produced smaller tone-poems for orchestra alone. These were surely deliberate compromises based on an acutely-perceived diagnosis of *le gout anglais*, with its insistence on traditional harmony and form.

For all this, Cooke is surely over-generous in attributing the invention of an 'English style' to Delius. Orchestral essays based on the actual absorption of 'folk-song' elements into a musical argument – as opposed to the mere literal quotation, ornamentation or variation of (for example) Stanford's *Irish Rhapsodies*, had started to appear several years earlier. Holst's *Somerset Rhapsody* dates from 1907; Vaughan Williams' *Norfolk Rhapsody* and *In the Fen Country* from 1906 and 1904 respectively; and a Tone Poem far more accomplished than any of these – *Cathaleen ni Hoolihan* by the twenty-year-old Bax – had been written a year earlier still.

[44] Granville Bantock to Delius, 23.12.07. Carley, *op cit*, p 325.

[45] Delius to Heseltine, 28.4.11. Add. 52547 pp 1-5v.

[46] Delius to Heseltine, 11.3.14. *Ibid* p 72.

[47] Delius to Heseltine, 20.9.14 and 23.11.14. *Ibid* pp 86-7 and 95.

[48] Delius to Heseltine, 15.10.16. *Ibid* p 155. (See also C Delius, *op cit*, p 196.)

[49] Delius to Heseltine, September/October 1915. *Ibid* p 127-31v.

[50] Until Russell's BBC film, no mention of Delius' syphilis was ever made in print or other public medium. Since then it has tended to be mentioned, but not discussed. More interesting, however is the hypocritical fact that Delius himself, for all his insistent preaching about absolute frankness in social relations, disguised his affliction even from an intimate friend and constant helpmeet like Heseltine.

[51] Delius to Heseltine, 21.12.15. Add. 52547 pp 137-38v; ('I love travel and adventure ... and the country I found it least was England, old Roast Beef Yorkshire Pudding England'.)

[52] Delius to Heseltine, 23.6.12. *Ibid* p 21.

[53] All examples taken from his letters to Heseltine; the quoted passage is from the very first (28.4.11.). But almost every letter of substance could be cited in support.

[54] Even most of his own 'camp' draw the line at acceptance of the *Requiem*, which they could only regard as spiritually blasphemous and culturally offensive, even when they admired the music. See, for example, Heseltine, p 115; Beecham, pp 172-73; Fenby's sleevenote to the recording on Seraphim (American HMV) S-60147. Its use of the Old Testament to attack belief in the Christian God, and its explicit support for female sexual equality were regarded as outrageous. Delius himself referred to the work as his 'Pagan Requiem' (Carley and Threlfall, p 73), and for some time provocatively demanded its performance in England.

[55] Delius to Heseltine, ?Spring 1919 and 26.12.20. Add. 52548 p 2 and 57v.

[56] Following many earlier examples, see, for example, Delius to Heseltine, ?Aug 1918, *ibid* 52547, p 166.

[57] Delius to Heseltine, 18.9.24. *ibid* 52548, p 92.

[58] This incident is disingenuously recounted by Clare Delius, all unaware of its real significance. She gives the name of the conductor as 'Dr Erchkleiber' (p 263). See also, McNaught, *op cit*, p 35.

[59] C Delius, *op cit*, pp 197-200.

[60] Delius to Heseltine, ?Spring, 1919, 24.3.20. and 10.4.20. Add. 52548 pp 2, 24 and 25v.

[61] Delius to Heseltine, 14.10.21. *ibid* p 70.

[62] Delius to Heseltine, 14.10.21, *ibid*, p 70. (Heseltine had written with this suggestion from a holiday cottage in mid-Wales.)

[63] C Delius, *op cit*, pp 203-06, 237-40 and 259. Her brother went so far in amusing himself as to ask her to find him an English butler for service in the house in Grez!

[64] Delius to Heseltine, 21.12.15. Add. 52547 p 138

[65] Jelka Delius to Heseltine, 8.9.26. *ibid*, 52549 p 53.

[66] Beecham, *op cit*, p 200; Carley and Threlfall, *op cit*, p 85; Jelka Delius to Heseltine, 14.1.26. Add. 52549 p 50.

[67] Jelka Delius to Heseltine, ?Summer 1929, *ibid* pp 61v-62v. Yet around the same time, Jelka admitted in a letter to Beecham that *An Arabeske* had been set originally to her *German* translation of Jacobsen's poem, made whilst staying at the conductor's house in Watford in 1914 (Jelka Delius to Beecham, 14.8.29. *ibid* p 71).

[68] Delius to Heseltine, 21.12.15. Add. 52547 p 137.

[69] Quoted by Tomlinson, *op cit*, p 27.

[70] Delius was doubtless influenced by Nietzsche's views on music itself, especially by sentiments such as: 'its chief promoters are princes whose aim is that there should not be much criticism nor even much thought in their neighbourhood ... next, societies [which] feel the need of spells ... thirdly we must reckon whole nations ...' (G Clive, *The Philosophy of Nietzsche*, New York 1965, p 303).

[71] Several essays in the volume edited by Colls and Dodd, already cited (n.20), and in T Hawkes's pioneering *That Shakespearean Rag* (1985) concern themselves with this theme. See also M Hughes' chapter in this book. Its specific relevance to the 'English Musical Renaissance' will be examined in a projected future study by Mr Hughes and the present writer to be published by Routledge.

[72] Delius's backers sensed that allegiance to Nietzsche was a more embarrassing disfigurement even than syphilis, and one which demanded meticulous cosmetic action. In an argument which Heseltine – above all others – knew to be specious, and which set a line faithfully followed by subsequent commentators, he maintained that Delius admired only Nietzsche the poet and not Nietzsche the 'Prussian' (or, later, 'Fascist') philosopher (Heseltine, *op cit*, pp 105-6; *cf* Beecham, *op cit*, p 219; Cardus, *op cit*, p 220).

[73] Delius and Jelka had met and been taken with (and taken up by) the Harrison family during the war. They pushed Delius's music throughout the 1920s and 30s, especially in the direction of the BBC. For substantial evidence of their energy and determination in such enterprises, see L Foreman, *Bax – A Composer and His Times*, Scolar 1983, pp 232-33, 276, 307 and 323.

[74] C Delius, *op cit*, pp 265-68 and 272-75.

[75] *Ibid* p 7 and pp 137-38.

[76] Fenby, *op cit*, p 14.

[77] Fenby to Elgar, quoted in Fenby, *op cit*, (above n 31). See also p 112-13.

[78] *Ibid*, pp 231 and 234.

[79] The first quotation is from Fenby's book (p 162); the second from his talk on Delius, issued on side 6 of the Angel recording of *A Village Romeo and Juliet* under Meredith Davies (SLS 966).

Paul Harrington

Holst and Vaughan Williams: Radical Pastoral

A composer's reputation can hang him. The notes themselves are often not enough; knowing what went on behind the music can influence our perception of it as much as our grasp of its style and form. Elgar became a figure we could take seriously once he was seen to share the early 20th century *Angst* of the central European masters; *Carmina Burana* forever loses its innocent freshness for someone aware of Carl Orff's war-time productions, and Wagner (as he did at almost every opportunity) speaks for himself. Any revaluation of the work and ideas of Holst and Vaughan Williams thus has to push uphill against the twee images and allegations of insularity that cling to their music. Ian Kemp, for example, writes of the earnest Pastoralism of the Vaughan Williams school,[1] which when it wasn't being earnest spent its time 'roysterdoystering' in mock Tudor pubs from Chelsea to Athlone, a good half-century behind its progressive continental contemporaries in creating a musical language that expressed the spirit of the time.

In his last years Vaughan Williams became a target for the young champions of the Schoenbergian revolution, the embodiment of everything provincial in British music. The young Donald Mitchell blooded his pen on the first performance of *Hodie* in 1955:

There is a level below which 'directness' and 'forthrightness' of utterance – qualities for which Vaughan Wiliams is praised – deteriorate into downright unacceptable primitivity ... It is doubly damaging when his contemporaries are so blind (or deaf, perhaps) that they mistake patent coarseness as evidence of exuberant genius.[2]

By 1955, Holst had been dead for more than twenty years and a concert devoted to his music, the first promoted by the Vaughan Williams Trust, left the Festival Hall half empty. Even in the year of Holst's death, conditions were right for Constant Lambert to lay in to the 'cowpat' school:

There is something about this music both unbearably precious and hearty. It precisely recalls the admirably meant endeavours of William Morris and his followers to combat the products of those dark satanic Mills with unpleasant handwoven materials, while its heartiness conjures up the hideous *faux bonhommie* of the hiker noisily wading his way through the petrol pumps of Metroland, singing obsolete sea-shanties with the aid of the Week-End Book ...[3]

1934 was late in the day for the pastoral style – Holst and Vaughan Williams had become victims of the very cultural independence they had spent their working lives trying to achieve. It is difficult, even now, to give the pastoralists – Howells, Moeran, Finzi, Hadley and the others – their due. The charge against their music, that it centres on that most futile of all emotions, nostalgia, is difficult to deny. So attuned are we to the Stravinsky-Schoenberg view of musical development that this enclave of post-Romanticism seems distant and unrewarding. The problem is ours. I believe it is possible to distinguish the 'sons of Ralph' from their model, and that the difference is deeply embedded in the period that saw the beginnings of the folk-song revival in Britain and a renaissance in socialist thought, the 1890s and early 1900s.

The pivotal figure of that time, William Morris, was already a fossil, shelved and dated by the time Lambert was writing *Music Ho!*. Lambert's inability to see the British national style as part of a broad cultural and political movement, generally related to what Morris was trying to do, was a major barrier to any attempt to understand the music of Holst and Vaughan Williams. And this failure to note the influence of Morris on the two composers has misled subsequent critics. In fact both of them were radicals from an early age.

At about the time of their first meeting in the autumn of 1895, the 21-year-old Holst, deeply impressed by his reading of Morris, joined the Hammersmith Socialist Club. 'Here', wrote Imogen Holst, 'he found a new sort of comradeship, and here he became aware of other ways of searching for beauty'.[4] Vaughan Williams, the older by two years, had been a 'radical' for a good while longer than this. 'When I was a boy at school', he wrote to the veteran socialist composer Rutland Boughton in 1952, 'I and another boy stood out as Radicals (as we were called then) against all the other boys. When I got to Cambridge in '93 I and a few friends read the Fabian tracts, and, in opposition to the majority of undergraduates, became socialists'.[5]

It is extraordinary that such a basic element in the make-up of two prominent composers should have become so thoroughly marginalised. In the early years of their careers socialism was at least as important for Holst and Vaughan Williams as it was for Tippett and Britten at the same stage of their lives, and its effect was enduring. This must transform our perception of many of their major works including pieces written long after the end of any active involvement in the politics of the left. The lack of acknowledgement of this aspect of their lives is partly explained by the attitude of Michael Kennedy and Imogen Holst, their most important critics, neither of whom have much inclination to look at their subjects in political terms. Perhaps the music itself has a tendency to invite listeners to approach it religiously despite the strength of evidence pointing in other directions. In addition, the British have a flair for absorbing rebels, reducing them to digestible size. Paul Foot has explored this tendency in relation to the 'castration of Shelley at British places of learning', and the anthologists' habit of 'extracting with devoted thoroughness every trace of political or social thought from Shelley's work'.[6]

Morris, ignored rather than assimilated after his death,

was one of the most articulate spokesmen for socialism in the late Victorian period, and his appeal was intense and widespread. He was an entirely English kind of socialist, unsophisticated by continental standards. Lacking in theoretical precision, he was also refreshingly undogmatic – probably a vital quality for anyone who would popularise socialism in Britain. Marxists have a strong case for claiming him as one of their own; he joined Hyndman's Social Democratic Federation for a short while before leaving with Eleanor Marx in 1884 to found the Socialist League. In the view of A L Morton, Morris believed that the ideas of socialism 'were always the ideas of Marxism.'[7] However it was the general ideas, rather than the systematic theory, to which Morris was attracted:

> To speak frankly I do not know what Marx's theory of value is ... and I am damned if I want to know ... It is enough political economy for me to know that the idle rich class is rich and the working class is poor, and that the rich are rich because they rob the poor.[8]

The socialism of Morris had its origins in guilt, the guilt of no longer being able to accept, in an age of unequalled prosperity, that severe poverty was inevitable. Britain at the end of the 19th century was a paradise for the entrepreneur. But profound popular disgust with the consequences of unrestrained capitalism meant that socialism was becoming an increasingly important force. 'You once said that you were so ashamed of yourself because your life seemed all holiday',[9] Holst wrote to Vaughan Williams in 1903. In those heady days accumulated capital gave thousands of people, Vaughan Williams among them, complete freedom from the necessity of work. Holst, however, several stages down the social ladder, slogged his trombone through orchestras and end-of-the-pier bands to support himself and his wife. In 1920, Vaughan Williams summarised these early days in an essay on Holst:

> It was Holst's strong sense of human sympathy which brought him when a young man in to contact with William Morris and the Kelmscott Club. The tawdriness of London, its unfriend-liness, the sordidness of its riches and poverty were

overwhelming to an enthusiastic and sensitive youth; and to him
the ideals of Morris, the insistence on beauty in every detail of
human life and work, were a revelation. No wonder that the
poetic socialism of the Kelmscott Club became the natural
medium of his aspirations; to Morris and his followers
'comradeship' was no pose but an absolute necessity of life.
And though as years go on Holst has grown out of the weak
points of Morris's teaching, yet his ideal thoroughness of beauty
and above all of comradeship have remained and grown
stronger.[10]

It thus seems likely that when Imogen Holst said her
father only remained in the Hammersmith club, 'for the sake
of good companionship',[11] she was doing him less than
justice. The principle of fraternity meant a great deal more
to Holst than simple good companionship, and in the singing
and playing of ordinary men and women he had the most
fulfilling musical experiences of his life. It is obvious why he
should have found the Morris group so congenial; indeed,
the socialism of Morris was always much stronger on
comradeship than ideology.

Holst and Vaughan Williams both came from what used to
be called 'free thinking' families. Holst's great grandfather
was an unwelcome liberal in early 19th century Russia and
came, like many after him, to England. His son quickly
acquired a resentment of blossoming bourgeois society
through providing music for fashionable 'At Home' concerts
where 'his patrons treated him with a snobbish discourtesy
that was almost unendurable'.[12] Holst's step-mother was a
Theosophist and as a child he inhabited a world where
progressive political thinking and a progressive approach to
spiritual values were inevitably linked.

Vaughan Williams' radical lineage is extremely impressive. The family's money was based on generations of
lawyers, judges, scientists and clergymen who included
Charles Darwin and the first judge of Common Pleas, John
Williams. The household atmosphere seems to have been
remarkably enlightened for a Victorian home on the
foothills of the English aristocracy. Vaughan Williams was

an atheist as a boy at Charterhouse. It can only seem very strange that the composer of the *Mass in G Minor* and *Sancta Civitas* should have been an atheist all his adult life, but it is really no stranger than a Catholic writing an opera about Orpheus or a Jew sculpting the risen Christ. Vaughan Williams saw Christianity in the same symbolic terms that had been applied to Greek and Roman religion for thousands of years. He was a non-believer deeply absorbed by the lyricism and huge idealism of faith. 'Who believes in God nowadays, I should like to know',[13] he declared to Bertrand Russell in Cambridge in 1892. The remark was scandalous in the Cambridge of Latin grace and clergymen dons but it was representative of the radical group of students of which Vaughan Williams was a member. His friends and contemporaries at this time included the historian G E Trevelyan, the philosopher G E Moore and the economist Maynard Keynes. And it was Russell who, when they were undergraduates, introduced him to one of the great enthusiasms of his life, the poetry of Walt Whitman.

It is difficult for us to appreciate the revelatory quality of Whitman's verse in England for the 1890s. He was, if we exclude the 'discovery' of Hopkins after the First World War, the last great blaze of the high romantic style in English, providing for the late Victorians the voice of exultant brotherhood and passion that Wordsworth had offered a hundred years before. Composers as different as Stanford (*Elegiac Ode, Songs of the Fleet*) and Delius were attracted to the vividness of his rhapsodic style, even if for no better reason than that it was vivid.

> Darest thou now O soul
> Walk out with me towards the unknown region,
> Where neither ground is for the feet nor any path to follow?
> No map there, nor guide,
> Nor voice sounding, nor touch of human hand,
> Nor face with blooming flesh, nor lips, nor eyes in that land.

Writing like this is grand enough and vague enough to appeal to innumerable sensibilities. Whitman's rhythms, absorbed undiluted from the King James Bible, and his joyful, heroic humanism made a powerful impact on socialists at this time. The words quoted above, from *Whispers of Heavenly Death*, became part of Vaughan Williams' first significant large-scale work, the 'Song' for chorus and orchestra, *Towards The Unknown Region* (1905-7). This is transitional music. Parry is a strong presence from the earliest bars. *Blest Pair of Sirens* ('my favourite piece of music written by an Englishman')[14] is an obvious model. It is his last work to be heavily dependent on the chromatic harmony that he and Holst had been trying to purge from their music for nearly fifteen years. The world of *Unknown Region* is utterly different from Stanford's Brahmsian classicism or Delius' nature painting; it is an impassioned, deeply personal appeal for courage and progress. We are dealing here with more than stock English nobility and late Romantic yearning. 'If Elgar's music', writes Michael Kennedy, 'captures one aspect of the Edwardian age – sounding its hollow note as well as its confident one – Vaughan Williams' pre-1914 choral works enshrine another, the growth of a wider sense of humanity's destiny and interrelationship'.[15] This 'sense of humanity's destiny' which dare not speak its name is, of course, socialism, and the group the composer represented was the 'alternative culture' of the Edwardian left.

Rutland Boughton, a committed Communist party member for most of his long life, also wrote a setting – later excluded from his list of works – of these same words. Vaughan Williams and Boughton had first met as students at the Royal College of Music and had come under the influence of Cecil Sharp, who was also a socialist. One of the great practical attractions of folk song for this generation was its complete contrast to the language of Wagner. Boughton, however, managed to get the worst of both worlds by combining folk-song-like directness with a Wagnerian concept of music drama and devoted eleven years to the establishing of an English Bayreuth at Glastonbury centred upon the huge cycle of Arthurian operas he was then composing. First encounters with *Tristan und Isolde* in the twenty years after its première transformed the life of any developing composer who heard it. In England folk song was the sound that broke the spell. Holst later described his largest work, the opera *Sita* (1899–1906), as 'good old Wagnerian bawling'[16] and Imogen Holst's account of it – *Sita* remains unpublished and unperformed – certainly suggests a severe case of *Götterdämmerung*.[17]

In 1905, Holst – in what seems to have been an almost compulsory right of passage – also made a setting of 'Darest thou now, O soul'. And in the same year he completed another Whitman setting, the Scena for soprano and orchestra, *The Mystic Trumpeter*. This is the work where we encounter the mature Holst for the first time. Most significantly, it is the celestial Whitman who evokes the characteristic response from the composer. The line, 'Floating and basking upon heaven's lake' is rapt in the frictionless infinities of *Neptune*. This isolated moment is the progenitor of what was to become Holst's characteristic mood, a detached and ascetic music liberated from romantic passion. In this respect Holst is fundamentally different from Vaughan Williams. In fact, given the similarity of their cultural influences, their two musical styles could not be less alike. Vaughan Williams was to learn a great deal from Holst's hard-won technical skill while Holst came increasingly to regret his self-imposed austerity.

In retrospect it must seem ludicrous that the major economic and imperial power of the world at that time should have had a folk song revival along the lines of colonial backwaters like Czechoslovakia and Hungary. And if we consider the state of British musical life at the turn of the century – only one international orchestra, one opera house, and a virtually non-existent native tradition of composition – it is miraculous that any sane person should choose composition as a vocation. British musical nationalism was built on a smaller cultural base than those of either Hungary or Czechoslovakia, yet by the time of Holst's death the careers of Elgar and Delius had come to an end, Vaughan Williams was in the middle of a hugely productive period, William Walton was well established and working on his *First Symphony*, Michael Tippett was writing his first published work (the String Quartet No 1) and the 20 year-old

Benjamin Britten was assembling the inspired juvenilia that
forms his *Simple Symphony*.

It was inevitable that folk-song should have come to seem
an irrelevance to the generation that came to maturity after
the First World War. But the situation was quite different
when Vaughan Williams began to collect traditional tunes in
1903. An art that was drawn directly from the very poor,
that contained the best of the common people, had an
inevitable appeal for anyone touched by the ideas of Morris.
There was nothing escapist about this attraction. Holst and
Vaughan Williams knew that the culture which had created
these songs had gone into terminal decline, but this was not
for them the cause of great grief that it was for a literary
figure with whom they are often compared, Thomas Hardy.

In his attachment to tradition and to rural Britain – South
West England in particular – Hardy does share a certain
feeling with the two composers, but he is more of a Victorian
figure than either of them. The pain of a religious
temperament enduring an uneasy humanism is the anguish
behind much of Hardy's work and his nostalgia – though its
edge is as sharp as a new scythe – is nostalgia none the less.
What attracted Holst and Vaughan Williams to Hardy was
his tone of unromantic heroism. This became the subject of
Holst's *Egdon Heath* (1927), and also, perhaps, of Vaughan
Williams' tragic last symphony. Beyond this the similarities
are superficial. Vaughan Williams set Hardy only once
(*Hodie*) while Holst did so only four times and not in any
major works. Holst's contact with Eastern religion gave him
a forebearance that extracts all the tragedy from Hardy's
doomed positivism: Hardy weeps under a Godless heaven,
Holst celebrates it. The difference is crucial. In both mood
and outlook the composer who comes closest to Hardy is
Britten. Like Hardy he makes nostalgia a cruel and deathly
thing. In his many folk-song arrangements and in the
Hardy-inspired orchestral suite, *A Time There Was*, the old
songs echo the futility of human desire, a lost and
unrecoverable Eden.

Vaughan Williams was aware of the limitations of the folk
song as a means of musical salvation as early as 1902. 'A
musician who wishes to say any thing worth saying must first

of all express himself ... English composers do not spring from the peasantry. Indeed, in England there is no true peasantry for them to spring from'.[18] But the old songs offered a unique continuity with a neglected tradition of English cultural life. 'Vaughan Williams' nationalism', wrote James Day, 'was rooted ... in a love for the underdog ... It may have been political at one remove; it was certainly (for want of a better word) 'anti-bourgeois' in its rejection of shabby, overdone ornament and second-hand values'.[19] At the same time, this music most emphatically faces forward; its lyricism is full of the world of possibilities. 'The object of art', as Vaughan Williams himself wrote, 'is to stretch out to the ultimate realities through the medium of beauty'.[20]

There is in William Morris a 'tough' pastoralism. For example, in the 1889 sketch *Under An Elm Tree* he wrote:

> The hay field is a pretty sight this month seen under the elm, as the work goes forward on the other side of the way opposite the bean field, till you look at the haymakers closely. Suppose the haymakers were friends working for friends on land which was theirs, as many as were needed, with leisure and hope ahead of them instead of hopeless toil and anxiety. Need their useful labour for themselves and their neighbours cripple and disfigure them and knock them out of the shape of men fit to represent the Gods and Heroes?[21]

A sensitive listener to the *Pastoral Symphony* and the *Lyric Movement* for viola and orchestra will know the ability of the pastoral style to convey genuine pain. 'It's really war time music', Vaughan Williams wrote of the *Pastoral*, 'not really lambkins frisking at all as most people take for granted'.[22] The harmonic language of *Job*, where the Devil himself stalks the patterned fields and hedges, has everything of this 'razor in the grain' effect.

Vaughan Williams claimed late in his life that the *Sea Symphony* owed a good deal to the language of Holst's *The Mystic Trumpeter*. There are moments, such as the modal tune that occurs at the mention of Adam and Eve in the Finale, that bring Holst to mind, but the emotional impact of this last great apprentice piece, willed into existence over six years, is far removed from the world that Holst had entered at this time in the *Rig Veda Hymns* and *Savitri*, his first fully characteristic works. In setting large extracts from Whitman's *Passage to India* in the symphony's Finale, a text larger than those used for the first three movements combined, Vaughan Williams set himself an almost impossible structural task. The choice of words was obviously significant for the composer as they demand a grandeur that the most sure-footed of composers would have found difficult to sustain. The explanation for this is revealed at the movement's monumental climax with the words:

> Finally shall come a poet worthy of that name,
> The true son of god shall come singing his songs.

This is perhaps the most passionate music Vaughan Williams ever wrote and, in its overwhelming statement of humanist values, it is the culmination of his pre-*Tallis Fantasia* work. To any one with a knowledge of Vaughan Williams' preoccupations over the previous twenty years the message could not be clearer. This remains true in spite of the sophisticated 1930s sarcasm of Constant Lambert:

> We are given the sea as a highly picturesque background to human endeavour and human emotion, a suitable setting for introspective skippers, heroic herring-fishers and intrepid explorers.[23]

The symphony does have certain technical and stylistic short-comings, but the force of the composer's vision and the vigour of its vocal writing have made it Vaughan Williams' most often performed vocal work. The music conveys the essence of its subject – which really has very little to do with the sea – even if the message has been blurred by the archaisms of the text and the passage of time.

Holst's political idealism was never as extrovert in its musical expression as this. His individual voice only began to be heard when he abandoned the trappings of late Romanticism completely in his Sanskrit pieces. Colin Matthews has written of these works,

Holst became interested in Sanskrit literature when he was in his mid-twenties and still very much an apprentice composer ... Holst who had earlier dabbled in William Morris's socialism and been fascinated by the visionary poetry of Walt Whitman, now added Hindu philosophy to his mental armoury'.[24]

One can not help but get an impression of immature dilettanteism from this extract. But the impressive Molto Adagio, *Elegy in Memory of William Morris* from the early *Cotswold Symphony* indicates the size of the debt that Holst felt he owed to Morris. This slow movement rises far above the range and achievement of the rest of Holst's music of the 1890s by sheer force of conviction. As Imogen Holst wrote in her biography of her father, 'listening to William Morris he realised that art must be part of the daily life of every man, to be shared by learned and unlearned, as a language that all people can understand'.[25] Elliot Carter has recalled Holst's look of incomprehension as he perused one of Carter's student scores at Harvard in the early 1930s. A music that apparently seeks no end but its own brilliance would have left Holst cold.

Holst's politics are inseparable from his spiritual beliefs. Theosophy is hardly understood at all today. 'It was', Don Cupitt has observed, 'progressive politically, founding schools and campaigning for emancipation on all fronts'.[26] Its origin, which can be traced in the remarkable career of Annie Besant who was an active socialist and a friend of Morris, Shaw and the Webbs, was in a disillusionment with a loveless institutionalised Christianity. The moral vigour of the movement can be gathered from the profound impact it had on Gandhi: It was only after speaking to English Theosophists in London in 1890 that he came to value Hindu scripture as more than the superstitious tales made of it by missionaries.

Holst's choice of text frequently reflected the concerns he developed in the 1890s. His longest mature vocal work, the *Choral Symphony* (1922-4) is a setting of Keats, an honorary Pre-Raphaelite:

'Beauty is truth, truth beauty' – that is all
Ye know on earth, and all ye need to know.

So proclaims the chorus at the Symphony's climax, a phrase as significant for Holst as Whitman's 'true son of god' had been for the composer of the *Sea Symphony*. Holst is celebrating Keats's 'Cold Pastoral', the temporal embodiment of eternity and it was to be his musical landscape for most of the remainder of his career. In 1925 he began to sketch a *Second Choral Symphony* to words by one of the great figures of late Victorian descent, George Meredith. Ill-health and fatigue are probably the main reasons for the work's abandonment. But it is also possible that its main text, 'The Woods of Westermain' from the 1883 collection *Poems and Lyrics of the Joy of the Earth* (which had provided 'The Lark Ascending' for Vaughan Williams ten years earlier) may have reflected too closely what Imogen Holst described as, 'the wintriness of his own chosen solitude'.[27] 'The Woods of Westermain' is a remarkable nature poem which extracts a Darwinian view of existence from a recognisable romantic landscape. Meredith is a more congenial poet for the later Holst than Whitman. He believed that humanity must find spirituality through a mind in touch with science and the whole of the physical world. It was Holst's ideal theme and the Symphony might well have become his *Mass of Life*. As the 1920s went by he came to realise that his music had only achieved part of Meredith's ideal, described here in a letter from early old age: 'I have written always with the perception that there is no life but the spirit; that the concrete is really the shadowy; yet that the way to spiritual life lies in the complete unfolding of the creature, not in the nipping of the passions'.[28]

Perhaps regular creative excursions into the Woods of Westermain, into 'a cold region where his brain was numb and his spirit was isolated'[29] was the last task that Holst wanted to set himself at this time. Much of the music of the mid-1920s, the choral ballets *The Golden Goose* and *The Morning of the Year* and some short piano pieces have a light cheerful air full of the pleasure of their composition. It was, however, with another Cold Pastoral, *Egdon Heath* that Holst achieved the perfection of his 'minimalist' style. A Webernian with a laser beam could not find an excess note to cut away.

Imogen Holst dates the crisis point in her father's awareness of the missing human element in his music to a performance of the Schubert String Quintet at the concert in 1929 where his *Songs of Humbert Wolfe* were heard for the first time. One of the pieces in the set, 'Betelguse', a meditation on the massive distant star, produces one of Holst's last great visions of eternity, a vision so huge as to utterly engulf anything as small as a human being.

Soon after, Holst wrote the work that is generally considered to mark the development of a less detached idiom, the *Choral Fantasia*, to words of Robert Bridges (1930). The economy of means in this music is still remarkable – the 31 pages of full score doesn't suggest at first sight a 17-minute choral work – yet the effects achieved are rich and at times ecstatic. The emotional climax of the work is the starkly positivist vision sung by male voices alone:

Man Born of desire
Cometh out of the night,
A wan'dring spark of fire,
A lonely world of eternal thought
Echoing in chance and forgot.

Imogen Holst tells us that her father had been feeling his way towards this music for nearly twenty years. I doubt if it is a coincidence that Holst found a newly invigorated language while working out a theme central to his political and spiritual values.

The remaining works of the 1930s show an increasing richness of expression, though pieces like the *Lyric Movement* and the orchestral version of *Hammersmith* remain rarities in the concert hall. It must be considered tragic that Holst did not complete the four movement symphony he was working on at his death, his first attempt at a full-length orchestral work since *The Planets*. The only completed movement, *Scherzo*, has a lightness and energy unique in his later music. Like Britten, he had in the last years of his life come out of a fallow period with a new creative strength. The struggle to earn a living over the previous 40 years had worn him down and it is a testament to his tenacity that he produced such a quantity of fine music. The circumstances that forced him into becoming a Sunday composer prevented him from ever realising his full gifts. In common with Tippett, who followed him to Morley in 1942 as Director, he became a composer as much through will as talent; unlike Tippett he had family responsibilities and perennially poor health to weigh him down. His outlook remained radical right up to the end, his loathing of the unimaginative and second-rate never abated and there is something entirely representative of the man in his comment in a note to his wife during a hospital stay in 1933 that he had spent Christmas in bed reading Trotsky and Jane Austen.

The great professional disappointment of Vaughan Williams career was the indifference that greeted his fifth opera, *The Pilgrim's Progress*. There have been very few productions since (and mostly, I would say, *because* of) its botched première at Covent Garden during the Festival of Britain. It is a seminal work for the understanding of its composer and forms one of his greatest achievements. The impression an opera makes in its first production, as Alexander Goehr painfully discovered with the première of *Behold the Sun*, can massively disadvantage its reception no matter what the quality of the music.[30] The choice of Bunyan as librettist is another point against *Pilgrim*. He is one of the least read of the major English writers, in fact he is probably one of the most disliked. I have known undergraduates plough through acres of roccoco moralising in *Clarissa* rather than face the holy horrors of Doubting Castle, Faith Hopeful and androgynous Christian himself. The poetic simplicity of the writing, for the modern generation at least, does not compensate for its aura of religiosity.

Vaughan Williams, as we know, was not a conventionally religious man. His resistance to several suggested cathedral performances of the work probably had at least as much to do with his secular purpose as the logistics of nave versus stage. During rehearsals for the first performance of *Job* in 1931 the composer's first wife, Adeline, wrote to a friend that the character of God was to be referred to as Job's spiritual self in the programme. It is a highly significant definition in terms of Vaughan Williams' religious music. The superb and very Holstian *Magnificat* of 1932 dramatises the annunciation as an encounter between a young girl and her lover, represented with Ravel-like sensuality on solo flute. In this instance the composer takes one of the most idealised events in Christian mythology and gives it a humanist interpretation through brilliant musical dramatisation. In *Pilgrim* he created an opera on a religious subject with much of the religion extracted. A great deal of Bunyan's Christian allegory is missing in the opera and Christian himself is simply called Pilgrim, 'because', wrote the composer, 'I want the idea to be universal and to apply to anyone who aims at the spiritual life whether he is Christian, Jew, Buddhist, Shintoist, or Fifth Day Adventist'.[31] His object was, in Tippett's words, to 'disengage some apprehension of spiritual treasure (which I would want to hold on to) from the elaborate costumes and dogmas associated with "belief" '.[32]

In *Arguments for Socialism*, Tony Benn cites an example of Bunyan's kind of radicalism with the case of a Lollard and twenty of his friends who were publicly branded on the cheek for Bible reading:

> For then, as now, in many parts of the world the Bible was regarded as a revolutionary book not to be trusted to the common people to read and interpret for themselves. No wonder then that the Levellers should regard the Bible as their basic text ... Divine teaching, as they read it, expressly prohibited the dominion of man by man.[33]

Bunyan's attack on bourgeois complacency and materialism is unrelenting, his Cromwellian principles militant and Bible-based. Vaughan Williams makes magnificent use of Bunyan's conceited middle-class man, Mr By-Ends of Fair-Speech, the son of a waterman who has now become a 'gentleman of quality', who in the Vaughan Williams version acquires a wife to double the folly. The By-Ends attempt to join Pilgrim on his journey but retreat when they are confronted with his purity of purpose. 'I will never desert my principles', sings By-Ends, 'since they are harmless and profitable'. It is a fine comic scene, cleverly underlined by a pompous *tua obligato* and as barbed in its ridicule of the smugly affluent as Bunyan's original.

Rutland Boughton saw the opera as essentially a rehashing of a worn set of symbols. Vaughan Williams was having none of that:

> As regards my opera, might I ask you at all events to read the libretto before you criticise it or me for writing it. And to what you accuse me of – i.e. 're-dressing an old theology', it seems to me that some of your ideas are a good deal more moribund than Bunyan's theology: – the old-fashioned republicanism and Marxism which led direct to the appalling dictatorships of Hitler, Stalin, and Mussolini, or your Rationalism, which dates from about 1880 and has entirely failed to solve any of the problems of the Universe.[34]

There are interesting parallels to be drawn between *Pilgrim* and operas which are genuinely religious in substance. Messiaen, for example, in *Saint Francis of Assisi* presents us with a truly religious work, the portrayal of an act of devotion upon the stage. It is music fundamentally not of this world, contemplative, joyously undramatic, an attempt to disclose revealed faith through the media of music and images. The same is true of John Tavener's *Thérèse*. The difference between *Pilgrim* and these pieces is immense. For an orthodox Catholic like Messiaen the ultimate questions of existence, revealed through sacred text and ritual, are known from the very start and the object of the opera becomes the revelation of the pre-existent and inevitable. *The Pilgrim's Progress* is a genuinely dramatic work, the struggle to fulfillment basically human. The heavens do not open, as in Pfitzner's *Palestrina* to offer divine inspiration; Pilgrim hauls himself forward upon a strength drawn from fidelity and good will. His great song in prison. 'O be thou not far from me', is an encapsulation of Vaughan Williams' genius – Pilgrim is freed by his inner faith, 'the key of promise' locked in in his heart. In the hands of a producer like Bill Douglas *Pilgrim* could shine as the great lyric masterpiece of brotherhood and moral courage that it is.

Immediately after completing *Pilgrim* Vaughan Williams began work on an entirely different kind of progress, the task of turning his music for the journey of Scott and his men into the *Sinfonia Antarctica* (1949-52). This is an entirely secular version of Bunyan's theme and has nothing whatever to do with the celebration of British heroism. Vaughan Williams had no time for the gentleman amateur that Scott obviously was. 'Ralph', wrote Ursula Vaughan Williams, 'became more and more upset as he read about the inefficiencies of the organisation; he despised heroism that risked lives unnecessarily and such things as allowing five men to travel on rations for four filled him with fury'.[35] The Antarctic enterprise was a great imperial blunder that became transformed into a British moral triumph. Vaughan Williams presents it as a tragic Odyssey, a metaphor for the greater human struggle contained in the quotation from *Prometheus Unbound* that heads the score:

> To suffer woes which hope thinks infinite,
> To forgive wrongs darker than death or night,
> To defy power which seems omnipotent,
> Neither to change, nor falter, nor repent:
> This ... is to be
> Good great and joyous, beautiful and free,
> This is alone life, joy, empire and victory.

Much though *Antarctica* depends upon atmosphere for effect, it is far from being an ultra-low-temperature *Alpine Symphony*. The austere post-war period in which this music was written was a time of great unease and uncertainty. In the end the values of moral strength celebrated in *Pilgrim* are not enough and Vaughan Williams came to realise that his original ending, horns and strings in radiant G major, was dishonest. The *A Minor Quartet* (1945) suffers from this forced radiance when its short, and admittedly very beautiful, finale fails to take up any of the grim questions raised in the preceding three austere and violent movements. In *Sinfonia Antarctica* the heroism is all in the struggle, but in human terms the failure is abject. The great luminous chords that close the Finale of the Ninth Symphony, the most difficult and least known of his major works, sound more for a battle fought than a battle won. 'There are no golden gates at the end of this symphony', wrote Hugh Ottaway, 'only human courage and defiance of the abyss'.[36]

It would be difficult to sustain that the mature Vaughan Williams and Holst were socialists in anything but a broad sense. Their distance from active left-wing politics can be seen in their reactions to the General Strike. Vaughan Williams was 'deeply troubled by the political situation and he was in doubt as to what part, if any, he should take when the strike happened. As it was, his work filled the foreground of his days.'[37] And when the General Strike came Holst 'was distressed that he knew so little about anything outside his own work'.[38]

The political outlooks of Holst and Vaughan Williams were quite opposed to the scientific rationalism of Shaw and Wells. Theirs is a view of life built on social obligation and good faith, and in this respect they emerge as much truer to the fraternal ideal than either Shaw, with his virtuoso back-biting, or Wells, whose treatment of women could be staggeringly selfish. Vaughan Williams was probably at heart always a Whig liberal with greater allegiances to personal principle than party. In a letter of 1952 he wrote to Boughton:

> Ever since I had a vote I have voted either Radical or Labour except once, after the last war when I was so disgusted by what I considered a mean trick of the Labour party in calling an election.[39]

Holst must be one of the great examples of a priestly disposition co-existing with a scientific and humanist mind.

Holst and Vaughan Williams did not flirt with politics, like many middle-class followers of Morris and the Webbs. In their music they effected an art that fully realised the best of the late Victorian days of hope – this is probably the only kind of radical action they were qualified to pursue. Their music, like the age that formed it, is widely misunderstood. But these late Victorian middle-class socialists, it must be confessed, fall to powder if we drop the full weight of the class struggle on their prim shoulders. Morris's transparent inadequacy as a man of action during the November riots in Trafalgar Square in 1887 is an indication of how cloistered and peripheral his movement really was. Holst and Vaughan Williams were children of this time and outgrew it, personally and musically, but the vision of the world they had in their twenties never left them. It is a position evolved almost entirely out of human sympathy and resentment of the status quo with barely a gesture towards the theory or practice of revolutionary action. When Vaughan Williams's great-uncle Charles graciously declined Herr Marx' request to dedicate *Das Kapital* to him he was making a gesture of which his nephew would have heartily approved.

After the Russian invasion of Hungary Rutland Boughton withdrew from the Communist Party with considerable pain and grief. Vaughan Williams adopted a conciliatory tone in a letter to him, at a time when he was in despair:

> It seems to me that all right-minded people are communists, as far as the word means that everything should be done for the common good. But communism has got to mean now so much other than that, which I, for one cannot subscribe to. Myself I see no reason why the Russian atrocities should prevent you from remaining a communist in the ideal sense of the word.[40]

Vaughan Williams died in one of the magnificent Nash terraces overlooking Regents Park where H G Wells spent his last bitter years brooding on what looked like the defeat of everything he had ever believed in. Wells was old and ill, the spirit gone out of him. Vaughan Williams never lost faith. In 1955, 60 years after the smoking-room radicalism of Cambridge, he was asked to arrange a concert for the Federal Education and Research Trust where he conducted the *London Symphony*. He wrote in the programme:

> ... a long and varied life has shown me that politically the world lacks a fresh vision of its own unity and it is often for the artist to show the way.

Notes

[1] I Kemp, *Tippett – The Composer and his Music*, Oxford University Press 1984, p 86.

[2] M Kennedy, *The Works of Ralph Vaughan Williams*, Oxford University Press 1964, p 331.

[3] C Lambert, *Music Ho! – A Study of Music in Decline*, Faber and Faber 1934, p 154.

[4] I Holst, *Gustav Holst, A Biography*, Oxford University Press 1938, p 16.

[5] U Vaughan Williams, *Ralph Vaughan Williams, A Biography*, Oxford University Press 1964, pp 322-3.

[6] M Foot, *Red Shelley*, Sidgwick and Jackson 1980.

[7] A L Morton (ed) *Political Writings of William Morris*, Lawrence and Wishart 1984, p 11.

[8] T L Jarman, *Socialism in Britain*, Victor Gollancz 1972, p 92.

[9] R Vaughan Williams and G Holst, *Heirs and Rebels – Letters Written to Each Other and Occasional Writings On Music*, U Vaughan Williams and I Holst (eds), Oxford University Press 1959, p 22.

[10] R Vaughan Williams, *National Music and Other Essays*, Oxford University Press 1963, p 135.

[11] I Holst, *op cit*, p 17.

[12] *Ibid*, p 2.

[13] R Vaughan Williams, *op cit*, M Kennedy's foreword to the second edition, Oxford University Press 1987.

[14] R Vaughan Williams, *op cit*, p 180.

[15] M Kennedy, *op cit*, p 112.

[16] G Holst, *Gustav Holst – Letters to W G Whittaker*, University of Glasgow Press 1974.

[17] I Holst, *The Music of Gustav Holst and Holst's Music Reconsidered*, Oxford University Press 1985, p 16.

[18] M Kennedy, *op cit*, p 30.

[19] J Day, *Vaughan Williams*, Dent and Sons 1961, pp 83-4.

[20] R Vaughan Williams, *op cit*, p 189.

[21] A L Morton (ed), *op cit*, p 189.

[22] U Vaughan Williams, *op cit*, p 121.

[23] C Lambert, *op cit*, p 41.

[24] C Matthews, sleeve note to Holst's *Rig Veda Hymns*, Unicorn 1986.

[25] I Holst, *The Music of Gustav Holst*, *op cit*, p 6.

[26] D Cupitt, *The Seat of Faith*, BBC 1984, p 174.

[27] I Holst, *The Music of Gustav Holst, op cit*, p 77.

[28] P Bartlett, *George Meredith*, British Council 1963, p 13.

[29] I Holst, *The Music of Gustav Holst, op cit*, p 88.

[30] For a more detailed treatment of this work see Nicholas Williams' chapter in this book.

[31] Quoted by M Kennedy, Introduction to the EMI recording of *The Pilgrim's Progress*.

[32] M Tippett, *The Music of the Angels*, Eulenberg 1980, p 53.

[33] T Benn, *Arguments for Socialism*, Penguin 1980, p 26.

[34] U Vaughan Williams, *op cit*, p 304.

[35] *Ibid*, p 279.

[36] H Ottaway, *Vaughan Williams' Symphonies*, BBC 1972, p 64.

[37] U Vaughan Williams, *op cit*, p 162.

[38] I Holst, *Gustav Holst, op cit*, p 117.

[39] U Vaughan Williams, *op cit*, p 323.

[40] *Ibid*, p 379.

Lionel Pike

Robert Simpson's Tenth Quartet: Politics, pacifism and the language of tonality

Simpson: an introduction

> One day we shall outgrow our present sensationalism and again
> ask for new music that is both an intellectual structure and also
> a qualitative comment on human existence. Then, no doubt,
> Robert Simpson's stature as a composer of just such music will
> be fully recognized.

We are as far from this happening as the day in 1973 when
Martin Cooper made these comments in the *Daily
Telegraph*: performances of music by this fine composer are
scarce, recordings of his work are rare, and there is little
knowledge of his music among the general public.

Robert Simpson was born in Leamington in 1921. At first
he studied medicine; and as a pacifist during the Second
World War he worked in London on a mobile surgical unit
during the Blitz. His earliest musical experiences were in
brass bands: when eventually he changed to the full-time
study of music he took lessons with Herbert Howells in
preparation for the external B Mus degree at Durham
University (though as a composer he is self-taught). His
Symphony No 1 was presented as his D Mus exercise. Most
of his working life has been spent as a producer for the BBC.
A born communicator who has been described as the new

Tovey, he has that happy knack of introducing and elucidating complex ideas in such a way that the non-expert can appreciate them.

He has always been something of a crusader; his perceptive musical mind has grasped such fascinating things in other composers' work that he has felt a compulsion to evangelise. This he did in his early days by founding the Exploratory Concert Society, in which he explored little known musical territory, avoiding the *avant garde* as well as received opinion as to what constituted the musical mainstream. His success in this venture led Sir Steuart Wilson, on the advice of Watson Forbes, to invite him to join the staff of the BBC in 1951. In the days when Bruckner was little played in this country Simpson waged a personal war on that composer's behalf to such effect that he is now well represented in the concert hall. Simpson then did the same thing for Nielsen, and so Nielsen's works are no longer the rarities that they were. A crusade on behalf of Havergal Brian included the gigantic undertaking of putting on the first professional performance of the *Gothic Symphony* – the largest ever written and calling for vast numbers of performers. There were many radio talks, including one (entitled 'The ferociously anti-pessimistic composer') that set out his *credo* as an artist. Alongside all this activity, composing had to be a sparetime pursuit; and Simpson, always dedicated to advocating other men's music, never pushed his own.

It is as a communicator of knowledge about other people's music that Simpson is at present best known. His monograph on Beethoven's symphonies and his pioneering books on Bruckner and Nielsen have been much admired: yet he denies that he is a musicologist. As he put it in *The Essence of Bruckner*: 'This book attempts to consider Bruckner through the ears of a composer ... It is my belief that the inner processes of music reveal themselves most readily to another sympathetic composer ...'[1]

His interest in symphonic processes, evident in the special regard he has for the music of Beethoven, Bruckner, Nielsen and Sibelius, made him the obvious choice as editor of Penguin Books' two-volume survey, *The Symphony*.[2]

Simpson himself contributed a brilliant essay outlining his view of the art form. For him, symphonies are works in which every element evolves in a logical manner; some admirable works with the title 'symphony' were excluded from the survey because they did not fulfil this criterion and something of a critical outcry ensued. As unrepentant as when faced by adverse criticism of his own music, Robert Simpson has always held to this position: indeed, his own works – and not only the symphonies – are notable for the sense of logical growth with which every element is imbued.

In 1980 Robert Simpson resigned from the BBC because of the corporation's musical policy – particularly the deterioration in the artistic policies which culminated in a plan to abolish five orchestras. Simpson also took issue with the Corporation over the administration of the Henry Wood promenade concerts. The book that followed his resignation – *The Proms and Natural Justice*[3] – caused an even greater stir than did *The Symphony*: but Simpson nevertheless maintained the justice of his point of view. This belief in himself, and the kind of integrity that makes a man resign a prestigious post on a point of honour, shines through his music too. Every page of his manuscripts is alive with confidence and with energetic strokes – even the pencil drafts seem to leap from the paper with a life of their own. He writes his music with Carl Nielsen's pencil, given to him by the composer's elder daughter. 'I hope', he says, 'that some of Nielsen's spirit will come through it'.

Too often this – and his love of Beethoven and Sibelius – has led commentators to the rather glib conclusion that Simpson's music is 'like' Nielsen's, or 'like' Sibelius's. One or two pieces, naturally, bear such traces: but Simpson's music is really only like Simpson, and it is less than just to a composer who writes everything with burning sincerity to suggest that it is merely a reflection of one of his mentors. It is usual that a single bar of Simpson's music is instantly recognizable as his own.

Nevertheless, certain procedures of his forbears affected him profoundly. He has always admired the sense of muscular forward motion found in the Viennese classics and believes that the secret of handling this kind of rhythmic energy has been lost to most 20th century writers. It is an art that he has tried to recapture in his own works. After some early serial experiments (the scores of which he subsequently destroyed) Simpson has found much satisfaction and endless possibilities in the tonal system, though it is often futile to attempt to pin-point actual keys in his works. His interest in Nielsen's 'progressive tonality' (which he prefers to describe as 'emergent tonality') has led him to explore means of playing off contrasting tonalities against one another. In all his large-scale works – there are at present ten symphonies and twelve string quartets, as well as much music for other forces, including brass band – it is the handling of tonality and the organic development of motivic material that most fascinates him.

His is absolute music in the sense that the processes governing its evolution rely on purely musical forces: yet it is not absolute in the way that Stravinsky meant when he said that music should express nothing beyond itself. It is clear that Simpson's music reflects the world around him: he insists on connecting music with life processes, and when discussing his own music he will often draw analogies with natural forces such as energy, or with some human predicament, or with astronomy (in which he has a profound interest): 'We must try to evaluate talent by what statements it makes about life as well as by its own skills ... [A composer] should not merely 'reflect' life; he should change it for the better if he can'.[4] The composers he most values – though not necessarily composers of 'programme music' in the normal sense – have, for him, this quality of evoking a better life: and his own music does so, to an unmistakable degree.

The necessity to communicate is as vital to Robert Simpson's music as to his scholarly pursuits: and for him 'communicate' means 'crusade'. He has said that 'No artist can be genuinely great unless his criticisms of life are positive and constructive'.[5] About his methods he says: 'If an idea feels wrong, chuck it out; if it feels right, keep it. It's purely a matter of intuition – it's *not* analytical, consciously, and it's *not* theoretical. That's work for other people, afterwards'. The result is that Simpson makes his appeal to the audience directly and unaffectedly: he insists that it is a composer's job at first to create a gripping sound – one that will attract the listener. In his music no less than in his exploratory concerts, he eschews the *avant garde* and has little truck with received ideas about what music should be like. He has the integrity to write the kind of music he feels and to fly in the face of those who tell him that 'tonality is dead', or that 'the symphony is dead'. To such comments, Simpson's uncompromising reply is: 'It's composers that are dead'.

The Tenth Quartet

Simpson wrote his String Quartet No 10 (For Peace) in 1983: it was composed for the tenth anniversary of the Coull Quartet, and is dedicated to them. These players gave the work its first performance at a concert in aid of the peace movement at Hazlemere, Buckinghamshire, on 22 September 1984. We do not need to be reminded of the horrors of war: Robert Simpson – who saw plenty of them during the Blitz – has said that the last thing he wanted to perpetrate was yet another of those shrilly protesting screams of agony so common in proselytising or propaganda works. In his programme note for the first performance he explained that the subtitle 'For Peace'

> refers to its generally pacific character and to the firm conviction, based on clear logic, that unless the human species makes a conscious and decisive choice against violence, the technology it now has (which cannot be unlearned and against which mere fear is no permanent safeguard) will sooner or later destroy it. Einstein's view that humanity must now change its way of thinking is at once compelling and pessimistic – he was not naive enough to suppose that this would happen. Nor is this composer. The music, however, is not an outburst of tormented anxiety; instead it tries to define the condition of peace. This excludes aggression but not strong feeling.

This is a much more pessimistic outlook than Simpson has previously expressed: but he still maintains that he is a ferocious anti-pessimist. He says, 'Although I have to accept that there is little hope, I insist on behaving as if there were – that is, I compose and I still go on trying to persuade other people of the menace we all face'.[6]

The programmatic representation of horrors with which we are only too familiar can easily be theatrical: but music has the potential to express positively the nature of peace, as many great composers have shown. An examination of Quartet No 10 will show how Robert Simpson has learned this lesson from past masters. A work by a composer whose normal language evolved from the dynamism of the traditional quartet medium, however, raises particular problems if it is to be dedicated to peace and the avoidance of conflict; for one associates the 'sonata principle' with dynamic contrast, if not with conflict and struggle. How, then, can a work dedicated to peace belong to the 'symphonic' tradition?

Before writing the tenth quartet Simpson had already begun to be interested in the possibilities of intervals, and to use them in place of tonalities in the construction of his large-scale music. In 1982, in a BBC Radio 3 discussion, he said:

> In earlier times I was interested in large-scale tonality, large areas of tonality: but now I'm trying to find what intervals themselves can generate, using the resonances inherent in simple intervals like the fifth, the fourth or the third. I try to generate something from that by feeling it in a novel way, by approaching the interval of a fifth as if I had never heard it before, and trying to find what can happen – or by using intervals against each other. Take two intervals, the second and the fifth, then you have a combination of intervals and you can use them in different ways against each other.

Simpson's eighth symphony and eighth string quartet are both examples of this kind of working:[7] indeed, the interval of a 5th played as prominent a part in the eighth string quartet as it had done in the seventh. The composer – who admits that, if he were condemned to write only one kind of work, he would choose string quartets – observes that many people who write for that medium nowadays do so without taking into account the fundamental nature of the instruments, and write *against* it. For instance, he maintains that the four instruments in a quartet are often treated as if they merely had different compasses and pitches instead of different characters. Many composers now treat all instruments – orchestral as well as chamber – without regard to their real natures; to Robert Simpson, writing badly for string quartet is not merely mistaking it for a string orchestra or a windband – it is failing to respect the very demands of the instruments themselves. Part – but only part – of the way in which Simpson tailors his music to the instruments is to recognise that each of them happens to have four strings tuned in fifths. Thus in Quartet No 7 the 'tonal norm' is that in which the open strings play the greatest part, and dynamic contrast is provided by moves away from areas that involve many open strings. The fundamental nature of the instruments themselves has thus suggested the formal logic of the piece.

This is a return to fundamentals also evident in another way in Quartet No 10. The slow and imitative nature of much of the music, and the interweaving of instruments, recalls Elizabethan and Jacobean Consort Music. It is not that the music is a pastiche of earlier styles, but the sinewy lines and the logical development of a few basic intervals (with their inversions), the use of canon, imitations by inversion with *arsin et thesin*, and the fugal writing, all help to make this a modern counterpart to the early 17th-century fantasias for viols. The concentration on the interval of a 5th (and its inversion, the 4th) constitutes a parallel return to fundamentals – the return to that fundamental basis of western music, the harmonic series.

The opening of the Quartet introduces us immediately to the ways in which Simpson appeals to tonal heritage. As Example 1 shows, the second violin begins on its lowest note; the viola, starting in unison with this note, moves downwards to fill in a 5th and end on its own lowest open string. (It is of some relevance that the viola precedes C natural with C sharp, sounding a tritone against G; for the tritone often acts as a foil to the perfect 5th. The tritone is at this point clearly stated as a combination of two minor thirds, G-E and E-C sharp). The open 5th, C-G with both notes played on open strings, is then left sounding, while the cello has a free imitation of the viola's opening line: this cello imitation reaches F, but treats it as E sharp moving upwards by a semitone to close on F sharp. (F sharp-C is another tritone, reflecting that between C sharp and G mentioned above).

Example 1.   First Movement, bars 1 - 9

What we have, then, at the opening of this work, is a statement of the two lowest notes of what we might call the 'tuning circle' – the circle of five 5ths (with the cello sounding an octave below the viola) to which the string quartet tunes. In tonal terms the lower end of this circle of 5ths is associated with the flatter key areas, and the higher with the sharper. We might therefore say that the Quartet's initial movement down a 5th from G to C gives a 'subdominantwards', 'flatwards', feel to the music; this feeling is capped by the further flatwards move on to F, one 5th *beyond* the flat end of the tuning circle. Perhaps this is why the composer does not at this stage dwell on the note, but lets it immediately move upwards to F sharp[8]; for as movement in a dominantwards direction is conventionally thought to be dynamic, it is customary to use it as the normal tonal shift in the early stages of sonata form works. By contrast, movement in a subdominantwards direction is conventionally considered relaxing – hence, perhaps, its relevance here in a work evoking peace.

Already, in the first few bars (see Example 1), the music's logic derives from the fundamental nature of the string quartet: the 'tuning' pitches give rise to the 5th used harmonically and melodically. Indeed, there is already a hint that it may work tonally as well, or at the very least, an indication that Simpson may use the 'tuning circle' in some way (differing, no doubt, from that already used in the seventh string quartet), and extend it beyond the five notes which constitute the 'tuning pitches'.

Playing any 'tuning' note against its next-but-one neighbour in the circle produces a 9th – an interval often inverted in this Quartet to produce a 7th: bar 2 of example 1, for instance, foreshadows the 9th in bars 7-8. Much use is made of the 9th (and its inversion as a 7th) in this piece.

It would be tedious to quote all the uses of the 5th in this work. Most obviously, it is used as a leap in many of the themes, as the interval of imitation, and also as the interval at which a part is doubled, sometimes replacing the more conventional octave doubling. In addition, an examination of those places where open strings are used prominently, and where the 'tuning pitches', though not necessarily played as open strings, have a prominent function in the music, will help show how the fundamental nature of the instruments themselves has helped shape the work. The composer describes the first movement as follows:

> [The music] is gently paced, in an unassertive sonata form, making use of repeated notes against flowing lines. Its one climax comes when the second subject is given an intensified recapitulation. Then the music relaxes into a slower tempo and finds a quiet close.[9]

'Unassertive' is an important word for our present purpose, since – as I have said – the sonata structure has to be written without undue conflict if it is to strive towards the condition of peace. In the first movement the open strings and the 'tuning' circle make an important contribution by replacing the more conventional tonal conflict. There is conflict of a very mild kind as the move towards the second subject is made (see Example 2).

The cello and second violin play their bottom open strings simultaneously, sounding an open fifth (C-G), while the viola adds an F to remind us of the extension of this flat end

Example 2   First Movement, bars 42 - 6

of the tuning circle by one more step. The first violin, however, by playing in a foreign tonality (one that revolves around a B natural, one 5th beyond the sharp end of the 'tuning circle', and thus countering the F natural), eventually forces the lower instruments upwards by a semitone, recalling the shift of a semitone that had followed the first cello E sharp (= F). The move to a more sharp area is emphasised by a series of slow octave-doublings played by the first violin, two of which contain open strings; there, octave E and octave D in bars 53-61, are at the sharper end of the 'tuning circle'. This pulling of the music towards the sharp side by the use of 'sharper' tuning pitches is a clear equivalent to the modulation to the sharp side found so often at the second subject area in conventional sonata form.

The development begins at bar 75 with a series of repeated B flats in viola and cello (playing an octave apart), soon joined by repeated Cs in the two violins (also playing an octave apart). The repeated notes which are a prominent feature of the Quartet are piled up here; we are reminded of the flattest note of the tuning circle, C, though here it is placed at the top of the quartet's compass rather than at the bottom. B flat, repeated in conjunction with C, is two 5ths flatter round the tuning circle, and makes a 7th against the repeated Cs.

There are two points of recapitulation in this movement; one involves thematic material, the other tonalities. The composer is himself not at all concerned about defining where the 'Recapitulation' starts: he is much more concerned with the idea of bringing back the second subject in an enhanced way.[10] As Example 3 shows, the combination of C with B flat below it, just mentioned as a developmental feature, is inverted at bar 112: here the thematic material of the opening is recalled, though with

Example 3.   First Movement, bars 112 - 120

a different, flatter, series of pedals. The omission of the first G and F of Example 1 means that the thematic material begins with E (rather than G): this would be unlikely to be played as the open E string, but nevertheless it is clear that the passage begins with the outermost tuning notes of the string quartet (though there are two 'foreign' notes included within that wide span). The pedals make two points of importance: the first is that they are, in a sense, more peaceful, static, version of the repeated notes which play a prominent part in the work: the second is that each extreme of the 'tuning circle' is accompanied by a note a 7th beyond it. Thus C, the flattest note of the circle, is accompanied by B flat, two 5ths beyond its end of the circle; and E, the sharpest note of the circle, is accompanied by F sharp (written as G flat), two 5ths sharper again. The resulting 7ths reflect the presence of many other 7ths (and 9ths) in the piece so far; and G flat in addition recalls the cello's move away from E sharp when, at the opening, it had veered away from the series of falling perfect 5ths by a semitone (see Example 1). The tension at this point is largely one of juxtaposing the sharp and flat areas of the tuning circle; there is no building of excitement such as one habitually finds at this point in sonata form.

The recalling of the original pitches at the point of greatest tension and excitement in fact occurs later in the movement: that is when, after the enhanced recapitulation of the second subject, the Coda begins on a massive octave G, with both violins playing on the open G string. In some senses, then, *this* is the Recapitulation (see Example 4).

Example 4.   First Movement, bars 231 - 42

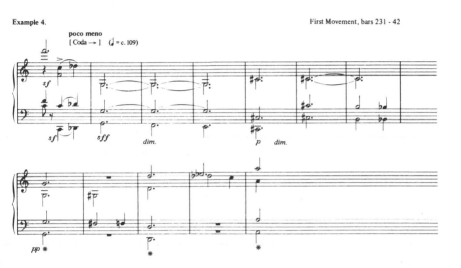

It has been prepared by the subdominant area rather than by the customary dominant, reflecting firstly the quite normal subdominant tendency of Recapitulation sections, and secondly the flatwards feeling of the movement which results from its 'pacific' nature. Open C strings in the viola and cello play some part in the preparation for the passage shown in Example 4, though the open G string of the violins is also in evidence. The actual arrival at the octave G – the most powerful stroke in the whole first movement – is approached from the open C string of the cello, and this creates a feeling of return from the 'relaxed' subdominant regions to which the music had moved at the beginning of the work.

Yet if we are to be quite accurate, the octave G which starts the Coda is approached via D flat, rather than directly from the subdominant C. This mutation of C upwards by a semitone is both a reflection of bars 7-8 in which E sharp was mutated to F sharp, and of the tritone G-C sharp in bar 3. Such a mutation of 'tuning pitches' on the flat side (or a 5th one degree beyond it) helps to weaken the flatter areas and so helps to steer the music into sharper ones. The process is very clear in Example 4, for the music moves from G down to C sharp, which is given all the weight of octave doublings, rather than C natural: this is a clear echo of bar 3.

Simpson now moves sharpwards through the 'tuning circle', with G, D, and A all being announced as unharmonised octaves (as indicated by the asterisks in Example 4). Clearly this tendency to pile 5ths on top of one another counters the falling 5ths which gave a subdominantwards feel at the opening of the movement. Some time later (in bar 258), an octave E is sounded, so completing the 'tuning circle'. The process of piling up the 'tuning 5ths' in a sharpwards direction, though, is made absolutely clear by the use of unharmonised octaves on those notes and on no others (except C sharp) at this point in the movement. By concentrating on particular notes rather than tonalities Simpson has created a nice parallel to the sonata principle of tonal motion away from a centre and an eventual re-establishment of that centre in such a way that the alternatives to it are banished.

The movement does not end with open strings, even though the final note is one of the 'tuning 5ths' and even though the viola's bottom C is part of a multiple pedal that precedes the final octave A. This C is central to the final bars, and is accompanied both by the 7th below (D in the cello) and the 7th above (B flat, in the 1st violin). The C natural has, however, taken over from a long high double pedal on F sharp and C sharp, resulting in a dichotomy between flat and sharp sides of the tonic.

Of the second movement the composer has said, 'A playful little scherzo follows, with syncopation and quicksilver quavers; this also has one climax, which vanishes as fast as it comes'.[11] The music starts at the point where it left off in the previous movement – on A. It is clear that the viola part at the opening is derived from the beginning of the viola part in the first movement, and of the Coda to that movement (see Example 5 and cf example 4): much other material is also built from ideas thrown up there.

Example 5.   Second Movement, bars 1 - 6

Prestissimo   ($\bullet$ = c. 144)

Scale Formations:

The two instruments start and end their opening phrases in the scherzo on notes that are part of the 'tuning circle', so that A (this is the only note that could actually be played on an open string, but is unlikely to be so played in this context), G, C and E are the notes around which the lines revolve. The two lines, indeed, mirror each other precisely – an idea to which we must shortly return. Like the first movement, the two-part counterpoint that starts this scherzo seems to emanate from a unison (the composer uses the same idea again in the Finale): moreover, the viola part at the start of the first movement fits neatly into the lower of the two 'scale formations' shown in Example 5. The composer also contrives to remind us of the 9th, for the widest interval in Example 5 – spelled enharmonically – provides one.

By mirroring the viola part exactly, the second violin in Example 5 falls short of filling up the perfect fifth by a semitone: in other words, just as the viola states C sharp in place of C natural in bar 4, so the second violin states E flat instead of E natural. Both parts, therefore, use the tritone in place of the perfect 5th. Such a 'mistuning'[12] of the 5ths to which the Quartet tunes reflects the frequent displacement of notes of the 'tuning circle' by a semitone that had happened in the opening movement; in discussing that earlier movement I had mentioned the shifts by a semitone up from a 'tuning pitch' which derive ultimately from the cello's E sharp-F sharp in bars 7-8. What also happens at times is that there is 'mistuning' of the 'tuning circle' note by a semitone down. Both these semitone 'mistunings' are evident in Example 5, for both the second violin and the viola fall short of stating the perfect 5th by a semitone. If, however, we take them as a pair, the perfect 5th *is* completed; for migrating between the viola and second violin we have the scale G-F-E-E flat-D flat-C, and migrating *vice versa* we have A-B-C-C sharp-D sharp-E (see the 'scale formations' in Example 5). Neither is a conventional scale – but the one is an exact inversion of the other.

Example 5 could scarcely be said to indicate a shift to either the sharper or the flatter end of the 'tuning circle'; or rather, because of the inversion it suggests both simultaneously. Yet the music does shortly move into sharper areas: the first violin, entering on B natural, moves swiftly (but not directly) to F sharp and to C sharp – a series of sharpward 5ths beyond the end of the 'tuning circle', and one that balances the Fs and B flats of the first movement. The perfect 5th is, indeed, a clear element in much melodic material of this scherzo; often the interval is filled in with a scale, using the Lydian instead of the perfect 4th (the upper scale of Example 5 without the C natural, in fact).

It is not that C natural and flat keys never appear in the scherzo – they certainly do; but the general trend is towards the sharp side. Nevertheless, the movement ends with a very high C in the first violin, at the other extreme of the quartet's range from the cello's fundamental C which had reintroduced the opening thematic material during the first movement. It is almost as if height had taken over from sharpness here; yet that cold, lone, high C cannot represent the sharp areas, especially as it is for a time supported by an A natural, a G flat and an E flat. The A and C of this chord are notes from the 'tuning circle', while the other two are a semitone away from the 'tuning circle' notes (one higher by a semitone, one lower). There is a tendency, then, to weaken the hold of the 'tuning 5ths'. Both the notes that weaken these 5ths have clear relevance to the work as a whole: E flat is the ultimate goal, though it is very distant at this stage; G flat is the enharmonic spelling of the note to which the cello had veered at the start of the first movement after reaching the first E sharp (= F natural), and it is also the dominant of B, a pitch one 5th beyond the sharp end of the 'tuning circle' of which much use has been made in this scherzo. Because of its layout, the final chord does not *sound* much like a diminished 7th; yet that is what it is. The chord is made up of a series of interlocking tritones, and so reflects the melodic outline of the thematic material of this movement, as well as the opening bars of the first movement.

Of the third (and last) movement Robert Simpson says:

After this brief contrast [ie, the scherzo] the work ends with a long adagio, growing out of a simple up-and-down phrase that rises through a natural (or flat) note and descends through a sharp one.[13] The whole movement explores the expressive possibilities of this quiet reversal of the usual expectations. As in the other movements there is only one climax, this time created by a sustained burst of passion. When this is at last supplanted by quiet, the first violin gives out a calm but graceful tune derived from everything else in the whole work. Then the music moves to a peaceful end.[14]

The Finale begins in sharp areas – but, as Example 6 shows, there are sequences which immediately attempt to veer the music towards flatter areas (see the asterisks in the Example). Thus the first real cadence is on F (bar 19), as far away from the opening B natural as can be, and yet it is only one 5th beyond the flattest of the 'tuning circle', just as B natural is only one 5th beyond the sharpest. Almost at once, therefore, the relevance of the tritones earlier in the work is made clear. Moving outwards from the 'tuning circle' by only one step in

each direction immediately produces a tritone: this interval, which negates the 5ths of the circle, had been introduced as early as the cello's F sharp in bar 8 of the first movement.

The opening theme of the Finale is a slow variant of that quoted in Example 5, though it is much more relaxed, being more consonant and avoiding syncopations. The 'rise through a natural (or flat) note and descent through a sharp one' is a further derivation of the scale formations shown in Example 5. The places where the instruments sound perfect intervals (without any other admixture of notes) are very instructive: in the first few bars of the Finale (see Example 6), octaves occur on E, D and G (a 15th rather than an octave in one instance), and perfect 5ths are built above G, F sharp, B and C. Perfect intervals are confined, therefore, to the 'tuning pitches' and the three 5ths next to them on the sharp side; B, F sharp and C sharp. The pitches beyond the 'flat' side of the 'tuning circle' are not used, nor are remote pitches used in octaves or 5ths.

The 5ths which have been so prominent throughout the quartet are often inverted to become 4ths in the Finale (Example 6 contains several); perhaps this reflects the 'inversion' of the 9th (two 5ths added together) to become a 7th, and the exact inversions of such lines as are shown in Example 5. The proof of the observation that 5ths have been inverted to become 4ths is shown in Example 7, in which the cello moves sharpwards round the tuning circle, though by

Example 7.

descending 4ths (they are marked by asterisks in the Example), while the viola uses rising 4ths moving in a flatwards direction. As at the beginning of each movement, two parts seem to grow out of a unison; and at this point there is a clear attempt to balance the sharpward and flatward tendencies. The underlying impression of bars 20-23 is of E flat moving on to D major, a progression that helps to prepare the final bars of the work. The flat-sharp dichotomy shown in Example 7 is pursued at some length in the Finale.

The teeming counterpoint of a big fugue some two-thirds of the way into the movement provides a late interruption of the prevailing quiet: it is carefully prepared by a series of short canons, which are mostly at the 5th and use the 5th prominently as a melodic interval. The canons gradually rise up through the quartet until they reach a very high point, at which stage the fugue begins with the viola's open C string. This loud low C signals the start of a new section by commencing on a clearly identifiable open string, a ploy used several times in the first movement. In view of the importance of 5ths to the Quartet as a whole, one might expect the fugal entries to be at that interval; but they are not. Moreover, while the fifth appears in the countersubject material, it is avoided in the subject itself. In fact, the entries are at the 7th, which, as we know from earlier movements, is an interval that results from juxtaposing two adjacent tuning 5ths; the first four entries, in C and B flat, G sharp and F sharp, make two pairs which clearly juxtapose pitches on the flat and sharp sides of the 'tuning circle'. The composer has suggested to me that the sharpwards tendency of this fugato is as anti-peaceful as its sustained fortissimo. The 'tuning pitch' E is twice emphasised by being presented as unharmonised octaves, and open strings and 'tuning-pitches' are also occasionally prominent (as, indeed, they are throughout the movement). At the very end of the fugue the only unharmonised octave that is *not* a 'tuning-pitch' is sounded: this is F, played by all the instruments, and it helps to compensate for the sharpness of much of the writing at the end of the fugue – a sharpness ushered in by the strident octave B natural in the first violin.

It is clear that the sharp and flat ends of the 'tuning circle' are again being played off against one another. In linking to the Coda the composer builds on this point by spelling B natural enharmonically as C flat, and then making the instruments descend by fourths on G flat, D flat, A flat and E flat. The last note of this progression then falls by a minor 3rd in order to start the tune of the Coda in A flat, a fall that has been prepared at several points in the movement, and is in any case an integral part of Example 1. The sense of integration and agreement between the sharp and flat areas at the end of the work is prepared by using C flat to usher in the very flat opening of the Coda; for C flat, spelled enharmonically as B natural, is the very pitch that was so prominent in emphasising the sharp end of the 'tuning circle'.

The tune that begins the Coda is Haydnesque with an apparent simplicity that belies the fact that it derives from all the preceding elements of the quartet. Its sense of well-being and quiet relaxation recall that found at a similar place in Simpson's First String Quartet, about which the composer said, 'I remember composing the whole of that Coda lying on my stomach on a sunny day in Regent's Park, feeling very pleasant'.[15] The tonality of the Coda is fluid, and conflict between the flat and sharp sides has evaporated. After a brief reminder of the opening theme of the movement, the music moves to a cadence on a chord of D major (with A in the bass); then two more chords bring the music to a close on E flat (with B flat in the bass).

Either the D major or E flat chords would seem to be quite suitable endings for this piece[16] – an extraordinary fact for a composer whose normal way of working for most of his composing life was based on tonality. It is not that this quartet is atonal – far from it; but such a balance has been struck between the opposing sharp and flat ends of the tonal spectrum by the end of the work that conflicts between them no longer exist. One other point of interest is raised by the end: the notes of the 'tuning circle' do not show up in any significant way at the close, even though they have played a large role in the rest of the work. The opposing views of the antagonists – pull towards the flat or sharp areas – have given way to a consensus embracing both.

The composer has said that the 'tuning circle' was not consciously part of his design when writing the work: but this does not invalidate the idea as an important element. It is a logical extension of the process used in the seventh string quartet, and so may well have lodged in the composer's subconscious mind. It is, in any case, well known that such 'accidents of construction' can occur in works of art created by experienced composers, artists, or writers. The use of the 'tuning circle' in this work has, moreover, great advantages. For one thing, it recalls the fundamental nature of the medium. But more than that, by concentrating on pitches and intervals rather than established tonalities Robert Simpson has – even if subconsciously – solved the problem of writing a work which can preserve the traditional formal principles of the quartet as a medium without the conflict between key areas which is a normal feature of that medium. By the end of the work, conflict has been so entirely removed that the flat and sharp sides of the 'tuning circle' coexist in peace – neither can be said to be predominant at the close.

Perhaps one of the greatest dreams one could ever have would be that of a world in which nuclear power had not been invented. Alas, such a thing is not possible now. But at least one might dream that all antagonists in the world had somehow agreed to differ in peace. It may be going too far to suggest that the processes of this String Quartet are connected with such a dream – that is only one listener's reaction to the music; and most composers would, I think, prefer not to have too precise a programme attached to a particular work. Yet perhaps the ordinary listener sometimes needs a programme. One of the ways in which a work can be 'of its time' is in suggesting contemporary relevance to the hearer: no composer, on the other hand, would wish his work to be relevant only to the time of its composition. But just as humanity has made God in its own image and made that image speak such things as we want to hear, so the contemporary listener is inclined to relate a work to his or her own outlook. We cannot attribute blame for this: but a work may have more relevance than a single listener can accord it. The job of poets or composers is to speak with relevance to their hearers. All a poet can do today, it seems, is warn.

This music is both an intellectual structure and also a qualitative comment on human existence: and there is love of music, love of life, love of tradition and love of peace in it. We are reminded by Mahatma Ghandi that 'hate can only be overcome by love'. The pacific character of the 10th String Quartet is Simpson's statement of belief in face of the dangerous situation in the world today. If a holocaust is not to engulf us, somebody – sooner or later – must take some steps back from the brink and look for peace.

The first part of this chapter is based on the author's article 'The ferocious anti-pessimist', *Times Higher Education Supplement*, 21 December, 1984, p 15.

Notes

[1] Robert Simpson, *The Essence of Bruckner*, Gollancz 1967, p 9.

[2] Robert Simpson (ed), *The Symphony*, Penguin 1966.

[3] Robert Simpson, *The Proms and Natural Justice*, Toccata Press 1981.

[4] See Hugh Ottaway, 'Third Symphony', in Edward Johnson (ed), *Robert Simpson, Fiftieth Birthday Essays*, Triad press 1971, p 15.

[5] *Ibid.*

[6] Robert Simpson, in a private letter to the author.

[7] Lionel Pike, 'Robert Simpson's New Way,' *Tempo*, June 1985, No 153, pp 20-29.

[8] The cellist of the Coull String Quartet tells me that he never thinks of bars 7-8 as F natural – always as E sharp.

[9] Programme note for the first performance.

[10] Public colloquium with the Coull String Quartet in Leamington, 8 March 1986.

[11] Programme note for the first performance.

[12] 'Mistuning' only in the sense that one might describe the opening of Saint-Saens *Danse Macabre* as employing a 'mistuned' E string.

[13] 'I pinched this from a misprint in Beethoven's *Hammerklavier* Sonata', says the composer.

[14] Programme note for the first performance.

[15] Hugh Ottaway's sleeve note for the recording of the First String Quartet.

[16] The members of the Coull String Quartet have commented that the E flat chord feels a more suitable ending than the D major one, because it is scored in a more 'relaxed' part of the Quartet's compass; and the viola and 'cello members of the group find the E flat ending particularly satisfying since both their parts return to the very pitch with which they started.

Nicholas Williams

Behold the Sun: The politics of musical production

Behold the Sun is the title of Alexander Goehr's second opera, premièred at Duisburg, West Germany, in 1985.[1] It is also a quotation from the writings of Gerrard Winstanley, founder of the remarkable communistic society of Diggers which flourished briefly in Cobham, Surrey, in 1649. Both the Diggers and the related movements of Ranters and Quakers were direct, if benign, descendants of the subject of Goehr's work: the violent Anabaptist uprising in the city of Münster in 1534, and the creation and catastrophic destruction there of the Kingdom of Zion. Goehr's title deliberately invokes the exalted faith in the dawning millennium and longed-for earthly utopia which was common to all these sects – a broad and persistent mode of thought in which humanity's very destiny seemed, in Winstanley's own words, to be 'running up like parchment in the fire'.

Every German schoolboy knows about the Anabaptists. Their origins amongst the poor and dispossessed and their novel ideas of social justice have long intrigued German philosophers, historians and novelists, even if comparable details of British history remain unfamiliar. So for the opera's first performance, Deutsche Oper am Rhein, who commissioned the work to celebrate their 25th anniversary, renamed it after its subject-matter – Die Wiedertaüfer. Not a serious change, on the face of it. Except that, in the context of the premiere, it appeared to many as if the shifting of emphasis from the spiritual to the prosaic was emblematic of a larger contradiction. Goehr had composed a full-length choral opera about the workings of religious fundamentalism; but what appeared on stage was a demonstrable violation of his text, and an implicit violation of his theme. Regardless of the work's intrinsic merit, the outcome of the production was unequivocal and immediate: withdrawn after only five performances, the opera was judged a failure. Not only was an opportunity lost; because of a flawed and ill-judged realisation, a work which had been ten years in the making was delivered up, tried and executed on false evidence.[2] An act of perjury, to widen the metaphor. But for the composer, it was nothing less than a fundamental artistic betrayal.

And there the story might have ended, but for a singular event: a symposium, organised by the Evangelische Stadtakademie Düsseldorf and the Theater-Gemeinde Düsseldorf, held shortly after the premiere in order to discuss the unique religious content of *Behold the Sun*.[3] The very existence of such a gathering was in itself both a handsome gesture and an indication of the seriousness with which the operatic form and the Anabaptist story are still regarded in Germany. Taking 'Religion and Fanaticism' as their theme, a distinguished panel of authorities considered the theological implications of Goehr's work. Inevitably, however, given its controversial presentation, their discussions were drawn from questions of theology to questions of form, content and artistic interpretation.

What emerged clearly in their debate was that they were not only considering the version of the work to be found in the score and the version seen on the Düsseldorf stage; they were also considering two fundamentally conflicting attitudes to the material. For Goehr, the Anabaptists possessed a symbolic significance not just as revolutionaries, but as vehicles for that universal revolutionary impulse and desire for a better world which the German philosopher Ernst Bloch defined as the Spirit of Utopia. Yet in the production of *Behold the Sun*, the evangelicals were presented in quite a different light – as an outrageous, bloodthirsty, irrational mob in whom the yearning for change was identified unambiguously with all that is most destructive of society and darkest in humankind.

The eminence of Bohumil Herlishka, the producer, was not in question. For seven years director of the Prague National Theatre, he came to the West in 1957 and established his reputation for originality and exuberance with a novel cycle of Janacek operas give by Deutsche Oper am Rhein. (According to one 65th birthday tribute, his stagecraft is characterised by a plethora of ideas and images balancing a fundamental conservatism.) Why then, in the case of *Behold the Sun*, did he choose to override the wishes of the composer? And even as an experienced man of the theatre rather than a theorist, did he possess the prerogative to transform a collective, apocalyptic vision of hope conceived in the tradition of Schoenberg's *Moses und Aron* and Stravinsky's *Oedipus Rex* into a conventional costume drama exploring a hallucinatory, expressionist, yet ulti-mately clichéd world of personal religious ecstasy familiar from Prokofiev's *The Fiery Angel* and, more recently, Penderecki's the *Devils of Loudon*?

The hybrid nature of the piece made these questions especially pertinent. Even on a superficial acquaintance, it would be difficult to think of another 20th century opera with a character more firmly established by its creator than that of *Behold the Sun*. In a detailed account of the work's compositional history, Goehr revealed to the symposium that from the start his conception of a non-naturalistic stage piece on a religious subject had been approved of and encouraged by the Intendant of Deutsche Oper at the time, Dr Grischa Barfuss;[4] that much of the libretto is found on Holy Writ as quoted by the Anabaptists themselves; and that words and music had grown together not in an artificial conjunction but as an inseparable stylistic unity of Biblical text and musical form. To manipulate the dramatic structure wholesale would be, *ipso facto*, to disturb the theological and political content. To do so on the grounds that *Behold the Sun* was in need of 'improvement' in order to make it effective theatre (as Herlishka's colleague Dr Ilka Kügler claimed was the case) was to beg the pertinent question. The matter of the opera's genre was specious; in the theatre, the genre that should count is that of accomplishment; and there is nothing in the carefully constructed scenario of the opera that is beyond reasonable technical resource. But there is a considerable dramaturgic challenge. Forcing Goehr's highly original musico-dramatic concept into the irrelevant category of costume drama neatly sidestepped the problem of form while allowing for presumptuous meddling with the content.

It was the producer's intention, said Dr Kügler, to render the work as a non-partisan parable. From this assumption, not cosmetic matters of staging and genre, arose the fundamental contradictions and travesties of the production – 50 minutes of music omitted, a key aria arbitrarily transferred between acts, gratuitous scenic elements. Art does not report, it interprets; the only fidelity it demands is fidelity to the text. To transform the ideological content of a work into its blatant antinomy and, under the guise of objectivity, to proclaim it as the truth, is to commit an egregious fallacy and an unjust deceit. In a word – censorship. The facts speak for themselves, beyond individual praise or blame. And for the benefit of the producers and consumers of opera the story of *Behold the Sun* demands to be generally known, not only as a vindication of the individual work, but as an object lesson concerning the interaction of art and politics in our time.

There was a sour irony about the comprehensive excision of the choral element at the première of *Behold the Sun*: for it was the excellent reputation of Deutsche Oper am Rhein's chorus in the 1960s and 70s under the direction of Georg Rheinhardt, and in particular a celebrated production of Moses und Aron and the personal enthusiasm of Dr Barfuss himself, which had been such formative influences on the opera's development. Nevertheless, the original impulse behind the opera lay even further back: in the political upheavals of 1968 and the composer's desire to write a work dealing with the revolutionary theme.

But this would definitely not be agitprop. That most

spontaneous and ephemeral of 60s categories was very far from his intention. A graduate of earlier and more sober Marxist ideologies, Goehr had embraced the general exhilaration of that time – the feeling that events in Paris, Berlin and the United States represented a great upsurge in radical thought and socialist action, in contrast to the corruption of the West and stagnation of the East – but had done so with a qualified optimism. The conviction of the student revolutionaries was beyond question; what was disputed was their motivation. For if the strength of the activists was their innocence (and their innocence lent them a romantic appeal denied to the traditional and declining left), it was also their weakness. As time has shown, naiveté blinded them to the realities of power, as the naiveté of the Anabaptists blinded them to destiny and their destruction. 'This is the season, this the day, the hour': the line is from Shelley's *Prometheus Unbound*, and is proclaimed by the prophet Bokelson in Act 3 of *Behold the Sun*. Bokelson takes it to be his moment of glory when he will ride in triumph to the 'Golden City'; but in reality it is his moment of downfall. Goehr would claim no prescience for his temperate view of history, but the truth remains: in today's world the radicalism of the 60s resembles less a glorious dawn than a fading and distant sunset.

When the composer first encountered the Münster story in the early 1970s through the pages of Norman Cohn's classic text, *The Pursuit of the Millenium*,[5] he was immediately struck by its epic scope and potential for superb theatre. More striking still was its contemporary flavour. In the struggle to understand the nature of recent events, this account of 16th century revolution acquired a special significance.

The violent Anabaptist revolution of 1534 was actually the culmination of many mediaeval movements of collective salvation, from the Hussites to the Waldensians, which preceded the protestant reformation. The millenarian ideal has always been a persistent if wayward thread in the history of European thought; but in the turbulent first half of the 16th century this condition of thought and action reached its apogee. The background was one of social fracture: the image of Europe under threat from without – the expansion of the Ottoman Empire; and from within – the challenge to mediaeval thought from Leonardo and Copernicus, and to mediaeval belief from Zwingli, Calvin and Luther. The potent instrument of unrest was the Word – literally – since 1455 liberated by Gutenberg as the most subversive vessel for freedom and exchange of thought. The Word is ever-present in *Behold the Sun*, from the use of actual recorded speeches of the Anabaptist leaders, to the opening image of a simple merchant's wife, alone, in deep contemplation of the scriptures set down in her native tongue. For in post-reformation Germany, Lutheranism could neither hold the allegiance of the poorer classes nor provide a satisfactory cohesion of its own to equal that of traditional catholicism. Replacing the mediating role of the priest by the new doctrine of salvation meant that the individual conscience of the faithful was as free to interpret the word of God as that of the clergy – and conscience led many to question the new order as much as the old.

It was from these social confusions that the Anabaptist movement derived a special strength, and in the Westphalian city of Münster matters reached a crisis point. The historical facts – scrupulously respected in the libretto of *Behold the Sun* – are these. Early in 1534, the baker Johann Matthys and the tailor and one-time actor Jan Bokelson, self-styled 'prophets' from Holland, arrived in the city to preach the imminent arrival of the millenium and the active destruction of the Godless by the sword of the elect. The status of Münster as a self-governing area within the general jurisdiction of a local prince-bishop made it no stranger to contemporary currents of evangelical feeling. But to the usual eschatological fantasies of the second coming prevalent at the time were swiftly added those of a darker hue. Matthys and Bokelson won legal recognition for their right to freedom of conscience, acquiring a growing band of followers and powerful political support from the city guilds. Iconoclasts began wrecking Münster's many churches; public outbursts of religious frenzy became commonplace (not least among the female converts); from all over Europe like-minded groups flocked to the New Jerusalem.

Encountering only limited opposition, the foreigners were able to achieve their ambition: the creation in Münster of a theocracy on the putative model of the early church. On 27 February, in the midst of a bitter snowstorm, the ungodly were driven from the purified city by Matthys, or forced to be rebaptised. It seemed that all prophecies were to be fulfilled save that of the wolf and the lamb. The following day the city was besieged by an army of mercenaries commanded jointly by the ruling catholic Prince-Bishop and the Lutheran Landgrave of Hesse.

Within the encircled city there followed the degeneration of idealism into terror. Confronted by the forces of antichrist, the prophets enhanced their power using classic totalitarian methods: mob rule, prescription and intimidation. (A blacksmith who dared to question was the first victim, slaughtered by the hand of Matthys: in the opera this act marks the symbolic betrayal of the people's hope.) Only the Bible was spared from the wholesale destruction of books; private property was abolished. If, briefly, a communistic, utopian society was achieved, it was at a terrible price. Yet the deeply revelatory nature of the movement can be felt in the death of Matthys himself (recorded at the conclusion of Act 2), killed at Easter in a sortie attempted after a vision of the Father had promised invincibility to him and his troops.

No such caveat could be applied to Bokelson, who seized control as a consequence. Whether or not unbalanced, he was an artful showman and a gifted tactician – but a ruthless egoist above all. As sympathetic uprisings in the Netherlands and Germany were crushed and the forces of the Prince-Bishop, now supported by the empire, tightened their grip into a blockade, the demoralised Anabaptists were witness to his ever more ironic charades and extravagant promises of deliverance – delusions and ploys which form the substance of Goehr's third act. In a cruel burlesque of the millenarian dream, he established Old Testament polygamy and had himself crowned an Old Testament prophet-king on earth: King John of Leyden. (But this was a ruler who gained sadistic gratification from the summary execution of unbelievers.) As a test of their loyalty, the people were ordered to march to the promised land, then subjected to the spectacle of an horrendous morality on the story of Dives and Lazarus (Goehr's 'play within a play') in which their ruler's murderous intentions become clear.

The situation could not endure. On 24 June 1535, helped by two traitors, the surrounding army finally broke through and exacted a terrible punishment. Neither women nor children were spared. The massacre of Anabaptists lasted two days. The execution of Bokelson, King John of Leyden, was reserved for a more suitable occasion.

Between the initial discovery of Cohn's account and the completion of *Behold the Sun* lay a dozen years of considerable creative evolution for the composer. But a single, basic principle remained clear in his mind throughout: that if a composer has anything urgent to contribute to the theatre, then it must be in the domain of his own expressive medium. For his own music he should accept only what is necessary; to reduplicate manifestations of poetic or theatrical brilliance is insufficient. The collaboration of composer and librettist may confirm the final identity of the piece, but that identity must stem from the essence of the music. Far from the conventional notion of a composer providing a 'setting' for a given libretto, the choice of text should in some way be predetermined by the nature of the music and realised in terms of a complex symbiotic relation arising between the two.

For a composer, this is the most basic truth. In the case of *Behold the Sun*, the determining nature of Goehr's musical inspiration was clear from the very beginning: a project for the revival of a Handelian conception in writing for the stage, eschewing more recent operatic models from Verdi to Alban Berg. Moreover, the kind of events with which he hoped to deal, and his decision taken early on to construct the libretto from the very Biblical exhortations and injunctions which the Anabaptists had tried to make real in their own lives, put the proposed composition squarely in the category of religious music.

His central vision was in terms of elaborations of the

single moment; the isolated statement and formalised gesture of the *Da Capo* aria, and the 'unnatural' intensification which comes about through the ornamentation and emphatic exaggerations of the repeat. And only by reviving the tradition of choral polyphony as it occurred in the great oratorios and passions – the choral fugue in particular – could he see a way to do justice to the over life-size and multi-referential character of the events and personalities of his subject. This would naturally involve a slower dramaturgie than has been acceptable to modern audiences – or so it is supposed. A treatment of this kind depends on the contrast between the suspension of action (while the music of aria and chorus gives full development to the moment of gesture), and the violently fast and unadorned moments of action. This is not merely a baroque conception: the second act of Wagner's *Tristan and Isolde* contrasts the long, sustained suspension of activity with a set of tumultuous events at its conclusion. But it is a conception specifically opposite to any adoption of cinematic techniques of montage; and quite different from any expressionist intention.

In fact, to have composed this opera with reference to the expressionist tradition would have been to glorify violence – the very antithesis of the composer's theme. He not only saw any attempt to revive a movement from before the First World War as epigonistic and intellectually feeble, but also believed that for *Behold the Sun* he should follow the example of Schoenberg in *Moses und Aron*. Here, the master expressionist found himself recreating a Handelian concept by means of double choruses and set-piece arias – archetypal and historically 'given' forms which provide a serious approach to this kind of material without the risk of descending into Hollywood phantasmagoria.

Yet because he did not feel that Schoenberg's approach of reconstituting these forms in a parallel serial methodology was possible, Goehr's challenge was to recreate for himself a viable manner of composing in this way, using common material.[6] But to put this material in quotes in a Bergian manner also seemed to place the composer in a false creative position as regards his subject matter – making it 'past'

history. He felt the need to write this piece in the same way –
though not as a pastiche of the same style – as Bach and
Handel. Goehr had already initiated the process by which he
would discover these structures for himself. To the artist's
imperative of 'making it new' he had, since the Psalm IV
cycle of the mid 1970s, urged a re-examination of the
inherent possibilities of ordinary, traditional material in the
belief that freshness might also be found in attempting
solutions to some of the age-old problems of music: a belief,
for example, that harmonic novelty might lie not so much in
new chords or new instruments as in originality of voice
leading or feeling for intervallic tension.

J S Bach might be the particular model for this kind of
activity: his genius for polyphonic elaboration created an
infinite harmonic variety from a strictly limited tonal
repertoire. Goehr's own fascination with Bach had already
been expressed in a number of pieces, not least the ensemble
work ... a musical offering (J S B 1985); in *Behold the Sun*
the chorale melody *In Gott Allein* (a familiar melody, and
much sung by the original Anabaptists) becomes the theme
for a sequence of increasingly rich harmonisations occurring
at strategic junctures throughout the opera. But the answer
lay not with the father but the son. From a study of Carl
Philipp Emanuel's theoretical writings, Goehr discovered
a new way of composing in which a transformation of the
traditional figured bass would control pace, articulation
and texture. The sheer architectural grandeur of the
polyphonic choruses sung by the turba confirm the strength
of this language and Goehr's success in recreating old forms
anew.

In contrast to the absolute nature of the musical intuitions
for *Behold the Sun*, the central element of religious
fundamentalism was, for a time, an enigma which could be
neither ignored nor fitted honestly into any convenient
scheme of German social history. Having rejected a number
of possible treatments for the theme of revolution, ranging
from a piece about the life of the Jewish false Messiah,
Sabbatai Zvi, to a musical based on Plato's Republic, Goehr
planned initially to present the Münster episode as a didactic
story for socialists and communists, using the example of a

Brechtian epic structure. (The particular model for this was Brecht's libretto for *Miseries and Splendours of the Third Reich*.) The religious texts, set as chorales and other sacred forms, would act as the equivalent of the signs and slogans which preceded scenes in the productions of the Berliner Ensemble. Independent tableaux derived from Cohn, Ranke and Loeffler would tell the Anabaptist story itself. The entire structure was intended to rest on four 'pillars': large-scale choruses which were the first parts of the opera to be composed and were performed separately in December 1979 as the oratorio *Babylon the Great is Fallen*.

By this time, however, the original plan had changed considerably. The composer had discussed his project with Dr Barfuss, who had made a number of practical criticisms concerning the original conception. Meanwhile, through the writings of Ernst Bloch, Goehr discovered a way of viewing the Anabaptist tragedy that differed from its conventional marxist interpretation and offered, for him, genuine insights into the workings of the revolutionary process. Often known as the 'theologian of the revolution', Bloch was himself a marxist, but of a most particular and idiosyncratic kind, working within a strongly Judaeo-Christian framework, blending elements of the messianic and transcendental in his philosophy of utopianism. In two great works, *Vom Geist der Utopia* (1918) and *Das Prinzip Hoffnung* (1954-59), he explained the nature of hope, its function in human affairs, and the importance of music as an expressive and non-conceptual correlative in which modern man might measure the nature of his aspirations.[7]

In many ways Bloch became the seminal figure in the creation of *Behold the Sun*. Working with this new perspective, Goehr came to see the previously embarrassing religious element as not only reconcilable with any political theme of social change, but as the theme itself. Rather than a classic socialist paradigm of class struggle and revolution, the horrific events at Münster represent every tragedy occurring when balance is lost and men exercise theory in the expectation of a better world; and even if it seems inevitable that such expectations will be corrupted, whether by individuals or institutions, the desire for a better world remains. Utopianism is less a factor in any teleological movement towards perfection than a psychological or spiritual truth about the human condition. To quote the opera's epigraph taken from St Paul: '... hope that is seen is not hope: for what a man seeth, why doth he yet hope for?'

With the significance of the religious element now clear in his own mind, the composer took the Intendant's criticisms to the playwright John McGrath, whose expertise ranged from left-wing theatre to devising the television series *Z Cars*. Together, by inventing an almost domestic circle of characters, the Berninck family, upon whom the historical events bear directly, they were able to meet the request of Dr Barfuss for a more life-like feeling within the dramatic framework. At the same time, these individuals acquire new force from the various aspects of the revolution than they represent. McGrath developed the conflict between older and younger prophets, Matthys and Bokelson, so that they clearly represent the deterioration from idealism to terror that revolutions have often manifested. And the wife they shared in real life, Divara, who married Bokelson after Matthys's death to become 'Queen of Münster', was chosen to represent the pure spirit of millenarianism. She observes the degeneration of the revolution into chaos under the leadership of her husbands; she suffers with the people and feels their pain as every murder becomes another denial of their utopian dream. Yet in the final pages of the opera, against a background of suffering and persecution as the city is ransacked, she delivers a new message of hope for the future. And the turba, united in their misery, witness a vision of Christ which means they must forever rise again.

Even in a decade prodigious of operatic premières, the debut of *Behold the Sun* in 1985 should have unveiled a work remarkable in conception and unexpectedly significant in content. At the time Goehr began his opera, the millenarian ideal might have seemed oblique to the realities of late 20th century secularism. But as the composer worked on his material, he saw the message of his work unexpectedly and violently mirrored in the world of events. Under the aegis of

a general ideology of extremism, Baader Meinhof
introduced the spectre of revolutionary terror to post-war
Europe; in America, the mass suicides at Jonestown showed
faith triumphant over reason in a most sinister way; above
all, since January 1979, a virtual theocracy came to exist in
Iran, instigated and guided in the name of Islam by a
modern-day prophet – the Ayatollah Khomeini. As vital to
man as the drawing of breath, the utopian spirit – innocent
or crazed, frequently turbulent – had once again become
contemporary in a striking and unpredictable way. But this
was not the case at Düsseldorf, where Bloch's Principle of
Hope became submerged beneath a mass of musical
alteration and scenic inconsistency.

It is necessary to observe the abridgements and
transpositions as a whole in order to understand fully the
musical and dramatic transformations that occurred in the
production. To find the key, consider the treatment of the
coloratura aria sung by the boy Christian – 'Behold the Sun'.
Taking its text from the same Winstanley source that
inspired the opera's title, this extensive, 13-minute refrain
structure was intended both as expression of the pure spirit
of millenarian revelation and as the keystone in the larger
form of Act 1 – the 'elaboration of a single moment' which
precipitates the actual outbreak of revolution. In the course
of a threefold cycle of sermons and choruses, Matthys and
Bokelson work the temper of the people to a fever pitch of
apocalyptic excitement. They respond with the proclamation
of pertinent lines of scripture: 'Great Babylon is fall'n and is
become the habitation of devils and the hold of every foul
spirit' (set as an extended triple fugue); 'For his Elect doth
God set up his kingdom and doth send a David for his
children'; 'Let the meek and gentle inherit the earth and its
riches'. Suddenly, experiencing in a flash of sunlight caught
in a weathervane a vision of God in his glory, Christian
exhorts them to confess their sins, renounce further
wrongdoing, and share in his ecstasy. Here at last is the
revelation of Divine purpose at work in the world. The
people respond with wonder and hysteria. At the conclusion
of the aria their expectation spills over into open
insurrection and the revolution has begun.

A virtuoso show-stopper in its own right, the aria has also stood alone as a separate concert piece. Within the complete opera it is pre-eminently an example of Goehr's novel dramaturgie. Although the action ceases while Christian sings, this section is nevertheless one of powerful agitation. A precise and detailed sequence of stage directions registers the quickening spirit of the Anabaptists – and provides first-hand evidence of the care with which the problems of a choral opera had been thought through by composer and librettist.

Two discrete yet related parts constitute this aria: Christian's vision of heaven, and his call for the Elect to embrace their destiny, expressed through powerful olfactory images – the sulphurous stench of tormented and burning flesh, and the perfume of celestial fire. In a sequence of carefully choreographed movements the chorus are directed to embrace; tear off their garments; imagine themselves whipped by an imaginary flail; and as the ultimate expression of their sexual and religious fervour – form themselves into a mighty cross and attempt to fly.

All this Herlishka's production ignored. Transferred to the third act, the aria was shortened by five minutes through the removal of that musical element identified with the revolution. At the symposium Dr Kügler's explanation was that in its original position it was too long, and that the transposition heightened its effect. But when scrutinised in the context of the production as a whole, the producer's terms for the definition of dramatic effectiveness may once again be called into question.

Put bluntly, the subversive content of the aria was no longer required. By removing 25 minutes of music from Act 1 (and this mostly from the ecstatic Biblical choruses), Herlishka had neutralised the theme of religious utopianism altogether. 'The lamb of God without blemish or spot ... the cherubims and a flaming sword ... the way of the Tree of Life', as witnessed in Christian's vision, were irrelevant to a mob supposedly inspired not by dreams of a better world, but by brutal feelings of hostility and revenge. Thus the removal of the aria was symptomatic of the wider ideological restructuring of the opera. And no less so was its new position in Act 3.

As conceived by the composer, it is in this act that the Anabaptists' apocalyptic fantasies, inspired by the Bible and preached by the prophets, are literally made flesh. Three times the trumpet sounds. The people adorn themselves in fine clothes, preparing to go forth to vanquish the enemies of the Lord and ride in glory to the Holy City. (In reality, they themselves will be vanquished, theirs is the city to be destroyed.) The atmosphere is one of uncontrollable hysteria; the climax of the opera is the turba's eleven-fold cry: 'Behold we go up to Jerusalem, and all things that are written shall be accomplished'. Musically, the tension is contained within a grand and elaborate refrain form, each return of the text a more elaborate contrapuntal variation on the chaconne bass. Yet in the performance, the turba's cry was heard once only. Absent was the bedrock of millenarian faith (and the sophisticated structural arch) embodied in the original extended choral framework. Instead, the entire drama was constructed as a tapestry of discontinuous vignettes – the starving population, the lamenting women, the play within a play – deprived both of outer sequential meaning and inner utopian fire.

Within this patchwork scheme, Christian's aria was presented as a supernatural episode. The boy has died of starvation within the encircled city. Over his corpse the mother, Mrs Berninck, and Divara sing an eloquent Purcellian lament in chaconne form. As they conclude their duet the ghostly figure of the son reappears behind and above them to sing what remains of his coloratura. The visionary figure becomes a spook, a condition reflected in the music, now reduced to a marginal existence by the omission of that very element which in the original gave it power. Curtailed and emasculated, the aria took its place not as the peripeteia but as meretricious ornament. And as with Divara's aria with decorated reprise, 'Comfort ye my people', and Bokelson's heroic celebration of kingship, 'This is the will of the Father', in Act 3 Scene 1, the consequence was clear: to divorce the explicit millenarianism of the texts from any wider resonance within the restructured message of the work as a whole.

If the musical alterations clearly revealed the producer's

intentions, scenically nothing gave more away than his introduction, quite against the composer's intention, of a pantomime. It was there to compensate for an overall dramatic lassitude. The direction of what little choral music remained from the original score was criticised both in the press and at the symposium as confused and undramatic. Restrained within a box-like set depicting the interior of the city, the actions of the chorus were rigid and unspecific, their identity scarcely established. Dr Kügler claimed that to sing properly the performers should remain motionless; in fact, they neither moved together (as did the chorus at the première of *Oedipus Rex*), nor acted individually, nor moved downstage in the traditional manner by which a choral group is asserted. With the factor of mass excitement eliminated, dramatic energy required a new focus: such was the function of the gratuitous if colourful troupe. Yet they were a contradiction both as a technical solution to a basic problem, and as an artistic function: the latter, the symposium heard, was to ensure the presence of Herlishka's special quality of non-partisan parable from beginning to end.

How was this accomplished? The mummers were introduced with the Anabaptists and accompanied them throughout the opera; they provided the people with their fine clothes and utensils, they assisted at their worship, and symbolically wrote down the sermons of the two prophets. Yet in their manner of doing these things it was difficult to perceive the quality of objectivity. On arriving at Münster in Act 1 Scene 2, the Anabaptists were immediately identified with the hippy movement of the 60s on account of their outlandish motley (in itself, scarcely an impartial interpretation of their doctrine and aspirations). They were preceded by the mime troupe, mysteriously garbed in white, scourging the ground with whips in the manner of flagellants. When the people prayed the mummers knelt with their backs to the audience, revealing emblazoned on their costumes the symbol of the death's head. Overall, as one anonymous member of the symposium audience objected, their presence in the production served to obscure the profound spiritual impact of the Anabaptists on the inhabitants of Münster, to diminish their collective energy, and in Act 3, in the episode of the play of Dives and Lazarus, to invite ridicule.

In the context of the composer's own account of the opera, and of what is contained in the score itself, these symbols of mortality and decay were contradictions of the original utopian content – Bloch's Principle of Hope. Yet their decadent ambience (more appropriate to Edgar Allan Poe than to a religious drama) was in accord with the producer's desire to stage a conventional, expressionistic costume drama in which the theme of millenarian expectation was rendered not only dramatically otiose but politically undesirable. Those who are inspired by the ideals of revolution, whatever their provenance, are identified as the destroyers of society; the prophets are all false prophets and the evolution of the terror becomes clear.

There is, in many works of art, a point when it can be felt that the creative mask has been dropped, and the unadorned voice of the artist can be heard. In *Behold the Sun* such a moment occurs in the final scene. The city has been overwhelmed, the people brutalised. With his retinue of soldiers and priests the Prince-Bishop stands in judgement. The crowd watch as Bokelson, Divara and Mrs Berninck are dragged in, chained and bearing the marks of harsh treatment. But when Divara sings she breaks free from her captors and comes forward to the front of the stage to address the audience in words which are part biblical, part the composer's own.

> If we have eaten darnel, or were blinded, would the sun lose its heat and die? Would the moon dim its beam or the powers in heaven cease? We reaped a poison harvest we did not sow. The well was tainted, the bread was foul. Our degradation is of your world ... But now we hear again the word we love, the voice in the night that brings us comfort, gives us hope ... And then again we go up to Jerusalem, to behold the sun. We eat your luscious poisoned fruit, hope becomes a Death's head. It begins again.

The message, clear from the text, is reinforced in the music by the return of the opera's opening phrase in the concluding bars. However regrettable the suffering and violence of revolution, however wasteful in human terms the result, the hope for something better – Bloch's spirit of Utopia – remains as constant and natural to humanity as breathing or the desire to make music. In the excesses of freedom rationality was abandoned and the realities of life ignored. The wells of hope became poisoned by the same loss of balance and respect for daily order as befell the Bacchae of Euripides in their Bacchanalian orgies. Yet if balance was lost, belief remains. And in Goehr's final scene, the source of that belief – 'the word we love' which is the word of God made literal flesh in the lives of the Anabaptists – is heard again. Regrouping behind Divara, the chorus discover their former ecstasy. Song returns. Over and above her vision is heard a singing of renewed expectation:

> And they shall see the Son of Man coming in the clouds, coming with great power and glory. And then shall He send his angels and shall gather the elect from the four winds, from the uttermost part of the earth to the uttermost part of heaven. And pray ye that your flight be not in winter.

This, if anything, is the composer's fundamental message. No surprise, therefore, to discover that while the music remained intact, in the Düsseldorf production the original ending was altered almost beyond recognition. The set was dominated by three enormous crosses bearing the bodies of the Anabaptist leaders in a simulacrum of the crucifixion. The effect, according to Dr Kügler, was to create an 'open' ending which, it was believed, was Goehr's intention. The practical result of the changes, however, was to promote not the producer's much-vaunted objectivity, but a final and most disturbing instance of the misunderstanding and manipulation of the opera's subject.

Thematically, the function of such forthright Christian symbolism was to act as a diversion. The opera is neither a sermon of the left nor of the right, nor a drama about the conflict of church and state as epitomised in Shaw's *Saint Joan*. Rather, it is a universal parable, a *Lehrstück*, about social theory corrupted by human practice yet sustained by belief, and about religious fundamentalism as experienced by ordinary people, and the pain and terror of the Bible literally read. The action is set within the city of Münster because it is only in isolation from the daily round that the application of such a theory might accurately be observed. Apart from a few minutes at the beginning of the second act, the chorus sings virtually from beginning to end. Before the opera's final scene there is scarcely a reference to established religion. Goehr's interest lies not in the conflict of contemporary secular powers, but in the apocalyptic religious faith of the Anabaptists.

Yet not so for Herlishka. By means of this set-piece crucifixion he shifted the focus of interest from the besieged community to events outside the city walls. Inevitably, the key text became obscured. It was impossible for Divara to free herself in order to speak directly to the public. And delivered from her position of execution, her message of hope was perceived by many as a message of despair and resignation. The producer took his cue from the initial exchange between Bokelson and the Prince-Bishop in which each questions the assumed role of the other.

The Prince-Bishop himself was seen clad in armour in front of the victims before donning his robe and mitre with the assistance of those ubiquitous bearers of objectivity – the mime troupe. Was the image of the cross to be taken at face value? Or was the intention ironical – a charade of the protagonists' spiritual pretensions? And having witnessed Mrs Berninck and Divara as bearers of insight and compassion throughout the opera, in contrast to the murderous Bokelson, were the audience now to discover that in fact each bore equal culpability?

In spite of the pain and fury of the defeated Anabaptists, all distinctions here were blurred. Ideology became a cynical facade. According to Herlishka's production, in this conflict between conservatives and revolutionaries neither side was the victor – no doubt a satisfactory conclusion to an argument of his own creation, but not the argument of Goehr's opera, in which the real conflict was confined within the city walls. Although Divara's prophecy was retained, and the music associated with Mrs Berninck and the revelation of the biblical word returned to complete the cycle, the stage picture rendered the final development of

Goehr's subject incomprehensible. The conclusion appeared confused and contradictory. Forced into the context of amoral secular antagonism, the turba's vision of a new heaven became superfluous. Once again the only message to be gleaned was that revolutions must always come to a bad end, and that for good politics any form of belief is a hindrance.

Even if such an attitude reflects a general condition of post-war German politics, the precise nature of any possible interaction between national feeling and operatic production must remain a matter for speculation. (Significantly, words such as 'compromise' and 'consensus' featured prominently in Dr Kügler's defence of Deutsche Oper's position.) Ultimately, however, the important issue remains not the attitude itself, but the dubious artistic morality behind its projection onto a fully-formed work of art. And in the case of *Behold the Sun*, censorship is not too strong a word for the result.

In composing an opera not only enriched by a chorus, but animated throughout by its presence – a 'passion without a protagonist' – Goehr set any producer a tough and imaginative challenge. A BBC recording of the complete work has revealed the consistent strength and variety of the music, and suggested that a suitable staging might involve a creative synthesis between baroque and 20th century theatrical techniques.[8] In addition, Goehr has never denied the practical necessity for cuts. Yet for the first performance, in spite of the long gestation and early enthusiasm of Dr Barfuss, Goehr was never consulted about any aspect of production; the producer's dilemma was solved by a retreat into the inappropriate genre of costume drama, and into a falsification disguised as objectivity and even-handedness. Therein lies the moral for which the opera should be remembered.

For in a free and open society, it is a subtle and corrupt form of censorship that masquerades as fairness and objective truth while rejecting as extremist propaganda all that with which it cannot agree. In such cases, the victim is not only the individual, but also the cause of truth. And in our world interests of truth and the fate of the individual are inseparable; their bond ensures the sanctity of the artist's message which remains the essence of our culture. In the world of opera it is a bond that must be upheld and renewed. The composer's individual vision depends for its successful realisation on the co-operation of the many, from producer to stage-hand; yet in the spirit of the Orpheus myth, the artist must retain the right to challenge, confuse and confound. If, as at Düsseldorf, this independence should be disregarded, why bother asking the artist to create at all? In the case of Alexander Goehr, an opera with a title rich in millenarian associations was renamed and presented in a form far removed from the composer's original vision. The work suffered, the audience suffered. *Behold the Sun* now cries out for a production in which this paradox will be removed, the original music restored, and justice done to the fullness of Goehr's imagination.

Notes

[1] Behold the Sun, Op. 44, an opera in 3 acts with libretto by John McGrath and the composer, was first performed by Deutsche Oper am Rhein at Duisburg, Germany, then transferred to their Düsseldorf house for subsequent performances. Goehr's first opera, *Arden Must Die*, to a libretto by Erich Fried, was first performed by the Hamburg State Opera on 5 March 1967.

[2] Although the unrepresentative nature of the production formed the main protest from the British press, with the exception of Reinhard Beuth in *Die Welt* (22 April 1985) and Gerhard Koch in the *Frankfurter All-Gemeine Zeitung* (24 April 1985), this aspect was scarcely mentioned by the unenthusiastic German reviewers. No doubt they relied on Deutsche Oper's publicity material for their information. A request from Goehr's publisher for the addition to the programme of the disclaimer 'The opera *Die Wiedertaufer* is performed here in a cut and altered version made without the composer's consent' was ignored.

[3] Held at the Haus der Kirche, Düsseldorf, on 10/11 May 1985. Apart from the composer, those involved in the discussions included Dr Ilka Kügler, Dramaturgin from Deutsche Oper am Rhein; Dr Leonore Siegele-Wenschkewitz, a theologian specialising in the survival of Christianity during the Third Reich; the Bach scholar Professor Dr Ulrich Siegele; Dr Martin Brecht, an ecclesiastical historian from Münster University; and Dr Dieter Wohlenberg from the Evangelische Stadtakademie. The present text is indebted to the minutes from this symposium, to which reference is made where appropriate.

[4] A Rumanian journalist who became Intendant of Deutsche Oper am Rhein in 1964, Dr Grischa Barfuss established a remarkable team of producers and musicians at Düsseldorf, which became one of the most dynamic forces in post-war German music-theatre. His initial enthusiasm for Goehr's project was entirely characteristic of a commitment to contemporary opera, in the light of which the subsequent complications are difficult to explain. Perhaps ill-health had a part to play.

[5] Norman Cohn, *The Pursuit of the Millennium* Paladin Books, 1970.

[6] See 'Working on Die Wiedertaufer: Alexander Goehr in Conversation with Bayan Northcott', *Opera*, April 1985.

[7] A selection of Bloch's major writings may be found in *Essays on the Philosophy of Music*, translated by Peter Palmer, with a valuable introduction by David Drew, Cambridge University Press, 1985.

[8] See, for example, Winton Dean's review of this broadcast in *The Musical Times*, December 1987.

Malcolm Barry

Ideology and Form: Shostakovich East and West

During his lifetime the greatest Soviet composer was already the stuff of legends – often of contradictory provenance. Thus we have the oppressed composer of Volkov's *Testimony*,[1] the embodiment of Soviet resistance at Leningrad in 1942, the tortured, nervous football fan (*passim*), the peace delegate (willing or coerced?) to the United States in 1950, and so on. Indeed it is possible to subscribe to the idea that any Russian cultural figure has to aspire to such Dostoyevskian significances to be taken seriously by the Western critical establishment, a group that, in preaching objectivity and value-free considerations, espouse a subjectivism and set of values no less pernicious for being largely implicit.

This is, of course, particularly true in the case of music, where remoteness from literary meaning enables both a concentration on the peripherals (biography at the expense of analysis) and an unverifiable ascription of 'meaning'. It is not only Deryck Cooke[2] who affects to interpret emotion and meaning by means of simple formulae: the greater subtleties of Meyer[3] and the semioticians betray an *angst* for meaning, at almost all costs. The late Boris Schwarz's book on music in Soviet Russia[4] remains, for all its faults, perhaps the best introduction to an extensive topic. But even he falls into the formalist trap – 'music, *per se*, cannot be ideologically right or wrong – it must be judged on its own, purely musical terms'[5] – a statement of ideology if ever there was one, which contrasts oddly with 'to understand Soviet music of the 1920's, one *must* analyse the forces that shape the composers – social, political and musical'. This implies that the anthropomorphic view of music '*per se*' is somehow divorced from its (or its listeners') creators.[6] At the same time one wonders why it is only Soviet music that '*must*' be analysed in this way. Schwarz, in describing other ideologies, is unaware of his own, perhaps the fatal flaw in his book.

Yet, even assuming such a mistaken idealist and 'autonomist' view of the language and literature of music, it is possible to regard the interaction of musical and political aspects in the assessment of the music of Shostakovich (and particularly that of the 1930s) in a way rather more positive than the usually accepted positions. By locating such a view in the context of explicitly committed aesthetics, there are lessons for other critical systems and, in particular, the autonomist view itself.

The tri-partite basis of the theory of socialist realism has been explored by C Vaughan James.[7] The link between *narodnost, klassvost* and *partinost* (attributes of people, class and party) provides a clear, logical progression, providing the essential tenets of Marxism and Leninism are accepted. It is in the application of the theory where problems begin. The first problem is to account for the link between theory and practice. Is socialist realism a theory of intention (ie, do committed artists prove their commitment by having these considerations at the moment of creation), is it a theory of judgement and criticism, or is it a theory of patronage, a policy guide? Of course, only a Western critic could make such a differentiation. For socialist realism in an avowedly socialist society can *only* be all three. Clearly the politicisation of the arts – the duty so to treat the arts – meant that a comprehensive approach to creation, perception and dissemination (production, exchange and distribution) was to be achieved. The second difficulty also lies in the application of theory to practice. For while it is easy to relate literature and visual arts (especially those in which figurative style was a pre-requisite in depicting the new Soviet man) to *narodnost* and *klassvost* features (and thus to *partinost* requirements), the application of a one-to-one relationship of theory to music is more problematic.

In fact so problematic was the application that, even as the theory was emerging, there was intensive debate between, on the one hand, the 'figuratives', arranged around the Association of Proletarian Musicians, and the 'modernists', whose centre was the Association for Contemporary Music. The former remained in the era of agit-prop and assumed a literal interpretation of the *narodnost* idea: a one-to-one relationship between the music *of* the people (folk music) and music *for* the people (large compositions). The modernists retained a belief, naive perhaps, in the links between progressive social organisation and 'progress' in musical language, espousing an almost value-free attitude towards that language and deserving the epithet of 'formalist'. Asafiev's treatise on intonations was an attempt at compromise but, significantly, was not written until after the lines had been defined, *in practice*, as they were during the 1930s.[8]

This last is an important point. For, despite this encompassing politico-aesthetic context, the attitudes of a composer – in this case Shostakovich – could only be demonstrated and assessed in practice by his compositions. His early work, of course, veers between the modernistic First Symphony, the programmatic Second and Third symphonies, and the more occasional other works of the period. Given the climate of the 1920s, though, it would be fair to count Shostakovich on the side of the 'contemporaries', intent on keeping up and even surpassing the purely formalistic concerns of the bourgeois West by means of an enhanced humanist consciousness. But, precisely because of the necessity of definition in practice, it is not to the heady 1920s that we should look for the exemplification of the application of socialist realism to music. That will much better be found in the 1930s and also in the immediate postwar period when questions of cultural politics were again high on the Soviet agenda. This occurred earlier for literature, theatre, cinema and the visual arts than for music. Hence the concentration, in the West, on 'key' texts for the application of socialist realist theory to music, and in particular on 'Chaos instead of Music' (1936) and the speech by Zhdanov to the Union of Soviet Composers Congress of 1948.[9]

The contradiction of Western criticism, though, is in fact exposed by this concentration on texts. For if music is value-free and autonomous of its context, then it might be reasonable to expect critics to focus on the *music* rather than on its political context and reception. It could be, for example, that *Katerina Ismailova*, the revised version, is in fact a more musically satisfying work than the original *Lady Macbeth of Mtensk*. It could be, perhaps, that in the early 1930s Shostakovich was undergoing a crisis of *musical language* and that this is expressed in the uncertainties of his work. Might it be that the Fifth Symphony – 'a Soviet artist's reply to just criticism' – is a better work than the Fourth Symphony withdrawn in rehearsal and not exposed until the 1960s? Before examining these questions further it will be useful to examine Zhdanov's 1948 speech in more detail, as an example of a politician talking theory and practice to a group of practitioners; and to trace the application of the theory of socialist realism to the position it had reached immediately after the Second World War. (This is, of course, before the astonishing sequence of works from Shostakovich which divided into the public (*Song of the Forests*) and the private (*From Jewish Folk Poetry*), and increasingly changed the definition of that differentiation (for example the Violin Concerto and the Tenth Symphony).)

In his 1948 speech Zhdanov summed up the discussions at the Conference of Soviet Music Workers, and made it quite clear what was expected of this category of Soviet citizen. He began by comparing, unfavourably, the situation in music with that in literature, cinema and the theatre: 'Some of the big journals are expressing real difficulties in using all the material in their editorial files ... worth publishing. No such "output" can be boasted of in music'. Some participants in the discussion had blamed organisational matters, others weaknesses of ideology. Whatever the reason(s), 'music has got left behind'.

The notion of progress, of development, may be located within an economically determinist view of culture. Just as the Soviet economy had to expand, within the post-war reconstruction, so music would have to develop. The difficulty is that Zhdanov's definitions – his criteria – are not of the clearest. He criticised the committee of the Union of Composers for 'abetting the formalist trend' while claiming to stand for the realist trend. In both cases he appended 'in music' to his talk of these respective trends. So there must be some underlying criteria.

Initially, as befits an *apparatchik*, he concentrated on organisation: the same old faces at the top stifling innovation. But he swiftly moved into peering into 'the crack [which has] appeared in the foundations of Soviet music'. This crack was caused, in Zhdanov's view, by the dominant position in Soviet music of 'the leading figures of the formalist trend, a trend which is fundamentally wrong'. These leading figures, including Shostakovich, Prokofiev, Kabalevsky and Khachaturyan, had established a cosy niche for themselves and their music – at this point Zhdanov was still concentrating on matters of organisation and patronage. He then moved on to his main point: this formalist trend ignores 'the classical heritage and in particular the Russian school, in the creation of a music which is realist and of truthful content and is closely and organically linked with the people and their folk music and folk song – all this combined with a high degree of professional mastery'. He contrasts this with a formalism 'alien to Soviet art ... innovation, a rejection of the idea of the popular origin of music'.

Here is the crux of Zhdanov's aesthetics as applied to music – not so much the dialectic between realism and formalism (as a marxist he should have approved of such a process) but a 'bottom-up' view of music and its origins. This was to be explored more technically and extensively by Janos Marothy.[10] The 'bottom-up' absorption of folk music by the classical composers had produced characteristics of 'truthfulness and realism', a 'blend of artistic form with profound content' and a combination of 'the highest technical achievement with simplicity and intelligibility'. What produces these desiderata is 'recognition of the fact that classical music has its sources in the musical creative powers of the people' [*narodny*]. Despite the neo-idealism of his language, there is the basis of a genuine materialist theory here. Classical music stems from the people and, furthermore, is characterised by its achieving a heightened 'intelligibility'. It is the *perception* which counts, rather than the intention. Citing great figures of the 19th century, Zhdanov noted the gulf between folk music and contemporary instrumental and symphonic music. The development of music, he averred, must derive from an interplay of academic and folk music.

Zhdanov then went on to discuss 'national' (by which he meant Russian) music and its relationship with foreign traditions. He dismissed 'contemporary bourgeois music' (presumably represented by Schoenberg and Stravinsky) as being in a state of decay and degradation, and argued that *true* internationalism would only be possible on the basis of a true understanding of national musical culture. He then cited programme music as being a characteristic of Russian classical music: the contemporary neglect of this was a matter for sharp rebuke. He poured scorn on experimentalism, whether in music or in education, believing that true innovation depended on surpassing the classics, but not by 'breaking away from laws and standards of music'. Although he was not completely clear as to what these latter might be, he offered some clues – works which 'approached classical music with regard to content, form, polish and beauty of melody'. Such purple prose is deeply unfashionable in sophisticated Western circles (although I venture to suggest that many self-styled 'music-lovers' would both know what he meant and agree, more or less, amongst themselves as to what constituted these qualities).

At the same time Zhdanov declared himself against 'crude naturalism' and, calling for support from Serov, asserted that the sound of cymbals and drums should be the exception and not the rule, going on to describe some contemporary compositions as sounding like 'a dentist's drill'. While some of this can easily be dismissed as politician's hyperbole, Zhdanov has a serious point to make when he goes on to assert that such music goes 'beyond the limits of the rational

... beyond normal human emotions ... normal human intellect'. This is a striking anticipation, not only of Stockhausen's attempt at super-rationalism in the early 1950s (see the early issues of the journal *Die Reihe*) but also of Meyer's application of information theory to 'the techtonics of serialism'.[11] Zhdanov equates musical experimentalism with theories of the more advanced states of pathological behaviour, and unequivocally equates 'musical work of genius' with the strength and breadth of its appreciation – 'the greater a work of music, the more responsive the chords it strikes in the human spirit', and 'the people do not need [sic] music which they cannot understand'. For Zhdanov, therefore, people do *need* music.

The final part of his speech dealt with professional skill and the tasks for Soviet music. In the nearest he came to purely technical criteria, he castigated music which was 'crude, ugly and vulgar, based on atonality and continuous dissonance' and 'false notes and combinations of false notes'. 'Melodiousness', he complained, 'is beginning to disappear' with 'a passionate emphasis on rhythm'. He called for balance between the various elements of music and for instruments and writing for the voice to return to 'normal' functions and standards. This is not simply conservatism, for Zhdanov's concerns stem from the view that 'departures from the standards of the art of music represent not only a violation of the fundamentals of musical sound' (he presumably equated the harmonic series and tonality with such fundamentals) 'but also an assault upon the basic physiology of normal human hearing'. In other words the perceiver had a vital role in music, and the characteristics, the *human* characteristics, of the perceiver needed to be borne in mind. The tasks for Soviet music were to reassert the classical heritage, to abandon the formalist trend and to turn towards the people for stimulus. Composers should keep track of what was going on in the West but 'prevent the penetration of bourgeois influences into Soviet Music'.

This speech, often cited, seldom considered, is remarkable in many ways. It could, with minor amendment, be taken as a middle-brow reaction to contemporary music that could be voiced almost anywhere in the world. But this very transferability might lead us to a more considered reflection: does such language make Zhdanov incorrect in his aesthetics? For his views, apart from stemming from his politics, also have an intellectual basis which is, at least in part, independent from that politics. He is a rationalist and a materialist, for whom music exists in the perceiver as much as in the creator. He recognises that music does not – cannot – exist independently of the circumstances surrounding its creation, performance and perception: it is a human endeavour. He has a view of the dissemination of musical formulae not unlike that of Asafiev, firmly locating music within language-related notions of communication. For Zhdanov, music is made for people.

This attitude contrasts strikingly with the neo-idealism prevalent in musical circles in Western Europe for most of the 20th century: Schoenberg, guided by 'the Supreme Commander', organising the Society for Private Musical Performances, inventing an apparently rationalist language in the interests of heightened (pathological?) expression, and saddling his music with a contradiction between the new language and the hyper-traditional articulation; the post 1945 avant-garde, firmly believing themselves on the side of progress and science, and espousing a neurotic hyper-rationalism that ended with one talented figure just this side of megalomania and another moving between a glittering attempt at didacticism in concert life and a glittering static sterility in his compositions.

Today's Western composers, insofar as they have rediscovered 'the listener' or even 'the community', have repudiated the anti-humanism of earlier in the century but remain confused, since all their training tells them there *must* be a Philosopher's Stone (a new musical language) – somewhere. And, following along in the rain, somewhat like a sweeper after the horse-drawn parade, come the critics, with 'value-free' judgements in which the weight of ideology bears so heavily that it obscures anything useful that might be said. This is not to assert that Zhdanov was infallible in his judgements and in his criteria, but his views, hyperbolic as they might be in the expression, do represent an alternative to this dismal catalogue of intellectual vacuity.

While Zhdanov can be quoted to illustrate the Soviet view of 20th century music *in theory*, there was, of course, *practical* application of his ideas, and related ones, during both the 1930s and 40s. As far as the 1940s are concerned it is a truism to say that Shostakovich was once more stunned into creative silence by the ferocity of the attack; and in subsequent years his output split into two, as was mentioned above. (There is danger of over-simplification in this, though: *From Jewish Folk Poetry* would have satisfied all of Zhdanov's *explicit* criteria and it was other factors in the political situation that rendered this cycle dangerous at the time. Further, the other 'private' works of 1948-1953 all demonstrate, albeit most often obliquely, a concern with the issues to which Zhdanov referred.)

But Zhdanov's underlying assumptions are not so specific in 1948 that they cannot be traced back to the 30s, and the origins of socialist realism and its practical applications. The usual example cited is, of course, 'Chaos instead of Music', the *Pravda* leading article that ensured the disappearance of *Lady Macbeth of Mtensk* from the Russian stage. Shostakovich shows, in his letters (or those of them that survive),[12] how shocked and appalled he was by this criticism, as vitriolic as it was pointed. Western commentators on the affair, however, in their haste to condemn the Soviet Government's interventions in 'free art' ignore two points.

First, in the Soviet Union, given the views taken of culture, the government has a *duty* to intervene in such matters. It is not a matter of arbitrariness or personal whim – the Party, being responsible for all activities, has no choice. Just as in 'a free-market economy' a government has a duty *not* to interfere, so, in a planned economy, the opposite is the case. We may hold differing views as to the righteousness (or even the wickedness) of this, but it is, nonetheless, a question of interpretation. The second point is that, even before 'Chaos instead of Music', there was considerable controversy over *Lady Macbeth* from outside the Soviet Union as well as within. To vilify *Pravda* for the criticism that 'on the merchant's double bed, all problems are solved' and for its continued reference to vulgarity, and at the same time to ignore the scorn poured on the work, for the same reason, by critics of the *New York Times* and the *New York Sun* is myopia. To describe the music as 'flimsily put together ... shallow tricks ... no originality or creative quality ... puerile, lurid, overdrawn naive' is criticism indeed. In fact this was the description by Olin Downes of the *New York Times* (quoted by Schwarz), not *Pravda*.

The 1936 article in *Pravda* in fact is remarkably similar to Zhdanov's speech of 1948 in its attack on petty bourgeois (as opposed to 'real') innovation. The basic criticism seemed to be, however, the programmatic quality of the music 'in order to express the amatory scenes as naturalistically as possible'. Perhaps the author of the *Pravda* article had a concern for human dignity (as perhaps did Downes): perhaps not. But, whatever the case, 'Chaos instead of Music' was not a simple piece of individual tyranny. Indeed the composer revised the work in 1963. It will be interesting to see whether, after *glasnost*, the original version is performed in the Soviet Union. And there could be more than one view of the respective merits of the original and of the revision. If, for example, a substantial body of expert opinion declared that the revision was a finer work (based on whatever criteria), might there not have to be a revision of the critical commonplace about the reprehensibility of 'Chaos instead of Music'? Could it be that the intervention, brutal and traumatic as it was, might have been *helpful* to the *composer*, even within the context of a 'value-free' approach to the music *as such*?

Just as the musical mode of expression is remote from the verbal (which has caused some masters of the dialectic such as Adorno to proclaim its utility as an instrument of social analysis), so such questions are likely to remain, for the most part, rhetorical. However, it might be profitable to investigate whether the 1936 intervention could have helped Shostakovich in developing the form most remote from programmatic significance, the symphony.

As with much Soviet history, myths abound. Just as Prokofiev did not sit with his back to Zhdanov during the latter's speech in 1948 (he was not present), so Shostakovich did not withdraw the Fourth Symphony in direct response to

'Chaos instead of Music'. Indeed, the symphony was not begun until 1935, when, according to Schwarz, conditions were already becoming difficult. Shostakovich had said in 1931 'there can be no music without ideology ... even the symphonic form, which appears more than any divorced from literary elements, can be said to have a bearing on politics'.[13] It is inconceivable therefore that he would not have been aware of the difficulties of the situation at the time of composing. Furthermore the symphony was completed some four months after the publication of 'Chaos instead of Music': it was withdrawn only after it had been in rehearsal and just before the première because, apparently, Shostakovich was dissatisfied with the finale. (A version appeared in two-piano score in 1946, but the entire piece, revised, was not performed until 1961.) Having started the work, of course, Shostakovich would have wished to complete it, even amidst the furore of 1936. But if outright tyranny was the order of the day, there seems no explanation for its going into rehearsal. And indeed there was no adverse press prior to the withdrawal. A naive political explanation for its withdrawal is thus unacceptable. There must be some occasions on which Shostakovich must be given the benefit of the doubt as to his honesty and musical integrity. Just as a comparison of the original and revised versions of the opera might reveal something other than cold-war prejudice, so might an examination of the differences between the fourth and fifth symphonies. The withdrawal of the fourth symphony might well have been caused by the long-term effects of the 1936 scandal but, equally, there might have been musical reasons.

There have, of course, been previous suggestions of this, notably by Tim Souster in 1966.[14] Souster takes as his starting point the macro-structural aspects of both the fourth and the fifth symphonies; he compares them, and finds the latter considerably more satisfying. That an avant-garde composer should so consider a symphony which was 'a Soviet artist's reply to just criticism' may seem surprising: what is less surprising, given the period in which Souster was writing, is that he concentrates on the *raison d'être* of music for such composers at that time – the form. Thus for Souster the fourth symphony, 'bursting with ideas', harbours a clash between experimentalism (referring back, of course, to Shostakovich's second and third symphonies) and structure, and the coda of the fourth symphony does not assist the finale. In a similar vein, Souster is somewhat surprised to find an 'even more idiosyncratic form' in the first movement of the fifth Symphony, but he judges it one in which the composer achieves, despite everything, a balance. The finale of the fifth, with its powerful coda, is pronounced superior.

Certainly posterity seems to agree with Souster: the fifth symphony is a popular symphony, perhaps the most popular 20th century work in this genre, both in terms of live performance and recording. The fourth remains something of a curiosity. But as well as Souster's structural concerns – and his criticism is as revealing of his *Zeitgeist* as it is of the object under criticism – there may well be other reasons for this. The fourth symphony, indeed, 'bursts with ideas' – melodic, rhythmic, textural and timbral; as Souster asserts, the ideas themselves strain at the structure of the work (and, in my judgement, break it). Apart from the second movement, while the piece may not be a simple medley of ideas, it sounds dangerously like one, largely because of the wayward and multi-directional character of the ideas themselves. For, in this piece, above all others, Shostakovich allows his imagination full rein – to run away with itself.

The fifth symphony, on the other hand, *sounds* like a symphony, largely because of the tightness of control imposed upon the ideas and the space in which they develop and come to a close, or half-close. It would need some lengthy analysis to demonstrate this tightness of motivic structure, but I think it can be perceived by most listeners. The fourth symphony composes itself, to use a metaphor: in the fifth Shostakovich is much more firmly in control. This may be seen in itself as a metaphor for the relationship between the state and the composer. At the same time, however, it is worthwhile recalling the criteria Zhdanov was to unveil in 1948 and to apply these to a comparison of the two works.

Firstly, the centrality of the perceiver must favour, on all the evidence, the superiority of the latter. I have already

referred to the popularity of the fifth symphony as opposed
to the fourth. To this must be added the greater coherence
and integrity of the fifth, as outlined by Souster. This, I
believe, derives ultimately not from the structural aspects
but from the coherence of the ideas themselves. Secondly,
although Souster finds the form of the first movement of the
fifth idiosyncratic, there can be no doubt that Shostakovich,
in this symphony, is paying careful attention to 'the classical
heritage'. Mahler is at least as present in the fifth symphony
as in the fourth (the finale especially), but Beethoven and
Tchaikovsky are also peering over his shoulder. The folk
influences are about equally balanced between the two
works but as 'a blend of artistic form with profound content'
the fifth must be preferred, as most listeners would surely
agree. Indeed, if the classical heritage is essentially 'bottom
up', the fifth, being a more classically satisfying piece, must
satisfy the folk-derived criterion to a greater extent.
Shostakovich's 'passionate emphasis on rhythm' occurs in
both works but is considerably more balanced by
organisation of other elements in the Fifth.

The 'Soviet artist's reply to just criticism' may be taken, as
Western commentators have done, as a response to political
considerations. But, as already argued, the chronology
suggests another factor at least as important. While the
self-preserving mechanisms common in totalitarian societies
might have been in operation (alternatively there might have
been pressure from sympathetic colleagues), another
possibility must be considered.

By the ideological lights of Western criticism Shostakovich
must be seen as an *individual* talent, or genius. According to
such criticism the great creative figure is the composer – alone
– wrestling with musical problems and (one hopes) solving
them. Thus it is possible to suggest that all the 'just criticism'
came from outside – from 'Chaos instead of Music', from
other hostile commentaries and vicious attacks. But I would
argue that this must have been balanced by 'just criticism'
from within. The fourth symphony bears every sign of a
work of crisis, both structurally and in content. Shostakovich
must have known this and, even if he did not yet fully
perceive the cause, external pressures must have aided him

in his decision to withdraw such a work of crisis. In other words, the internal and external criticism combined to beneficial effect and helped to produce – in the fifth symphony, the early quartets and the Piano Quintet – a series of works that, in answering Zhdanov's criteria, also answer needs in the Western musical public.

None of this can be proven, of course. The 'true' picture may be that of the browbeaten and terrorised composer so necessary to Solomon Volkov's account. But an examination of the music itself seems to indicate that the balance of just criticism – internal and external – proved highly beneficial to Shostakovich's development.

There is, however, another aspect of the 1936 intervention, and indeed of Zhdanov's speech, which repays examination and prevents these from being seen as simple historical problems. For in a world in which an American university composer can write an article entitled 'Who cares if you listen?' there does seem some need to re-assert the human basis of music. Paradoxically, perhaps, socialist realism attempted to do just that. In the West there is a neo-idealistic world in which music, as an autonomous language, has a life and development of its own and thus becomes 'unloved by millions'; on the other hand, there is the commercial world, the techno-pop horrors (whether muzak or industrial pop based on transnational record companies). In this context the case for an explicit basis for criticism of music should at least be heard. I have elsewhere suggested the futility of the 'autonomous' view of the history of music and, by implication, the dishonesty of a musical elite which proceeds according to implicit and undiscussed notions of value: the rhetoric of 'standards', 'quality' and the rest, signally undefined within a hieratic cosiness.

Against this, brutal as some of its applications may have been, stands the honesty and the *explicit* nature of socialist realism as a philosophy of art. If the basis of Western criticism – individualistic and ultimately class-based – is superior to such honesty, then it should be able to demonstrate this; and it should do so on a basis of discussion of values, rather than on assumed superiority or alleged freedom from value-judgments.

Notes

1 S Volkov, *Testimony*, Hamish Hamilton, 1979.

2 D Cooke, *The Language of Music*, Oxford University Press, 1959.

3 L B Meyer, *Music, The Arts and Ideas*, Chicago University Press 1965.

4 B Schwarz, *Music and Musical Life in Soviet Russia, 1917-1970,* Barrie and Jenkins 1972.

5 *Ibid*, p 75.

6 *Ibid*, p 61.

7 C Vaughan James, *Soviet Socialist Realism: Origins and theory*, Macmillan 1973.

8 For a discussion of this theory see J R Tull, *B V Asafiev's Musical Form as a Process, Translation and Commentary*, PhD thesis, Ohio State University, 1977.

9 The source of this account of Zhdanov's speech was *Speeches by A A Zhdanov to Cultural Workers* (in English translation), published in Moscow in the 1950s. I am grateful to the late Cornelius Cardew for making this book available to me.

10 J Marothy, *Music and the Bourgeois, Music and the Proletarian*, Budapest 1974.

11 L B Meyer, *op cit.*

12 D Shostakovich, *Erfahrungen*, K Mayer (ed), Leipzig 1983.

13 Interview in the *New York Times*, 20 December 1931, quoted in Schwarz, *op cit.*

14 T Souster, 'Shostakovich at the Crossroads', *Tempo*, no 78, 1966, p 2.

Alastair Williams

Music as Immanent Critique: Stasis and Development in the Music of Ligeti

Any discourse concerning itself with the relationship between music and politics is likely to be fraught: it must tread a thin path between the mistake of simply mapping a political interpretation onto musical experience, and the corresponding error of regarding music as an autonomous domain separate from other spheres of life. It is a challenge to think about music in an incisive manner, with a political edge that does not evaporate into concentric spirals of hopeless dissatisfaction, or dwell on some relatively minor symptom. There is no doubt that the tradition of Western art music is tainted by purist values which exclude the underprivileged, but to dismiss it on these grounds would be to write off one of the richest veins in Western culture. If the social, with its inbuilt political ideologies, is regarded as the context and raw material of music, a totality through which music is thought, then it becomes easier, or at least more necessary, to mediate conflicting processes. It is Theodor Adorno's great achievement to have revealed the affinity between philosophical and musical thought, and hence, by distilling musical processes through the mesh of social functions, to have realised music's ability to undermine closed thought-patterns which are the medium of political repression.

The first section of this chapter will attempt to outline the major tenets of Adorno's music criticism with a view to reaching a model of the contemporary interaction between music and politics, from which to consider the potential in the music of György Ligeti for a decentring of pervasive ideology. The deconstructive thought of Jacques Derrida is used as a means of expanding Adorno's frame of reference, and as a particularly fluid methodology or praxis, which is germane to Ligeti's musical concerns. Similarly, ideas drawn from other thinkers are treated not as complete bodies of thought, but rather as starting-points for critical reflection, which have assumed a certain independence from their original context. Political and indeed musical discussion can easily get bogged down in its own terminology: it is hoped that the present approach in which music, politics, philosophy, and semiotics are played off against one another will result in a situation where stagnant areas of each discipline receive a reviving jolt.

In accordance with Adorno's appropriation of the Hegelian dialectic of identity and non-identity, any system contains a conceptual breach (the conceptual itself can only be construed in terms of the non-conceptual), a rupture which allows for critique of that system in terms of itself. Furthermore, because no system of thought is identical with itself, its immanent critique will reflect other systems of thought and behaviour. Such an interpenetration of domains is highly characteristic of Adorno's thought, and his writings, over half of which are devoted to musical issues, display no clear dividing-line between the musical-aesthetic and the philosophical. For Adorno, the fate of Western art-music and philosophy (though both tend to be German oriented) are inextricably bound up with each other; philosophy articulates conceptually that which music articulates non-conceptually. The potential for both musical and philosophical ontologies to tear themselves apart from within (which Adorno recognised in both media) becomes apparent in their mutual interaction.

This deconstructionist tendency in creative thought is a powerful force in the last two main works of Adorno's career, *Negative Dialectics*[1] and *Aesthetic Theory*.[2] These represent, respectively, a culmination of the philosophical and artistic impulses in his output. The oscillation between identity and non-identity thinking is a constant theme of *Negative Dialectics*, in keeping with a continual examination of the contradictory nature of truth, which functions as a central tenet throughout Adorno's work: 'our best thoughts are, every time, those which we are not fully able to think.'[3] The basic contradiction emerges out of the fact that:

> The name of dialectics says no more, to begin with, than that objects do not go into their concepts without leaving a remainder, that they come to contradict the traditional norm of adequacy.[4]

This remainder leads Adorno to attack ontological thought in general, in particular through the quarrel with Martin Heidegger. For Adorno the 'ontological need' is a need to deny the rationality of history and invoke the irrational model of prehistorical authority, in which the sufferings of contemporary society cannot be objectively negated, but are rather accepted in the name of 'freedom' – as the way things are. Thus the autonomy of the individual becomes submerged under the generality of Being.

> The dialectics of Being and entity – that no Being can be conceived without an entity and no entity without mediation – is suppressed by Heidegger.[5]

That Being can only be perceived in terms of its difference from entity, but that in order to maintain its primal status it must somehow include the notion of entity within itself, is regarded by Adorno as the central paradox in Heidegger's ontology. Heidegger tries to surmount this problem by ontologising the paradox itself, by 'ontologizing the ontical.'[6] The paradox is inverted so that the being of an entity, whose unity should be guaranteed by that of Being, becomes a critique of itself; the internal becomes the external and vice-versa, a contradiction which cannot be resolved without resorting to a higher level, or transcendental signified, by which to contain it.

Derrida and the Ontology of Presence

The sleight of hand[7] concealed in the metaphysics of Being and presence, which Adorno exposes in Heidegger's imposition of a transcendental signified, has also become the overriding concern of Jacques Derrida's deconstructive practice. Derrida regards the problem of ontology in Heidegger as the manifestation of a suppression symptomatic of the whole of Western metaphysics; hence his texts are shot through with Heideggerian references to Being and presence. Thus, to use a source common to Adorno as well, Derrida tends to invoke Heidegger in his reading of Nietzsche, which takes the form not so much of a dispute with Heidegger, but rather an attempt to reveal the heterogenous qualities in Nietzsche, which erupt if Heidegger's premises for discovering a unity are driven to their limits.[8] Derrida's intellectual position is couched in terms of the tradition of semiotics and structuralism, and thus offers another angle on Adorno's critique of ontology. One of his main objections to ontology is derived from Saussure's observation that signs function in a differential system where a sign is defined by the fact that it differs from other signs, and not by its own particular identity or presence. Thus language exists in a continual state of substitution, for which there is no grounding basis.[9] Derrida's insight is that this structure of difference can be extended to include the difference between the signifier and the signified, which require the presence of simultaneity that Derrida considers to have been imposed by the Western emphasis on the 'naturalness' of speech over the supposed artificiality of writing.

Derrida's broad understanding of writing emerges from a detailed examination of the work of Jean-Jacques Rousseau, particularly the *Essay on the Origin of Languages*.[10] Rousseau contends that articulation is the defining feature of language in its pure state, in which it functions as a means of articulating expression. This is problematic; the fact that language needs articulation at all implies a lack in its purity which has to be filled. Articulation is not a manifestation of affect, but an expression of it, constituting a structure of deferral which in turn is a function of writing, and thus antithetical to language as natural, unmediated expression.

> Writing naturalizes cultures. It is that precultural force which is at work as articulation within culture, working to efface a difference which it has opened.[11]

The supplementary role of writing can, however, become so advanced that it assumes its own self-presence, as is sometimes the case with notational systems, thereby rearticulating the lack which it is trying to fill at the origin.

In Derrida's text, the notion of writing or *arche-writing* is largely in keeping with his usage of the terms *trace* and *differance*, amongst others, which are intended to convey the unthinkable lack of an origin at the origin, or non-simultaneity of the signifier and signified, an intrinsic part of the process of signification. *Differance* is a variant spelling of *différence*, which is intended to draw attention to the instability of the sign and to indicate the dual function of both differing and deferring. Though Derrida's critique is directed at language as the defining medium of our thought, its emphasis is on structures of repetition which are fundamental to the conception of language. The ultimate significance of Derrida's work is that an arche-writing or trace operates in all thought processes: therefore the spacing of writing already operates in the immediacy of music, even of non-literate music. The apparent spontaneity of improvisation already contains the articulatory features which will be the separate marks of notation.

> This interval is what might be called *spacing*, the becoming space of time, or the becoming time of space (temporization).[12]

The space between the marks in a temporal medium already displays the supplementary qualities of space and time, a substitutive relationship which music is particularly well equipped to explore.

Art as Mediation

It is in its power to articulate the limits of metaphysical

closure that Adorno locates the critical force of art. The following discussion is based on his posthumously published *Aesthetic Theory*, which is a theoretical exposition and development of the principles underlying Adorno's profuse and voluminous music criticism. Although the *Aesthetic Theory* deals with art in general, and the author expressed a wish to dedicate it to Samuel Beckett, the impulse and terminology is manifestly musical. Derrida's argument concerning the way in which interior and exterior structures determine each other is central to Adorno's theory of art, where it is generated from within the dialectic tradition, and from his acute perception of the problems facing contemporary music. Adorno's thought is presented in the state of appearance: it emerges out of the fragmented fabric of a text riddled with pregnant juxtapositions of meaning and irregularities. One is directed towards the teeming mass of conflicting components in the sub-text as if the text itself had been turned inside out. In the same way that Adorno's music criticism functions less as a commentary than as an extension of the creative process, so the *Aesthetic Theory* employs the fragmented processes which comprise the inner workings of an art work, yet glimpses the absolute which art is capable of touching.

The crux of Derrida's argument is that metaphysics imposes the necessity of its own critique; this is precisely the position that Adorno takes with respect to art. Furthermore he argues that the necessity of the critique entails the conceptualisation of philosophy; therefore the immanent critique of both metaphysics and art become inextricably bound up with each other. 'Art is – or was, until recently – what metaphysics always wanted to be.'[13] If this is the case then art should be susceptible to the same sort of deconstructive tendencies in terms of itself as metaphysics; Adorno realizes this implication:

> What if metaphysics were to predict that art will die along with metaphysics which used to guarantee the existence and substantiality of art? What if the survival of art hinged on the fate of metaphysics?

Derrida's deconstruction of Rousseau's *Essay on the*

origin of languages is part of a more ambitious project to demonstrate that metaphysical thought is inherently bound up with the notion of presence. It is significant that the critique is to a large extent directed towards Rousseau's conception of the totality of nature. The relationship of nature to art is central to Adorno's *Aesthetic Theory*, in which it is claimed that the omission of a consideration of the beautiful in nature is one of the biggest faults in aesthetics since the decline of Idealism. Art mediates between the fear of being dominated by nature and the danger of repressing it. Art both dominates nature in the form of an image, and simultaneously transcends this repression in the form of objective beauty. Only as polar opposites are art and nature mediated through one another in the subject. Because, like Idealism, art locates the reconciliation with nature in the subject, Adorno posits art as the model for philosophy and not vice-versa.

> Art imitates neither nature nor individual natural beauty. What it does imitate is natural beauty as such. This puts the finger on the paradox of aesthetics as a whole, which is intimately tied up with the paradox of natural beauty. The subject matter of aesthetics, too, is defined negatively as its undefinability. That is why art needs philosophy to interpret it. Philosophy says what art cannot say, although it is art alone which is able to say it: by not saying it.[15]

Art's unique quality is to be able to touch the sensuous quality of mimesis in a rational manner. As Albrecht Wellmer[16] has put it:

> Art and philosophy thus denote the two spheres in which mind, by linking the rational with a mimetic moment, breaks through the crust of reification. To be sure, this process of intertwining occurs in both cases from opposite poles: in art, the mimetic moment assumes the form of spirit, while in philosophy, rational spirit tones itself down to take on a mimetic-reconciliatory character.

For Adorno it is the way in which art articulates its relationship with nature and society that determines its truth content and hence validity. This integrity is revealed by the immanent content of a work which functions simultaneously as a rejection and an embodiment of nature and society. By externalising itself from nature and society art embodies them as immanent content, so that in every perception of nature there is actually embodied the whole of society.

> How can works of art be like windowless monads, representing something which is other than they? There is only one way to explain this, which is to view them as being subject to dynamic or immanent historicity and a dialectical tension between nature and domination of nature, a dialectic that seems to be of the same kind as the dialectic of society.[17]

Thus it is only by rejecting society that art can realise the paradoxes contained within it – 'the unresolved antagonisms of reality appear in art in the guise of immanent problems of artistic form.'[18] Art's peculiar quality is that it is caught in the same paradox as that which Derrida draws out of Rousseau; it is animated by a desire to recover the bliss of a lost world but can only convey this desire by letting in the violence of the reality which it is trying to escape. Art then sets up the illusion of a totality and of immediate presence. It brings nature into being by the progressive move away from its shapeless form, but this natural moment returns in its amorphous state when the work is viewed closely, and substitutes the illusion of totality for the complementary illusion of immediacy: 'In order to be purposeful music requires the purposelessness which is illusion'.[19] The network of paradoxes is increased by the fact that art presents this illusion of totality in itself, a microcosm of perfection, while at the same time pointing to a Utopia beyond itself which would be its ultimate realisation, a being other than itself.[20] The truth, value and validity of art lie in this paradox.

The paradoxical character of art is further complicated by the fact that the autonomous art-work which determines its own internal organisation and points to something beyond itself is an artificial product. The artist must tread a very thin line between social awareness and the rejection of society. Adorno puts the artist in the privileged position of being allowed to participate in a material fetish which would normally be condemned as reification of the social order, since it is through this obsession with technique that the antagonistic properties of society work out their own laws in terms of immanent content. Adorno is also sympathetic to both compositional virtuosity and the demands that it often makes on the performer, which he terms a *tour de force*, as it represents the art-work's attempt to push beyond its own artificiality as a human product. The art-work strives for autonomy as it is a reflection of the need for individuality in a repressive society. This autonomy results in usurpation of the artist's intention to the extent that the art-work decides its own structural necessity and decides its own response in terms of a dialectic in relation to society and the style in which it functions, which is also a product of the prevailing social order.

Presence in Music

The implications for a musical understanding of Adorno's conception of the social role of art can most clearly be seen in the two figures around whom his musical criticism gravitates, namely Beethoven and Schoenberg. The issue upon which this relationship rests is an understanding of Beethoven's late style in which Adorno locates a tendency that was to be realised in Schoenberg's 'alienated' music. Central to Adorno's understanding of the late style is the essay *Alienated Masterpiece: The Missa Solemnis*,[21] which is one of the few detailed studies of a particular piece of music that Adorno undertook. It is difficult to ascertain just what is Adorno's final diagnosis of the *Missa*: he ranges from talking about its impotence and false totality, comparing it unfavourably with the 'compositional daring'[22] of the late quartets, to adhering finally to Beethoven's assessment of it as his greatest work. At any rate Adorno certainly views the *Missa* as problematic, since it refutes the notion of total synthesis sought in the middle period works such as the *Eroica* and *Fidelio*, in which he perceives a genuine revolutionary force attuned to the prevailing social context. The degree of freedom which Beethoven attained through the dialectical mediation of subjective content and objective form, though at times somewhat forced in the concluding tonic affirmations of the middle period works, becomes utterly untenable within the confines of a mass setting.

> It [the human idea] calls upon positive religion for help whenever the lonely subject no longer trusted that it could of itself, as pure human essence, dispel the forward surging chaos of conquered and protesting nature.[23]

In the face of Beethoven's intrinsic awareness of the increasingly splintered qualities of his musical medium, archaic polyphonic procedures unsuited to processes of dialectical transformation are called upon to supply a musical salvation of ontology. As Martin Jay has pointed out, this

> registered the failure of the bourgeois emancipation from its pre-enlightened past ... he called into question the bourgeois subject's achievement of a genuine autonomy.[24]

The problematical aspect of the *Missa* is embedded in its rejection of that which 'critically endorsed Being in the classically symphonic'.[25] Instead it endorses a 'taboo about the negativity of existence',[26] through its use of archaic methods of organisation. Unlike the late quartets which demand of the listener involvement in the fragmented style, in the musical problem of unity, the authority of the mass setting tends to preclude participation in the musical conflicts. In terms of semiology, the manifestations of Beethoven's late style might be described as a realisation of the differential qualities of musical syntax (writing). The union of the signifier and signified has been split, so that the stability denoted by the tonic triad, or dominant-tonic relationships, is no longer determined stylistically, but rather has become hypostatised as a predetermined quantity. The extent to which the late works rely on fragmented musical procedures indicates an attempt to escape generalised units of meaning.

The legacy of Beethoven which proved so burdensome to many 19th century composers was that of being left with the inimitable qualities of the late works and the debris of the spectacular middle period. Rose Rosengard Subotnik[27] has suggested that Adorno's elision of the alienated qualities of late Beethoven with Schoenberg's early atonal works, in terms of the latter's historical realisation of the implications inherent in the former, led Adorno, despite, and because, of his emphasis on the necessity of historical progress, to regard the intervening musical events of the 19th century as essentially static. Certainly, the model of 19th century music to emerge from Adorno's overview is one in which the attempt to reinvigorate the procedures of middle period Beethoven results in a musical style characterised by structural rupture rather than continuous process. In view of this Subotnik goes on to suggest that, notwithstanding widely differing intentions, in its results Adorno's understanding of 19th century music falls essentially within the synchronic world view of French structuralism. It would seem, however, as several writers have pointed out,[28] that given the emphasis on heterogeneous fragments which is so characteristic of Adorno's thought in general, there is a stronger link with poststructuralist tendencies, particularly those of Derrida, for whom any type of stable structure, including rigidly historical or ahistorical models, becomes problematic.

Adorno's model of 19th century music is able to cope with the idiosyncrasies of individual works and the developmental tendencies which lead from one to another. This is an advantage denied to the two figures chosen by Subotnik to represent French thought, Lévi-Strauss and Foucault, the former unable to recognise the particular qualities of an individual myth, but having to negotiate it as representative of a norm, and the latter encountering similar problems with the details contained within an episteme.

Diachronic tendencies have a certain immanent process which is lost to an epistemic historical model reduced to the chance outcome of simultaneous synchronic events. If Adorno's understanding of 19th century music did fall within a structuralist static world view which changes only by rupture, in which the individual (entity) remains frozen in a pre-established system (ontology), then it would effectively loop the loop (volte), in rather the manner that Adorno diagnoses in Heidegger. Just as the ontological can only be conceived in terms of the ontic, so the structurally static can only be conceived in terms of the historically progressive.

In view of the loss of the apparent logical consistency of classical musical arguments, the emergence of programme music in the 19th century is explicable in terms of providing an external frame of reference on which to hang musical form, to act as ballast against the dissolution of necessity in the music itself. Furthermore, the principle of musical autonomy which emerged with Beethoven becomes a fetish of art as religion, in which the creator (the genius) takes on the ontological aura that has become musically problematic. The epitome of this tendency is found in the art-religion of Wagner, in which the prehistorical authority of myth is invoked. For Adorno, Wagner should thus represent the utmost in musical regression, but it is significant that Adorno's discussion of him displays the familiar response of evincing deep admiration however hostile the express comments. Wagner's mythical discourse yearns for a lost presence, but is articulated in a musical medium which, though frequently structurally static, abandons the tonic-centricity of tonal harmony. The passage from Wagner to Schoenberg is marked by a rupture on the formal, stylistic level (the latter doesn't attempt to resort to an archaic order), but on the level of process a degree of continuity exists in Schoenberg's reappraisal of Wagnerian chromaticism (a similar model of rupture and continuity is discussed later in relation to Ligeti's appropriation of advanced serialism). This ambivalence about Wagner indicates a conflicting trend in Adorno's understanding of the nineteenth-century music in general; an acknowledgement of the historical development of tonality that Schoenberg was able to seize upon, despite the static and repetitive forms through which it evolved. If this dichotomy can be identified in Wagner, it cannot be excluded from 19th century music altogether.

Alienated Music and Beyond

Schoenberg, as heir to Beethoven's late style, is able to

articulate the negation that was taboo in the *Missa Solemnis*. He is only able to do so, however, in terms of the debris of late Romanticism: the poignant sevenths and ninths that function at the limits of tonality, though retaining their tonal meaning as discrete semantic units, become alienated from the context which provides that meaning, by functioning within the environment of atonality. The principle of continuous development is thereby renewed; the elements have to create their own syntax without the aid of a stylistic context. By thus cutting itself off Schoenberg's free atonal style was able to function as alienated social critique. Schoenberg's numerous testaments to this feeling of standing on the edge point to a need for the security of a compositional technique, which was constituted by serialism.

Adorno's stance with respect to 20th century music is not really comprehensible outside the framework of the Frankfurt school formulation of the *Culture Industry* as a nomenclature to convey the ideological permeation of commodity values which increasingly penetrate the consciousness of day to day living. The main exposition of this pernicious process occurred in the chapter entitled 'The Culture Industry: Enlightenment as Mass Deception' in *Dialectic of Enlightenment*, and it was to remain operative in Adorno's subsequent musical writings. In fact Adorno states that the *Philosophy of New Music*, should be regarded as an extended appendix to *Dialectic of Enlightenment*.[29] It is in the face of the blanket values offered by mass media, and the subsequent infiltration and determination of people's personal desires, that Adorno saw the enhanced political necessity of contemporary music. For Adorno, the only valid response from an artist living in an alienated society is to produce alienated art. This stance led him to be deeply suspicious of popular art whose effortlessly assimilated sheen of well-being enforces the stranglehold of commodity reproduction which designed it in the first place.

> Art for the masses has destroyed the dream but still conforms to the tenets of that dreaming idealism which critical idealism balked at.[30]

The culture industry has succeeded in producing a mental state which is constantly reproduced by commodity values, and whose expectations are continually met by mass art. Given this context, Schoenberg's music, particularly the free atonal style, represents an entrenched stand against the machinations of mass culture. Adorno considered it to be progressive in its respect for tradition, which involved an abandonment of tonality, the very medium in which that tradition exerted its force, and in its historical urge towards the paradoxical technique of serialism which, though a logical outcome of the composer's development, in some ways compromised his earlier achievements. Adorno recognised that serialism

> enchains music by liberating it. The subject dominates music through the rationality of the system, only in order to succumb to the rational system itself.[31]

In its obstinate exposure of the explosion of the organic art work, yet its retention of the autonomy principle, Schoenberg's best music performs the function of an art that can still point to that unity beyond itself, which it affirms as being illusory. To realise this chink in a seemingly hopeless situation is the awesome task that Adorno demands of contemporary art if it is to survive. Though he has in effect recognised the Derridean claim that any metaphysical formulation is undermined by itself, for Adorno there is a *telos*; as Wellmer points out, 'the presence of a reconciling spirit in an unreconciled world can only be thought of aporetically'.[32] This emancipatory dimension does not, however, hark back to an origin but is only hinted at by philosophical distillation of the mimetic moment offered by art. Such a reconciliation of humanity with nature suggests the ahistorical, but would be reached historically, and would be a Utopian moment rather than a passive acceptance of a static world view. The static qualities of Adorno's music criticism thus reflect a failure to meet the demands of history, rather than an abandonment of the historical framework.

The intrinsically temporal quality of music makes it an ideal vehicle for articulating the force field between the stasis of play and the process of history, which, indeed, has become a preoccupation of post-war composers. This body of music displays the extremes of both Cagean games, and total serialism, which at their limits tend to rearticulate each other. It is ironic that Adorno levelled charges of abandoning the historical perspective, and succumbing to governing principles of static repetition, at the compositional activities centring around the Darmstadt school, as this music in many ways responds to the same problems that beset his own thought. The conflicting forces which operate in Adorno's music criticism, and indeed in his general philosophical outlook, are crucial to the musical concerns of Ligeti, which reflect the composer's intellectual and personal acquaintance with Adorno.

The Music of Ligeti

The collapse of the Hegelian identity in non-identity by thought displaying deconstructive tendencies is highly apposite to the music of György Ligeti, which might be characterised as musical dialectics with the hub knocked off; a dialectic in which the moment of *Aufhebung*[33] remains operative within the thought structure, but fails to take place. This preoccupation with the sameness and difference of identity becomes apparent in the terminology which has been used to portray the off-balance feeling created by Ligeti's music: 'structures in structural dissolution',[34] 'changing unchange'[35] and 'non-diatonic diatonicism',[36] to mention a few. As Martin Zenck points out,[37] Ligeti's realisation that determinacy and indeterminacy are expressions of the lack in each other, became assimilated by Adorno in the *Aesthetic Theory*.

The pertinence of thinking about Ligeti's music in terms of philosophical functions is vindicated by the fact that the music dating from his arrival in the West amounts to an almost Cartesian[38] re-examination of the parameters of music: what happens when one eliminates harmonic and rhythmic delineation (*Atmosphères*), when many different metrical layers are superimposed (*Poème Symphonique*), or when the governing principle becomes continuous motion

(*Continuum*)? At the same time this *tabula rasa* is tempered by a lively awareness and assimilation of tradition. The probing and retraction from the limits of metaphysical thought which were examined in the first half of this chapter emerge as the overwhelming concern of Ligeti's musical constellation. The dissolution of the sign as a stable unit becomes realised by a musical style in which discrete musical units are often hazy and continually threaten to transform themselves. Ligeti's strong urge to move forward rather than merely to consolidate earlier achievements displays an awareness of the risk of hypostatising, and hence reconstituting the closure of thought by precisely the means that were used to decentre it earlier, a risk against which Derrida fights a running battle. It is in its refusal to become hypostatised and fall into a system that Ligeti's music can be reckoned to have some political significance.

In an article entitled *On Music and Politics*,[39] Ligeti has denounced demands that music should be used as a political vehicle, strongly refuting claims to the effect that if music is not politically engaged, then it automatically serves the establishment. Ligeti acknowledges that a Mozart quartet may reflect the prevailing social situation from which it emerged, but is anxious to avoid direct correspondences between musical and social/economic structures.

> the social situation, or if you wish, the conditions of production, the economic conditions which in Marxism constitute the substructure or base, that obviously is related – when we talk about music – with that which is musical structure, but it is not identical with it and the two are not interchangeable.[40]

This is a fair point which amply quashes vulgar marxist tendencies to regard music as little more than a manifestation of prevailing conditions of production. Ligeti's final argument in the article, however, in which he points out that the same melody with different words was used both by the 'ultra-reactionary' Rumanian monarchy and by the Albanian partisans, for conflicting political ideologies, thus suggesting that the theme itself is apolitical, takes a somewhat narrow view of the political potential of music, at least from someone familiar with the work of

Adorno. It is understandable that a composer who lived through the horrors both of the Nazi domination of Hungary and of the Zhdanov purges under Stalinist rule should wish to remain separate from politics; but one senses that the article is a response to jibes at the expense of the musical avant-garde from leftist activists, and that Ligeti underestimates the radical impulses in his own work. Similar charges of aestheticising at the expense of any real social concern have been levelled at Adorno and Derrida. Though not totally unfounded this criticism tends to miss the radical potential in these thinkers; and Ligeti's music has the alleviating feature of being fairly accessible whilst at the same time responding to exacting listening.

Perhaps a more accurate portrayal of the role of politics in Ligeti's music might be gleaned from a conversation with the composer cited by Ulrich Dibelius, in which the political is listed along with other elements of everyday reality which are assimilated by music.

> Everything contributes in some manner [Ligeti has just mentioned politics], but only ever halfway: it is pulled out, seized, and dropped again. It is like a dung heap, in which one digs and brings out some wrecks, – or like a child at his toy cupboard which has got into a state of total disorder.[41]

If the concept of the political is expanded from the intentions of those in power, to include social ideology, which determines norms of behaviour and consciousness, then this statement by Ligeti corresponds more closely to Adorno's view of art as both the embodiment and rejection of social structure, in which the social/political is mediated through the immanent content of a work of art. The shifting of levels, the radical decentring of Ligeti's musical discourse, offers an immanent critique of the stagnant recalcitrant values of the culture industry, with its cult of the forever new but essentially the same.

Static Music

The consideration of developing and static forms which emerged as the major theme of the first section of this

chapter is of fundamental significance to Ligeti's compositions, which have a complex relationship to Adornian
musical standards; on the one hand recognizing the force of
tradition precisely by reacting against it, on the other
abandoning values of continuous development and hierarchical organisation, apparently succumbing to the
temptation of static non-developmental music. It is
significant that Ligeti cites Debussy's *Jeux* as a formative
influence, thus stepping out of the Adornian mould,
according to which Schoenberg drives the tradition of
Western music forward. *Jeux*, which was to become a
seminal work for the Darmstadt circle in general, rather
than representing an ongoing unfolding of structural
possibilities in time, takes the form of an essentially static
organisation which Ligeti has likened to 'a tropical tree
whose wildly growing aerial roots grow downwards back into
the soil'.[42]

Rather than a rejection of Adorno's criteria, Ligeti's
adherence to static constructional principles, especially in
his earlier Western European music, might be symptomatic
of the same forces which had ground Adorno's own dialectic
to a halt: a society which is governed by the incessant
sameness of commodity exchange (repetition), will produce
alienated static music. Yet typically, in view of the
paradoxes with which Ligeti's music is riddled, and which
are one of the most potent qualities of it, the terms
alienation and static are problematic. Ligeti's music is
undoubtedly alienated in its refusal to fall back on hollow
platitudes of certainty, a fact that is strengthened by his
refusal to entertain the possibility of writing film music,[43] (at
least not intentionally),[44] under conditions of financial
hardship; yet the fact that the Requiem and *Atmosphères*
were successfully used as film music points to a sensuous
immediacy in this music which, though indicating a
splintered totality, suggests a desire to break through the
confines of elitism. Ligeti has likened his music to 'frozen
expressionism',[45] suggesting that a musical medium which
has ground itself to a halt can only express emotions which
are similarly jammed, resulting in a disinterested commentary. Though this may be a valid response to the social

commodification of emotion, it is ultimately untenable, for just as stasis can only ultimately be thought of in terms of motion, so frozen expression can only be grounded in some experience of genuine emotion.

Unlike the ritualistic acceptance which pervades Stravinsky's ostinati and tableaux, Ligeti's approach to static music is akin to a creative inquiry into the qualities of stasis which must to some extent include their antitheses. The early cluster scores, notably *Atmosphères* and parts of the Requiem, achieve a preponderance of the synchronic at the expense of the diachronic, precisely by pushing the diachronic (polyphonic) to its limits, at which point it becomes self-defeating; the sheer density of lines (*Atmosphères* includes a 56 part canon, starting bar 44), excludes any possibility of the traditional polyphonic interplay of individual lines. The convoluted five-part fugue of the Requiem's Introitus, in which each part is sung by four voices in canon with themselves, results in a sense of huge pulsating slabs of sound that merge with and emerge from one another. This *tour de force* on the diachronic level, which obversely results in an emphasis on the synchronic, finally performs a back-flip in which the suppressed diachronic level reasserts itself: as one becomes immersed in these static textures, one's perception becomes attuned to fluctuations which move across the grain; the main fugal entries of the Introitus, which are pointed up by orchestral doubling, glance across the dense weave before submerging back into the sound-web. Derridean terminology here threatens to become rather confusing as it is couched in terms of language which does not have a physical vertical dimension. For Derrida the space of writing constitutes the actual gaps between the words themselves, which may correspond to the gaps between fugal entries, or smaller units, but is basically inadequate in terms of the spatiality of atemporal music. Bearing this in mind, the ahierarchical spatial vision of these scores cannot exclude the temporization (Derridean spacing) of the diachronic. Temporality appears as the supplement at the origin of spatiality.

The realisation that an impenetrable wall of cluster formations constitutes a static background which enhances the perception of events moving against it (provided that they are sufficiently defined not to become swallowed up in the process) becomes a determining principle of *Lontano* and *Melodien*. In the case of *Lontano*, the canonic technique by which voices imitate at the unison and the octave creates a slowly changing pitch configuration, against which strata consisting of several lines, distinguished by pitch association and/or orchestral timbre, emerge. A particularly clear example of this procedure occurs at bar 145, in which a void opens out of the dense orchestral texture, from which the timbral strata of three distant horns emerges, an effect that Ligeti has compared to the similarly placed emergence of a horn quartet in the coda to the slow movement of Bruckner's Eighth Symphony. Typically, new features start imperceptibly, rather than being structurally accented.

Various metaphors have been used to describe the transformational process which takes place in the general sonority of *Lontano*, such as the iconic concept of a slowly rotating diamond whose overall shape remains apparent, but which appears transformed as light catches different angles,[46] and Ligeti's own image of dissolving crystalline structures.[47] The latter has distinct resonances from Thomas Mann's *Doctor Faustus*[48] in which the rigid structures of the later Leverkühn's music are anticipated by the strange organic-inorganic growth of crystals cultivated by his father during childhood, and from the metaphor of crystalline structure which Edgard Varèse used to describe his own music.[49] Ligeti seems to have taken on board the Adornian retraction into a frozen dialectic, but to have found a response to it in the interplay between events (*Ereignisse*) and transformations (*Wandlugen*),[50] where the ossified structure exists in a state of flux. Although *Lontano* does exude a sense of distanced unchanging change, of non-developing development, real events do take place in real time; lines or clustered strata of several lines definitely evolve before gradually submerging again. The oscillations between background and foreground, stasis and development, are revealed as intrinsic expressions of the lack in each other; the new pitch sets are introduced out of notes common with the previous set – a manifestation of the role of the other in Derrida's notion of difference.

Ligeti's development as a composer since his flight from Budapest follows a trajectory in which the expelled parameters of his earlier drastically reduced scores are reclaimed. The virtual annihilation of separately identifiable lines which marks *Atmosphères* leads to the situation in *Lontano* where the slightest deviation from the sound-mass is heard as a potential temporal development. It is as if having knocked out harmonic and rhythmic functions, reducing his resources to a heaving conglomerate of sound, Ligeti can start to reintroduce these factors within the organisational possibilities gleaned from his experiments in privation. The strata which function as foreground temporisation in *Lontano* become thinned out and glimpsed as melodic shapes amidst the jostling mass of melodies which constitute *Melodien*. The composer asks for every part to be played with an 'inner vitality and a dynamic agogic shape of its own',[51] thus reaffirming the identity of each level, which operates on its own substratum, but which nevertheless must coexist with other similarly independent lines, moving out of phase with each other. Various gradations of transformation operate simultaneously and individually. The sustained notes (described by Ligeti as the background level) ensure a continuous sonority against sometimes fragmented textures, and function in the traditional role of a static pedal, but at the same time exhibit the most defined harmonic motion in the score. The ostinati and melodic levels further distinguished by Ligeti (the former described as middle-ground, the latter as foreground), the distinctions between which are often subtle, have the static qualities of superimposed repetitive figures – which are often very fast – but the temporal demarcation and transformation of pitch content characteristic of clear lines. *Melodien* also exhibits an increasing tendency towards rhythmic differentiation, the individual configurations remaining fairly imperceptible, but the interaction of levels resulting in combinatorial rhythms surfacing and sinking in a similar manner to the melodic content.

Musical Aura

Ligeti's idiosyncratic handling of musical temporality, and his layering of events is illuminated, and to some extent politicised, by another thinker who shared his convoluted commitment to the modern, one who lurked in the wings throughout the earlier discussion of Adorno's theory of art, namely Walter Benjamin. It is significant that many commentaries on Ligeti's music tend to use terms, such as aura and constellation, which reverberate throughout Benjamin's thought; and more concrete connections between the two men have been made.[52] The link would seem to be strong enough to sustain a detailed study, but for the present purposes Benjaminian themes will function as an undercurrent to be tapped through the immanent content of Ligeti's music, in the context of the interplay of stasis and development drawn from the earlier discussion of Adorno and Derrida.

Of particular relevance is Benjamin's understanding of history, which emerges throughout his writings but receives its most succinct (indeed aphoristic) exposition in his *Theses on the Philosophy of History*.[53] Ligeti's fascination with the notion of stopping time and the covert Messianism which becomes explicit in pieces such as the *Lacrimosa* (Requiem) and *Lux aeterna* receive a radical twist from Benjamin's conception of the rich nowness of the present (*Jetztzeit*), as opposed to the presence of empty repetitive time (*Gegenwart*). In his Derridean recognition that synchronic and diachronic time are supplements of the lack in each other, and in his subsequent doomed attempts to fold them into each other, Ligeti may be seen as reaching for the *Jetztzeit* which remains equally as unthinkable as Derrida's trace, but which yearns to overstep that 'whore called "once upon a time" in historicism's bordello'.[54] For Benjamin the 'concatenation of discrete events taking place within a posthumous explanatory order' which constitutes historicism, is merely the product of historicism, rather than any innate justification for its existence. Benjamin posits a new kind of historian who stops telling the sequence of events like the beads on a rosary. Instead, he grasps the constellation which his own cra has formed with a definite earlier one. Thus he establishes a conception of the present as the 'time of the now' which is shot through with chips of Messianic time.[55]

Benjamin outlined his notion of the aura of a historical object in terms of natural objects, in his essay 'The Work of Art in the Age of Mechanical Reproduction', as 'the unique phenomenon of a distance, however close it may be.'[56] This distancing effect of history is juxtaposed to the striving of the culture industry to examine everything closely and hence destroy the aura of uniqueness through reproduction.

To pry an object from its shell, to destroy its aura, is the mark of a perception whose 'sense of the universal equality of things' has increased to such a degree that it extracts it even from a unique object by means of reproduction.[57]

One of the main structural features of the Horn Trio is a fascination with the relative distancing of tradition, which is evoked by the dedication, 'Hommage à Brahms', coupled with the sound aura of the horn and its network of association. Both these preoccupations are central to Benjamin's understanding of aura. Ulrich Dibelius[58] points out that the 'horn fifths' of classical two-part horn writing (which became a standardised motive in their own right), are used as a structural resource and reference point for this work. Ligeti[59] has drawn attention to the horn fifths in the coda of the first movement of the *Les Adieux* sonata, whilst acknowledging that the influence of Beethoven's late sonatas and quartets is 'somehow always there'.[60] These influences can be thought of as operating on a distanced horizon, parts of which are telescoped into view (though invariably through a distorted lens), thereby setting up further implications peculiar to the present context.

The aura of pre-mechanised history is felt in the Horn Trio's extensive use of open horn harmonics; the modern double horn is in effect used as twelve natural horns. The notes, which are out of tune in a tonal context, become inbuilt micro-tones for a post-tonal medium. Further, the horn sound evokes distant Romantic sonorities for Ligeti, particularly those of Bruckner and Mahler. The effect of a warm horn tone emerging from a huge orchestral sonority is conveyed by the frequent use of muting and of sustained pedals. This sense of aura does not always remain filtered; the raucous horn fanfares which invade the reprise of the 'Scherzo' retain their bucolic hunting flavour thereby imparting a certain rough immediacy. Though the aura of these techniques from the past remains recognisable in many places, frequently it becomes blurred, and the material itself functions as immanent musical content: the intervals which constitute the distorted 'horn fifths', and the linear movement of the two parts, become musical material detached from their context. Similarly the Second Quartet, which is in many ways a modern commentary on Beethoven's late quartet style, explores the potential of material which in Beethoven's context is used for articulating larger formal concerns.

Benjamin's conception of aura became a tenet of the Frankfurt School in general, and was particularly useful for Adorno, who shared his friend's fascination with Proust's conception of memory. In this respect, Kropfinger has offered some useful points of access to Ligeti's music by drawing upon Adorno's ideas of 'spontaneous memory' (*unwillkürliche Gedächtnis*),[61] and 'present forgetting' (*gegenwärtige Vergessen*):[62] those of 'recollection in forgetting' (*Erinnerung im Vergessen*),[63] in conjunction with a description of aura as a dialectical coupling of 'dissolution and restoration' (*Auflösung und Wiederherstellung*).[64] This configuration, in which the past fades into the distance but can be reclaimed and constellated in the present, could have been formulated as a precise description of Ligeti's fluid crystals. The constellating principle itself becomes assimilated as an immanent dynamic, used as a generative musical principle, rather than a rigid realisation of a predetermined formula. The sense of the past applies not only to the auratic appearances of tradition, but to the temporality of the music itself, in which past events can be reclaimed. The matrix of melodic figures of which *Melodien* is comprised, operates as a background (past) within the piece which can be drawn upon to throw melodies into the present of the foreground. There is an uneasy tension between Benjamin's distancing of aura and the stripping of its uniqueness by the 'contemporary masses'[65] – the process by which it is partially defined. *Melodien* pushes up elements from its background and subjects them to the kind of scrutiny that enables them to become reproducible ostinato figures which, however, refuse to hypostatise and thus avoid 'commodification' by collapsing back into the fabric.

Ligeti's use of micro-tones has much to do with Benjamin's notion of the stripping of aura characteristic of everyday life. In the minute details of *Ramifications*, scored for twelve strings, half of which are tuned a quarter-tone sharp, traditional intervals are, as it were, brought closer and examined microsonically by being presented simultaneously in two different tuning grids. Ligeti has compared this weird effect of clashing tuning to a body 'in a state of gradual decomposition',[66] a simile suggesting the detached observation of detail central to Benjamin's understanding of the erosion of aura. Zenck has suggested that the elision of past and present, foreground and background, even if ultimately unrealisable, has the potential for political significance in its disruption of everyday perception (*Alltagswahrnehmung*).[67] In this context he points out sections in the Second String Quartet in which the distancing effect of soft sustained harmonies is juxtaposed with frantic, jagged, often loud, figures which have the violent immediacy of the present.

Repetition and the Culture Industry

An oblique parallel to Benjamin's diagnosis of contemporary society can also be seen in Ligeti's somewhat skewed and ambivalent relationship to technology. Upon his arrival in Cologne, Ligeti quickly utilised the resources of the electronic studio there, but the only piece to become part of the electronic repertoire, *Articulation*, though using the reservoir of sounds being developed by the composers sharing the studio, departs, in its detached self-mockery, from the euphoria of new found opportunities then prevalent. The early experiments in the studio remain

Ligeti's only venture in the electronic medium, his subsequent encounters with technology being restricted to those instrumental portrayals of manic little machines that play a seminal role in his elisions of time and space. Ligeti's obsessive machine-driven ostinati are pertinent to both sides of the Adorno/Benjamin debate concerning the relationship of art to present-day technology, but in no sense achieve a happy medium between them, rather drawing out the conflicts between the two positions. In his use of machine-like motion Ligeti seems to be accepting, like Benjamin, advances in technology as revolutionary in their potential for the immediacy of enjoyment; this is coupled with the camera-view 'orientation of the expert',[68] reflected by Ligeti's close-up examination of the inner workings of ostinato patterns. On the other hand, by using traditional instruments Ligeti is rejecting the actual technology itself, and by using an instrument with such distinct bourgeois associations as the harpsichord, he is flagrantly refusing to abandon aura into the arms of repetition. Instead the present and past constellate, illuminating both eras across the space of history. If the assimilation of the ceaseless self-perpetuating motion of culture industry represents a sliding of Adornian values, it also represents an outspoken vindication of them, a critique of alienated repetition which must perforce tear itself apart.

A principle of Ligeti's earlier harmonic transformations is the recognisably serialist striving to avoid repetition which inherently places perceptual emphasis on the repeated element, thus resulting in hierarchical organisation. Though no element acquires sufficient self-identity to be recognisably repeatable in these net transformations, there is a sense in which the whole transformational process is itself repeated. Ligeti's ostinato figures would seem at first blush to be diametrically opposed to any principles of non-repetition, yet they too illuminate the contradictory notion of a unique sound event. Each repeated event, simply because it takes place in its own moment of time, is in a sense unique; it is as if Ligeti, like Cage, is trying to eliminate repetition through repetition. In keeping with Cage and Boulez, Ligeti acknowledges the influence of

Artaud's Theatre of Cruelty,[69] which strives for the impossible uniqueness of unrepeatable events. In an essay on Artaud's Theatre of Cruelty Derrida has the following to say:

> Being is the form in which the infinite diversity of the forms of life and death can indefinitely merge and be repeated in the word. For there is no word, nor in general a sign, which is not constituted by the possibility of repeating itself. A sign which does not repeat itself, which is not already divided by repetition in its 'first time', is not a sign. The signifying referral therefore must be ideal – and ideality is but the assured power of repetition – in order to refer to the same thing each time.[70]

A gloss on this passage might be found in the use of minimalist techniques which, while presenting an easily digestible 'high' of hyper-activity antithetical to large scale development, at the same time offer a genuine new sense of layered rhythmic complexity – at least to Western music. Undoubtedly the most interesting feature of minimalism is its gradual phase shifts, which are comparable, on a different parameter, to Ligeti's methods of harmonic transformation. The harmonic sensation of becoming imperceptibly aware of the growing prevalence of a particular pitch set is matched by a comparable shifting of rhythmic placement, which has the added dimension of a sudden gestalt shift to a new metric contour. In Ligeti's first experiments with superimposed metres, which have yet to realise the potential of minimalism, such as the two organ études (1967/69), the repetition of ostinati, like the dense polyphony discussed above, results in a repression of the diachronic through saturation in favour of the synchronic. Again a reversal takes place in which the ostinati come to be heard as a background that highlights anything which might be perceived as temporal movement against it. In the case of the organ études the temporal foreground is limited to the shifts between rhythmic patterns which tend to remain somewhat local, and hence do not add another dimension to the music. A process takes place on the metric plane in *Continuum for solo harpsichord* which is similar to what takes place on the harmonic plane in *Lontano*; the intrusion of the diachronic into the synchronic becomes a generating force. Again there is a struggle to fold the diachronic into the synchronic, to fold the near into the distant – the interaction of the rapid ostinati against each other throws up a cumulative gestalt rhythm which moves temporally against the static background. The shifts themselves are not notated in the score, and are difficult to predict accurately in reading; they rely on the immediacy of performance. The minutely examined repetitive patterns which are instantly reproducible have forfeited any sense of aura, but by interacting produce a temporal dimension which, if not unique, at least has some distinguishing features.

Minimalist techniques are assimilated into Ligeti's idiosyncratic style, the ceaseless activity of *Continuum* depicting a frantically neurotic little machine working at full capacity, in which the clanking of the harpsichord action provides a third rhythmic layer (over the notated patterns and their gestalt shifts), whilst the audacity of its technical demands gives the piece in performance the aura of virtuosity. If the ostinato plane is thought of as the vanishing past, and the gestalt plane as the immediacy of the present, there is a sense in which the sheer desperation of the speed tries to break through the limits of continual repetition, to 'blast open the continuum of history',[71] and constellate it with the present. The fact that Ligeti usually works within a network of formal concerns and meanings allows him to deflect the frequent drab monotony of minimalist techniques: the separate lines in the Six Etudes for piano, or the Vivacissimo of the Horn Trio, interact with each other while retaining individual interest. The impulse of minimalism remains very strong in *Selbstportrait* (2nd piece, *Drei Stücke für zwei Klaviere*); however, it becomes lopsided through the use of blocked keys, whereby silences can accurately be introduced into ostinati by the playing of the silent keys, thus enabling highly complex metric layers to be superimposed without the rigours of precise notation. Ligeti is always guided by immanently musical considerations, and is thus able to blast Chopin's B flat minor sonata, opus 35, out of history, and constellate it with minimalist concerns at the end of this movement. This is no last-ditch resort to

Chopin in a state of rigor mortis; the sonata appears as a living tradition which interacts reciprocally with Ligeti's music.

The fact that this frenetic, almost satirical, use of layered structures should occur in a movement entitled *Selbstportrait* points to an endearing feature of Ligeti – his ability to parody and laugh at himself – something that definitely does not stem from the influence of Adorno. Though the ridiculous and satirical pervades Ligeti's music, there is a body of works in which what might be called the Dadaist impulse is particularly prevalent, the most prominent examples of which were all composed in the first two years of the 1960s; *Fragment* for ten instruments, *Trois bagatelles* for pianist, *Die Zukunft der Musik* for lecturer and audience, and *Poème symphonique* for 100 metronomes. However, this influence is also very marked in *Aventures, Nouvelles aventures*, and *Le grand macabre*. If *Fragment* is a parody at the expense of Ligeti's own musical techniques, and perhaps the idea of a fragmented totality, *Poème symphonique* was designed as a skit on the futile (as Ligeti saw it) influence of chance procedures in music, which were infiltrating the European avant-garde at the time, from the example of Cage. *Die Zukunft der Musik*, in which an audience responds to instructions such as 'crescendo' chalked on a blackboard, is again directed at Cage (this time the happenings), but is also perhaps an expression of the frustrations facing contemporary music. The germinal aspects of these pieces for the composer's later development have often been pointed out – the use of silence in *Trois bagatelles*, the layering of rhythmic strata in *Poème symphonique* – but in place of the essentially political assault on institutionalised art which, as Peter Bürger has argued,[72] runs through Dadaism and Surrealism, there is a sense of hopelessness and humorous acceptance. Ligeti's extremism within the area marked out by the concept of art indicates a frustration with these confines, but not a radical desire to shatter them.

Musical Limitations

The *tour de force* of contained extremism functions as a strong impulse in Ligeti's oeuvre, where it combines some of the most powerful moments in his music with a frustrated pacing around the cage of possibility. The Requiem outlines a trajectory from the extraordinary deep pulsating clusters with which the Introitus opens, to the more transparent high (celestial) textures with which the Lacrimosa dissolves. A microcosm of this process is presented by the violent registral contrast of the Dies Irae. Extreme registral oppositions are characteristic of Ligeti's vocal settings: the four ecstatic cadences of *Hälfte des Lebens*, the first of the *Drei Phantasien*, require all voices to take tigers' leaps into the registral extremes, '*Tutta la forza*' (bars 15-17, 20-21, 23-27, 49-50, of which cadences two and three are diametrically opposed to the plunging bass line which connects them). The Horn Trio (bars 80-81, first movement) takes the violin up to such high harmonics that the tone disappears into 'a noise like a breath', whilst the final sustained horn pedal G (fourth movement) makes formidable demands on the player's breathing capacity. These musical extremes, including other areas of virtuosity, are matched by the sheer physicality of involvement in performance, where the performer is taken to his or her limits – a manifestation of Adorno's *tour de force* where art strives through virtuosity to reach beyond its own material limitations. Ligeti's almost Messianic striving to transcend the illusionary artificiality of music is apparent in his frequent recourse to silence, which is only interrupted by one note in the case of the *Trois études*; it is an almost mandatory requirement at the end of compositions (often notated by blank bars), though it also occurs elsewhere, for example, the first five bars of *Monument* are silent. The cut-off is a frequent feature of Ligeti's ostinati-based music, where the incessant babble of repetition is suddenly juxtaposed with silence. In an article on 20th century chamber music, in which Bojan Bujić discusses Ligeti's second string quartet, it is argued that chamber music provides a composer with the opportunity for personal exploration by stretching the medium, and striving for a

> not actual but possible music – music that sounds in the mind of
> the composer and the performer as an ideal possibility before it
> has been curbed by the limitations of notation and
> performance.[73]

In the case of Ligeti, this chamber music impulse interacts closely with his philosophical exploration of the nature of sound, pervading all his musical thought.

The yearning to break out of metaphysical/ideological enclosures, together with the acceptance of the unavoidability of playing within them, illuminates Ligeti's fraught experiences with totally determined structural musical devices. In his rejection of open forms, Ligeti retains a link with the autonomous art-work: the desire to break through strictures is conveyed by the interplay of fragmentary processes within the confines of forms, neither of which can totally exclude the other. As Kaufmann has pointed out in the context of *Aventures* and *Nouvelles Aventures*, there is an attempt to fold open and closed form into each other – 'when the form apears closed it opens'.[74] Ligeti's most fastidiously organised music, though requiring meticulous accuracy, actually takes into account and requires human error: the huge vocal clusters in the Requiem exploit the microtonal ingredient of mistuned intonation to create the desired impenetrable wall of sound. If notated, such micro-tuning would make the parts so difficult as to be detrimental to performance.

Ligeti's response to total serialism accords well with his general tendency towards decentred assimilation stimulus. It takes the form of another non-supercessionary dialectic, of serialism in non-serialism, or as the composer describes it, 'serialism without a series'.[75] From his early Darmstadt days Ligeti was aware of the tendency for the all-determining devices of total serialism to eliminate compositional choice from the composer, paradoxically in a similar manner to the chance procedures prescribed by Cage.[76] Further, Ligeti recognised that the application of predetermined procedures to all parameters becomes somewhat self-defeating because large-scale formations tend to level out the row functions of a particular line; thus the small scale internal organisation which was a primary feature of Schoenberg's twelve-tone method becomes somewhat arbitrary. Absolutely determined, supposedly universal systems unwittingly let in arbitrary elements which have the power to undo the presence on which the whole structure is based, to collapse the whole edifice; they are the irritating hairline fracture into which a Derridean lever can be inserted that might just rift the whole system wide open. The flood of arbitrary relationships released by this levering action is utilised as the medium of chance music, which in its turn threatens to undermine itself by having to take structured precautions to ensure that compositional procedures are in no way determined by personal choice. Total serialism thus rearticulates the catastrophe of writing: in moving away from the self-presence of immediacy, 'law supplements nature', and reappropriates the origin from which it had moved away. 'Total alienation is the total reappropriation of self-presence'.[77] Thus the consequences of Schoenberg's realisation of the tendencies inherent in late Beethoven led to the formal reconstitution of that presence, which Beethoven had recognised as inadequate.

This paradoxical situation where the other cannot be excluded, where arbitrariness seeps into total determinacy, and determinacy leaks into chance procedures, is mirrored by the transitions from structuralism to poststructuralism, in which the universal structures of the former already house that terrible knowledge which the latter will release.[78] The mere notion of global structures cannot but encompass awkward details that will have to be generalised to some extent, in order to climb up the hierarchy of a structural network. Similarly, the significance of a deconstructionist unleashing of a plethora of free-range significations can be realised only in terms of an exploded structural totality. Deconstruction is both a continuous transformation of the premises of structuralism, and a violent rupture which blows these premises apart. The subterranean current and the jagged tear are both to be found in Ligeti's music, which has glimpsed the potential to abandon meaningful discourse, but has retracted to some form of structural coherence without relinquishing the threat of chaos, perhaps holding out some hope by reaching for the intangible *Jetztzeit*. *Atmosphères'* much acclaimed negation of serialism is both a rupture, an abandonment of serial procedures, and a realisation of the potential for obsessive organisation of musical parameters to result in their very dissolution.

The tendency for much commentary on Ligeti to talk about his musical techniques in terms of universal laws and natural organic forms becomes decidedly problematic when thrown into the thicket of poststructuralist discourse. The composer himself does discuss the use of golden section principles in *Apparitions*, and the general use of constructivist small scale building principles,[79] but later comes to the conclusion that other principles would equally well have sufficed. Undoubtedly, large scale logical procedures do occur in Ligeti's music, but they operate in a context which threatens their very existence. The fact Ligeti has recognised that tonal and chromatic functional harmony are played out, and similarly serialism contains the seeds of its own demise, should indicate that (though he may be dealing with traditional problems in a different guise) fixed and immutable musical laws do not exist for him.

> My feeling is that both diatonic and chromatic music have been worn out. I do not think that we need to look for other tonal systems – I abhor all fixed systems.[80]

The Hegelian *Aufhebung* of middle period Beethoven is frozen, and the internal coherence of serialism chokes itself. To suggest that Ligeti has recognised the limitations of total serialism and hence gone on to articulate higher universal forms, is to out-structure serialism on its own terms, to recognise that it defeats itself, but at the same time to make the same mistake, and to try and look down upon it from a higher innate structure. If any transcendental signified does look down upon Ligeti (under erasure of course), it must be that of historical necessity, an immanent distorted reflection of the social and intellectual concerns of contemporary society. It would not be gratuitous to draw a parallel between Ligeti's insights into totally determined musical organisation, and his experience of totalitarian states, which in their levelling out of experience cannot account for potentially disruptive individual activity, which might just gain sufficient momentum to seriously threaten ideological values.

The exposing of ideological presuppositions, which has been drawn out of Ligeti's musical constellation, becomes the explicit concern of the absurd libretto in *Le grand macabre*, which also deals, in its half-mocking, half-serious way, with questions of temporality and death, though scorning anything resembling an insight. The detached, clichéd puppet-character depictions create the ideal situation for a Derridean play of signs. If the Day of Judgement does not take place, which is one interpretation of the opera, death itself can be understood as dying on the fictitious Day of Judgement, thus revealing itself as a fake, lacking identity, operating in the continual tangle of deferral constituting signification: it is the unknowable other through which the trace must be thought, but which fails to become a stable sign conferring metaphysical significance on the opera. The day of judgement collapses into the duplicity of difference; the two lovers (*Epilogue*) emerge from the tomb, in which they have been copulating during the preceding two scenes, indifferent to the end of the world, unsure whether they are still awaiting judgement, or whether they have died, yet nothing has changed. In Gheldrode's original play Nekrotzar is explicitly revealed a charlatan, but Ligeti's distillation of the drama introduces the element of doubt; this pathetic parody of a monster, though ridiculing the machinations of dictatorship, might just be real. In either case death remains the unthinkable other which presence requires.

Beneath the distorted reality of *Le grand macabre* lie typically human situations. In many ways the issues which occupy Ligeti might be described as those which have always concerned composers and artists in general, yet Ligeti composes in an age which is marked by its own self-awareness, an age in which the central themes of philosophy are considered through analysis of the very means used to articulate them, in which music has similarly turned in upon itself to examine its own constitution, and in which the gruesome manifestations of political ideology have been explicitly revealed. The flood of information which saturates everyday life turns most attempts to deal creatively with human truths into parodies of themselves, clichés of the greater achievements of the past. These great monuments for the past are themselves commodified, and their very existence threatened, as they are wheeled on as paradigms of profundity in a society for whom the experience of profundity is squeezed out by the ideology of reality – the way the world is. In such an all-embracing system, music is faced with a choice between being overtly and simplistically political, continually facing the danger of becoming engulfed by the system it tries to criticise, or of operating with the self-awareness that consistently covers up its own tracks, and which refuses to become hypostatised.

Ligeti's musical development emerges as an enormous ongoing constellation which transmutes itself from within, and accretes new ideas to itself on its path, but in which no previous discovery becomes entirely submerged. His music is not therefore neatly reducible to a manifestation of any of the thought structures outlined earlier; rather such ideas exist in conflicting clusters whose simultaneity is antithetical to the narrative presentation of a text. It is in this elusive ability to provide glimpses of a self-determined whole which remains always out of reach, that Ligeti's music remains the bane of any ideological totality. It continues to exert that possibility which Adorno identified in music, of remaining troublesome in the face of standardised emotions and responses. Listening to the music of Ligeti will not erase gross political injustices, but it might disrupt the ideological pressures which threaten to crush individual thought, and though it strives for that impossible beyond of art that reveals its own illusion, it might feed the hope that things could be better than they are. The process by which Ligeti musically sifts through the dung heap of reality might just disturb the stagnant crust of reification.

Notes

[1] Theodor Adorno, *Negative Dialectics* (trans. E B Ashton), Routledge and Kegan Paul, 1973.
[2] Adorno, *Aesthetic Theory* (trans. C Lenhardt), Routledge 1984.
[3] Adorno, *über Walter Benjamin*, Suhrkamp Verlag, Frankfurt am Main 1970, p 160, reference from footnote in Kropfinger (1973), p 134, see notes 38 and 64.
[4] *Negative Dialectics*, p 5.
[5] *Negative Dialectics*, p 115. I have substituted 'mediation' in place of Ashton's translation of 'Vermittlung' as 'transmission.'
[6] *Negative Dialectics*, pp 119-122.
[7] A section of *Negative Dialektik* has the heading 'volte' (pp 121-123) which is given as 'looping the loop', pp 115-117, in the translation.
[8] Derrida's critique of Heidegger on Nietzsche is contained in *Spurs: Nietzsche's Styles* (trans. Barbara Harlow), University of Chicago Press 1979.
[9] Ferdinand de Saussure, *Course in General Linguistics* (trans. Wade Baskin), Fontana 1978.
[10] This discussion is contained in *Of Grammatology* (trans. Gayatri Chakravorty Spivak) Johns Hopkins University Press, 1977. For a more extensive account of this issue, see Norris's (present volume) discussion of de Man's *The Rhetoric of Blindness: Jacques Derrida's Reading of Rousseau*. Also of relevance is Hirschkop's (present volume) account of Bakhtin's dialogical linguistics, and by extension Sollertinsky's dialogical views on music.
[11] *On Grammatology*, pp 301.
[12] Derrida, *Margins of Philosophy* (trans. Alan Bass), Routledge and Kegan Paul 1978, p 13.
[13] *Aesthetic Theory*, p 47.
[14] *Ibid*, p 467.
[15] *Ibid*, p 107.
[16] Albrecht Wellmer, 'Truth, Semblance, and Reconciliation, Adorno's Aesthetic Redemption of Modernity' (trans. Maeve Cooke), *Telos*, 62, 1984-85, p 92.
[17] *Aesthetic Theory*, p 7, Adorno derives this simile for the autonomous art work from Leibnitz.
[18] *Ibid*, p 8.
[19] *Ibid*, p 149.
[20] For a more overt though no less knotty view of the Utopian potential of music, see Norris's (present volume) discussion of Bloch's musical thought.
[21] Adorno, 'Alienated Masterpiece: the *Missa Solemnis*' (trans. Duncan Smith), *Telos*, 27, 1976.
[22] *Ibid,* p 116.
[23] *Ibid*, p 120.
[24] Martin Jay, *Adorno*, Fontana 1984, p 144.
[25] Alienated Masterpiece, p 122.

[26] *Ibid*, p 119.

[27] Rose Rosengard Subotnik, 'The Historical Structure: Adorno's "French" Model for the Criticism of Nineteenth-Century Music', *Nineteenth-century Music*, ii, p 1, 1978. The static qualities of Adorno's music criticism are also discussed in Subotnik's papers 'Why is Adorno's Music Criticism the Way It Is?', *Musical Newsletter*, vii, p 4, 1977-78; and 'The Cultural Message of Musical Semiology (Some Thoughts on Music, Language, and Criticism since the Enlightenment)', *Critical Inquiry*, iv, 1978.

[28] See Jochen Schulte-Sasse 'Theory of Modernism versus Theory of the Avant-Garde', foreword to Peter Bürger, *Theory of the Avant-Garde* (trans. Michael Shaw), Manchester University Press 1984, pp xv-xxix. Schulte-Sasse distinguishes between two philosophical and historical modes of understanding the avant-garde; one represented by Breton, Artaud, Barthes, Adorno and Derrida, the other by Brecht, Benjamin, Negt and Kluge. See also Michael Ryan, *Marxism and Deconstruction*, The Johns Hopkins University Press 1982, pp 72-81, for a discussion of the similarities and differences between Derrida and Adorno. Terry Eagleton discusses the extent to which Adorno's thought anticipates that of Derrida in *Walter Benjamin, or Towards a Revolutionary Criticism*, Verso 1981, p 141. Derrida himself has acknowledged parallels with Benjamin, and thus by association with Adorno: 'Ein Porträt Benjamins', in *Links hatte noch alles sich zu enträtseln ...' Walter Benjamin im Kontext*, Burkhardt Lindner (ed), Frankfurt 1978.

[29] Adorno/Max Horkheimer *Dialectic of Enlightenment*, (trans. John Cumming), Verso 1979, Adorno, *Philosophy of Modern Music* (trans. Anne G Mitchell and Wesley V Blomster), Sheed and Ward, 1973, p xvii (preface). See also Adorno, 'On the Fetish Character in Music and the Regression of Listening', *The Essential Frankfurt School Reader*, Andrew Arato and Eike Gebhardt (eds), Urizen Books, New York 1978.

[30] *Dialectic of Enlightenment*, p 125.

[31] *Philosophy of Modern Music*, p 68.

[32] Wellmer, *op cit*, p 92.

[33] Hegel, *Phenomenology of Spirit* (trans. A V Miller), Oxford University Press 1977. *Aufhebung* is translated as 'supercession', as opposed to the previous 'sublation'.

[34] Harald Kaufmann, 'Strukturen im Strukturlosen', *Melos*, December 1964, also in Kaufmann, *Spurlinien. Analytische Aufsätze über Sprache und Musik*, Vienna 1969.

[35] Erkki Salmenhaara, 'Das Musikalische Material und Seine Behandlung in den Werken Apparitions, Atmosphères, Aventures und Requiem von György Ligeti', *Forschungsbeiträge zur Musikwissenschaft*, Gustav Bosse Verlag, Regensburg 1969), xix, p 99.

[36] Ulrich Dibelius, 'Ligeti's Horntrio', *Melos*, 1984, 45, quoted from a conversation with the composer, 15 July 1983.

[37] Martin Zenck, 'Auswirkungen einer "Musique Informelle" auf die Neue Musik zu Theodor W Adornos Formvorstellung', *International Review of the Aesthetics and Sociology of Music*, x, 2, 1979, p 149.

³⁸ Klaus Kropfinger, 'Ligeti und die Tradition', *Zwischen Tradition und Fortschritt über das musikalische Geschichtsbewußtsein, Veröffentlichungen des Instituts für neue Musik und Musikerziehung*, 13, 1973, p 136, quotes a passage by Ligeti in which he discusses his music in Cartesian terms.

³⁹ Ligeti, 'On Music and Politics', *Perspectives of New Music*, 2, Spring-Summer 1978, p 21.

⁴⁰ *Ibid*, p 21.

⁴¹ Dibelius, *op cit*, p 59, quoted from a conversation with the composer, 15 July 1983.

⁴² *Ligeti in Conversation*, (trans. Gabor J Schabert, Sarah E Soulsby, Terence Kilmartin, Geoffrey Skelton), Eulenburg 1983, p 42.

⁴³ *Ibid*, p 24.

⁴⁴ The Requiem and *Atmosphères* were used in Stanley Kubrick's film *2001*.

⁴⁵ *Ligeti in Conversation*, p 18, p 65.

⁴⁶ Bruce Reiprich, 'Transformation of Coloration and density in György Ligeti's *Lontano*', *Perspectives of New Music*, 16, 1978, p 180.

⁴⁷ *Ligeti in Conversation*, p 98.

⁴⁸ Thomas Mann, *Doctor Faustus* (trans H T Lowe-Porter), Penguin, 1968, pp 23-24.

⁴⁹ Schwartz, Elliott, and Barney Childs (eds), *Contemporary Composers on Contemporary Music*, Holt, Rinehart, and Winston, New York 1967, p 203.

⁵⁰ Ligeti '*Zustände, Ereignisse, Wandlungen*', Melos, xxxiv, 1967.

⁵¹ Notes to score of *Melodien*, Schott, Mainz, 1971.

⁵² See Kropfinger, *op cit*.

⁵³ Walter Benjamin, *Illuminations, Essays and Reflections* (trans. Harry Zohn), Schocken Books, New York 1969.

⁵⁴ *Ibid*, p 262.

⁵⁵ *Ibid*, 263.

⁵⁶ *Ibid*, p 222.

⁵⁷ *Ibid*, p 223.

⁵⁸ Dibelius, *op cit*, p 47.

⁵⁹ *Ibid*, p 46.

⁶⁰ *Ibid*, p 45.

⁶¹ Adorno, "Tradition"', 'Dissonanzen. Musik in der verwalteten Welt', *Gesammelte Schriften*, Suhrkamp Verlag, Frankfurt am Main 1973, p xiv.

⁶² *Philosophy of Modern Music*.

⁶³ Kropfinger, *op cit*, p 133

⁶⁴ *Ibid*, p 134. Kropfinger quotes from a letter to Benjamin from Adorno, 29 February 1940: see note 3.

⁶⁵ *Work of Art in the Age of Mechanical Reproduction*, p 223.

⁶⁶ *Ligeti in Conversation*, p 54.

⁶⁷ Martin Zenck, 'Entwurf einer Soziologie der musikalischen Rezeption', *Die Musikforschung*, 23, 1980, p 269.

⁶⁸ *Work of Art in the Age of Mechanical Reproduction*, p 234.

⁶⁹ *Ligeti in Conversation*, p 54.

[70] Derrida, *Writing and Difference*, p 246.

[71] *Illuminations, Essays and Reflections, op cit*, p 262.

[72] Peter Bürger, *op cit* p 28.

[73] Bojan Bujic, 'Chamber Music in the Twentieth Century: Cultural and Compositional Crisis of a Genre', *The British Journal of Aesthetics*, xxii, 2, 1982, p 115.

[74] *Spurlinien, op cit*, p 141.

[75] *Ligeti in Conversation*, p 131.

[76] Ligeti, 'Metamorphoses of Musical Form', *Die Reihe 7*, 1965; also a bit later, 'Form in der neuen Musik', *Darmstädter Beiträge zur neuen Musik*, x, Mainz 1966.

[77] Derrida, *On Grammatology*, p 295.

[78] For a more detailed discussion of the relationship between structuralism and poststructuralism see Perry Anderson, 'Structure and Subject', *In the Tracks of Historical Materialism*, Verso 1983.

[79] *Ligeti in Conversation*, p 43.

[80] *Ibid*, p 54.

Claire Polin

Why Minimalism Now?

'In the past one imitated the masters; today one searches for the singular'

Valery

'Old music has to do with concept and communication; the new with perception'

John Cage

In the late 1950s and early 1960s a new movement in the arts emerged which stripped language, music and painting of all peripheral aspects down to the fewest possible essentials. Labelled 'minimal art', it sought to narrow the gap between audience and observer/listener by presenting a more 'accessible' art in which the fewest possible components formed the message.

In painting, the reductive tendencies of a Rothko, who covered large canvasses with one or two large colour areas, were carried further, into the realm of virtually complete exclusion of all painterly elements (narrative, representation, perspective). Ad Reinhardt, a mystical artist influenced by oriental philosophy, in 1957 wrote of the new aesthetic: 'no texture, no drawing, no light, no space, no movement, no object, no subject, no symbol, no form ... no pleasure, no pain'.[1] Followers, like Olitsky, produced works of unnameable luminous mixed colours that appeared to float in infinite space, or in a spaceless infinity, recalling Pascal's words: 'the silence of infinite space fills me with terror'. One feels a weariness of the human spirit, a desire to escape into an enfolding quietude from the pressures of a frenetic, discordant world, a world which, according to Carl André, 'contains too many objects, and now requires some blankness, some tabula rasa'.[2] Viewed in moments of depression, much contemporary painting suggests only nihilism and chaos. Thus Picasso revealed decay in human forms as biological and historical phenomena, while Giocometti's skeletal forms tended towards reduction and void, revealing speechless fear when reduced to needle-thin figures, 'endowed with neither action nor feeling'.[3] Hence, a minimal art. Even in Delaunay's *Nude Descending a Staircase*, elements of mental or sensuous meaning have been drastically suppressed, again creating a minimal art. Other minimalists, appearing to be tongue-in-cheek, such as Rauschenberg, Warhol, Johns or Lichtenstein, reduced the familiar subject to an environment of images which glorified the mundane – soda pop bottles, movie posters or comic strips, blown up to monumental and horrifying size and placed in unfamiliar contexts. 'Such art can attack the senses directly and vehemently transmit profound intimations of both order and disorder'.[4] The minimal self, states Lasch, in his book of same name, longs 'to merge into its environment in blissful union, or to remake the world'.[5] Overwhelmed by the cruelty, disorder and sheer complexity of modern history, the artist retreats into a state of uneasiness and chronic anxiety. The minimalist sensibility originates in a mood of retrenchment. By refusing to feel pain or pleasure, the artist has adopted the voice and eyes of a survivor.

In music, a search developed for a kind of objectivity, almost anonymity, in the use of pure sound alone. 'Music freed itself from artistry and taste, by excluding expression, drama, psychology'.[6] The origins of such a radical anti-music, in which little happens that is musical, allowing nothing but the auditory experience of pure sound, may have come from a rebellion against the super-organised serial music which dominated the avant-garde scene both in the United States and in Europe during the first half of this century. Evidently there was some human need missing from this highly organised, super-intellectual music which failed to satisfy the less intellectual listener. Milton Babbitt, for example, took this to extremes in advocating that the contemporary composer should prepare for a total withdrawal from the public world into one of private performance, completely eliminating the public. When the intricacies of serialism reached a level of confusing complexity and exclusivity, sated audiences turned to its opposite number – oversimplified accessible music with no continuity, and with forms that were not bound up with memory.

It may be useful at this point to examine some of the lines of continuity that link minimalism to some of its precursors such as John Cage. Cage was perhaps one of the first composers whose rebellion directed him to use minimalist techniques. Influenced as he was by Satie (whose *Vexations* for piano require a chord to be repeated 840 times), by abstract painting and Zen Buddhism, and by non-western ritual music, it is natural to attribute to him conceptual and indeterminate music which were the genesis of minimalism. Indeed Cage, as an extraordinary advocate of new methods and techniques, exercised a powerful influence on the avant-garde. One has but to note his early usage of 'prepared' piano and other instruments, attuning our ears to new pitches and to noise as musical sound; and his use of collage, of radio superimposed upon other instrumental sounds, or of musical excerpts and sound detritus combining to create a new phonic-metric experience.

Minimalists' preoccupation with eastern music, partly based on the search for more contemplative modes, may be traced back to Debussy's 'orientalism' which was readily absorbed into western music. Of particular significance were the raga and tala studies of Messiaen (*Technique de mon language musical*) which conceptualised more complex tonality and rhythmic strata for western ears – although ultimately, he too sounded more western than eastern. In the United States, Cowell, Hovhaness and Varèse experimented with trance-like, immobile harmonies, or melodic configurations which circled around a central tone, purporting to sober and quiet the mind. Eventually, even the supreme serialist, Stockhausen, was deeply impressed by the music of the orient, resulting in works of extreme contemplative withdrawal, like *Stimmung*, whose six singers repeat six electronic tones, unchangingly and immobile for 75 minutes, aiming to induce a yoga-like state of peaceful non-perception. As Terry Riley observed, the restless inquietude of European avant-garde music had never been able to give the world those moments of peace which were its greatest current need. Minimalists tend to have in common the use of eastern or African rhythms (Messiaen, Cowell), of Balinese instrumental timbres and tunings (gamelan music), and of microtonal scoring of small cellular motifs (Partch).

The blending of popular and classical styles, of jazz and serious music, are also a feature of minimalism. During the first half of this century there were experiments in this direction (notably by Stravinsky and Milhaud, by Copland and Weill) which developed later into a much more densely 'busy' music (in the hands of Berio, Foss, Rochberg, Davies and Crumb). This now added to its over-all complexity the inclusion of improvisation, quotes and collage effects. Berio's *Sinfonia* is an example of a multi-layered piece with a most complicated network of overlaid collages (employing instruments, noise, singing, chanting, speech, whispers, etc), which its composer explains as an exercise in the relativity of perception of music history. Its constant changes in textual comprehension, in multiple melodic fragmentation, in metrical confusion, all contribute to a state of frenzy in the listener. In structure and scale it is the very antithesis of minimalism but some of its technical preoccupations were undoubtedly an influence. No doubt, the breakdown of durational notation (Feldman's and Brown's graph pieces) and the introduction of indeterminacy also contributed to the rise of minimalism.

The relationship of minimalism to politics is complex. During the past three decades there has evolved an approach to music which implies that in order to be meaningful, music must be either directly political (or ecological) in orientation, or else divorce itself completely from life. New music, and the avant garde, has often been criticised for its tendency to avoid real concern for the ills of

the world. Some European composers, however, like
Henze, Nono and Cardew, viewed their writings in a
political light, recognising the artist as an outlaw in society,
an outcast and a dreamer, whose purpose was to incite
reactions and demonstrations while stressing the dehumani-
sation of contemporary life. They evidently agreed with
Langer that 'music is meant to evoke emotional response,
[which] at its highest, though clearly a symbolic form, is an
unconsummated symbol'.[7] That is to say, music may lack
any specific or programmatic content but still have powerful
transformative effects on the listener's consciousness. In the
United States, Cage presented this kind of strong political
involvement in his music. In a review of his work *HPSCHD*
in 1975 we are informed that the listeners are bombarded
with a mass of uncoordinated information which results in 'a
state of confusion, maximum isolation, loneliness – not an
attempt to bring order out of our chaos, but to wake us up to
our own life'.[8]

The rise of minimalism in America however is essentially
the rise of a non-intellectual movement. Although the
United States was founded by a group of intellectuals, such
as Adams, Franklin and Jefferson, throughout its history the
intellectual has been treated as an outsider.[9] Jefferson was
considered by his opponents as unfit for the presidency
because he was a philosopher who also indulged in multiple
intellectual interests and inventions. John Quincy Adams
was also regarded as unsuitable for office because he had
studied in European capitals and later taught at Harvard.
Franklin Roosevelt was the first president to employ
intellectuals as a body of experts in government, while
Kennedy's dinner honouring Nobel Prize winners at the
White House was without precedent. The Horace Greeley/
Andrew Carnegie type of untutored, yet rich and successful,
man was to remain the American stereotype well into the
first half of this century. Until the Second World War,
scholarship and arts were regarded as embellishments, while
teaching was considered an unmanly profession. Although
Dewey, the first educational philosopher, pleaded, earlier in
the century, for a well-rounded education as a preparedness
for life together with the ability 'to stretch the mind', the

Puritan code of practicality and the ideal of the independent, self-made man left little room for an intellectual tradition to develop. In a sense, then, the intellectual area always remained Europe. And to the American popular mind, Europe in the second half of this century continued to represent oppression while America represented freedom and vitality. Hence minimalism had a particular attraction for American composers. At the same time it is as well to be aware that this attraction is politically ambivalent and liable to be misunderstood by European commentators.

Historically, one of music's chief uses has been in the service of propaganda.[10] Plato advocated the teaching of 'the affirmative modes' for the education of a future elite, while Confucius felt music represented the ethical level of a people. Beethoven's only opera, *Fidelio*, dealt with the advocacy of civil liberties and feminine valour. 'Music', said Ilya Ehrenburg of Shostakovich's Eighth Symphony, 'without mentioning anything can say everything'. But in late 20th century Western Europe – as Adorno clearly recognised – this relationship can no longer be as straightforward and transparent.

Can the artistic mind function if it is bound up with a political ideology? Undoubtedly, in a totalitarian society the state plays a decisive role in the making of an art-work. 'Revolutionary songs lead to revolutionary action.'[11] Art must be carefully evaluated as to its message, lest it leave people discontented and render them unfit for the work of the State. Repressive societies tend to view artists as potentially politically dangerous types. For Shostakovich, for example, there could be no music without ideology, because music's purpose, according to Lenin, was to be a means of unifying the masses. One may also observe that in industrial societies order and harmony are prized in art, while in newly developing ones art is often encouraged to divert people from their hard labours.

In America, the music of the 60s was also politically oriented, as were the protest songs, dealing with alienation, racial bigotry, ecology, war, civil rights and similar temporally urgent subjects. The message the music conveyed was that people were not alone nor powerless. But in popular music it was the words, sung by the Beatles or Baez, which uniformly delivered the message rather than the music itself. Other music ridiculed conformity, or made us aware of our ecological losses, or addressed itself to student unrest and disillusionment. (Berio's quotes from rioting Sorbonne and Harvard students make the message of *Sinfonia* very potent.) Protest songs of that era were political confrontations – true propaganda. The contemporary composer became a social critic. Even in the Soviet Union, where Shostakovich and others suffered repression at one time or another, the composer still managed to communicate (as in his Thirteenth and Fourteenth Symphonies which dealt with 'unpopular' subjects such as death and holocausts) because of the significance of both the music and the message. In Europe, Henze and Nono's operas revealed powerful anti-war statements, while Penderecki dealt with both social and religious concerns in his *Threnody for the Victims of Hiroshima* and his *Dies Irae* recalling the horrors of Auschwitz. In the sphere of the arts, it now seemed that there could be no values which were completely independent, neutral or nonpolitical. In the 1960s, the social and moral aspects of music took precedence over aesthetic considerations. Music could no longer serve as an end in itself, but was required to express something extra-musical. Neumeyer's dictum of the 1950s, that 'art tends to move away from contemporary cultural realities, even to the point where the artist creates for himself worlds that have not existed before',[12] simply would not hold true, either in Soviet society, or in the world musical trends of the 1960s, until the rise of minimalism. This new music was undoubtedly radical in style and technique, but its political content was not so easily decipherable.

Since that time, the path taken by the minimalists has differed sharply from that of Cage. A great deal of Cage's music remained improvisatory or capable of being diagrammed or under-notated. The music of such minimalists as Reich or Glass is precisely notated, demanding a high level of control and coordination in its performance.

Disenchanted with the inaudible structural complexity and extreme difficulty of performance of serial music of the post-Webernian era, their recourse was to turn to simple structures whose repetition provided an ease of performance. By the early 70s the trend in this music was to create clear, elemental motifs, which grew and altered slightly over a long period of time, almost imperceptibly. (These somehow crept into the vocabulary of such former die-hard serialists as Boulez, Stockhausen and Ligeti.) In other words, minimalists were aiming for a fusion of the western concept of time, passing from one sound-structure to the next, with the eastern notion of cyclical phrases, circular return or simple stasis. It is interesting to note that so widespread has been the influence of this fusion, that even some of the younger Soviet composers (Schnittke, Pärt, and Martinev) share an interest in minimal techniques if not in its ideology. Schnittke predicted 'a meeting of styles in the future', indicating that 'composers who wrote very traditional music in the past now are eagerly assimilating new techniques'.[13]

This endlessly repetitive and meditative music is an attempt to express metaphysical ideas rather than to provide sensuous pleasure. It appeared first in the music of LaMonte Young, an experimental jazz musician whose ensemble, as early as 1962, performed stretches of sound of seemingly endless durations, often over a drone-bass. Creating a kind of 'dream music' of two or three frequencies which drifted aimlessly in a phase relationship, Young's purpose was to 'tune ourselves to the cosmos'. His *'Composition No. 7'*, in 1960, directs the performer to hold the tones of B and F-sharp 'for a long time'. His experiments were directed at creating electrophonically aural environments relating to Indian philosophy, much of which would leave the listener in a near catatonic state.

Terry Riley was at one time part of Young's ensemble of the Theatre of Eternal Music, where he also functioned as a solo improviser. His music is also made up of a few pitches and much repetition, sometimes, as in *A Rainbow in Curved Air*, preserving the tonal immobility by the use of perpetual *ostinati. In C*, with its 53 tiny motifs against a background of

C octaves, gives the effect of gradually changing figures proceeding through a landscape. A discernible difference in Riley's music was its encouragement of meditative improvisation over immensely long stretches of time to induce trance-like states, yet permitting the performer to begin or end the patterns wherever desired. Differing from other minimalist works in that it was participatory, it acted as a sort of musical hypnotism of the 60s, bypassing anecdotal meaning, so that, true to McLuhan, the message was in the medium.

Today, the most significant and dedicated minimalists are Philip Glass and Steve Reich. Both have refined and redefined the techniques of minimalism, meanwhile keeping open the bridges between pop and classical audience appeal. In the music of Glass, a melodic unit is established which alters and extends gradually over a period of time. By studying Eastern principles of music and the tabla with Ravi Shankar, Glass worked on adding, repeating, or removing units to produce harmonic stasis. Glass has his own ensemble which he trains to play simple patterns which change minutely and constantly. At the same time, his music is played rather loud and fast, producing a forward motion with apparent jerks where tiny metric changes occur. The result is very like Balinese gamelan music, combining additive procedures with cyclical patterns. Although it is harmonically static, the introduction of rudimentary counterpoint and textural density sets this apart from Riley's or Young's music. In a sense, it is an outgrowth of Ravel's *Bolero*, whose single melodic pattern is perpetually altered by timbral changes. In Glass's operas, notably *Einstein on the Beach*, the same process takes place, in this case for a duration of more than four hours!

Glass's operas centre around characters who represent historical and moral outlooks in society (*Satyagraha* in 1980 and *Akhnaton* in 1984), yet in his minimalist techniques he seems to join the crowd in repudiating the history of music; this means that ultimately he remains a slave to his own style. His music admits the existence of a harmony without any reference to western tradition; and at the same time it relates to pop groups in its deafening remorselessness, while rhythmic units fly by so fast that the players must concentrate and play with precision. And as someone once pointed out, a minimal piece by Glass lasting three hours might have no more 'happening' to the few pitches and rhythms than happens in a maximal piece by Webern lasting three minutes.

What is the clue to Glass's popularity? For one thing, his music is closer to rock, while his operas exhibit an open tunefulness. All transformations of the original motifs are easily perceived. In Glass's 1981 album, *Glassworks*, the materials and process can be described in the simplest terms: in 'Opening', the repeated piano soft minor triads gradually become seventh chords, using dynamics to promote a feeling of change. In 'Floe' the horns sustain tones while the orchestra gradually changes the chords, meanwhile building up a feeling of direction by sheer timbral accretions (flute, piano, organ, saxophones), until the piece ends abruptly. In 'Islands', repetitions of the motifs of flute and lower strings end in a decrescendo *al niente*. The very rapid arpeggios and mixed timbres of organ and saxophones lend it a more aggressive liveliness. 'Facades' has some of the loveliest sounds, while 'Closing' ends with the piano in mixed hemiola rhythms. One gets the impression of naïvety, of comprehending too easily. Only by literally sleeping through the music does one gain a sense of perceivable deeper layers of meaning. Reminiscent of looking at sepia photographs of one's family, the familiar seems misplaced in time. One can hardly believe that such simple music is to be taken seriously. The 'harmonic' resolutions to adjacent steps, a sort of secundal progression, gives a sense of medievalism, as do the slightly 'sweet' chromatic dissonances which dissolve immediately. Timbres of saxophone and clarinet in minor thirds lend it a 'Klezmor'-like quality. One feels that the sweet placid sounds are best appreciated when not listened 'to' but 'through'.

Steven Reich studied African drumming at the University of Ghana and also Balinese gamelan playing. His music creates a sense of naïvety and adherence to musical fundamentals similar to that of Glass. He differs from Glass in weaving continuous changes rather than abrupt alterations, producing what he calls 'psycho-acoustic byproducts of repetition and phrase shifting'. Its appeal and limitation, like that of Glass, lies in the simple repetition of pitches and rhythms. To Reich, the art of making the music is an end in itself: 'with everything happening slowly enough, there is no difference between the process and the piece'.[13] The slow changes, 'like sands running through an hourglass', form his response to the neuroses of an over-competitive society. A very effective description of Reich's musical aesthetic appears on a flyer advertising a recent London concert[14] of his music: 'Take a sound, any sound with a regular pulse. Take the same sound but a bit faster. Put them together: there's an overlapping, dovetailed pattern of pulses. And that is about as minimal as minimal music gets.' It is easy to understand why the concert was advertised as 'hauntingly hypnotic'.

Observe the process used in other works of his: *Clapping Music* – five minutes of two interwoven rhythms; *It's Gonna Rain* – based upon recorded loops of a preacher's voice with gradually shifting phrase relations between two or more identical repeating patterns; *Slow Motion Sound* – very gradually slowing down of a recorded sound to many times its original length without changing pitch or timbre; *Drumming* – in four sections without pause, lasting about 90 minutes, the use of four pairs of bongos with male voice, followed by three marimbas with female voices, then three glockenspiels, whistling and a piccolo, ending with all of these combined. The object of the piece is, first, the gradual substitution of beats for rests within a constantly repeating rhythmic cycle; secondly, the gradual changing of timbre while the rhythm and pitch remain constant; thirdly, the simultaneous combining of different timbres; and finally the use of the voice which imitates the pitch of the instruments.

Reich has written intelligently about his musical aesthetic and process – a phenomenon rare in young composers. Compared with Glass, Riley or Young, Reich seems to be the most intellectual and critical personality, trained in philosophy and natural sciences. Like Glass, he represents a cross-over phenomenon of replacing traditional audiences of serious and new music with masses who attend pop concerts, a convergence of elite and mass appeal. This, consequently, becomes a type of pop music for intellectuals. But Reich does not extrapolate himself from history, and openly acknowledges the influences of Perotin, Stravinsky, Baroque music's rhythmic propulsion, as well as jazz, rock, polyrhythms derived from African drumming, Indonesian gamelans, and lately, Hebrew cantillations of the Bible. In his rather thorough analyses of his own music, he writes of his interest in music 'which works exclusively with gradual changes in time ... I am interested in a perceptible process. I want to hear the process happening throughout the sounding music ... the distinctive thing about musical processes is that they determine the note-to-note [relationship] – think of a round, or an infinite canon ... my musical structures are rigorously organised in advance, with little or no improvisation by the performer'.[16]

Later he states his belief that 'non-western music is presently the single most important source of new ideas for western composers', with its basically different systems of rhythmic structure, scale construction, tuning and instrumental techniques. He also advocates a strong preference for live performance over electronic sounds, and believes that aural or rote teaching is better than teaching from scores exclusively. Reich predicts that non-western music will serve as new structural models for western musicians: 'Schools should offer instruction in the practice and theory of all the world's music'. He favours meticulously worked out scores.

After 1976, Reich started to compose lengthier melodies made up of smaller units. An intensive study of Hebrew and Torah cantillations had a profound effect upon his musical style. His adoption of traditional melody was an indication of his abandonment of strict minimalism, for in 1980 he wrote of the importance of studying the past, particularly that of one's own traditions. Reich created a new style in his setting of Psalms in Hebrew, notably in the work *Tehillim* written in 1982. He creates a historical distance by using ancient Hebrew, and now abandons excessive repetition of small units. Constructive forms are employed here, canon and variation being the dominant ones. Despite the ambiguous modality, a feeling of tight organisation pervades the work, especially as each verse is conceived as an independent canon. Setting four women's voices with six woodwinds, six percussions, two electronic organs and five amplified strings, his canonic imitations are so well-wrought that it appears that the melodic lines gradually grow longer. It is composed 'of short repeating patterns with no fixed metre … the rhythm comes directly from the words'.[17] It is well set. His extension of melodic lines, use of imitative counterpoint, functional harmony and full orchestration suggests renewed interest in earlier western musical practices. The non-vibrato vocal part is reminiscent of music prior to 1750. Word painting abounds: for example, the word for 'good' in Hebrew ends in an A-flat major triad while the word meaning 'perverse' is set in C-sharp minor with a G-natural tritone. What could be more Bach-like? In the final section and the Hallelujah part, only four tones are used: G,A,D,E, which, repeated in 4-part canons, yield areas of D minor, C major, G major and D major. Reich explains that, 'the text demands this type of setting. I use repetition as a technique when that is where my musical intuition leads me'.

Reich represents the minimalist who has come full circle from serialism. His reply to Babbitt's earlier quoted pessimism and withdrawal from the world is eloquently stated: 'I believe that music does not exist in a vacuum … I rely on … the popular, naïve reaction … My work and that of Glass and Riley comes as a breath of fresh air to the new music world'. How right he is!

Beyond rebellion, minimalism today represents a critical reaction to the condition of humanity in a complex and uncontrolled society. Despite its ability to offer escape, its true power lies in its affirmation of the value of clear structures and rigorously planned processes. And it has put us in touch, directly and simply, with the music of a large part of the world which the west would otherwise have made no attempt to explore or comprehend. At the very least, it has been a learning experience about cultures and philosophies very remote from our own. At best, it may offer composers a richer, composite language for music of the future.

Notes

[1] Ad Reinhardt, 'Twelve Rules for a New Academy', Whitney Museum catalogue, New York 1957.

[2] Symposium at Windham College, Putney, Vermont 1968.

[3] Alfred Neumeyer, *Search for Meaning in Modern Art*, Prentice Hall, Englewood, New Jersey 1964, p 52.

[4] Daniel Mendelowitz, *History of American Art*, Holt, Rhinehardt, New York 1970, p 456.

[5] Christian Lasch, *The Minimal Self*, Norton, New York 1984.

[6] *Ibid*, quoting Christian Wolff, pp 164-5.

[7] Suzanne Langer, *Philosophy in a New Key*, Mentor Books, New York 1948, pp 176, 195.

[8] *Musical Times*, London, January 1975.

[9] Richard Hofstadter, *Anti-Intellectualism in American Life*, Knopf, New York, p 145.

[10] Arnold Perris, *Music as Propaganda*, Greenwood, Westport 1985, pp 4,67.

[11] Howard Becker, *Art Worlds*, University of California Press 1982, p 166.

[12] Neumeyer, *op cit*, p 2.

[13] Claire Polin, 'Interviews with Soviet Composers', *Tempo*, London, December 1984, p 13.

[14] Steve Reich, 'Music as a Gradual Process', *Perspectives of New Music*, Princeton University Press, Vol xix, pp 373-92.

[15] By the Contemporary Music Network.

[16] Steve Reich, 'Writings about Music', *Perspectives of New Music*, Princeton University Press, Vols. xix and xx, pp 38-61.

[17] Review of Reich by Koch in *Tempo*, June 1984.

David Matthews

The Rehabilitation of the Vernacular

In the scherzo of his Second String Quartet, the work in which he brought tonality to its breaking point, Schoenberg unexpectedly quotes the well-known Viennese popular song 'O, du lieber Augustin'. There are compelling personal reasons for this quotation. At the time he was writing the quartet, Schoenberg's wife Mathilde had left him to live with the painter Richard Gerstl, from whom Schoenberg had been taking painting lessons. The tune and its bass contain hidden references to the names Arnold Schoenberg, Mathilde and Richard,[1] and the significance of the repeated refrain 'Alles is hin' ('it's all over') is obvious. But we can hardly help reading a different meaning into 'Alles ist hin'. For the new language that Schoenberg was nurturing in his Second Quartet, and which would soon burst into ripely-perfumed flower in the Five Orchestral Pieces and *Erwartung*, would have no use for simple diatonic melodies like 'O, du lieber Augustin'. For Schoenberg at least, the vernacular language of popular and folk music, which had stood behind the melodies of European art music until the end of the nineteenth century, was indeed over.

Schoenberg proposed his new totally chromatic language as a complete substitute for diatonicism ('every expression and characterization can be produced with the style of free dissonance'[2]). Unlike Webern, who soon began to advance a stage further, towards athematicism, Schoenberg continued to regard melody as a vital element, both in his 'free atonal' music and in his twelve-note music. In his essay 'Heart and Brain in Music', he proudly quotes the twelve-note theme of the Intermezzo of the Third String Quartet alongside the E major theme of the slow movement of the First Quartet as examples of melodies from the heart.[3] Schoenberg's earliest pieces (for example the D major string quartet) were firmly diatonic, and his mastery of diatonic melody may be heard in a tune such as 'So tanzen die Engel' from *Gurrelieder*. But in choosing to develop Wagnerian chromatic language, Schoenberg soon left diatonicism behind. In Wagner's mature music there is no sense of chromaticism *replacing* diatonicism; rather, the two languages are used for different purposes. On the one hand there is a diatonic language rooted in the vernacular and used for such elemental statements as the Sword motive from *The Ring*; on the other, an unprecedentedly heightened chromatic language of the emotions. Wagner dramatically juxtaposes the two languages, above all in *Parsifal*, where the diatonicism of Faith eventually triumphs over the chromaticism of personal anguish and sin. In Schoenberg's early music there is a similar, and effective, juxtaposition: for instance in the scherzo of the First Quartet, with its sturdy, almost folk-like main theme standing out against a densely chromatic background. The straightforwardness of this light-hearted theme, which at times dances for joy (see pp 29-31 of the score) is in strong contrast to the use of 'O, du lieber Augustin' three years later: Schoenberg can now use the vernacular only for satirical purposes.

Schoenberg's new totally chromatic language was developed by his successors – above all by Webern and Boulez – to a point where the vernacular is no longer even a ghostly memory – as it is, poignantly, in some Schoenberg works, such as *Pierrot Lunaire* or *A Survivor from Warsaw*. In his didactic writings Boulez has, with characteristic Gallic severity, excluded all those who did not follow the narrow paths of modernist orthodoxy that lead to himself – through Schoenberg and Webern on the one hand, and Debussy and Messiaen on the other – from serious consideration. But Schoenberg was the only major composer of the early

twentieth century to take such a deterministic view of
musical history. Other composers continued to make use of
the musical vernacular in various ways. Nationalists such as
Bartók, Stravinsky (before he turned to neo-classicism),
Vaughan Williams and Janáček consciously exploited the
folk music of their own countries as a basis for melody.
Many composers, including Stravinsky, Hindemith and
Tippett, were attracted by the new vernacular language of
jazz, and a few outstanding composers emerged who were
totally immersed in the jazz and popular music world:
Gershwin, Ellington, Weill. Some composers continued to
write as if there was no early twentieth-century crisis at all:
outstanding among them was Britten. By the 1960s,
however, most European composers found themselves in
Schoenberg's position in 1908, either totally divorced from
the vernacular or else able to use it only in nostalgic or ironic
quotation.

In this essay I shall consider whether the vernacular has
any future in European art music. My starting point is
Deryck Cooke's *The Language of Music*, a book that greatly
influenced me in the 1960s. Cooke wrote *The Language of
Music* in the late 1950s in response to Stravinsky's notorious
dictum that 'music is, by its very nature, powerless to *express*
anything at all, whether a feeling, an attitude of mind, a
psychological mood'.[4] This was then a fashionable attitude.
As a Romantic who had grown up in an anti-Romantic
period, Cooke was concerned to revalidate a theory of music
that upheld the primacy of expression. From a distance we
can now see that Cooke's and Stravinsky's attitudes to music
are complementary rather than conflicting. Stravinsky's
statement is consistent with his intention as a confirmed
anti-Romantic to suppress emotion in his music. The
awesome monumentality of Stravinsky's finest music was a
result of this deliberate suppression. Cooke's attitude as a
Romantic, which leads him to associate music closely with
life, does not invalidate his basic perception of music as a
language of the emotions. But Cooke went further, in
suggesting that music can communicate emotion in a precise
manner; that there are certain 'basic terms of musical
vocabulary' which operate in a way analogous to verbal

language. These terms – intervals, melodic phrases – have been used again and again by Western composers from the late middle ages up to the present and, he claimed, they have particular intrinsic emotional meanings. But in attempting to name the emotions these musical phrases express, many critics of the book – and I would agree with them – have felt that Cooke went too far. Mendelssohn was right when he said that what is expressed in music is too definite to be put into words: Cooke was asking musical language to yield up something that should not be demanded of it. As his friend Hans Keller pointed out, conceptual thought is always hostile to musical thought: Mozartian 'tragedy', as in the G minor symphony or the D minor quartet, is always sharply distinguishable from tragedy itself.[5] Keller nonetheless accepted the general validity of Cooke's theory; and certainly an essential part of the theory, that there exists – or at any rate existed – a vernacular language from which almost all composers have derived the basic building material for their music is, I believe, confirmed by the many music examples Cooke produces to support it.

Cooke was pessimistic about the future of the musical language he had tried to codify. In two subsequent articles for *The Listener* (reprinted in *Vindications*, the posthumous collection of his essays), he observed, to his personal regret, that most young composers were taking the non-vernacular path instead of following those composers such as Britten or Shostakovich whose music was still based on the vernacular. For Cooke, Schoenberg's new musical language was an unsatisfactory substitute for the old language. Cooke compared it to Joyce's artificial language in *Finnegans Wake*, noting that whereas the majority of writers had not chosen to follow Joyce but still continued to use comprehensible English, in music this had not been the case. In order to find a fresh and lively contemporary use of the vernacular, Cooke had to resort to popular music, and in particular to the innovative music then being written (this was 1968) by the Beatles.[6]

Cooke's views on contemporary music are shared by many of the concert-going public to whom Webern and Boulez are as inaccessible as *Finnegans Wake*. Which may mean nothing more than that Webern's or Boulez's music, like *Finnegans Wake*, is likely to remain a minority interest, because there is no immediately accessible surface layer in Webern or Boulez as there is, for instance, in a Mozart symphony. The majority of the concert-going public, it can be argued, are as likely to miss the deeper, structural level in Mozart as in Boulez. But is the surface layer – the melodic line – of a Mozart symphony superficial? Hardly; Mozart's melodies are the keys that give access to the deeper levels in his music. Beethoven's late quartets are arguably the richest and deepest works of music in existence: Joseph Kerman has noted how Beethoven's frequent use of recitative in the late quartets 'testifies to the overpowering strength of his need for immediacy of address';[7] he also points out that in the dance movements the thematic material is often very simple and close in style to popular music: 'We are to respond to these childlike strains as unguardedly as children to nursery rhymes, we are to be swept away by the *Volkston* of the half-dainty, half-clownish country dance.'[8]

The loss of such accessible, singable melody in the music of Schoenberg and his successors is a devastating blow to its comprehensibility, and also a limitation to its comprehensiveness. To return for a moment to the two Schoenberg string quartet melodies referred to earlier: without trying to evaluate them as melodies, there is no doubt that few of those who can sing the First Quartet's tune would also be able to sing the Third's. Fewer still would be able to sing any melody by Webern or Boulez. Again, does this matter? I believe, with Deryck Cooke, that it does; there is something very wrong with contemporary music if its melodies cannot be sung by those who can sing Mozart's or Wagner's or the young Schoenberg's.

> But there is nothing I long for more intensely (if for anything) than to be taken for a better sort of Tchaikovsky – for heaven's sake: a bit better, but really that's all. Or if anything more, then that people should know my tunes and whistle them.[9]

Schoenberg again, writing to Hans Rosbaud in 1947. A sad

letter, and an unrealistic hope; for the melodies of contemporary music will be whistled in the street only if there is a return to the vernacular.

During the last twenty years a number of developments have taken place which have brought about a *rapprochement* with the vernacular, if not the radical renewal of melody which is contemporary music's most urgent need. An entirely new music based on the vernacular has appeared, that of the American minimalists. It began as a reaction against what were felt to be the excesses of European modernism, and therefore made a point of reverting to the simplest possible means of expression: the first significant piece of minimalist music is Terry Riley's *In C* which, taking up Schoenberg's famous aphorism with a vengeance, never moves from that key in its half-hour (or more) duration. In recent pieces by the outstanding minimalist composer so far, Steve Reich, such as *The Desert Music*, modal and chromatic harmony is developed to a more sophisticated level; though Reich's melodies, like all minimalist melodies, remain primitive, and subordinate to the insistent rhythmic ostinati which are his chief concern. Nor has a solution to the melodic problem been found by other American neo-tonalists. In David Del Tredici's huge piece for soprano and orchestra, *Final Alice*, it is the virtuosity of the orchestration and the sheer effrontery of the concept that impress; the melodic material is obsessionally restricted, a single, intentionally banal tune being repeated endlessly over and over again.

But here at least is another musical language based entirely on the vernacular, and though it is almost wholly late-Romantic pastiche, it is pastiche raised to such an extraordinary level that it becomes something altogether different. Del Tredici's mixture of innocence and irony, and his outrageous musical punning, have something in common with the later songs of The Beatles. Reich's music too has affinities with rock music. Its relaxed, hedonistic tone is close to The Beach Boys, who were also discovering harmony afresh in the 1960s, with stunning results on the small scale (for example 'God only knows' or 'Surf's up'). More recently, Reich has had a productive influence on the music of Laurie Anderson, whose records seem to demonstrate that minimalism is at its most effective in a popular context – though Reich himself (not to mention his downmarket disciple Philip Glass) is something of a cult figure, with a larger following than any composer in Europe.

Much recent European music shows a renewed relationship with the past that is partly nostalgic, certainly; but more importantly there has been a wish to rehabilitate much of what was lost in modernism's exclusive striving for purity. I hesitate to call this music postmodern, since I am emphasising here a creative dialogue with the past, and with tradition; whereas the tendency of postmodernism is to what Denis Donoghue has called a 'promiscuous cool', where allusions are simply decorative, and devoid of content or meaning. In this country, Robin Holloway's music is passionately involved with the past, and especially with nineteenth-century Romanticism. Holloway is by temperament himself a Romantic, sharing many of the Romantics' ideals, tastes and aspirations; but he can also look on their world with scholarly detachment, and it is in the tension between identification and detachment that much of the fascination of his music lies. Holloway has often deliberately composed with what he calls 'commonplaces of tonality' – melodic and harmonic clichés, scraps of the vernacular; and his work is full of wryly affectionate glances at favourite pieces. His introduction of irony as a check on excessive emotion recalls Del Tredici, with whom he shares a taste for occasional shock effects. Two slightly older composers, Alexander Goehr and Nicholas Maw, have widened their vocabulary to include much more explicit references to tonality. Goehr's music has evolved distinctively from its Schoenbergian starting-point: in the last ten years he has become preoccupied with the fugue, and in doing so has sometimes chosen to use a modal language which has drawn him more closely and comprehensively within the contrapuntal tradition. Maw's latest work, his vast symphonic poem *Odyssey*, contains a slow movement of Brucknerian dimensions and scope, with an eloquent main theme in a clear G sharp minor, harmonized in triads, that goes straight to the heart. Maw has long been concerned with the rediscovery of musical archetypes – singable melodies, dance rhythms, tonal harmonies – which can be used in new ways while retaining their traditional resonance. Using a language capable of broad, generous gestures, Maw aims to restore a sense of wholeness to music; he rightly sees that a language such as that of Boulez, a language of the nerve-ends, remote from music's origins in dance and song, cannot become universal.

Some quotations from other European composers will indicate a correspondence of ideas, an area of mutual agreement. From Kurt Schwertsik:

> We need to learn to understand once again the roots of that compact which for millenia made possible the comprehension and the appreciation of music. If we do not succeed in reinvigorating these roots, then sooner or later the genre of so-called serious music will cease to be 'contemporary' at all.[10]

From his compatriot H K Gruber:

> For my part, I can only say that I try to give the attentive listeners the clearest possible signals, especially in complex situations. Ultimately, simplicity is always the ideal, but comprehensibility is the first objective ...[11]

And Alfred Schnittke:

> Contemporary reality will make it necessary to experience all the musics one has heard since childhood, including rock and jazz and classical and all other forms, combining them into a synthesis. This has not happened in my generation ... The synthesis must arise as a natural longing, or through necessity.[12]

Gruber and Schnittke have both written violin concertos in which tonal epiphanies emerge at the end as calm resolutions. In Gruber's Concerto, the concluding E major statement of a popular song of his own parallels the 'Es ist genug' of Berg's Violin Concerto, as David Drew has noted[13] (and Berg's Concerto is itself a key work in the rehabilitation of the vernacular). Schnittke's Third Concerto also resembles Berg's in following its central climax, which is its point of maximum tension, with a C major clarinet

melody in limpid thirds and sixths that recalls Brahms or
Mahler. Other Schnittke pieces have similar benedictory
endings: the Piano Quintet; or the Second String Quartet, a
memorial piece for a friend, whose material is taken from
sixteenth- and seventeenth-century Russian church music
and whose ending, again in C major (Schnittke has made this
key as much his own as did Britten) reaches heavenward in
almost unattainable violin and viola harmonics.

Minimalism has its European practitioners, though it has
been chiefly an American phenomenon: it seems more
natural for Americans to cast off tradition and begin anew,
just as America is the natural home of born-again religious
sects. In Britain composers who work with simple means are
loosely grouped under the 'Experimental Music' label; one
of the best of them, Howard Skempton, has produced some
perfect miniatures comparable to Beach Boys' or Beatles'
songs.

Whatever the limitations of minimalism, and they are
considerable, for the heights and depths of music seem
beyond its scope, the cross-fertilisation between 'serious'
and 'popular' languages is one of its attractions. But can
rock, which is fast becoming a popular musical language for
the entire world, be of real value to other 'serious'
composers today, as Schnittke hopes? One may regret the
passing of folk-song, the old vernacular, as a living tradition,
and envy composers in those few isolated areas of Europe
where it is still a vital force in the musical culture (in
Moravia, for instance, where the present generation of
composers in Brno are still able to draw on the tradition that
nourished their great predecessor, Janáček, at the
beginning of the century). In this country, traditional
folk-song had ceased to be a vital force by the 1930s, at
about the same time that Vaughan Williams was writing that
folk-song must be 'the foundation on which all our art must
rest'.[14] Folk-song did not, however, simply disappear into
the museum culture of the Cecil Sharp Society and morris
dancing. In the 1950s and 1960s, young people began to
revive folk music at the same time as they began to listen to
and to play rock, the new popular music derived from black
American blues and white Country and Western music.

Blues, rock and folk-song from Britain and North America united into a common new vernacular language. It is a true vernacular, for its new music has largely been written by the musicians who play and sing it, unlike the popular music of the first half of the century which was for the most part the product of non-executant composers.

The last major British composer to use folk-song as a foundation for his music was Tippett; but Tippett was also deeply affected by 1920s blues and jazz, and an intriguing feature of the Concerto for Double String Orchestra, for instance, is its dual vernacular background in folk-song and jazz – as well as Elizabethan madrigal and eighteenth-century concerto grosso.[15] Tippett's incorporation of folk-song and blues into his music of the 1930s was part of a conscious desire to popularise his musical language, to try to make it accessible to the working class with whom he was at that time politically involved. Perceptively, Tippett came to see blues and rock as a viable alternative vernacular to folk-song, and several of his works of the last twenty years demonstrate this belief. In the Third Symphony, the last movement contains a 'transmogrification' (Arnold Whittall's term) of Bessie Smith's version of the 'St Louis Blues', with Louis Armstrong's cornet solo metamorphosed into a flugelhorn that also carries echoes of Miles Davis. The music has become entirely Tippett's own, but its background in a blues he especially loves is as magically potent as Beethoven's references to popular song in his late quartets (and the passage is given still richer allusive meaning by the specific modelling of the movement on the finale of Beethoven's Ninth Symphony).

I think it is fair to say that Tippett is less happy with rock than he is with blues, because he did not grow up with it. I find the electric guitar – together with an attempt at Dylanesque language – introduced into *The Knot Garden* and *Songs for Dov* faintly embarrassing, though I warm to Tippett's intentions. My own generation, those born during and immediately after the Second World War, encountered the beginnings of rock as we were emerging from childhood into adolescence, and for many of us it was a crucial event. Some of my earliest genuine musical experiences were of hearing mid-1950s rock – Elvis Presley and Little Richard: the effect on me of this wildly orgiastic music, so different from anything I had encountered in my cosy suburban childhood, was overwhelming. The Beatles were hearing and absorbing this music at the same time, as well as other kinds of popular music, including folk-songs and sea shanties that were still sung in Liverpool pubs. One of the earliest recorded Beatles' songs, 'I saw her standing there' is, as Wilfrid Mellers has remarked, pure folk monody: an utterly simple four-note melody with prominent flattened sevenths.[16] It was through songs like this that my generation was reintroduced to the folk tradition.

Exactly how composers of my own and younger generations should make use of the vernacular that is embedded in our consciousness I am not going to try to prescribe, except that I am certainly not advocating a crude fusion of rock and 'serious' music of the kind that is occasionally indulged in by over-ambitious rock groups. But I am convinced that the solution to the problem of melody in contemporary music will come from some kind of reintegration of the contemporary vernacular. Twenty or thirty years ago such an idea would not have been seriously proposed; modernism seemed to hold the only possible answers. Today, modernism may be seen in perspective as a historical movement whose apex has passed, and whose most notable achievements, such as Webern's late works, Boulez's *Le marteau sans maître*, Ligeti's *Atmosphères*, can be objectively judged as attempts to pursue particular areas of experiment to their limits. And it must be recognised that if music as a whole is, as Deryck Cooke defined it, 'primarily and basically a language of the emotions, through which we directly experience the fundamental urges that move mankind',[17] then the areas that modernism has chosen to explore are marginal to human experience, and can only be of marginal interest. Mankind's fundamental urges seem at the moment to be more the concern of rock music than of 'serious' music; yet rock is, by its nature, severely limited in its ability to treat them. But there seems now no reason why contemporary musical language should not once again be able to communicate with more than a handful of initiates. If

Deryck Cooke were alive today (and his premature death ten years ago was an irreparable loss to British musical life), he would, I am certain, have far less reason for disillusion.[18]

Notes

[1] See Michael Graubert, *Tempo* 111, December 1974, pp 47-8.

[2] Arnold Schoenberg, *Style and Idea*, Faber 1975, p 245.

[3] *Ibid*, pp 70 and 74.

[4] Igor Stravinsky, *An Autobiography*, Norton 1962, p 53.

[5] Hans Keller, *Music Analysis* 2: 2, 1983, p 228.

[6] Deryck Cooke, 'The Lennon-McCartney Songs', in *Vindications*, Faber, 1982, pp 196-200. Cooke's analysis of 'Yesterday' is the best writing on The Beatles I know.

[7] Joseph Kerman, *The Beethoven Quartets*, Oxford University Press 1967, p 199.

[8] *Ibid*, p 201.

[9] *Arnold Schoenberg Letters*, edited by Erwin Stein, Faber 1964, p 243.

[10] Kurt Schwertsik, 'Looking into the Mirror', *Tempo* 161/2, June and September 1987, p 67.

[11] H K Gruber, 'Conversations in Berlin', *Tempo* 131, December 1979, p 3.

[12] Alfred Schnittke, *Tempo* 151, December 1984, p 11.

[13] David Drew, 'H K Gruber', *Tempo* 126, September 1978, p 22.

[14] Ralph Vaughan Williams, *National Music and Other Essays*, Oxford University Press 1963, p 40.

[15] See Wilfrid Mellers's illuminating comments on this work in his essay 'Song and Dance Man', in *Michael Tippett: A Celebration*, The Baton Press 1985, pp 28-9.

[16] Wilfrid Mellers, *Twilight of the Gods*, Faber 1973, pp 34-5.

[17] Deryck Cooke, *The Language of Music*, Oxford University Press 1959, p 272.

[18] The rehabilitation of the vernacular has continued since this essay was written in 1987, and I should like to mention two more British composers whose use of the vernacular in recent pieces has been especially interesting: Judith Weir, whose basically diatonic musical language draws on various folk musics, including her native Scottish, and whose opera *A Night at the Chinese Opera* has a Brittenish clarity and melodic freshness; and Jonathan Lloyd, whose Fourth Symphony, for instance, is an intriguing collage of simple diatonic fragments and references to popular music and jazz.

Alan Durant

Improvisation in the Political Economy of Music

Improvisation in Music and Society

Perhaps more than any other aspect of music-making today, improvisation questions dominant directions of musical change, fully across what are often conceived as discrete, separate forms: classical, jazz, folk, pop. As a procedure, it raises fundamental issues by putting continuously into question – moment by moment, within the activity of music-making itself – the processes of deciding what to play and how to organise or shape musical events or performances. As a social practice, through its challenge to the production and distribution of music in commodified forms, it questions how relationships of music-making are to be represented: economically, legally and aesthetically. These are genuinely fundamental concerns for a whole formation of music, since together these aspects of procedure and practice, rather than matters of form alone, make up the basic parameters of what 'music' is.

To some degree, improvisation exists within virtually all forms of music. But the 'fundamentalist' capacity it possesses to reach down to foundational decisions and processes of music-making is, in its clearest forms, a recent phenomenon. During the last 25 years of Western music, improvisation has emerged from its role of being merely one dimension of music which is for the most part composed and notated, to become a specific form in itself: improvised music, 'free collective improvisation', 'free jazz'. Over two decades, it has opposed tendencies which conceive of music less as a social process than in terms of kinds of resulting representation or 'text': as a series of compositions, records, videos. By contrast, improvised music foregrounds – in its practice as well as in its name – the relationship between the *product* of performance (the musical 'text') and the *process* through which that product comes into being: it sets the notion of music as something to which you listen back in the context of music made by someone. As something people do for themselves, too, improvisation stresses independent activity rather than passive consumption. For these reasons, improvisation plays a central part in the process of transition (as Jacques Attali outlines in *Noise: The Political Economy of Music*) from a current period of 'repeating' into what Attali calls (slightly paradoxically, given the importance to it of improvisation) the coming period of 'composing'.[1]

The challenge posed by improvised music might thus be thought to have large-scale political or epochal reverberations, linked to changing circumstances in which music is produced, circulated and heard. The advent of recording technology and broadcasting earlier in the century led not only to the development of new audiences, but also to new kinds of musical *text*: the record, the broadcast, the music tape and cassette, more recently the music video. In doing so, they introduced what Attali has called the order of 'repetition'. At the same time, in a process common to many technological developments where the technology is redirected towards purposes other than those for which it was originally foreseen, recording technology made possible new creative relationships in the making of those new kinds of text: shared creative composition directly into recorders; recorded (and so fixed and replicable) spontaneous extemporisation; selection and discussion in editing after the take. These areas of practice produced a pressure against dominant directions stimulated by the technology, and by the interests of those developing the technology. Partly in consequence of, and partly in opposition to, those major directions, techniques of production, as well as conditions of ownership and rights over music, continue to change. As they do so, they establish new institutions for funding and royalty collection. In turn, these new conditions mark out for musicians different and changing positions in their music through a series of complicated realignments and struggles. Together, such processes can be thought of as actively redefining the music industry within broader terms of national and international economies of leisure and entertainment.

Changes in technologies and institutions of music influence musical styles, and so have an effect on what we understand by idiom or genre. Musical forms themselves, which we generally take to be the stuff of music, are always the result of complex conditions and determining process of the kind described above. So as music is heard and played differently or in new circumstances (eg, in new forms of amateur or domestic performance, as well as on radio, as television soundtrack, and as musak in shopping malls) it is not surprising that various kinds of crossover take place between 'high' music traditions (eg opera, concert music) and 'popular' music (eg, jazz, rock, pop). This kind of formal hybridisation has the effect of changing our ideas and connotations of particular musical styles, and leads to major redirections in our understanding of what musical *form* is, of what *audiences* – giving what kinds of attention – music is addressed to, and of what type of *representation* music should or might make of other levels or concerns of modern societies.

It is precisely the relations between music and other levels of social formations which improvisation, perhaps more than any other aspect of music-making today, investigates and disrupts. We already know that relations between music and society are more complicated than those of simple determination or reflection. Reflection theorists claim that music, as a part of ideology more generally, is a reflection of real economic relations; but the interpenetration of economic, aesthetic and ideological aspects of music suggests a more complicated and difficult relationship – a changed conception which has major implications for both musical practice and theory. Jacques Attali's work provides an interesting example of the kind of shift in theory to which this changing theoretical perspective might lead. Attali avoids the reductionism inherent in the idea of music as simply a 'reflection' of the economic level, whilst still linking music with the social infrastructure. He divides the history of music into four periods with differing modes of organisation which represent simultaneously fundamental forms of social structure or order ('sacrificing', 'representing', 'repeating', 'composing'). Far from suggesting that music *reflects* what is happening at a more basic, economic level of society, Attali argues that music can be an important premonitory guide to changes *about to happen* in society:

> Music is more than an object of study: it is a way of perceiving the world. A tool of understanding. [...] My intention here is thus not only to theorise *about* music, but to theorise *through* music. The result will be unusual and unacceptable conclusions about music and society, the past and the future.[2]

Difficulties common to both the 'reflectionist' and 'prefigurativist' positions remain, of course. Codes of interpretation connecting different aspects of social formations work through systems of metaphor rather than by virtue of literal identity or resemblance: 'dissonance' and 'harmony' in society do not necessarily correspond directly to 'dissonance' and 'harmony' in music. To take music as possessing properties such that it 'heralds' or is 'prophetic'[3] is to mediate the relationship between music and society through conventions of a historically and regionally specific musical rhetoric. (The very idea of such 'communicative' rhetorics invokes questions about the possibility of music being a kind of 'language' at all.)[4] Even as it points beyond reflectionism Attali's work sidesteps the central problem of analysing the explanatory power of the interpretative rhetoric it provides. Summing up the task of new kinds of music commentary for the future, Attali simply affirms: 'What must be constructed, then, is more like a map, a structure of interferences and dependencies between society and its music'.[5]

Questions of rhetoric afflict all representations of music and its interventions in other levels of social practice and understanding. If improvisation appears to offer possibilities for a fundamental questioning and alteration of current ways of conceiving music, it is therefore important to examine the ideologies of music-making it embodies as much as those it opposes, and to explore the systems of musical representation by which arguments for it are underpinned. In the comments which follow, I will try to work through some of the main forms of argument which have grown up around improvisation in recent years. I will consider less those arguments which concern improvisation as a procedure integral to music-making based principally on composition than those which see it as an autonomous and revolutionary aesthetic form, 'improvised music'. In order to do this it will be necessary nevertheless to refer at a number of points to practices of improvisation within established idioms of composed music. My reason for focusing on abstract arguments surrounding this area of music, rather than cataloguing styles or achievements of particular performers, is that if – as I have suggested above – improvised music challenges conventional distinctions between musical form and political practice, then considering the premisses of this specialised area of activity serves to explore political dimensions of contemporary music more generally.

The Word 'Improvisation'

The term 'improvisation' itself frequently complicates musical discussion. Having interviewed a wide range of improvising musicians from very different spheres of musical activity (including organ music, flamenco, jazz, Indian classical music, etc), the improviser Derek Bailey suggests that the word 'improvisation' is actually disliked and even avoided by improvising musicians:

> There is a noticeable reluctance to use the word and some improvisers express a positive dislike for it. I think this is due to its widely accepted connotations which imply that improvisation is something without preparation and without consideration, a completely ad hoc activity, frivolous and inconsequential, lacking in design and method.[6]

It is worth beginning, therefore, by trying to account for the difficulties presented simply by the word itself.

Etymologically, the word 'improvisation' comes from a Latin past participle, *improvisus* (related to the verb *providere*, to foresee). In classical Latin, *improvisus* had the sense of 'unforeseen'. The word passed into Italian, and also into French, where it produced a verb, *improviser*, to act without foresight or foreplanning, usually used in the context of some kind of artistic invention. In English, the word did not gain currency in the vocabulary of music-making until the late 18th and early 19th century. At that time, it arrived as part of a larger borrowing of specifically artistic loan-words. At first, 'improvisation' carried the neutral sense of musical extemporisation, or extempore performance of poetry or ballads with extensive embellishment or elaboration. By the 1850s, however, the word had also acquired a negatively valorised sense, that of 'the production or execution of anything off-hand', or 'doing things spontaneously, on the spur of the moment', with an implication that the degree of preparation is insufficient (cf, 'an improvised shelter', 'an improvised solution').

Another complication in the word also existed from its earliest loan usages; that 'improvisation' is ambiguous, as a possible reference to either a process, or to a product (the end-result of that process). The word can be used to indicate either a procedure for the activity of *making* music, or a concrete *piece* of music that has been achieved through extemporisation. (In this respect, the words 'improvisation' and 'composition' have important parallels, as well as the more usually noted important semantic contrasts.)

These changing senses of the word cause difficulty in modern discussions of musical practice. For example, the attitudinally marked sense affects discussions of financial reward for largely or completely improvised music-making. It is sometimes used – in conjunction with appeals to the requirement of very specialised musical training and rehearsal for other kinds of music-making – to discredit improvised performers on the question of parity of fees with other musicians. It is frequently the connotations of the word, as much as any developed argument about music or preparation for performance, which are making the case.

A similar problem arises as a result of the distinction between process and product. The sense of a set of procedures for an activity – involving interactive relationships between participants – collides with the fact that with the product 'improvisation' – the piece of improvised music performed or recorded – you only know about the interactive, creative relationships by inference. What is for the performer a matter of process and practice is for the listener a completed *form* which unfolds through time, as composed music also does. Participating in an improvisation differs quite fundamentally from listening to one; and this drives an important wedge between two aspects of contemporary practice which are often assumed, usually without argument, to be directly complementary. In addition, for the listener it is often very difficult (even impossible) to distinguish whether a piece of music was totally composed, partly composed and partly improvised, or completely improvised: matters of procedure which may be crucial to the event for the performer can be of marginal concern to, or even unnoticed by, a listener. Critically, this conflict between the perceptions of a performer and those of a listener frequently feeds back into musical argument in the view that improvisation may be a pleasure for musicians, but is boring for audiences. This argument raises fundamental issues not only about the nature of the activity of improvisation, but also about the nature of the activity of music in general: whether it is principally a participatory activity, like sport or certain kinds of therapy, or whether it is primarily a representational activity, with specialised producers and large numbers of more passive consumers. The relationship between these two ideas of music – as with dance and theatre – has varied from period to period, and between societies. But it is possible to say that the role ascribed to 'improvisation' is central to the process of codifying the relationship between the two divergent possibilities.

Improvisation in the History of Western Music

Noticing that complications in the word 'improvisation' have been worked through differently in various periods and societies is a reminder that improvisation plays a role in virtually *all* music. But if improvisation is almost universal in this way, providing continuity across cultures, is it not then reasonable to assume that it defines something of the essence of music?

Certainly there is a temptation to think that at some deep level improvisatory activity might define the essence of human creativity in music. But what is perhaps most striking in looking at relevant musical history and ethnography is that improvisation plays very *different* roles in different periods, cultures and types of music. Far from suggesting any underlying common denominator, these differences indicate a social and historical specificity of musical practice which challenges the essentialism of conceiving of improvisation as the musical root of the human or the self. So it would seem more useful to concentrate on specific social relations of improvisation rather than on any power of the activity to strip off the social and reach an underlying human commonality.

Nobody would dispute the fact of the pervasiveness of improvisation in music throughout the world. But that pervasiveness is nevertheless often neglected in histories of music – especially in histories of Western music – and replaced with discussion purely of the development of compositional and instrumental techniques. Even restricting attention to Western traditions, nevertheless – where improvisation is perhaps least evident in comparison with other musics – we see that improvisation took place extensively: in music of the ancient Greeks; in mediaeval religious and secular music (including Gregorian chant and rounds); in all kinds of Renaissance music (for example in 'divisions' around well-known melodies or compositions, as well as in songs, and in organ and other kinds of instrumental music); and in Baroque music (where there seem to have been links between the amount of latitude allowed in performance and the particular stage of development of notational techniques). Beyond reasonable doubt, we know that improvisation existed to some degree in most periods and forms of Western music from the mediaeval period until the 18th century (as it has in virtually all other musical traditions). It took the various forms of melismata, troping, and other kinds of melodic ornamentation, as well as of continuo playing, thorough-bass, added arpeggios and contrapuntal embellishment. This was all in addition to what we now generally think of as improvisation: large-scale melodic, harmonic and rhythmic extemporisation.

From the mediaeval period until the 18th century in Western music, then, improvisation provided the possibility of variation by participants on relatively known and predictable forms, which were themselves in part structured in accordance with social rituals or ceremonies of performance (eg, for prayer or dancing). The challenge to this general conception – the challenge which dislodges improvisation from its centrality to Western music-making – comes only when these shared patterns of formal repetition and permutation are replaced by a far more fully calculated uniqueness of formal development. Gradually latitude for the performer is reduced by increased sophistication of notation; and improvisation tends to become the display of exceptional technical talents and imaginative fantasy by individual performers. Especially in cadenzas, these displays are gradually codified, and are then frequently planned out in detail in advance of a performance and notated. In the development of the new concert forms of the 19th century, which were coupled with larger changes in conceptions of art and the artist in society, the participatory possibilities invited by earlier concert forms are displaced by individual compositions whose concern is less to act as a spring-board to creative performance by the musicians playing on any particular occasion than to record individual insights already achieved by the composer.

For Western concert music, this transition is decisive, at least until the recent resurgence of interest in improvisation. After this period, it is possible to follow a history of improvisation almost only in popular cultural forms – in the 20th century especially in folk music, jazz and rock. Whereas in the 'high' cultural traditions improvisation becomes controlled and limited (surviving to any extent only in organ playing), in popular music (frequently organised around song-forms and harmonic sequences or simple repeated figures), variation remains a convenient way of extending performance time to suit locally changing needs of the occasion, as well as for practising. In this respect, the watershed for improvisation in Western music coincides closely with the elevation of music in 18th and 19th century concert performances to the status of an art, and of a primary rather than ancillary focus of interest: in concert-music after this, improvisation plays little role. The different directions taken in 'serious' music and in 'popular' music from this time onwards offer an interesting comparison with, for example, Indian music, where improvisation is retained in both high and popular forms, or with Javanese gamelan music, which incorporates improvisation as one of the essential elements in devising a piece to perform over a long period of rehearsal, so enabling the music to represent specific and changing kinds of social relationships and aspiration.

Arguably jazz and modern popular musics represent a persistence of improvisation which results partly from the influence on their musical conventions of traditions from outside this specifically European history. As is well known, jazz and rock music developed in a transplantation of practices of performance and improvisation from African music, through the spirituals and blues forms of the slavery and post-slavery periods, into the increasingly urbanised and commercially exploited forms: urban blues, jazz and rock'n'roll.[7] As greater high-cultural claims have been made for these musics over the last twenty years, the integral role in them of improvisation has been taken more seriously, as has their realisation through constantly changing collaborative relationships in small groups (leading in the 1970s, for example, into the explicit ethic of 'DIY production' central to punk). Throughout the same period, nevertheless, a process in the other direction has also been taking place, most clear in 'tin-pan alley' popular music traditions: an emphasis on the 'work' as a commodity over which commercial rights can be exercised, and which subordinates improvisation, or the specificity of music to any particular occasion, to the demands of reproducibility and general commercial availability and attractiveness. This is the continuing pressure underlying Adorno's criticisms of popular music, and underwriting what Attali has called the period of 'repeating': a pressure towards social control over, and subjection of, mass audiences, to be achieved through saturation with mass-produced, generally anodyne musical products.

Although the historical changes between ancient Greece and the present, which I have summarised in these paragraphs, are often represented as development (sometimes as musical evolution), they define different roles for music in society, and confer on music different degrees of status and quite different functions. (Consider, for example, the difference in social standing – as also in modern cultural connotation – between a collectively sung chorus in a folk sing-song and a cadenza by a famous virtuoso.) What is curious about the Western concert-music tradition in this context is how it becomes detached and isolated from the range of earlier social rituals, and from the kinds of musical and theatrical entertainment and folk music from which it developed, to become increasingly represented with a degree of idealisation, having no connection to its actual history. In looking at both the history which precedes concert-music, and at its own developing conventions, there is a tendency towards dehistoricisation and abstraction: the construction of an impersonal ceremony of 'classical' music, and of the seemingly timeless rituals of the concert-hall; and the creation of a myth in which earlier 'folk music' sub-strata are made imaginary, as a musical world not itself also socially constructed. What is therefore important to note is that these kinds of circumstantially specific 'folk' musics (spreading fully across the social stratification of feudal and early capitalist societies) were in fact linked to very specific kinds of social ceremony. Just as concert-music has particular social roles, cultural resonances and class connotations now, so folk music of earlier periods functions as a form of accompaniment within very precise frameworks of social significance: of gesture, custom, ethics and religion. Music has only ever been an expression of humanity through the process at the same time of being an expression of particular forms of social organisation.

Improvisation and Frameworks of Interpretation

In all periods and places specific philosophies of music-making have governed instrument design, conventions of musical form and rituals of performance. As conditions of music vary, therefore, improvisation is embedded in new and changing kinds of social mythology or ideology. In all forms of music-making *before* developments of the last twenty years, improvisation developed within pre-existent controls on decision-making which followed from conventions governing the 'meanings' or social function of any given idiom. A clear example of this can be found in the expressive properties of classical Hindu modes, which link the effect of an improvisation with conventional characteristics of the particular mode in which the improvisation takes place, each mode having its own historically established cultural connotations. Similarly, in ancient Greece improvising around the *nomoi* and *tonoi* took place in accordance with imagined emotional and ethical effects to which the modes were believed to be connected. (It is these Greek modes which are carried through from Plato and others into the thinking of Plotinus, Boethius, and other mediaeval theologians, and so – in reworked forms – into the music of the mediaeval church). Or again, consider the idea that musical scales repeat and embody a 'music of the spheres', or musical harmony created as the celestial spheres rotate round the earth – a notion which has the effect of prescribing what forms of music will be consonant with the harmony of the universe, and ruling out alternative musical scales which would otherwise be possible. Or still again, consider the complex symbolisms to be found in almost all cultures permeating other aspects of music-making such as harmony, instrument design, conventions of idiom or genre, and so on. In each of these social codes of interpretation improvisation works as variation within a socially constituted framework or 'language' of music which provides general reference points of intelligibility.

The particular conventions which provide frameworks of reference for improvisation are varied: they can be *formal* conventions (scales, keys, variation around a repeated figure); they can be compositional *dynamics* such as performance contours or particular moods (crescendo then diminuendo; certain tones, textures, etc); they can be *technical* roles assigned to individual instruments (registers, relative density of notes played, kind of attack, etc); or they can be *metaphysical* or *political* schemas or functions (cf the metaphorical interpretations of harmony and dissonance cited above, or, in one sort of Brecht-Eisler model, the exploitation of musical connotations to confront an audience with contradictions in its social and musical life). Each of these frameworks limits and defines possibilities for creation and for reception, and gives meaning to improvisation in contributing to the formation and reproduction of images of the world and of human and social purposes through music.

But what of improvisation in jazz in these terms? Jazz does not appear to have any obvious superordinate system, beyond the local conventions of its musical idioms, to regulate it. In this sense it could be argued that jazz was the first form to break away – perhaps through some force of alienation in urban living – from social codes governing musical performance.

However, not everyone who has commented on this music agrees that there is a tradition of anything in jazz that can properly be called 'improvisation'. In reviewing 50 years of what he describes as 'jazz' during the 1960s Theodor Adorno made the criticism that its famed improvisation is in fact much less improvisation than is generally thought.[8] Adorno's argument, broadly, is that jazz involves rigid formulae successfully repeated with only superficial change over a long period, in a diversity of pretentiously differentiated 'styles'. Adorno argues that improvisation provides merely 'frills' and an appearance of spontaneity: 'what appears as spontaneity is planned out in advance with machinelike precision'.[9] The music which results is

> the more or less feeble rehashing of basic formulas in which the schema shines through at every moment ... The range of the permissible in jazz is as narrowly circumscribed as in any particular cut of clothes.[10]

He goes on to argue that, particularly in jazz which keeps to a basic beat, improvisation is not liberating but liable to induce regression in listeners:

> The ban on changing the basic beat during the course of the music is itself sufficient to constrict composition to the point where what it demands is not aesthetic awareness of style but rather psychological regression.[11]

This idea picks up Adorno's arguments elsewhere – especially in 'On the Fetish Character in Music and the Regression of Listening'[12] – that in popular music well-defined formulae lead to a subjection of the listener which drastically simplifies and obstructs his or her musical response. In turn, the fan projects that subjection in a fetishisation of everything to do with the performer: personality, stylistic traits, etc. In Adorno's view, this structure of regression makes a contribution to the development of authoritarian societies: jazz, he says, stems 'not by accident' from marches and the syncopated dance-steps of military bands, with the implication that the regression this music induces can lead to mass regimentation and so totalitarianism. In a series of speculations, Adorno then suggests a range of connections between psychoanalytic patterns of castration and the liking for jazz.[13] Far from challenging the order of musical 'repetition', improvisation in jazz colludes with demands of commodification and popularisation, and in this sense its claims to cultural prestige are misplaced. For Adorno, only certain kinds of modern concert-work genuinely engage the listener, and for this reason a radical politics of music would have to find its impetus not in improvisatory, popular forms, but in certain kinds of experimental concert composition. What follows is a response to Adorno which also attempts to explore some of the more ambivalent aspects of contemporary improvisation.

'Free' Improvisation

Even the most recent edition of *Encyclopedia Britannica* asserts that some framework of conventions is a necessary precondition for improvisation to be intelligible at all. But,

unlike earlier forms of music-making (in which improvisation appears a kind of permutation of established
material or codes), contemporary 'free' improvising has
become established in quite explicit opposition to such
conventional frameworks. Pointing to this clear contrast
between two approaches to improvisation, Derek Bailey
distinguishes what he calls 'idiomatic' improvisation, which
works within an overarching framework of generic
expectation or conventions, and 'non-idiomatic' improvisation, which does not.[14]

Express opposition to idiomatic frameworks of activity
and interpretation, then, is what distinguishes, in Britain,
Western Europe and the United States, a school aiming for
completely free, collective improvisation or spontaneous
music. The history of this emergent movement has involved,
in Britain, performers such as Derek Bailey and Evan
Parker, the Scratch Orchestra and groups such as AMM or
the Spontaneous Music Ensemble, in addition to many other
jazz, rock and concert-music performers; in the United
States, the movement grew during the 1950s in loft jazz and
through initiatives by Bill Dixon, Archie Shepp and Ornette
Coleman, into work by Cecil Taylor, Don Cherry, Albert
Ayler and others. In schools of contemporary concert-
music, there is work by Earle Brown, John Cage, Karlheinz
Stockhausen, Christian Wolff, Cornelius Cardew and a
range of other 'composers'.

Two important conditions appear to have made the
development of these experiments with non-idiomatic
improvisation – which cut across the performers' established
idiomatic preferences – historically possible. Firstly, within
modern concert-music, aleatory and indeterminate compositional methods appeared in opposition to total serialism and
to the increasing technical difficulty of performance in
contemporary concert-music. Graphic scores in particular
provided one point of transition into free improvisation.
Their visual attraction for the performer linked music with
changing visual codes of interpretation in other plastic arts
(such as abstract and kinetic painting and design), and
opened up ways for the performer to 'interpret' the score
rather than simply follow it – so rehumanising what had

become an increasingly mathematical formalism in serialist music. Underlying this use of graphic scores is a reinvestigation of the role of notation: the idea of the score as a fixed 'language' which pairs symbols and responses (a tradition developing from use of notation simply as a mnemonic, but leading to a behaviouristic idea of performance) is turned into active personal interpretation of symbols (the score's 'code' can only be read through a problem-solving, discovery approach). Graphic scores insist on a performer-centred concept of notation, suspending what had become the post-war conventional will to determine as many ·parameters of the musical event as possible. Whereas in 18th century music some degree of improvisation inevitably existed irrespective of aesthetic preferences because notational techniques were inadequate to prescribe all aspects of performance, in the 20th century interest in graphic and indeterminate scores is part of a subversion and aestheticisation among many of the musically highly literate of the extremely sophisticated notational formalisms which have now been devised.

But it would be a misrepresentation to suggest that contemporary interest in improvisation is solely the result of dissent by some musically-literate musicians against certain post-war compositional orthodoxies – many very eminent musicians in recent years, especially in jazz and rock music, have been notationally illiterate. The second major influence on improvised music has come from the informal, changing character of groups of musicians within jazz, rock and pop, especially as creative relationships in rock groups allowed expansive formal experimentation in the late 1960s and 1970s on a scale previously only possible in jazz. Building music simply from bass riffs, chord sequences and drum patterns allows for a degree of variation and embellishment which reduces the role of advanced planning in musical arrangement, and results in a constantly changing balance between material planned in advance and spontaneous extemporisation. Coupled with the changing creative possibilities presented by recording, mixing and editing described earlier, this alternative tradition of music-making works extensively through extrapolation from minimally

worked-out forms. In becoming established as a major commercial and cultural force during the 1960s and 1970s this
tradition of popular music contributed to a re-establishment
of the view that Western music can be entertaining and
rewarding even to people without much formal training.

But collective improvisation remains beset by a range of
conceptual difficulties which surround any activity that seeks
to disconnect itself from any framing backcloth of 'conventions'. In general, these follow from the fact that the 'meanings' of any social practice are created as much by its context –
by the framework of activities surrounding it and by its
contrasts and oppositions with other related activities – as by
internal, formal properties of the practice itself.

The 'meanings' of improvisation – and in particular its
investigative and therapeutic potential – lie precisely in
relations between the choices made by musicians moment by
moment during a performance and surrounding frameworks
of alternative possibility. Like the analysand's discourse in
psychoanalysis, completely improvised music is framed only
by silence on the one hand, and by noise on the other. Its
significance lies in particular choices of what to do, and in the
way the large-scale dynamics and kaleidoscopic patterns
which emerge simultaneously close off other options which
might otherwise have occurred. And there is another similarity with concerns of psychoanalysis here, too. Aside from
determining professional pressures, desire to gain pleasure in
some form acts as the immediate stimulus to play music of any
particular kind. What then distinguishes improvisation from
idiomatic performance is that in it this desire always exceeds
the culturally charted routes to gaining pleasure through
which it passes: to play is to find pleasure in a polyphony of
different voices and evanescent and evasive possibilities over
which no individual performer ever has final control. What
remains critically at issue as regards explaining pleasure in
improvisation is whether in continually alluding to but never
grasping a fund of existing musical associations, improvisation relativises and reconstructs their musical codes for
the performer and the listener, or whether it deconstructs
them to a point at which it offers musical escape from any
code at all.

Three Arguments for 'Free' Improvisation

A range of detailed arguments have been made in recent years about how 'free' improvisation works and what it can achieve. I propose to isolate here three recurrent strands of debate: strands which I will call 'improvisation as liberation', 'improvisation as discovery' and 'improvisation as dialogue'. These strands are 'types' or 'repeated forms' within arguments rather than particular formulations: each *foregrounds* specific properties and aspirations of improvisation. As parts of arguments rather than as complete defences or explanations, they usually occur in compound forms; and in discussion they sometimes appear and disappear evanescently in larger arguments, too briefly or contingently to be considered directly. I am of course aware that presenting such models or part-arguments rather than referring to specific formulations of them is open to charges of reductionism, replacing accuracies of history with simplistic stereotypes and idealisations. Against this inevitable risk, however, needs to be set the argument that the material force of ideas often lies in popular forms in which they are used rather than in originating, often more sophisticated, forms from which they are derived. In any case, my purpose is not to destroy these arguments as straw-persons, but to try to separate out particular lines within larger patterns of musical discussion in order to piece together something of the overall contemporary case for and against improvised music. In fixing on the three argument 'types', I am simply trying to interrupt the process of discussion in order to focus briefly, and in effect statically, on isolable argumentative elements. After brief discussion of each in this way, I will try to comment on the larger discussion in which they are interconnected.

Improvisation as Liberation: Improvising as a procedure does not determine improvisation as musical form. Improvising describes how something is done, not *what* is done; it is in principle possible to improvise – in a minimal sense such as 'create music without pre-existent or prepared material' – an infinite range of musical results, and to engage in an infinite range of possible inter-relationships among participants. It is this sense which gives the idea that in improvising you are free to do precisely what you want.

A number of difficult consequences follow from this view. There is, for instance, the classical problem of resolving the conflict between different aspirations which are liable to exist within such 'freedom'. In addition, holding to such a minimal definition would involve a commitment to complete relativism on the question of variable achievement or value in specific acts of improvisation.

There are, of course, several kinds of libertarianism with which this minimal definition fits comfortably; and quite a number of contemporary improvisers profess to holding some version of this view. For them, improvisation is a human activity which gains value exactly from the fact that it constructs no versions of hierarchy or competition, no ensnaring conventions or intrinsically detrimental value judgements; it frees the human from the social. This escape from judgement and value has the currently attractive political force of dissent. It is a point of counter-identification against systems of control, hierarchy and subordination. But the question then arises of what kinds of principled connection between improvisation and surrounding social structures are implied by this view. Clearly, music is not held to be *reflective* of an economic or political 'base': its ability to evoke freedoms which do not exist, and hence its radicalism, follows directly from this fact. Rather, the 'improvisation as liberation' view holds to the idea of a connection between music and society in which music can be prophetic or premonitory of a desirable condition or utopia to come: it can represent a liberating alternative to actual forms of oppression embodied in differentiation, regulation, and judgement. But if this 'improvisation as alternative' connection is taken as more than the loosest of metaphors, the politics of completely improvised music becomes naive: no social formation will involve no conventions at all, or will thrive on the abolition not only of any kind of hierarchy but also of conventions for differentiation and comparison. Whereas at present the 'improvisation as alternative' view takes its 'meanings' from specific contrast with actual forms, if ever the alternative 'freedom' was achieved, such resources for differentiation would no longer exist. In any case, material conditions of being will always impose forms on formless abstractions: differences create possibilities for meaning as well as inequalities between meanings that are created. Without structuring differences and distinctions, meanings of any kind are impossible. A politics of 'liberation' is one of counter-identification and can signal directions for relative change, but it cannot be a condition to which to aspire.

In practice, there is another source of confusion in this 'prefigurative' view of an anarchic alternative: that between the idea of latent musical potential in *all* human beings, and the view that musicians now improvising are a minority who can nevertheless speak provisionally on behalf of a more general human liberation. While it is often suggested that exemplary performances by such musicians galvanise listeners into improvising, and so have an educative as well as an entertaining function, what remains in question – following on from the ambiguity between process and product – is whether the *practice* of improvising can be taken from the experience of listening and developed, or whether it will be one particular set of musical conventions or anti-conventions which will be appreciated and later imitated. The contradiction is the recurrent one in educational and political activities of someone standing as an example of how people are to help themselves. If *procedure* is imitated, performance combines values as artistic display or exploration with encouragement to others, gradually undermining the importance of the exemplary performers themselves; if on the other hand it is the *product* which is imitated, improvised performance offers simply one more template for imitation, providing a form of prescription or convention for music-making quite alien to the improvisatory ideals of freedom from convention for which the practice is adopted.

Improvisation as Discovery: In frameworks of argument which prioritise invention and novelty as the particular forms of freedom from convention to which improvisation should aspire each improvisation might be expected to differ from previous ones, rather than to repeat familiar areas or dynamics of performance which are merely comfortable and pleasurable to the musicians involved.

From the point of view of considering improvised music as a quest for the new, it is interesting that sceptical audiences often suggests that the music 'all sounds the same'. Many critics of improvisation point to its tendency towards repetition as the major drawback of this form of music-making, and improvising groups themselves frequently dissolve and reform in new combinations precisely in order to stimulate new kinds of interactional chemistry. Naturally judgements that music 'sounds the same' depend on the scope of comparison being made: an improvising group is far more likely to sound like previous performances of its own than it is likely to sound like music by another group in another genre; even the contrast between evident symmetries of composed music and asymmetries in non-composed music may be a basis for comparison here. But while a narrower comparison brings out the degree of newness in an improvisation, at the same time it diminishes the scale of achievement that can reasonably be claimed on behalf of its 'novelty' or 'discovery', since in larger contrasts what is noticeable remains more the degree of repetition than of invention.

What does 'newness' mean, in any case, when used to describe an improvisation? One possible emphasis here is that novelty is achieved by efforts towards complete escape from the expected or the conventional. But this is a difficult view of performance to sustain, especially over the period of time of a series of performances. As regards any given performer, there inevitably exist reflexes, pre-dilections and habits which shape the activity of improvising, giving it distinctive symmetries and patterns of repetition. In this sense, what constrains the kind of improvisation likely to be made is a history of the performers' experiences, training and preparation, rather than a set of more obviously social conventions of genre. These personal histories – with their movements of desire and given economies of pleasure – constitute an invisible set of conventions and regularities, and point to a further likeness between improvisation and psychoanalysis. It would even be possible to take the view that such subconscious or subliminal templates for musical activity shaped by the personal histories of individual performers, and by their physical reflexes and aptitudes, are forms of bodily and psychical 'notation' or 'score'; to do this would be to rule out 'improvisation' as discovery in any strong sense of *novelty* altogether.

Hidden regularities within the 'newness' aspired to in the 'improvisation as discovery' argument also cuts across the activity of listening. Sometimes the view is expressed that in listening 'newness' involves liberation from connotations with which sounds are burdened in all other forms of music. (In this respect, improvisation would share intellectual aspirations with some kinds of abstraction in painting.) But this idea is made problematic by the fact that as soon as a sound is made it will be *perceived* in relation to a set of distinctions, contrasts and terms which are already socially and historically constructed: as mellifluous music, as resembling some particular idiom or genre, as reminiscent of something. Perceptions of music are saturated with culturally constructed meanings of one kind or another. Even where specified musical connotations do not exist already – and given any scenario of performance these connotations are already very likely to be mobilised – an overall connotation may be ascribed to them as part of a general, mythological connotation of 'musical avant-gardism', or simply as noise.

Undoubtedly disruptions take place to such categories: this is how conventions of musical 'meaning' change through time. (Massive changes in ideas of what is 'dissonant' and what role dissonance should play in music are a clear case of this.[15]) Nevertheless, as regards developing a politics of improvised music on the grounds of 'novelty' and the possibility of escaping strictures on conventional sound associations, what seems clear is that novelty exists only in situationally specific relationships of transgression and transformation of existing codes, rather than as some 'pure' alternative to them: there is no new musical realm to discover that isn't at the same time a restructuring or reconstruction of the old.

Improvisation as Dialogue: In this emphasis, the interest and value of improvisation is thought to lie less in any particular arrangement of sounds than in the forms of human relationship and interaction which the activity of improvising involves. Improvisation's capability to give pleasure and to educate is believed to lie in the way its processes of decision-making and collective problem-solving foreground a concern to explore and negotiate forms of interpersonal relationship.

It remains a complication of this approach in any simple form, however, that in a procedural description of improvisation such as 'improvisation as dialogue' or 'improvisation as problem-solving' there are no guidelines concerning what will be a 'problem' or what might constitute a resolution of any such problem. Psychological and educational work with problem-solving generally relies on frameworks of loosely established objectives. In improvisation, on the other hand, the attractiveness of the activity – as well as its claims to stand as a liberating 'free' alternative, or as a way of discovering new sounds and new musical 'meanings' – lies precisely in *not* having pre-ordained objectives. Apart from purposes locally or provisionally agreed between individual groups of musicians, the principal objective of improvising appears to be the general one of gaining pleasure. But this creates a difficulty of relativism for the 'improvisation as dialogue' view. What may seem a state to be resolved or transformed to one player may well seem a point of comfortable or pleasurable equilibrium to another. Negotiation of changing situations within an improvisation whose basic definitions are not established offers interesting opportunities to improvisers; and it also ensures that there can be no single assessment of 'problem' and 'resolution' for a listener – in listening there will be contradictions rather than any resolving moment or single direction through a performance. But does this apparent open-endedness in fact disguise clandestine appeals to a broader, authorising theory or ideology of musical aesthetics or politics?

It seems that there *is* a determining, broader theoretical or ideological assumption in the 'improvisation as dialogue' view: a view of the nature of desirable human relationships and interactions (eg, co-operativeness, freedom from aggression, etc). And such a view may perfectly well be shared by particular groups of improvisers or by any audience group. In this case, though, the music itself merely dramatises and endorses an already established framework of values, rather than constructing or investigating them. To follow this line of thinking is to move back from claims that improvisation has a unique investigative or therapeutic potential to the more orthodox view that music-making *represents* particular ideas, feelings or values. The 'investigative' and 'therapeutic' claim about improvisation is that it is precisely the nature of interpersonal relationships and routes to pleasure that improvisation enables us to explore and discover, rather than simply confirm and represent. But decisions about social values and models of interaction made in advance or held by presumption appear preemptive of improvisation's investigative and therapeutic properties. If on the other hand, no shared objectives are agreed between musicians, then what improvising provides is a forum in which all kinds of interaction can be explored. But if improvisation provides a forum, rather than some more specific directive towards a particular paradigm or set of values, then it provides a vehicle for all varieties of human relationship – involving both community and conflict – to expose themselves equally (possibly even in a musically 'darwinist' way), without being thereby subjected to any musical process of discrimination or judgement.

The political implications of the 'improvisation as dialogue' view appear to be towards either a moral politics in which improvisation dramatises and so represents a model of desirable human interactions, or else a 'therapy' in which the process of improvisation itself, rather than any particular pattern of emerging interpersonal relationships, justifies the activity. One consequence of either line of thinking is undoubtedly a priority for developing new ways of thinking about compatibility (in terms of patterns of pleasure rather than in terms of repertoire or technique) when joining together in performance groups. Certainly the logic of all shades of the 'improvisation as dialogue' view is that wherever possible people should become involved in improvisation as an activity – like therapy or sport – rather than expect to consume improvisations as a traditional 'artistic form' of performance. This new conception of musical *activity* pulls improvisation away from conventional ideas of music as a representational art, with producers and consumers; it fits with Attali's observation that no genuinely new music can be made without at the same time fundamentally changing music's present conditions of production and distribution.[16]

Conclusion: Musical Form and Musical Practice

Dogmatic observance of any of the three views outlined above would be simplistic and misguided. Yet this does not mean that improvised music can have no genuine political impact or force, as is suggested by Luciano Berio. In writing about the improvising group New Phonic Art, he argues that these musicians represent themselves as

> a little commando group of musical guerrillas who infilitrate enemy lines to shake up the subscription holders and incite revolt among the young. But 1968 was a long time ago, and improvisation can provoke neither revolutions nor crises of conscience, above all when it is (or was) those same subscribers who invite and pay the improvisers.[17]

Following on from the three strands of argument presented above – and despite the difficulties with each of them I have indicated – improvisation does appear to have political force in two main ways: firstly, in disrupting expectations of musical form, especially as these establish musical rhetorics which allow us to think that music can represent states of mind, feelings and thoughts about the world; secondly, in questioning dominant procedures through which music is made and consumed, especially in challenging established roles for composers, musicians and audiences.

Consider improvised music's disruptions to formal conventions and expectations first. Improvised music stands in clear opposition to traditions of thinking of large-scale formal symmetries as the necessary architecture of musical argument. Even where contrast between improvisation and composed music is reduced, when both are reproduced on tape or record (with the effect that the improvisation can be known in as precise detail as can the musical composition), the difference between the two kinds of music remains important: through its formal irregularities, improvisation insists that pleasure need not only come from perceiving and construing symmetrical patterns as an informed listener, but can also lie in not knowing which musical directions will be developed, which musical elements are thematised or what precise musical register or idiom a piece is intended to be in. Overall, what improvisation suggests is that it is possible to find musical pleasure not only in knowing where you are in a piece of music but also as a 'decentered' listener: in false starts, contradictory reactions and labyrinthine routes through the music's haphazard and unresolving formal patterns. [18]

Many musicians, especially composers belonging to or influenced by the Darmstadt School, however, have argued that in not following worked-out developing patterns improvised music fails to meet requirements of what modern music should be. Luciano Berio, for example, argues that music should involve musical 'thought', and that musical 'thought' is made up of deliberate formal patterning at different levels:

> by musical thought I mean above all the discovery of a coherent discourse that unfolds and develops simultaneously on different levels. [19]

Improvisation in such a view lacks the coherence an informed listener might want and expect, and instead involves merely a crude psychological dynamic of gesture and emotion. In a similar vein, the composer Pierre Boulez writes:

> Improvisation, and especially improvisation where there is a degree of sympathy between the individual members, always follows the same curve of invention: excitement – relaxation – excitement – relaxation. In so-called primitive societies a similar situation exists in religious ceremonies whose relatively simple form involves a building-up of psychological tension followed by relaxation ... [20]

By using only such simple, 'primitive' formal contrasts, this psychological conception of form 'only shows up the most basic side of the individual', and Boulez goes on:

> At present improvisation is a sequence of negations. If a lot of things happen in register A, for the next few minutes A will be avoided and we shall have B; then, after B has had its outing, it will disappear and we shall have C instead. It is the opposite of what happens in composition, where one combines elements A, B, and C sometimes in an extremely complex way. But mixing is excluded by this type of instantaneous, improvisatory creation, as a result neither of aesthetic nor of any other deliberate policy but simply of inadequate memory – because the mind is incapable of mixing certain elements.[21]

But according to Boulez it is not only memory-limitations which are the problem for improvisers; his view of 'invention' differs quite fundamentally from any process of interaction and discovery likely to be involved in improvised music:

> Instrumentalists do not possess invention – otherwise they would be composers. There has been a lot of talk of 'improvisation', but even taken in the best sense of the word it cannot replace invention. True invention entails reflection on problems that in principle have never been posed, or at least not in the manner which is readily apparent, and reflection upon the act of creation implies an obstacle to be overcome. Instrumentalists are not superhuman, and their response to the phenomenon of invention is normally to manipulate what is stored in the memory. They recall what has already been played, in order to manipulate and transform it.[22]

In these passages, Boulez repeatedly implies that interest in music lies in posing and solving intellectual problems. But playing and listening to music are material activities, and also involve potential cross-fertilisation between intellectual, sensual and physical pleasures. For all its own unresolved conceptual difficulties, it has been a major accomplishment of improvised music that it has helped wrest contemporary musical argument away from increasingly arid post-serialist debates over formal complexity and artistry into more direct consideration of issues of pleasure, which can come just as effectively from repetition and simple contrast as from complex combination or transformation. The idea of taking pleasure as freely from repetition as from permutation and combination – which is fundamental to jazz, rock and most non-Western musics – challenges the formalist ideas of composers such as Berio and Boulez; and when these alternative ways of gaining pleasure then combine with pleasures of physical activity in *making* music, a challenge is also made to the distinction Boulez everywhere confidently assumes between categories of 'instrumentalists', 'composers' and 'audiences'.

In rejecting traditional relationships between performer and performer, and between performer and score, improvisation not only disputes conventions of form but also challenges dominant social relations in which music is made, reproduced, circulated and represented. And if this is so, then it must be a correspondence between problem-solving in improvised music and in other areas of human experience which gives improvisation this critical power. If social problems are of the kind presented in an improvisation, then improvisation undoubtedly has an important contribution to make not only to heralding new kinds of social order, but also more immediately – as a part of 'progressivist' education – to contemporary music education: suitably organised, improvisation in the classroom should help locate lessons in harmony and instrumental technique in the broader context of music as a process of combining practical techniques with decision-making and formulations of individual and group purpose.[23]

Whereas improvised music makes possible perceptions of pleasure in the context of thinking about musical form, when it comes to questions of connections between music and society, the role of pleasure in improvisation poses a problem. For improvising appears to provide opportunities to explore practical situations radically different from and impossible within, everyday extra-musical experience. This is the case to the extent that the aim of improvising of giving pleasure differs from the primary purpose of most other social activities in which it is necessary to solve problems. And if there are major differences between the 'experimental' situations in making music and 'real' situations in other spheres of activity, then no close correspondence can reasonably be claimed between problem-solving in improvised music and ways of seeking solutions to problems outside it. Improvising could still be a very valuable activity, in a range of ways: it might, for example, provide a therapeutic safety-valve, or the possibility for counterfactual or imaginary experimentation. Nor would this imply that there is no connection between music-making and other social practices. But it would alter the political claims that can be made about improvisation.

The formal and procedural dimensions of arguments over improvised music finally meet in this issue of 'correspondence' between musical improvisation and other areas of social practice. Human relationships are explored in improvisation by being mediated through musical conventions, styles and connotations. At the same time as practitioners are relating to one another, they are also relating to a set of already socially established musical options, and the kinds of resonance created by choices between these. Improvisation cannot, therefore, provide a general paradigm of social experience. It can, however, explore possibilities and implications of different forms of interpersonal relationship with respect to given parameters of music-making in and for a particular time and place. There are then likely to be inferrable connections and influences from these forms of relationship into other areas of social practice and notions of self-identity. What is important – and what is not sufficiently acknowledged in existing political arguments made for improvised music – is that although these larger connections certainly exist, they cannot be read off from musical activity in any simple way which would authorise the confidence of a traditional marxist politics of the kind taken up by many improvising musicians.

Jacques Attali includes improvised music – alongside an emphasis on the informal, constantly changing small groups and do-it-yourself production associated with punk music – in his idea of a challenge to the era of mass music or 'repeating' which will lead into a new and preferable musical (and then social) epoch of 'composing'. To conquer habits of the period of 'repeating', Attali suggests, two major preparatory conditions need to be met: firstly, a condition of 'autonomy', in which listeners are free from the craving for mass music which is stimulated by advertising and other forms of publicity; and secondly, a condition of 'tolerance', in which listeners will feel able to tolerate the music of others even if they do not like it.[24] When Attali claims that the movement of free improvised music which began in the 1950s and 1960s has virtually failed, he attributes this failure not to any inherent contradiction in the music or bad faith on the part of improvising musicians, but to a split between the impulse towards self-determination through independent organisation of venues and record production and the impulse to capitulate to the wishes and requirements of impresarios and major record labels.[25] Whatever the current condition of such compromises, however, it seems beyond doubt that improvised music has a continuing role to play – in alliance with strands of popular music, experimental concert-music and jazz – in challenging mass music and the order of 'repeating', if the era of 'composing' is to be more than a convenient postmodernist fantasy.

An earlier and shorter version of this article was presented as a paper to a forum organised by the Association of Improvising Musicians called 'Improvisation: History, Directions, Practice'. That forum was held at the Institute of Contemporary Arts, London, on Saturday 31 March 1984. Papers from it were published by the Association of Improvising Musicians in the form of a booklet (contents: articles by Christopher Small, Alan Durant and Eddie Prevost).

Notes

[1] Jacques Attali, *Noise: The Political Economy of Music* (trans. Brian Massumi), Manchester University Press 1985.

[2] Attali, *op cit*, p 4.

[3] *Ibid*, p 4.

[4] For a discussion of this issue, see Alan Durant, *Conditions of Music*, Macmillan 1984, chapter 1.

[5] Attali, *op cit*, p 19.

[6] Derek Bailey, *Improvisation: Its Nature and Practice in Music*, Moorland Publishing in association with Incus Records 1980, p 15.

[7] For detailed accounts of the history of jazz and blues, see for example, James Lincoln Collier, *The Making of Jazz: A Comprehensive History*, Macmillan 1978, and Paul Oliver, *The Story of the Blues*, Barrie and Jenkins 1969, republished Penguin 1972.

[8] Theodor Adorno, 'Perennial Fashion – Jazz', in Theodor Adorno, *Prisms* (trans. Samuel and Stierry Weber), Neville Spearman 1967, pp 121-32.

[9] Adorno, *op cit*, p 123.

[10] *Ibid*, p 123.

[11] *Ibid*, p 123.

[12] Theodor Adorno, 'On the Fetish Character in Music and the Regression of Listening', in Andrew Arato and Eike Gerbhardt (eds), *The Essential Frankfurt School Reader*, Blackwell 1978.

[13] Adorno, *Prisms*, pp 129-32.

[14] Bailey, *op cit*, p 4.

[15] For detailed discussion of this issue, see Durant, *op cit*, chapter 3.

[16] Attali, *op cit*, chapter 5.

[17] Luciano Berio, *Two Interviews*, London 1985, p 84.

[18] For a contrast between composed music and improvisation described in terms of the metaphor of making a journey, see Christopher Small, *Music-Society-Education*, John Calder 1977, p 176.

[19] Berio, *op cit*, p 84.

[20] Pierre Boulez, *Conversations with Celestin Deliege*, London 1976.

[21] Boulez, *op cit*, p 115.

[22] *Ibid*, pp 113-4.

[23] For a very different, and less enthusiastic account of the place of improvisation in arts funding and in education, see Malcolm Barry, 'Improvisation: The State of the Art', *British Journal of Music Education*, volume 2 number 2, 1985, pp 171-5.

[24] See Attali, *op cit*, p 145.

[25] *Ibid*, pp 138-40.

Ken Hirschkop

The Classical and the Popular: Musical Form and Social Context

From where does a politics of music start? How do you organise 'music' when that means performances in the Royal Festival Hall by the London Philharmonic, recorded pop on BBC 1, live bands in small London or Liverpool clubs and traditional folk produced in the most casual of circumstances? All of this is musical and yet, in their aesthetic feel and social tone, these activities seem almost incommensurable. And it is precisely the social differences and the political distinctions they entail which we are least able to discuss, because the heritage of music criticism and analysis is a largely formalist one. When the 'notes themselves' are the exclusive focus of interest we lose the sense of music-making as communication taking place at particular occasions and among particular groups. While we now have 'linguistic' theories of music we still need a 'sociolinguistics' of music, a kind of analysis which could describe how the various kinds of musical utterance work within their distinctive social contexts.

But to start we could borrow the politicised sociolinguistics of Mikhail Bakhtin (1895-1975), whose work is now the subject of quite animated and occasionally fierce discussion in university literary circles. Cultural theory is not a word he used, or probably would have used, but it seems to describe the direction his work took between 1925 and 1941, a period during which he composed books on Dostoevsky and the

German *Bildungsroman*, a dissertation on Rabelais and popular carnival and several long essays on the political and cultural role of the novel, while participating (in what capacity is still unclear) in the writing of book-length critiques of Freud, linguistics and Russian Formalism.[1] Thus Bakhtin was part of the very intense debate that took place in the Soviet Union at that time over the role of culture in a socialist society, a debate which was prematurely concluded with the official rejection of modernist experimentation in favour of socialist realism. There are two sides of his work which are relevant to what I want to discuss here. First there is his critique of linguistics: an argument that we should study texts as instances of discourse, as contributions to an ongoing social dialogue made in a particular historical situation, and reflecting that social and historical location in their style. Secondly, Bakhtin connected this critique to a history of the politics of culture, in which he claimed that popular resistance to official culture was manifested in 'novelistic' verbal forms which foregrounded this social and historical 'feel' of discourse in order to undermine any pretensions to universality found in the discourse of political and cultural authority. These positions were developed in a literary context, but they were carried over into musical questions by one of Bakhtin's friends and colleagues, Ivan Ivanovich Sollertinsky, who attended meetings of the unofficial Bakhtin Circle throughout the 1920s.[2] Sollertinsky himself was a much more prestigious figure than Bakhtin until very recently: among the positions he held were professor at the Leningrad Conservatory and artistic director of the Leningrad Philharmonic. A student of Boris Asafiev in the 1920s, he went on to become a major defender of modernist composition during the 1930s, even after this became a risky and unpopular position. He wrote enthusiastic studies of Mahler and Schoenberg in 1932 and 1934 respectively and became embroiled in the controversy over Shostakovich's *Lady Macbeth of Mtensk* in 1936.[3] In what follows I want to use Sollertinsky as a pivot for the application of Bakhtin's work to problems of musical politics. This article is meant only to suggest some possible routes towards a more socially orientated approach to music, so my remarks are mostly theoretical with only brief allusions to particular works and forms. Let me begin with an account of Bakhtin's position.

According to Bakhtin linguistics conceived of its object as a system of stable grammatical forms which referred, so to speak, outwards, to objects or concepts. The speaker would pick out appropriate forms in order to convey the desired message; in such a scheme meaning was actually a property of language itself. And yet in reality the situation is much different because:

> any concrete discourse (utterance) finds the object at which it was directed already so to speak, spoken about, argued about, evaluated, enshrouded by either the obscuring mist or the 'light' of other words already spoken about it.[4]

Speaking, therefore, is not a process of pure naming or expression, but is the making of responses to other utterances. We speak 'dialogically', in relation to previous utterances and in anticipation of later ones and this context of 'alien' words is essential to understanding the meaning of anything we say:

> The living utterance, having taken meaning and shape at a particular historical moment in a socially specific environment, cannot fail to brush up against thousands of living dialogic threads, woven by socio-ideological consciousness around the given object of the utterance; it cannot fail to become an active participant in social dialogue.[5]

So meanings are never definite or stable because 'Each word tastes of the contexts and context in which it has lived its socially charged life.'[6] A speaker doesn't pick out available forms of expression but 'appropriates' them, refracting meanings established by past contexts to suit his or her present context. Given this basic condition 'there are no "neutral" words and forms ... language has been completely taken over and shot through with intentions and accents.'[7]

From this perspective, the grammatical, syntactical and lexical traits of language reflect not the logic of thought but very specific social and historical usages of discourse, usages in which one takes up a particular position or point of view. It is easy to think of examples of this stylistic fact of life: expressions or kinds of pronunciation which indicate social superiority; a kind of language which enforces respect for expertise or, alternatively, indicates a sense of being outside 'society'; even the difference between everyday speech and the discourse of the academic article. In all such cases socially defined ideologies and specific contexts of speech play themselves out in the choice of particular linguistic forms. So our language is not homogenous but 'heteroglottic', as Bakhtin puts it, crisscrossed by competing intentions and interests:

> Thus, at any given moment of its historical existence, language is completely heteroglot: it is the embodied coexistence of socio-ideological contradictions between the present and the past, between different epochs of the past, between different socio-ideological groups of the present, between tendencies, schools, circles and so on.[8]

As Bakhtin here speaks of contradictions, it should be clear that he is claiming not only that there are different languages but that languages are in many cases defined against each other, in a struggle for some common ideological territory. This kind of open struggle of interested social languages is not a very promising basis for political authority in class and gendered societies, but at the same time the actual differences are there for anyone to see. So ruling institutions produce an official discourse, a body of texts, which takes account of these different languages but arranges them in a hierarchy, so that the subordinate popular languages appear as deviant, uneducated, hysterical or savage in relation to a valued high or correct language. The texts by which this is accomplished Bakhtin called 'poetic', and the strategy of this hierarchising discourse he called 'monological', because it sought to extinguish the natural dialogism of discourse. Poetic texts erase 'any sense of the boundedness, the historicity, the social determination and specificity of one's own language.'[9] Bakhtin did not mean to imply that anything written in verse was oppressive, but one can see why he might suspect the standardised metrics, rhythm and rhyme schemes of pre-modern poetic language. In poetic, monologising texts one linguistic form, taken to be more expressive, refined or rational, frames all opposing forms; it acts as the language of truth or narration, against which everything else appears subjective, deformed by its peculiar social location (the discourse of the Artful Dodger in *Oliver Twist* is perhaps an ideal example of the latter). In the cultural sphere such a tendency ultimately crystallises in the establishment of a national vernacular literary language, which can set a standard for both texts and conversation.

Beyond the realm of this official 'poetic' discourse is 'the social life of discourse ... in the open spaces of public squares, streets, cities and villages',[10] which finds artistic expression in a novelistic discourse 'aimed sharply and polemically against the official languages of a given time.'[11] And although Bakhtin was referring to the canon of literary prose, or at least certain works within it, these literary works were seen as grounded in the 'low' cultural institutions which embodied popular resistance to political and ecclesiastical authority:

> On the stages of local fairs and buffoon spectacles, the heteroglossia of the clown sounded forth, ridiculing all languages and dialects; there developed the literature of the *fabliaux* and *Schwanke*, of street songs, folksayings, anecdotes ...[12]

The defining characteristic of these 'low' novelistic genres is that they trade in discourse 'still warm from that [social, KH] struggle and hostility',[13] marked by all the signs of a definite historical moment. Stylistically, the novel should always refer beyond itself, either to a text or language it refracts or to some dialectical opposite (sacred in comparison with its own vulgarity) it implicitly bounces off. The one thing Bakhtin demanded of the novel is that it be fundamentally incomplete, in the sense that it could only be comprehended as a contribution to an ongoing dialogue. What this precluded was the ideal of a self-contained aesthetic totality, that central fetish of bourgeois culture.

From this summary it would seem that the ideal of a 'classical' musical tradition, which was established in the late

18th and early 19th centuries, shares the ideological strategy of poetic-monological discourse. But two words of warning are in order. First, it would be a mistake to regard 'classical' music (in the broad sense of the term) as the only or even the leading form of official musical culture. Bakhtin wrote in a country and at a time in which there was no established commercial mass culture. In our current situation it may well be that Top of the Pops does the lion's share of the ideological work; however, it doesn't use the poetic strategy of putting itself at the top of a hierarchy of languages. Second, the 'classical' musical tradition is in fact made up of very different musical works; when we speak of a 'classical' kind of musical discourse we are referring not to the works themselves but to a way of experiencing those works. The emerging champions of the aesthetic sought to represent what was a socially and historically determinate musical experience, dependent upon all kinds of limiting contextual factors, as a universal one: this was the key to 'monologisation'. Yet at the same time a contrast had to be maintained between serious 'art' music and the noise of popular songs and ditties. If musical works with an undoubted force could be stripped of their social and historical connotations then they could be prized as examples of the 'aesthetic', which would now partially fill the gap left by the demise of other forms of social authority. The paradigmatic theorisation of this practice is probably Kant's *Critique of Judgment*, in which the aesthetic work is defined as the right balance of spontaneous creativity and formal discipline, perfect enough to persuade the listener that it is possible to reconcile individual subjective freedom with natural scientific necessity. In music this means works in which the spontaneous development of melody and harmony accords magically with the ultimate structural unity of the whole.

This apparently natural harmony of musical law or structure with human 'subjective' expression is an aesthetic effect today so deeply ingrained that it is hard to see what might be ideological about it. Yet it was only as a result of a struggle with an earlier official musical practice, different in its occasions and purpose, the Baroque, that the 'classical' achieved its dominant position. The formal differences between the two imply different effects for the listener. Alan Durant has described how 'The continuous kaleidoscope of polyphonic interest was gradually displaced by structures of formal and psychological drama'.[14] As is well known, this entailed the transformation of voice-leading – horizontal movement or movement through time – into melody and melodic development supported by a background harmonic rhythm. The new music aimed for a kind of internal dramatic shape, a structure of tension and resolution which was reproduced at the various carefully periodised levels of phrase, section, movement and work and which appeared to be a consequence of nothing but the music itself. This formalism, the supposed self-referentiality of the musical language, was, so to speak, the ideological point for the emerging concert audience of bourgeoisie, aristocracy and middle class. It separated *music*, cultivated sound, and its listeners, cultivated men and women, from sounds which were too 'academic' or ecclesiastical, that is, connected to visible social power, and from sounds which were insufficiently refined or vulgarly connected to everyday needs. If the tending of the natural qualities of sound – pure musical elaboration – led to such divine works, this was an assurance that cultivating nature led to pleasing results in all spheres. Theodor Adorno, the Marxist philosopher and cultural critic, argued that the music in fact betrayed these aesthetic goals.[15] As he saw it, the pure elaboration of musical ideas, the subjective pole, represented in the classical music of the Vienna School by the motivic development which drives the work along, was in fact drastically curtailed by the need to preserve a finished off tonal structure. Even Beethoven, legendary for the working out of 'germinal' motives, discharged his 'polyphonic obligations' only in the development and coda sections of his movements. To Adorno's mind the reason for this is that free musical development would not necessarily produce the reassuring wholes which the bourgeois aesthetic consciousness needs. If indeed there is such a perfect fit between spontaneity and structure then each thematic content, freely developed, should lead to a differently formed work. The fact that this didn't happen implies that there is a certain amount of arbitrariness in the mode of composition, a limitation in the principle of musical elaboration which means that the theme could be changed or substituted without altering the large-scale structure of the work. This implies not the kind of open historical development of the music which we could call dialogical but a prior interest in producing copies of an ideal self-contained 'monological' work which leads nowhere in particular. Now some may argue that the music of Romanticism has just this formal openness and variety. But although the fixed forms recede in importance the primary categories of musical dynamics which they embodied – harmonic tension and resolution, motive and development – remain, dictating the shape, if not the exact means, of the music in advance. The essence of the project of 'classical' music, then, would be the continual dramatisation of the possibility of an unfolding or elaboration which always ends happily, with some formal tonal closure. In this it mirrors the ideal form of bourgeois history at both the personal and national level: development and maturation only really serve to display what was there in the beginning.

But this does not happen without a struggle, the pathos of which must be communicated in the aesthetic experience. The fact that individual aspects of the classical work don't refer to anything external doesn't mean that the work as a whole can't. Sollertinsky described the central ideological complex of 19th century official musical life as 'symphonism', an appropriate term if we think of how central that particular genre was and is to the public culture of the middle and upper classes. Like Adorno, he identified Beethoven as the apex of this tradition, and connected his success in composition with the heroic energies generated by the French Revolution in the 18th century. The symphony is a musical working through of the 'ecstatic knowledge of human brotherhood', a 'great collective idea' animated by 'immediate revolutionary enthusiasm'; as such it appears as a natural product of petty bourgeois revolutionary ideology.[16] It appeals to humanity at large on the basis of a supposedly universal musical language, yet it affirms the need for a 'revolutionary' development: the forcefulness of the musical movement implies a struggle which belies the claim of actual human brotherhood. Sollertinsky went so far as to call Beethoven's symphonism 'dialogical' and 'polyper-sonal' (a term clearly kin to Bakhtin's idea of the 'polyphonic' Dostoevskian novel) because it depicted 'reality and the struggles taking place within it'.[17] Insofar as Sollertinsky is claiming that Beethoven's symphonies represent various wills, something extra-musical, rather than a conflicted state of musical language, it is difficult to decide how seriously we should take the idea of dialogism here (the relevant article is quite short). But he narrates a history of unmistakable descent from these heights to the 'Byronized', subjective work of the Romantics, one which corresponds to the politi-cal failure of the petty bourgeois democratic project over the course of the 19th century. Mahler's symphonies figure as the last futile attempt to revive the tradition of the Beethovenian symphony and its ideology of human brotherhood, a problem I will take up again further on.

The coexistence of these two values, formal perfection and heroic struggle, in the ideal classical work can be accounted for within the context of Bakhtin's theory of the poetic work. Poetic style is 'cut off from any mutual interaction with an alien language'[18] so as to ensure the 'unity and singularity' of its own.[19] The corresponding fiction in music is that tonality and musical form constitute a musical language consistent and unified across Europe and the 19th century, the vari-ations within which are matters of self-development rather than social and historical conditions. Yet at the same time this illusory unity of musical language makes possible an immedi-acy of expression, that sense of heroic drama, which grips us with a force seemingly independent of any convention. People may disagree about whether the *Eroica* has a specific historical referent but they are less likely to argue about its dramatic shape: the play of tension and resolution, stasis and movement appears as at once an immediate emotional expression and a property of the music itself. But the expression, the aesthetic experience itself, is unqualified only because the listener

... is not able to oppose his own poetic consciousness, his own intentions to the language that he uses, for he is completely within it and therefore cannot turn the limits of the style into an object one is conscious of, reflects on, relates to.[20]

So far as the classical tradition goes, consciousness of these stylistic limits is a matter of recognising the actually existing social and historical diversity of expression within it. The real disunity of the tradition and of the musical language within it is a fact which must be constantly explained away by an ever-broadening definition of the aesthetic and principles of Western 'art' music. Even its essential core, the classicism of the Vienna School, did not come into being through the gradual elaboration of some basic musical materials – scales or harmonic properties – but was constituted by the recontextualisation of an older, already elaborated discourse which had different goals and purposes. Durant describes how classical forms were developed by detaching forms of dance music, dramatic music (masque, pastoral and opera) and religious music from original contexts in which they had a different expressive function.[21] This typifies the dialogical, recontextualising moment in all composition. But this re-use of available materials can take very different forms. If you look on the existing conventions as givens which define the possibilities of expression, then composing is a matter of providing subjective content for these accepted forms. By contrast fully dialogical composition should require hearing the conventions themselves as historically limited languages, which can be spoken in such a way that they express themselves as a certain social and historical moment or attitude. The choice of musical style involves a very different type of commitment once 'Consciousness finds itself inevitably facing the necessity of *having to choose a language*.'[22]

Even composers committed to a fairly classical notion of the aesthetic were forced to acknowledge this necessity over the course of the 19th century. They did so by 'subjectivising' (to use Adorno's term) the existing musical conventions, most notably the practices of tonal harmony.

These took on the expressive role formerly reserved for melody in the compositions of Debussy and Wagner, and in so doing they surrendered their claims to be the external *structuring* principle of the work. If harmonic movement – the old basis of musical structure – becomes expressive, then the whole work begins to sound like a giant utterance. But even earlier Beethoven, in works like the late quartets, questioned the gestural basis of musical expression, the familiar techniques whereby music signifies 'transition', 'statement' or 'ending'. The series of broken, halting gestures with which Beethoven tries to finish Opus 131 calls attention to the very convention of ending. One could even say that it becomes music about ending, taking its own procedures as an object of investigation. When music does not merely represent but finds its own language represented as an object, when, to cite Adorno again, 'all sensuous immediacy reduces itself to mere foreground, to allegory', the result is the kind of distanced, indirect expression associated with the late quartets.[23]

Sollertinsky, in his short works on Mahler and Schoenberg, identified the work of the former as the true *Schwanengesang* of 'symphonism' and its musical language.[24] At the outset, however, it is worth pointing out that Sollertinsky's attitude to this symphonism varied significantly between the 1930s and the 1940s (he died of a heart attack in 1944). In the books mentioned above, the end of the petty bourgeois project of symphonism is final, and leads to a new form of orchestral writing which he calls chamber symphonism.[25] But in the essay 'Historical Types of Symphonic Dramaturgy', composed around 1941, Mahler, together with Tchaikovsky, is said to provide the materials for a revival of the classical project of symphonism, a revival which will take place in the Soviet Union.[26] Between these two positions lies, among other things, the codification of socialist realism in 1934 and the attack on modernism and its defenders, including Sollertinsky, in 1936.[27] One aspect of this theoretical shift in Soviet policy was the claim that the Soviet artist would now be the true heir of the classical humanist tradition of aesthetic achievement, and it is impossible not to see a connection between Sollertinsky's

change and this one. Be that as it may, Mahler figures in all
these works as the composer who poses 'the very problem of
the symphony' as an ideological form; his is the last attempt to
resurrect the utopian symphony of Beethoven 'addressed to
all of humanity'.[28] The attempt fails because the old musical
language of dramatic tension and resolution can't, in the
context of pre-war imperialist Europe, be spoken with conviction. It isn't just that tonal procedures changed radically in
the intervening years; the whole idea of dramatising the
accord between subjective struggle and objective unity and
reconciliation falls into disrepute. Instead there is the familiar
duality in Mahler's symphonic work: the 'ecstatic sermonizer
... crying in the desert' on one hand, and the sarcastic parodist
on the other.[29] The lyrical and dramatic elements in Mahler
veer almost into self-parody, estranging the convention of
this kind of musical pathos. 'The method of direct lyric',
Sollertinsky observed, 'begins to be combined with the
method of indirect or eccentric lyric, in which the lyric isn't
presented frontally but is masked by a grotesque intonation.'[30] This phenomenon could be called 'external dialogism', as could the earlier example of Beethoven's late style.
In both cases the estrangement or distancing of musical
conventions – for Beethoven the gestural language of resolution, for Mahler the discourse of lyrical pathos – comes not
from any confrontation between different musical languages
within the work but from the work's inability to 'take itself
seriously' and provide an immediate, poetic form of expression. The music refers implicitly to its own historical limits.
'Internal dialogism' would then refer to situations where
musical languages other than the 'classical style', drawn from
popular or folk music, are cited within the body of the piece
itself. The funeral march from Mahler's First Symphony and
the scherzos from his Ninth are examples of such a 'Mahlerian
grotesque'.[31] The popular genres inserted into these symphonies are double-voiced: there is their usual direct musical
sense as well as a parodic overtone which condemns the
'idiotic monotony of vulgar tunes'.[32] Mahler, like the
novelist, expresses himself through a socially alien language;
as Adorno says, 'his themes are expropriated ones'.[33]

Both Sollertinsky and Adorno regarded Mahler's work as a

prototype for modern progressive musical practice precisely because of these dialogical elements. The contrast between an already fading aesthetic pathos and lively yet philistine popular forms seems to endow the music with a 'feeling for the social and historical concreteness of living discourse'.[34] The depth of this dialogisation derives from the fact that not only are the inserted genres double-voiced but the framing discourse itself – classical Beethovenian symphonism – is thrown into question. It is almost as if we are confronted with 'musics', none of which is quite adequate on its own, at a time when the reassuring sound of classical aesthetic 'music' was no longer possible. But although Mahler was able to confront the social and historical limits of Central European high culture in his music, he was unable, and probably unwilling, to do anything to disturb its actual social basis. The rest, as they say, is history. In Europe the bourgeoisie emerged victorious, if bloodied, after the political crises of the First World War period and after. The institutional basis of their cultural dominance remained in place and through it 'classical' musical discourse was given a new lease on life, albeit one which depended almost entirely on works of the past. Today, Mahler is consumed as an orchestral showpiece with no 'social' significance what-soever. The lesson is clear: to really dialogise music in an effective way you have to bring in not just musical language from popular social contexts but actual institutional elements of those social contexts themselves: forms of performance, reception and composition.

The actual institutional basis of 'classical' music has been critically analysed by Alan Durant and Jacques Attali (in his recently translated *Noise*).[35] They suggest that what unifies classical musical discourse is not tonality but a particular social context: the spectacle of performance in the concert hall. It is the separation of music from its symbolic role in public and ecclesiastical ceremonies and its corresponding transformation into a product, a commodity to be bought and sold, which monologises music. Music appears as pure form, self-contained and devoid of social meaning, because it becomes an object of consumption, capable of being used without reference to a supporting political or cultural ritual.

This endows music with an autonomous *value* (a key term in the argument), asserted and measured in the act of exchange (payment for performance or 'representation' as Attali calls it). But for this purely 'aesthetic' music to come into being, several institutional changes are necessary. Beginning in the late 17th century, but most significantly during the 18th, concert halls are developed as the exclusive sites for the performance of official music. Although at first this applies only to 'art' music, during the second half of the 19th century popular music undergoes a similar process of confinement and pricing through the establishment of cafe concerts and cabarets. A condition for this commodification is legal status for the musical work itself, guaranteed by the establishment of copyright for music. Whereas in ecclesiastical and courtly contexts the 'body' of the composer was owned by his employer (as with Bach and Haydn), in the 19th century the dominant practice becomes the sale of separate musical works, owned by the composer or publisher at the outset. This seems straightforward enough until we stop to think about what the musical work now legally recognised actually is. It's not quite the same thing as the notations of a score but then again it's not exactly equivalent to the sum of its actual performances. An intangible commodity, neither flesh nor fowl, which can be 'represented' in a performance and sold for a price. In this new order, music is no longer a continuum of melodies, ornaments and instrumental techniques which can be drawn upon by an improvisatory practice, but a collection of discrete, individual, performable works. And this in turn implies the notion of a repertory which can extend in space (as it does when Liszt begins to perform the works of others in 1830) and through history (as it does when Mendelssohn revives Bach in 1829). So many works and performances implies a market and from there it is a short step to the competitive star system which so visibly dominates public music today.

Sollertinsky did not confront these institutional realities in his defence of the modernism of Mahler and Schoenberg or in his later plan for an 'epic symphonism'. This latter was a scheme for what in many respects sounds like a true 'musical novel'. The epic symphony was to be a *lyric of the whole people*, the whole culture, a lyric which crystallises over the course of a century, which is bound up with national-heroic traditions and the great historical past of a people.[36]

In other words it was a symphonic work which would blend together the popular musical life of a nation. As a plan for composition the idea is interesting, but without a parallel plan for the democratisation and popularisation of musical institutions one can only assume the epic symphony would find the same fate as Mahler. Like the classical aesthetic to which it is too closely bound, epic symphonism assumes that musical practice is mostly a matter of the 'notes themselves'.

But punk and New Wave music, American country-and-western and Appalachian bluegrass, opera, jazz and rap differ not only in terms of their technical musical resources and conventions but also in terms of form of production (live, recorded), relation to capitalist imperatives (profit-making, subsidised, tolerated), context of performance (as part of a spectacle, as part of a casual get-together, as part of a political movement), concept of repertory (common stock of alterable tunes and rhythms, unique performances, changing list of hits) and, of course, in terms of the size and social composition of their audience, and of the explicit ideological content of the lyrics, if any. It is easy to assert that each of these is a distinct social practice from which the music cannot be simply abstracted; but it is much more difficult to characterise the actual social and historical meanings at stake, because musical meaning itself remains a hazy and ill-defined thing. In speech, tone of voice, rhythm, pace of conversation and like factors all determine how we feel or relate to the strictly ideational or conceptual content of the utterance; they combine it with a certain affective force. Similarly music alters or reinforces not just ideas but the conscious or unconscious physical and emotional responses bound up with them. To borrow a term from the literary criticism of Raymond Williams, music deals in 'structures of feeling': not raw experience but forms – dramatic, narrative or lyrical – which organise our response to that experience. Elvis Presley was not just a great set of chops but the explosion of a new kind of sexuality – popular, youthful, aggressive, visible – into white popular musical consciousness. It wasn't just music about sex but music which drew on sexual energies and images in order to come up with a new form of erotic musical pleasure. And no one is in any doubt about the degree to which this musical pleasure depended upon certain contextual factors: the visual image of Elvis himself, the existence of an excited 'crowd' of fans, and so on. All these factors distinguish the musical sexuality of his work from that at work in the music of Cole Porter, or in rural Southern blues. Each is a presentation of sexuality with a distinctive socio-ideological feel.

So any adequate sociolinguistics of music has a rather hard road ahead. There is no single musical logic to discover: this mistake is a consequence of the institutional separation of music from its obvious social functions in high culture. Instead there are a variety of social practices in which musical technique is a central, though variable element. To grasp musical meaning is to understand: what does Top 40 mean when we hear it on the car radio? How does bluegrass affect those who play and hear it in Appalachian communities? What does Muzak mean (if that is not too strong a word) to people in dentists' offices and supermarkets? But it also means knowing how and how much the various elements of a practice contribute to the overall sense. Then we are in a position to guess what the effects will be of recontextualising a musical practice, whether this be bringing rap music into a white disco in London, putting orchestral performances on TV or combining folk traditions on a record.

This is the fundamental dialogism in all musical practice. Even the most formal classical performance, lacking any open sign of social or historical location, translates its force into socially specific beliefs about man's heroic struggle with fate or the virtues of culture, although this process may be mediated by a number of cultural and educational institutions. But although it produces social meanings with definite historical consequences, it may not produce them as 'consciously social' and this distinguishes it from the 'novelised' forms of musical practice usually, though not exclusively, found in the 'open spaces of public squares and streets'. These latter start from a feeling for the emptiness of the dominant musical discourse, the distance between its structure of feeling and the needs of popular groups under intense political or economic pressure. They therefore mark a division between the popular and the official, emphasising the social rootedness of the discourse on each side of the divide. By conscious opposition or parody they dialogise an alien musical culture which they must acknowledge, given their subordinate status.

The actual materials for this kind of musical novelisation or open dialogism appear to be abundant beyond measure. It is hard to imagine anything to rival the sheer productivity of popular musical practice: the by now established forms of blues, jazz, rock, folk and popular song have, in the last 20 years, been subject to quite conscious and innovative transformations. Punk, ska and rap involved not merely new musical conventions but changes in the total practice of music with conscious social and political overtones. In different ways popular musical practices may express the distance between popular and official ideologies, but not all of them become foci for open social and political discontent. For this kind of novelisation I think we can hypothesise some general requirements.

There must be some open challenge to a dominant ideological value, an articulation of an opposed structure of feeling around some common ideological territory. Examples of this which come easily to mind are Grace Jones's contestation of the canons of acceptable female sexual behaviour or the use in punk of a sound quality consciously opposed to the slickness and production values of commercial rock. Whatever else the novel might have been to Bakhtin it was always profane; the word 'desecration' almost sums up the ideological impetus of the novel. But the desecration was always of a particular 'philosophical' (as Bakhtin liked to call it) kind, which contrasted some kind of popular 'common sense' with the ideological pretensions of official society. So one has to avoid, on the one hand, the simple organisation of an alternative set of values (utopianism) which never faces up to the struggle around key ideological points, and on the other, a denial which does not lead in the direction of some systematic 'common-sense' alternative.

Many of the central values of official musical culture have been challenged by composers whom we now think of as part of the unified classical tradition supporting it. I have already pointed out Mahler's dialogisation of the Romantic aesthetic but he was just one of a number of late 19th and early 20th century rebels. The new Slavic national traditions as well as older French and Italian traditions were anxious to separate themselves from the 'pure' music of the Germanic mainstream. Most remarkable, however, is the range of early and mid 20th century modernism: Schoenberg creating a form of expression which reconstructs musical dynamics; Ives literally overwhelming his work with 'extra-musical' public noise; Satie's open parodies. But these critiques, like Mahler's, never really gained a foothold and were eventually incorporated into the concert hall repertory, albeit rather unevenly. Their negations of musical values, unlike those of the true novel, never achieved an audibly social feel (except perhaps in the case of Ives), probably because they did not look on their problems as anything other than aesthetic questions. In the novel, if the questioning of language is not to be merely 'rhetorical' then it must be 'fertilised by a deep-rooted connection with the forces of historical development which stratify language'.[37] The challenged musical discourse must not merely appear conventional and limited but it must become, in the hands of the novelist, 'speech from speaking lips, conjoined with the image of a speaking person', with a definite social and historical identity.[38] If the difference between Satie and Impressionism or Schoenberg and Romanticism does not appear as a *social* difference then it loses its necessary leverage. This second general requirement bears on a lot of the borrowing and influence which goes on in popular music and in some 'postmodern' forms. Musical language must be identified closely enough with a social context and a social ideology to carry the taste of that context with it even when it enters foreign musical territory. The specialisation of music as a separate discipline threatens this kind of social identity.

Once marked off from social life in general, musical techniques become stylistic resources available for aesthetic manipulation. They acquire and maintain 'social and historical concreteness' when they are integrated into a more general cultural or social movement. Michel Foucault, admittedly not known for his rock criticism, felt this concreteness was part of the current scene: 'to like rock, to like a certain kind of rock rather than another, is also a way of life, a manner of reacting; it is a whole set of tastes and attitudes.'[39]

This brings us to the most obvious and crucial general precondition for musical dialogisation: freeing popular musical activity from the circuit of capitalist production and finance. Since the advent of a mass recording industry, popular activity has provided the raw materials for the musical trends which are the lifeblood of commodified music. The diversity and innovation in performance and reception typical of popular music is erased when the music is abstracted and placed onto the capitalist circuit of radio playlist, promotional tour and record/cassette/CD sales. Without real control over composition, production and conditions of performance, it is impossible for the creation of musical sound to respond to cultural and political needs, and recognition of this fact has led to popular movements organising their own production and distribution: the setting up of Olivia Records by feminists in the 1970s, the attempts to organise an alternative small club circuit in certain cities, and the many attempts to marry musical activity to political agitation (Rock Against Racism and the like) are some typical instances. It was Adorno's great virtue that, however deep his allegiance to the project of Western classical music, he recognised that a similar insertion into the recording industry had destroyed whatever critical edge the great aesthetic tradition might have had.[40] In both cases commodified music may still embody ideological meaning, often of a very progressive kind, but the intensity of the response is instantly transformed into the desire to consume or experience the music itself, it never, so to speak, leads beyond the record.

This prevents a lot of the music we love from reaping its

best effects. Often aspirations which are wholly incompatible with a capitalist society are encoded in musical forms
and kinds of performance which drain away any sense of
tension between these values and those they oppose. The
essence of a contribution to a musical dialogue should be an
internal incompleteness: it should be a work which cannot
be understood except in the context of its struggle with the
dominant culture. As these struggles are unresolved and
daily refought in social life so we should expect the music
which articulates them to be characterised by a certain
historical unfinishedness. One possible consequence of this
is a lessening of interest in producing finished works and an
increase in an interest in a flexible form of music in constant
tension with the dominant culture. Many popular forms are
characterised by open and participatory forms of performance; there may be no set score but a beat, or a skeletal chart
around which improvisation can take place. The recent
explosion in technical resources has expanded these
possibilities. Now we all perform the work as we play with
the little dials and switches on the amplifier, although our
intervention is limited to constructing some ideal sound
quality more or less irrelevant to anything the music might
actually mean. But at the same time a lot of the most striking
innovation in rock and hip hop centres on these new
possibilities in the electronic manipulation of sound.
Presenting or performing music is no longer a question of
the interpretation of single works; a more appropriate model
might be the social questions raised when a DJ decides how
to mix which records together.

But even performance in the old-fashioned sense can do
with a sense of redirection. These days Haydn plays the role
of light opener while composers as diverse as Beethoven,
Shostakovich and Debussy might provide the 'aesthetic'
backbone of a concert programme. The social gulf
separating these forms of expression is enormous and needs
to be reopened, so that some of the scandalous force of these
works might be revived. This shouldn't mean simply yoking
some extract from the classics to a political movement (and
the 1987 Labour campaign demonstrates just how horrible
that can be) but trying to explore the social dimensions of

aesthetic experience, in order to discover the reasons why we find Haydn trivial, Strauss disturbing, Debussy arousing. The points of pleasure and tension in our musical experience should lead to questions, linked to our social experience in general, rather than to aesthetic satisfactions which lead nowhere.

Although its precondition is a 'spontaneous' gap between needs and current dominant modes of expression, all musical dialogism is the fruit of sustained cultural and political thought and organisation. This article is analytical but most of the actual exploration of the social and political questions I have raised takes the form of artistic decisions, made in the act of composition, performance and presentation. The pleasure of music-making, itself a powerful weapon of solidarity, is not in the end separable from wider social and political goals. Often music is most satisfying when it is part of the collective identity of a group which knows it has a long struggle ahead. But music, no less than any other practice, will not be perfected without accompanying political and social change. Because music is so deeply entangled in the web of history it cannot help but be part of a larger social dialogue. But this, Bakhtin would surely have agreed, is its strength, for it is from aspirations and desires formed in the everyday struggle in public squares and streets that it receives its greatest creative impetus.

Notes

[1] These works have been translated as: *Problems of Dostoevsky's Poetics*, Manchester 1984; *Rabelais and His World,* Cambridge 1968, reprinted Indiana 1986; *The Dialogic Imagination*, Austin 1981, these being the essays on the novel; *Speech Genres and Other Late Essays*, Austin 1986. The works whose authorship is disputed are V N Voloshinov, *Marxism and the Philosophy of Language*, New York 1973, reprinted Cambridge 1986; P N Medvedev, *The Formal Method in Literary Scholarship*, Baltimore 1978, reprinted Cambridge 1986; V N Voloshinov, *Freudianism*, New York 1976. For biographical information on Bakhtin see Katerina Clark and Michael Holquist, *Mikhail Bakhtin* Cambridge 1984.
[2] See Clark and Holquist, *op cit*, pp 49, 104-5.
[3] See Boris Schwarz, *Music and Musical Life in Soviet Russia 1917-1970*, New York 1972, pp 119-32.

[4] Bakhtin, 'Discourse in the Novel' in *The Dialogic Imagination*, p 276, translation altered.

[5] *Ibid*, p 276.

[6] *Ibid*, p 293.

[7] *Ibid*, p 276.

[8] *Ibid*, p 291, translation altered.

[9] *Ibid*, p 285, translation altered.

[10] *Ibid*, p 259.

[11] *Ibid*, p 273.

[12] *Ibid*, p 273.

[13] *Ibid*, p 331.

[14] Durant, *Conditions of Music*, Macmillan 1984, p 42.

[15] See Adorno, *The Philosophy of Modern Music*, New York 1980, pp 54-60 and 'Arnold Schoenberg 1874-1951' in *Prisms*, Neville Spearman 1967, pp 152-7 for examples of his argument.

[16]See Sollertinsky, *Gustav Mahler*, Leningrad 1932, pp 4-7, 21 and the essay 'Historical Types of Symphonic Dramaturgy' in *Muzykalno-Istoricheskie Etyudi*, Leningrad 1956.

[17] 'Historical Types', *op cit*, pp 303-4.

[18] *The Dialogic Imagination, op cit*, p 285, translation altered.

[19] *Ibid*, p 286.

[20] *Ibid*, translation altered.

[21] Durant, *op cit*, pp 41-2.

[22] *The Dialogic Imagination, op cit*, p 295.

[23] *Prisms, op cit*, p 169.

[24] See *Gustav Mahler, op cit*, pp 4-8 and *Arnold Schoenberg*, Leningrad 1934, pp 41-2.

[25] *Arnold Schoenberg, op cit*, p 42.

[26] 'Historical Types', *op cit*, pp 307-8.

[27] See Boris Schwarz, *op cit*.

[28] *Arnold Schoenberg, op cit*, p 41.

[29] *Gustav Mahler, op cit*, p 25.

[30] 'Historical Types', *op cit*, p 307.

[31] *Gustav Mahler, op cit*, pp 26-9.

[32] *Ibid*, p 28.

[33] 'On the Fetish Character in Music and the Regression in Listening', in Andrew Arato and Eike Gebhardt (eds), *The Essential Frankfurt School Reader*, Blackwell 1978, p 297.

[34] *The Dialogic Imagination, op cit*, p 331.

[35] See Durant *op cit*, pp 29-44 and Attali, *Noise: The Political Economy of Music*, Manchester University Press 1985, pp. 46-86.

[36] 'Historical Types', *op cit*, p 309.

[37] Bakhtin, *The Dialogic Imagination, op cit*, p 325, translation altered.

[38] *Ibid*, p 336.

[39] Michel Foucault and Pierre Boulez, 'Contemporary Music and the Public', *Perspectives of New Music*, Fall-Winter 1986, p 8.

[40] See 'On the Fetish Character in Music ...', especially pp 277-80, 284.

Christopher Norris

Utopian Deconstruction: Ernst Bloch, Paul de Man and the politics of music

The signs are that Marxist criticism is at present undergoing one of its periodic shifts of theoretical vision. What is at stake is a widespread revaluation of utopian or visionary thought as it bears upon the Marxist project of historical understanding. This amounts to a questioning of the received view that utopian reverie was a kind of infantile disorder, an escape from the problems and exigencies of materialist critique into a realm of unanchored speculation where thinking encountered no resistance to its wildest dreams. This attitude was supposedly warranted by Marx's scattered allusions to utopian mystics and ideologues like Saint Simon, Fourier and Robert Owen. It was also based on a decidedly selective reading of Engels's *Communism: scientific and utopian* (1880), where the argument for Marxist 'science' in fact goes along with a qualified respect for the genuine emancipatory impulses embodied in utopian thought.

Fredric Jameson's book *The Political Unconscious* (1980) sets out to reclaim a positive or future-oriented version of Marxist hermeneutic, a philosophy of principled utopian faith to set against the purely demystifying drive of so much recent theoretical work.[1] He is even willing to enlist various patristic, theological and other-worldly schemes of interpretative thought, provided these can be effectively coopted into a master-narrative whose ultimate terms are secular and Marxist. Thus Jameson argues for a reappropriation of the traditional four 'levels' of exegesis – the literal, moral, allegorical and anagogical – as stages on the path to an enriched understanding of Marxist hermeneutic method. History remains, in Jameson's words, the 'untranscendable horizon' of thought, the point towards which all meanings converge in the quest for some ultimate 'totalising' grasp. Dialectical materialism is the only standpoint from which these various partial narratives and perspectives can at last be seen as composing a history that makes sense of them in adequately complex and non-reductive terms. Otherwise Marxism is always in danger of imposing a monological scheme of understanding, either through some variant of the crude base/superstructure model, or – as in Althusser's case – by reducing consciousness, history, culture and subjective agency to mere effects of a dominant structural complex whose workings can only appear under the aspect of detached theoretical knowledge.[2]

Jamesons's ideas are expressly indebted to the greatest of modern utopian thinkers, the German Marxist and visionary philosopher Ernst Bloch. There is a well-known passage from one of Marx's letters that Bloch was fond of quoting, and that indicates something of his own close but ambivalent relationship to Marxist thought.

So our slogan must be: reform of consciousness, not through dogma, but through the analysis of that mystical consciousness which has not yet become clear to itself. It will then turn out that the world has long dreamt of that of which it had only to have a clear idea to possess it really. It will turn out that it is not a question of any conceptual rupture between past and future, but rather of the *completion* of the thoughts of the past.[3]

This passage is remarkable for the fact that it prefigures all the major themes of Bloch's utopian thinking. It is also of interest, in light of what I have said so far, for rejecting the idea of revolutionary change as a rupture with past ways of thought, or as striving to achieve, in Althusserian terms, a decisive 'epistemological break' that marks the transition from lived ideology to genuine theoretical knowledge. One can read Bloch's work as a sustained, indeed lifelong, effort to give substance to the kind of alternative vision held out by these comments of Marx. That they strike a note distinctly alien to most subsequent versions of Marxist thought is a fact to which Bloch's own fortunes, and the reception-history of his writing, bear eloquent witness.

Up to now it has been difficult for the monoglot English reader to obtain more than a hazy impression of Bloch's enormously ambitious and wide-ranging work. Apart from Jameson's pioneering chapter in *Marxism And Form* (1971), the main source was through Bloch's various debates and polemics with other Marxist thinkers, notably Adorno, Lukacs and Brecht.[4] The sheer bulk of his writings, as well as their charged poetic style and resistance to orderly exposition, have so far conspired against his entering the mainstream of Western Marxist debate. However, this situation has now begun to change with the appearance of two major texts in English translation. One is Bloch's magnum opus *The Principle Of Hope*, a three-volume work which ranges over the entire compass of his thinking, from the politics of popular culture and everyday life to philosophy, religion, aesthetics, psychoanalysis and every sphere of thought where Bloch detects the latent signs of an as-yet unrealised utopian potential.[5] The other is a collection of essays *On The Philosophy Of Music* which brings together work from his early 'expressionist' period with pieces written much later when Bloch's thinking had undergone a shift toward more overtly Marxist concepts and categories.[6] Between them, these volumes make it possible at last for the English reader to grasp the full extent of Bloch's innovatory thinking.

In what follows, I shall concentrate on those aspects of his work most directly concerned with music in its political or utopian-redemptive aspect. For Bloch, as for others before him in the German philosophical tradition – notably Schopenhauer and Nietzsche – music was at once the most humanly-revealing form of art and the form most resistant to description or analysis in conceptual terms. But this was no reason, he argued, for retreating into an attitude of mystical irrationalism which denied music any kind of cognitive import, or (conversely) for adopting the formalist standpoint which reduced it to a play of purely abstract structures and relationships devoid of expressive content. If musical aesthetics had hitherto tended to vacillate between these extremes, it was not so much by reason of some ultimate deadlock in the nature of thinking about music, but more an indication of the limits placed upon thought by its present confinement to a rigid categorical logic and a subject-object dualism incapable of transcending such antinomies. Bloch sees an example of this limiting perspective in the way that Bach's music has been praised alternately for its qualities of 'pure' mathematical structure, and its power to move emotions by a kind of affective contagion quite beyond reach of analysis.

> Utterly wrong though the romanticizing which occurred in Mendelssohn's rendering of Bach is, equally an understanding of Bach cannot be achieved by mere dead dismissal of romanticism, as if nothing remained after it but reified form.[7]

Here Bloch concurs with Adorno's argument in the polemical essay 'Bach defended against his devotees'.[8] Critics and performers who celebrate Bach in the name of 'absolute music' are in fact submitting their judgment to those forces of inhuman abstraction and reification which mark the latest stage of capitalist social relations.

> This 'new objectivity' in relation to Bach reproduces with a supposedly positive significance the judgment which was common half a century after Bach's death and which in fact submerged him as the greatest musician.[9]

And such excesses always lead to a swing in the opposite direction, in this case toward a style of sentimentalised performance which lacks any feeling for structure or form. Thus

> a poorly overcome romanticism took revenge by again introducing expressive interpretation, but now not even in the Mendelssohnian style but in the style of the sentimental bower.[10]

This reception-history is for Bloch symptomatic of everything that presently stands in the way of an adequate musical response. It reflects the kind of bad dialectic, the shuttling back and forth between extremes of 'objective' and 'subjective' response, which leaves its mark on every thought and perception in an age of commodified cultural experience. Bloch would no doubt have found this judgment amply confirmed had he lived to witness the present-day obsession with 'authenticity' in musical performance. Such ideas can only be deluded, he would argue, in so far as they substitute a dead, monumentalised concept of tradition for the living, evolving, dialectical process of change which has come between us and the cultural products of an earlier age. The jargon of authenticity is in fact nothing more than a kind of self-defeating nostalgia, a harking-back to ideas and practices that are falsified as soon as one sets them up as absolute, ahistorical values.

For Bloch, the only way to transcend such reified notions is by a new kind of listening, one that effectively opens the path toward a state of redeemed utopian promise. This 'surplus' of future-oriented meaning was ungraspable, he thought, within the terms handed down by Western philosophical tradition. Certainly music had figured at various points in this tradition as a kind of qualitative touchstone, a name for whatever surpassed or eluded the powers of abstract conceptualisation. For Schopenhauer especially, music gave access to a realm of primordial experience – the Will in all its ceaseless strivings and desires – which the other arts (painting, architecture, poetry) could only express at a certain distance of formal representation.[11] Thus music was the truth to which philosophy aspired but which could never reach the point of articulate understanding since language itself, and philosophical language in particular, dealt only in concepts or abstract figures of thought. And there is a deeper ambivalence about Schopenhauer's attitude to music, since he commits himself to the following contradictory propositions: that the highest point of human wisdom and felicity is to achieve detachment from the restless activity of Will, this state to be arrived at through a kind of self-disciplined contemplative repose, much akin to the Nirvana of Buddhist teaching; that music most directly embodies the unconscious, inarticulate strivings of Will; and yet, despite this, that music is the highest form of art since it dispenses with the various intermediary concepts and representations which characterise other kinds of aesthetic experience. All three propositions are integral to his thinking, but there is no way of squaring their plainly contradictory entailments.

This problem has been recognised by Schopenhauer's commentators, even the more sympathetic among them, who treat it as a curious logical flaw in his otherwise intensely single-minded philosophy.[12] For Bloch, on the other hand, it is a sign of Schopenhauer's failure to grasp the utopian or forward-looking element in music, its appeal not to a realm of archaic, instinctual desire that precedes articulate thought, but to that which lies beyond the aporias of self-conscious reason and which draws thinking on toward the promise of transcending all such antinomies. Schopenhauer can conceive of no ultimate good save that which comes of escaping the Will, putting away all objects of desire and thus enjoying that long-awaited 'sabbath' from the penal servitude of instinct when 'the wheel of Ixion stands still' and the mind achieves a state of perfected stoical indifference. But what then of music, the experience of which – as Bloch says, paraphrasing Schopenhauer – 'speaks of the exclusive essence itself, weal and woe only, the universal Will and that alone as the most serious and the most real thing of all we can find'?[13] This desperate conclusion is forced upon Schopenhauer by his equation of 'reality' with the dark, destructive, self-preying nature of human instinct, and his total disbelief in the redemptive power of history, politics or secular reason. By renouncing all hope in the future, by ignoring the utopian dimension of music and hearing it only as a record of archaic struggles and defeats, Schopenhauer condemns his own philosophy to self-contradiction and ultimate nihilist despair.

Bloch's argument can be seen as the affirmative counterpart to Schopenhauer's gloomy metaphysics of will and representation. He concurs in treating music as the source of primordial truths that can as yet find no voice in philosophy or the other arts. This power he attributes to music's peculiarly inward character, its capacity to call out feelings and responses that have hitherto existed only in confused or inchoate form, but now find expression in the realm of ordered sound. Such is the capacity for 'visionary listening' (*Hellhören*) that can work to transfigure the very conditions of human sensuous awareness. What music embodies in potential form is 'a figuring-out *in fonte hominum et rerum* that is utopian and fermenting, in an area of intensity that is open only to music'.[14] For music provides the most striking intimation of that always-conditional future state when subject and object, mind and nature might yet be reconciled beyond their present, divided condition. Like Schopenhauer again, he contrasts this inwardness of musical experience with the external, phenomenal or visual character pertaining to other art-forms. Of course this is not so obviously the case with poetry or literary language. But in so far as these partake of *representation* – of that which, according to Schopenhauer, exists only at a certain remove from the primordial experience of Will – they are likewise to be thought of as mediated forms of expression which lack the sheer intensity of musical experience.

This is not to say that Bloch in any sense devalues literature, or sets up the kind of rigid hierarchical system that one finds in Schopenhauer's theory of art. Indeed, some of his most powerful writing in *The Principle Of Hope* is devoted to Goethe's *Faust* and other such works where the impulse of utopian thought is expressed through images of secularised mystical experience or promethean overreaching. But it is in music that his thinking finds its elective homeground, a domain where the subject-object relation takes on a peculiarly charged and prophetic character. That is why its meaning eludes any theory based on notions of 'absolute form', or of structural relations, numerical proportions and so forth, as the ultimate constituents of music. Such ideas are *theoretical* in the root sense, going back to the Greek terms for seeing, contemplation and other essentially visual metaphors raised into concepts of purely intellectual knowledge. As Jacques Derrida reminds us, these sublimated figures so permeate the discourse of

Western philosophy that it is impossible to escape their influence.[15] But we can, according to Bloch, at least imagine an alternative realm of experience, one which points beyond the kind of static ontology enforced by these visual analogues, and which thus opens up a more active, transformative grasp of the subject-object dialectic.

> Music is, for a deeper reason than was hitherto evident, the latest of the arts, succeeding visuality and belonging to the formally eccentric philosophy of inwardness, its ethics and metaphysics ... This means objectively penetrating to the core of the listener instead of the savant, instead of mere form-analysis ... Both the existence and the concept of music are only attained in conjunction with a new object-theory, with the metaphysics of divination and utopia.[16]

Thus music holds out the promise of a radical transformation, not only in our habits of aesthetic response but in every sphere of thought – ethics and politics included – where the relation between knower and known is a field potentially open for creative reimagining.

Of course there are problems in coming to terms with any philosophy which stakes its faith on such a leap outside all past and present categories of thought. The difficulty is posed most acutely by Bloch's attempts to explain the 'dialectic of nature' in terms of an envisioned utopian overcoming of the subject-object dualism. This might seem to place him in dangerous proximity to that current of vulgar-marxist materialism which naively conflates the dialectical process of thought with the antagonistic forces (or so-called 'contradictions') of external nature. In fact Bloch is everywhere alert to such confusions, and regards them as determined in part by the inadequate heritage of formal, post-Aristotelian logic, and in part by the pitiless divorce between subject and object imposed by an alien, dissociated sense of how thinking relates to the world of sensuous experience. His reiterated *noch nicht* ('not yet') is therefore both a kind of logical shifter – designed to bring about a qualitative change in the order of classical logic – and a means toward imagining the ultimate transcendence of human alienation from nature. (In this respect Bloch comes close to the position adopted by the early Lukacs in *History And Class-Consciousness*, although their paths diverged sharply when Lukacs came to repudiate his own 'idealist' leanings in the name of Stalinist orthodoxy.) Yet this transcendence can only be achieved through a veritable leap of faith, since Bloch's arguments depend absolutely on a speculative concept of nature and a logic (as some would say, a pseudo-logic) whose potential is as yet unrealised in any presently-existing system of thought.

These problems are addressed by Wayne Hudson in the only full-length study of Bloch yet to appear in English. If it is not possible, as Hudson says, 'to extract much emancipatory potential from the dialectical process of nature in its present form', then there is always the risk that this process will be 'arbitrarily transferred to history, despite the fact that in history, unlike nature, a subjective factor has emerged with conscious purposes'.[17] In a sense this criticism undoubtedly hits the mark. One could cite from almost every page of Bloch's writing sentences which metaphorically double back and forth between images of natural growth and development on the one hand, and figures of utopian-redemptive promise on the other. Very often they strike an apocalyptic tone which does indeed suggest that these metaphors are carrying a burden of meaning that resists articulation in more prosaic terms, and that might appear largely nonsensical if so treated. The following passage may stand as a fairly representative instance:

> Only the musical note, that enigma of sensuousness, is sufficiently unencumbered by the world yet phenomenal enough to the last to return – like the *metaphysical* word – as a final material factor in the fulfilment of mystical self-perception, spread purely upon the golden sub-soil of the receptive human potentiality.[18]

Such writing is clearly open to the charge that it works by assimilating nature – or a certain quasi-dialectical image of nature – to a language shot through with metaphors of human purpose, activity and conscious striving for change. To this extent it bears out Hudson's argument that Bloch is in danger of collapsing ontological distinctions, treating history as a kind of organic process, and thus producing a mystified account of those social and material forces that shape human existence.

One response to this charge might be that Bloch is after all attempting nothing less than a full-scale revision of the concepts and categories that have hitherto governed what counts as 'rational' argument. This takes him back to the heritage of German metaphysical and speculative thought, to those philosophers (Kant, Fichte, Schelling and Hegel) in whose work there unfolds a dialectical debate on the relationship between subject and object, knower and known. It also leads to his revisionist account of those ancient, medieval and renaissance thinkers whom Bloch regards as having opened up a space for utopian divination. In his late work *Experimentum Mundi* (1975), he explores the lineage of an 'Aristotelian left' which worked to convert the 'immaterial forms' of a Platonizing Greek philosophy into an 'active form-laden matter', a realist doctrine which nonetheless rejected any notion of the real as fixed in terms of its presently-existing attributes.[19] For Aristotle, reality is not exhausted by giving an account of what offers itself to immediate knowledge and perception. It must also include an aspect of future possibility, a dimension wherein things are latently other than they seem, and where knowledge takes on a forward-looking modality adequate to this sense of the capacity for change possessed by objects in the natural world. Aristotle's potentialist metaphysics was largely lost to view through the subsequent growth of more narrowly empirical philosophies of mind and nature. But its promise was maintained by those heterodox thinkers – notably Avicenna and Averroës – who continued to develop a kind of utopian materialism, one that held out against the reification of matter as inert substance, and the consequent reduction of knowledge itself to a passive contemplation of external forms. Even where this tradition led into byways of mystical and pantheist thought – as with Bruno and renaissance neo-Platonism – there was still, Bloch argues, a materialist subtext of unrealised hopes and desires which might yet be reclaimed by a Marxism open to such heterogeneous sources.

But there remains a real problem with any such use of organicist or naturalising images and metaphors. This problem takes on a political edge when one considers the role played by such analogies in the history of aesthetics – and especially of musical aesthetics – in the wake of German romanticism. For Schopenhauer, as we have seen, music gave access to a realm of experience beyond words or concepts, a realm of ultimate truth, to be sure, but of a truth which could never find expression in articulate form. For Nietzsche likewise, music holds out the promise of a knowledge beyond mere conceptual reason, a knowledge forgotten since the time of Socrates, when Greek tragic drama entered its period of decline and philosophy, in the shape of Socratic dialectic, asserted its claims to rational mastery.[20] Nietzsche is very firm in rejecting what he sees as the world-weary quietism and escapist ethos of Schopenhauer's thinking. Music – and specifically Wagner's music – brings with it a force of creative renewal which will make of nineteenth-century German culture a second great age of world-historical achievement, one in which the two great opposing impulses – the Dionysian and Apollonian – will again be interlocked in the kind of titanic struggle that engenders great works of art. Up to now, Nietzsche argued, this vital energy had been lost through the predominance of the Apollonian principle, of everything that belonged on the side of form, self-discipline, abstraction and rational control. Hence the conventional view of Greek culture promulgated by scholars like Winckelmann, the notion that its highest attainments consisted in the 'classical' ideals of harmony, grace, perfected balance and proportion. What was lost to sight through this civilising process was precisely the repressed Dionysian element, the dark side of irrational energies and drives which could scarcely be contained by that other, form-giving principle.

Such is the pseudo-historical myth of origins that animates the argument of Nietzsche's early tract, *The Birth Of Tragedy from the Spirit of Music*.[21] It seeks to transform the very nature of thought and perception by asking us to hear, in Wagner's music, the signs of a new aesthetic dispensation that would overcome all forms of conceptual abstraction,

including the subject-object antinomy that had plagued the
discourse of philosophy from Socrates to Kant. In this
respect Nietzsche is simply pushing to its extreme that
high-romantic faith in the synthesising powers of creative
imagination that typifies the work of philosopher-critics like
Goethe and Coleridge. Aesthetics takes over the burden of
achieving what cannot be achieved by any form of
theoretical reason, namely that union of sensuous experience with concepts of pure understanding which had figured,
since Kant at least, as the main preoccupation of philosophy.
Kant himself had claimed to resolve this problem in some
notoriously obscure passages where he appeals to the
'productive imagination' as a faculty that somehow manages
to synthesise the forms of *a priori* knowledge (for instance,
our concepts of causality, time and space) with the concrete
data of phenomenal experience which alone give substance
to those concepts.[22] Otherwise thinking would soon become
lost in the toils of metaphysical abstraction, in those airy
regions of speculative paradox which Kant describes under
the heading 'Paralogisms of Pure Reason'. And this would
lead inevitably to the dead-end of epistemological scepticism, the despair of discovering any valid or necessary link
between concepts and phenomena. Hence his dictum that
'concepts without intuitions are empty; intuitions without
concepts are blind'. But this claim is made good at crucial
points in Kant's argument (including the 'Transcendental
Aesthetic' that lays out his groundwork for the *Critique Of
Pure Reason*) in terms that derive, more or less obliquely,
from the discourse on art and the modalities of aesthetic
experience that will occupy Kant in the Third *Critique*.[23]

So it was that such questions were installed at the heart of
subsequent (post-Kantian) philosophy of mind and knowledge. In Hegel, Schopenhauer and Nietzsche, aesthetics
comes to play an increasingly central role, as the emphasis
shifts from a critical account of reason, its constitutive
powers and limits, to a kind of expressionist philosophising
that tries to make sense – narrative or mythical sense – of the
various forms and manifestations of human creative activity.
Two themes in particular emerged in the course of this
development: the pre-eminence of music as the highest

realm of aesthetic experience, and the superiority of Symbol over Allegory in terms of artistic beauty and truth.[24] And these assumptions went together to the extent that language in its symbolic mode was treated, like music, as a means of overcoming the otherwise insurmountable split between thought and perception, subject and object, concepts and sensuous intuitions. If literature henceforth aspired to the condition of music, then it did so in the shape of a symbolist aesthetic which dreamed that language might at least momentarily transcend these hateful antinomies, thus managing to reconcile the world of phenomenal perception with the realm of noumenal reason. And this remains the belief of those modern interpreters for whom the Romantic ideal of 'unmediated vision' retains its considerable seductive power. In the words of M H Abrams,

> the best Romantic meditations on a landscape ... all manifest a transaction between subject and object in which the thought incorporates and makes explicit what was already implicit in the outer scene.[25]

Such moments can only come about through the power of language to fuse organically with nature and the objects of sensory perception, so that meaning is experienced as somehow consubstantial with the images, memories or natural forms which evoke these visionary states of mind. The relation between signifier and signified is no longer conceived (in Saussurian terms) as an arbitrary link, one that exists solely as a product of linguistic and social convention. Rather, it is thought of as a constant struggle to transcend that unfortunate condition, to achieve a kind of hypostatic union between thought, language and reality where all such distinctions would at last fall away.

Paul de Man's classic essay 'The Rhetoric of Temporality' sets out to deconstruct this high-romantic dream of origins, truth and presence. De Man mounts a case against the Symbolist aesthetic which draws attention to the blind-spots of argument that recur in the various programmatic statements put forward by its past and present-day adherents. Such thinking is a potent source of ideological mystification, a habit of thought that persistently ignores or represses those aspects of language that resist assimilation to an order of transcendent, ahistorical truth. It does so primarily by masking the temporal aspect of all interpretation, the fact that knowledge can never achieve such a moment of ecstatic visionary inwardness with nature. In the criticism of neo-Romantic theorists like Abrams it is made to seem at times as if

> imagination did away with analogy altogether ... and replaced it with a genuine and working monism. 'Nature is made thought and thought nature [Abrams writes] both by their sustained interaction and by their seamless metaphoric continuity'.[26]

But such ideas are undermined by a reading that shows how the Symbolist aesthetic cannot in the end make good its claims; how language itself undoes the illusion that mind and nature might ever attain this kind of idealised organic relation. For it always turns out, according to de Man, that the passages in question depend for their effect on tropes and devices which stubbornly resist this will to aesthetic transcendence. Chief among these is the figure of allegory, treated condescendingly by critics and philosophers like Goethe, Coleridge and Hegel. For allegory works precisely by insisting on the arbitrary character of signs, the lack of any ultimate or quasi-natural bond between signifier and signified. To interpret a text allegorically is to read it as an artificial construct whose meaning unfolds in a narrative or temporal dimension, and where signs point back to no ultimate source in the nature of 'organic' or phenomenal perception.

Thus allegory serves as a powerful demystifying trope, one that resists the truth-claims vested in Romantic or Symbolist conceptions of art. In these latter, 'the valorization of symbol at the expense of allegory' can be seen to coincide with 'the growth of an aesthetics that refuses to distinguish between experience and the representation of experience'.[27] This can never be the case with allegorical modes of understanding, marked as they are by a constant awareness of the gap that opens up, as soon as we begin to interpret, between subject and object, nature and language, the desire for a purely self-originating source of meaning and the knowledge that no such source can be found. Thus

> the prevalence of allegory always corresponds to the unveiling of an authentically temporal destiny ... [and] this unveiling takes place in a subject that has sought refuge against the impact of time in a natural world to which, in truth, it bears no resemblance.[28]

In this relatively early (1971) essay, de Man has nothing explicit to say about the political or ideological values that attach to these opposing conceptualisations of language. But his later work brought a sharper awareness of the ways in which aesthetic ideology worked to mystify the relationship between history, language and the processes of critical thought.[29] For it was, he argued, precisely by construing that relationship in terms of an organic or quasi-natural principle that various forms of post-Kantian aesthetics had managed to avoid any rigorous reflection on the historicity or temporal predicament of all understanding. And in the case of allegory, conversely, it is the material resistance that language puts up – the discrepancies between what a text actually *says* and what a mainstream, traditional or conformist reading would predictably have it mean – that opens a space for political or counter-hegemonic readings.

Hence de Man's claim that such textual complications in some sense 'generate history', a claim that is all too easily misread as a species of mystifying 'textualist' rhetoric designed to head off any serious thought about the relationship between literature, politics and history. In an essay on Rousseau's *Social Contract* he even goes so far as to assert that

> the political destiny of man is structured like and derived from a linguistic model that exists independently of nature and independently of the subject.

And yet, the passage goes on,

> contrary to what one might think, this enforces the inevitably political nature, or more correctly, the 'politicality' (since one

could hardly speak of 'nature' in this case) of all forms of human
language, and especially of rhetorically self-conscious or literary
language.[30]

For it is language that works to promote the various forms of
ideological misrecognition, forms whose common feature is
this habit of confusing the cultural-linguistic with the
natural-phenomenal realm. But it is language also that
provides a model for deconstructing that conservative
mystique, for showing how organic or naturalising
metaphors begin to break down, and how history effectively
reasserts its hold at the point where understanding is forced
to recognise its own temporal condition. And this conflict of
interests is sharpened and intensified when language has to
bear – as it does in all versions of aesthetic ideology – a
weight of significance tied up with its presumed capacity to
articulate the claims of sensuous cognition and conceptual
understanding.

> What gives the aesthetic its power and hence its practical,
> political impact, is its intimate link with knowledge, the
> epistemological implications that are always in play when the
> aesthetic appears over the horizon of discourse.

This excursion into the province of literary theory may help
us to grasp what is at stake when Bloch insists that the
meaning of music can only be grasped in allegorical terms.
For there is, as we have seen, a strong countervailing
tradition of post-romantic thought, one that treats music as
the highest form of art on account of its unique expressive
power, its capacity to fuse the phenomenal sound-world of
sensuous experience with a sense of some ultimate
significance beyond the grasp of mere reason. When
literature seeks to emulate this condition, it does so in forms
– like that of lyric poetry – where language seems closest to
the lived actualities of sensuous experience, where the sound
(in Pope's phrase) is supposedly 'an echo to the sense', and
where subjectivity is felt to exist in a peculiarly intimate
relation to the objects of outward, phenomenal experience.
As the language of Symbolism takes precedence over that of

allegory, so the lyric achieves absolute pride of place in a scale of hierarchical values which tends to demote those other, more extended or narrative forms where language cannot possibly achieve this degree of aesthetic formalisation.

Michael Sprinker has addressed this topic in a book that seeks to articulate the claims of deconstruction with those of Marxist ideological critique.[32] He shows just how close was the perceived relationship between music, lyric poetry and those versions of the Symbolist aesthetic that found their way into literary criticism through the precepts and practice of poets like Gerard Manley Hopkins, writers who determined to break with the conventional forms of their day and achieve a more 'musical', sensuous or immediate quality of language and style. To their way of thinking,

> lyric poetry not only aspires to the condition of music, it offers instances (in meter and in its various phonic devices) of genuine musicality.[33]

But what Sprinker finds in his reading of a Hopkins sonnet is evidence that language resists this kind of ultimate musicalisation; that meaning cannot in the end be assimilated to the order of phenomenal perception, since language turns out to signify in ways that exceed and complicate the presumed correspondence between sound, sense and the realm of phenomenal experience. The standard exegetical line with Hopkins is to argue that the poetry achieves such correspondence to a quite remarkable degree, and can thus be said to manifest God's presence in the world through a kind of literalised incarnationist metaphor.

> Nothing is more familiar … than [this] claim for the aesthetic unity of a work based upon the congruence of the work's phonic and semantic features.[34]

But in fact, as Sprinker shows, such readings are highly selective, ignoring those dissonant details of sound and sense that cannot be reduced to such a preconceived order of aesthetic harmonisation. When read deconstructively, with an eye to such details, the poetry can appear to suggest just the opposite: that language is not so much an 'organic' phenomenon as a field of conflicting rhetorical forces where unity is achieved only through a naturalised habit of reading that ignores these signs of internal disruption. Like de Man, Sprinker locates the source of this delusion in a form of deep-laid 'aesthetic ideology' that blinds critics to the various ways in which language inevitably fails to 'harmonise' with the world of phenomenal cognition. And it is precisely in so far as it encourages such forms of aesthetic mystification that music comes to occupy its privileged place in post-symbolist aesthetic theory.

This is why Bloch in the end asserts his distance from the potent ideology inscribed in such forms of organicist thinking.

> Nothing in his [Schopenhauer's] account is more obscure than 'the ineffably inward nature of music', and nothing is more incomprehensible than 'the profound wisdom it contains as a language which reason does not understand', but which Schopenhauer still claims to have fully decoded.[35]

Such notions are at odds with his own belief that music is not a 'natural' phenomenon, or at least not one whose nature could ever be theorised in terms borrowed from the realm of perceptual experience. They are regressive in the sense that they betray the listener back into a world of inchoate sensations, emotions and fantasies where thought – as in Schopenhauer – becomes the mere plaything of archaic instinctual drives. In Wagnerian opera Bloch hears something like a full-scale programmatic realisation of Schopenhauer's aesthetic creed. Only rarely is this music

> attuned to a signal of liberation that would break Nature's spell ... Nearly all Wagner's creatures are at home in the volcanic world of impulse, in the Schopenhauerian Will, acting and talking from within this natural dreamstate.[36]

As Bloch understands it, this confinement to a realm of dark, destructive, elemental passions is a price that is inevitably paid for the identification of music with nature, and of nature in turn with those inhuman forces that exist beyond hope of redemptive change.

So Bloch's utopianism doesn't at all imply that the history of music as we have known it so far has been a progress toward ever more refined or humanly adequate means of expression. Such ideas are just a version of the shallow optimism which equates the utopian element in music with the signs of mere technical advance, like Wagner's exploitation of hitherto unknown harmonic and chromatic resources. They are thus bound up with that same aesthetic ideology which identifies the ultimate meaning of music with its power to evoke ideas directly through sensuous intuitions, without (as in the case of other art-forms) any detour by way of mere words, concepts or mediating representations. Bloch never ceases to denounce the idea that musical progress can be read off as so many stages on the path to some ultimate fulfilment that had always, so to speak, been latent in its nature as an organically evolving language. On the contrary, as he writes:

> social trends have been reflected and expressed in the sound-material, far beyond the unchanging physical facts ... No other art is conditioned by social factors as much as the purportedly self-acting, self-sufficient art of music; historical materialism, with the accent on 'historical', abounds here.[37]

Organicist ideas of music tend to go along with evolutionist accounts of musical history, both being governed by the same root metaphor, one that traces the development of forms and expressive styles through a process of quasi-natural growth and fruition. This metaphor is particularly prevalent in treatments of the German line of succession from Bach, through Beethoven to Brahms, Wagner, Mahler and Schoenberg. Often it is presented in terms of a struggle for legitimacy, a debate as to where exactly the line runs, or which composers are the rightful heirs. Thus loyalties divided over the rival merits of claimants like Brahms and Wagner, the one representing a development primarily in formal or structural terms, the other seen as extending the harmonic resources of musical language to a point of extreme chromaticism that was always latent, just waiting to be realised, in earlier stages of the same evolution. Hence Schoenberg's polemical essay 'Brahms The Progressive', intended both to rescue Brahms from the misconceived devotions of his more conservative admirers, and to establish the claims of his own (Schoenberg's) music as deriving simultaneously from Wagner and Brahms, and thus carrying on the high destiny of German musical tradition.[38]

This argument is connected with Schoenberg's attempt to establish the legitimacy of atonal and twelve-tone music by deriving its harmonic innovations from the very nature of the sound-material that composers had to work with. If such music encountered widespread resistance, it was only because it reached out into more remote regions of the overtone series, renouncing the desire for home-keys and familiar tonal centres that continued to exert a regressive hold upon listeners trained in the old expectations. Thus Schoenberg's defence takes the form of an appeal to nature as the ground of all musical experience, the source of phenomenal perceptions whose validity is beyond all doubt, since they correspond to what is actually given in the sound-world of music itself.[39] His own passage from a post-Wagnerian chromaticism, through atonality to twelve-tone technique can thus be presented as the outcome of a dynamic process set in motion by the very nature of music, but finding its highest, most evolved forms in the great tradition of German composers from Bach to Schoenberg. One can trace the emergence of this organicist doctrine through the various theories and critical approaches devised by 19th century commentators in the effort to make sense of music that defied analysis on the older, more conventional terms.[40] It took hold at about the same time that post-Kantian philosophers and literary theorists were elaborating an aesthetics of the symbol that likewise claimed to reconcile concepts with sensuous intuitions, or to provide a bridge between the natural world and the realm of articulate thought. And indeed, the two developments are closely allied, since they both locate the ultimate value of aesthetic experience in the power of art to reconcile otherwise disparate orders of experience. History itself can then be viewed in a providential light, as the process whereby certain languages, art-forms and cultural modes of expression evolve toward a state of organic unity in which ⌐ consciousness discovers its authentic relationship to nature. ⌐ And it is, as we have seen, very often in connection with music – or with various images and metaphors drawn from the realm of musical experience – that this aesthetic ideology ⌐ achieves its most seductive and plausible form.

Bloch holds out against all versions of this organicist creed, whether applied to individual works of art or to the history through which these works come into being. 'A rudimentary musical theme', he writes, 'however well chosen, sharply delineated and productive of movement, is no acorn from which ... the forest of the symphony will grow.'[41] His reason for resisting such analogies is that they carry along with them an inbuilt tendency to treat the work as something closed, finished, possessed of its own self-determining principle and thus incapable of taking on a new significance. And when this same aesthetic ideology is extended from art to history itself – as occurs in the discourse of late romantic criticism – then history is likewise immobilised, reduced to an outcome of natural forces whose origin is thrown back into a mythical past. Bloch is implacably opposed to such ideas, and for much the same reason that Walter Benjamin offers in his 'Theses on the Philosophy of History'. Benjamin rejects any notion of future time as continuous or homogeneous with our knowledge of past events. 'Historicism' and 'universal history' are the characteristic forms of this Hegelian drive to assimilate the future to a kind of organic temporality where nothing can possibly come as a shock to our settled beliefs and expectations. For Benjamin, on the contrary, 'history is the subject of a structure whose site is not empty, homogeneous time, but time filled by the presence of the now'.[42] And again:

> to articulate the past historically does not mean to recognize it 'the way it really was'. It means to seize hold of a memory as it flashes up at a moment of danger [which] affects both the content of the tradition and its receivers.[43]

Superficially there might seem little enough resemblance

between Bloch's utopian outlook and Benjamin's dark-hued meditations. But in fact Bloch perceives quite as clearly as Benjamin the risk that any hope stored up in past meanings and memories will be repossessed by the forces of cultural inertia; that tradition will assert its hold once again as a weapon of those with the power to dictate what shall count as authentic history. And one major form in which this power stands revealed is the notion of history as an organic process, a providence whose meaning unfolds through time in a series of exemplary figures, meanings or events.

In musical terms, this leads to the idea of Wagner as in some sense fulfilling the destiny prefigured in earlier composers like Bach, Mozart and Beethoven. Bloch very firmly rejects this idea, asserting that Beethoven

> is as superior to Wagner as Kant is to Hegel, and as the restless *a priori* in man is to any kind of prematurely fulfilled objectivism'[44]

These analogies, though presented in cryptic form, will I think stand up to a good deal of conceptual unpacking. Wagner's music is Hegelian in the sense that it seeks to transcend all antinomies through an ultimate merging of mind and nature, subject and object in a realm where no such distinctions any longer obtain. In Beethoven, conversely, the will to transcendence is encountered in a restless, dynamic form which precludes such a false or premature sense that this state has actually been achieved. Again we can turn to de Man – especially his late essays on Kant – for a better grasp of how these issues in the province of philosophy connect with Bloch's understanding of music. De Man brings out very clearly the ways in which Kant is forced back upon allegorical or figural modes of explanation at exactly those points where his argument is most concerned with questions of epistemological and ethical truth.[45] Kant's very desire not to be seduced into forms of premature identification – as between the realms of phenomenal cognition, understanding and practical (ethical) reason – obliges him to resort to such figural strategies despite his repeated warnings elsewhere against what he sees as their seductive and misleading nature.[46]

This is not the place to rehearse de Man's arguments in detail. But their upshot can be summarised as follows: that allegory is the one authentic mode of reading in so far as it acknowledges the inevitable failure of all attempts to make meaning coincide with the realm of intuition or phenomenal self-evidence. To read allegorically is always to recognise that understanding is a temporal process, one that takes place not on the instant of punctual, self-present perception but through a constant anticipatory awareness of what is lacking in the present. Thus

> allegory designates primarily a distance in relation to its own origin, and, renouncing the nostalgia and the desire to coincide, it establishes its language in the void of this temporal difference.[47]

For de Man, as indeed for Bloch, it is only by accepting this condition of deferred interpretative grasp that thought can hold out against the delusive promise of fully achieved understanding. This is why notions of 'organic form', however refined or elaborate, always tend to seek their ultimate grounding in a principle of order which denies or suppresses the restless, utopian, forward-looking character of musical experience. Such ideas cannot account for the meaning of music, 'any more than logic and a theory of categories account for metaphysics'. They treat the formal element as something implicitly there from the outset, given as part of the work's thematic material, and subject to development only in so far as that material contains *in nuce* every detail of its own unfolding. Whereas for Bloch, 'the theme is not found at the start but overlies it like an *a priori* that is working from a distance'.[48] And this means that any analysis of musical form based on notions of organic unity or self-contained thematic development will be closed to whatever potential the work may possess for renewing our perceptions through repeated acts of creative listening. What then takes hold is

> the same fatalism and occasionalism, the same transfer of 'efficient cause' to the first principle alone as applies in all other reactionary Romantic systems.[49]

In its place Bloch proposes something more like an Aristotelian teleology, one that treats music in terms of its 'final cause', the end toward which everything strives in the effort to realise its full potential.

It is in Beethoven especially that Bloch discovers this resistance to preconceived ideas of what does or should constitute musical form. He takes the first movement of the *Eroica* symphony as an instance of how such ideas break down when confronted with music that everywhere exceeds their explanatory grasp. Thus

> the question of sonata design is primarily focused ... on the problem of the new, unsuspected, productive element, the dissipating, mutually overriding and self-surmounting sequence of events in the development section ... He is under no binding obligation toward either an individual theme or even to all the initial themes. He can restrict himself to mere thematic fragments of motifs, can even depart from the guiding thread of tonality ... provided that after all his divagations he does reestablish the surrendered key, the secret and, in the end, triumphantly emerging end-cause of the entire harmonisation.[50]

This passage gives a fair impression of Bloch's style, his use of open-ended syntactic patterns and phrase-structures which gather momentum from point to point, and thus prevent the reader from resting content with what has been said so far. It is a style, once again, that enacts *allegorically* the distance between musical meaning and verbal description, in this case by deferring the moment of ultimate grasp through a sequence of fragmentary hints and suggestions that cannot be reduced to any straightforward sense of thematic coherence. Thus Bloch rejects any appeal to 'programmatic' elements as such, even in a case like the *Eroica*'s first movement, where the extra-musical associations are particularly hard to ignore. For 'the dictatorship of the programme' leads, as he argues, to 'an almost entirely unmusical line of reasoning', one that produces an essentially fixed, preconditioned habit of response, and thus ignores what is going on from moment to moment as the music reworks and transfigures its thematic material.

He is equally opposed to any kind of analytical criticism

which seeks to articulate musical structure in terms of some quasi-mathematical ideal or rule-governed formal procedure. The fallacy here is the assumption, going back at least to Pythagoras, that music is the sensuous embodiment of laws, ratios and harmonic proportions which exist in nature – as witnessed by phenomena like the overtone series – but whose true character can be best be divined from their kinship with pure mathematics. Again, this may remind us of Schoenberg's attempt to deduce the predestined historical emergence of twelve-tone composition from its supposed grounding in the realm of phenomenal perception. Bloch's main objections to this whole way of thinking are to be found in his 1925 essay 'On the Mathematical and Dialectical Character in Music'. Here he rejects every version of the analogy between music and mathematics, pointing out that wherever such thinking has prevailed it has also tended to arrest musical history by laying down laws of harmonic proportion that supposedly reflect a natural, immutable order of things. One example is the Pythagorean ban on intervals of the third and sixth, felt to represent a destabilising force within the quaternary system of harmonic-numerical consonance, and hence proscribed as a matter of ethical as well as musical decorum.

> Mathematics remains the key to Nature, but it can never be the key to history and to those self-informings by the non-identical and the asymmetrical which number was devised to counter, and for whose gradual objectification the human spirit ultimately produced great music.[51]

It is precisely where music takes a heretical turn, where it outruns all the laws of harmonic good form, of preconceived symmetry and structural proportion, that it becomes open to this transformation by a process whose character is *historical* through and through, and not subject to any such formal-transcendental laws.

> It was only the need of polyphonic song, which did not worry about mathematics, that resorted to the forbidden third, thereby attaining the major chord, that cornerstone of all harmonic development.[52]

And such changes come about, not in answer to some
principle of historical inevitability, but through music's
responsiveness to new configurations of social and historical
hope.

It should be clear by now that Bloch's utopian outlook is
not to be confused with the kind of wishful thinking which
treats every setback on the road to enlightenment as a mere
local aberration. In fact it is more akin to Benjamin's sense
of future time as momentarily prefigured in the present, as
offering itself to a redemptive vision that must seize its
opportunity on the instant if everything is not to fall back
under the sway of cultural inertia and reaction. But it is
Adorno, not Benjamin, who provides the most obvious
point of departure for assessing how far Bloch's philosophy
stands up to the rigours of negative critique. For Adorno,
the very notion of affirmative culture – of art as an index to
the liberating power of human creativity – had to be
renounced in the light of such evidence as modern history
afforded. Hence the relentlessly self-denying character of
Adorno's thought, his insistence that the only kind of truth
now available is that which unmasks the delusive
truth-claims of all aesthetic ideologies and other such falsely
positive systems of thought.[53] Since Schiller, philosophy had
held out the notion of art as a healing or reconciling power, a
realm of experience where the conflicts and antinomies of
alienated consciousness could at last find an image of perfect
fulfilment in the 'free play' of human creativity, of sensuous
cognitions in a state of ideally harmonious reciprocal
balance. This ideal had once possessed a genuine
emancipatory force, as in works like *Fidelio* or the Ninth
Symphony, music where the ethos of liberal humanism
found expression not only in dramatic terms, but in every
detail of the work's dynamic tonality and structural form.
But this moment had passed irrevocably, Adorno thought,
with the advent of a modern 'culture-industry' which had
taken over these musical resources, adapting them to the
purposes of passive consumption and utterly negating their
original redemptive character. Henceforth they could only
be heard as hollow gestures, as a language whose apparent
spontaneity, vigour and force were in fact mere symptoms of

cultural regression, of a music that recycled past styles and
forms in a mode of more or less unwitting self-parody. The
best that philosophy could do in face of this massive
reification was to denounce all forms of commodified
culture, maintain an intransigently negative attitude, and
thus keep faith with the critical spirit that had once found
authentic expression in the works of an earlier, more
hopeful epoch.

Schoenberg's music served Adorno as a measure of what
art might yet achieve in this implacably critical or
deconstructive mode. That is to say, it expressed the alien
reality of modern social conditions by refusing all forms of
aesthetic transcendence, by extending a tight compositional
control over every aspect of structure and style, and thus
giving the lie to notions of art as a source of compensatory
freedoms untouched by the grim truth of historical events.
In Adorno's words,

> The total rationality of music is its total organization. By means
> of organization, liberated music seeks to reconstitute the lost
> totality – the lost power and the responsible binding force of
> Beethoven. Music succeeds in so doing only at the cost of its
> freedom, and thereby it fails. Beethoven reproduced the
> meaning of tonality out of subjective freedom. The new
> ordering of twelve-note technique virtually extinguishes the
> subject.[54]

Thus Schoenberg's very 'failure', the fact that his music
cannot make good the Beethovenian promise, is also –
paradoxically – the source of its ultimate value and truth.
Max Weber had described the process of increasing
'rationalization' that marked the development of music in a
culture long subjected to the order of bourgeois social
relations, to the work ethic and its forms of instrumental or
means-end reasoning.[55] For Adorno, this process arrives at
its most advanced point in the serialist claim to derive all the
parameters of a musical work from a single generative source
(the tone-row) whose permutations would then account for
every aspect of its style and form. Such music 'fails' in so far
as it defeats its own object, negates the very impulse of
'subjective freedom', and thus falls prey to an extreme form

of reification which reflects the worst, the most inhuman aspects of present-day rationalised existence. But it also succeeds – and for just that reason – in exposing those conditions, forcing them to the point of manifest self-defeat, and thus closing off the various seductive escape-routes provided by music in its other, less taxing contemporary forms.

For Adorno, philosophical thinking is subject to the same necessity, compelled to keep faith with the values of enlightened reason but always in the knowledge that those values have been falsified, turned to inhuman or destructive ends, by the advent of a social order founded on eminently 'rational' means of surveillance and control. Hence Adorno's 'negative dialectics', a relentlessly self-critical habit of thought which interrogates its own procedures at every stage, resisting any kind of residual attachment to method or system.

> The life of the mind only attains its truth when discovering itself in desolation. The mind is not this power as a positive which turns away from a negative ... it is this power only when looking the negative in the face, dwelling upon it.[56]

This is not Adorno but Hegel, or rather it is Adorno quoting Hegel very pointedly against himself, against that version of Hegelian dialectic that identifies the present (for Hegel, Christianity and the Prussian nation-state) with a final overcoming of all antinomies. For Adorno, on the contrary, any suggestion that thinking might *presently* achieve such a state is at best mere utopian reverie, and at worst a delusion complicit with the forces that work to produce this predicament of chronic bad faith. As Fredric Jameson writes in his commentary on Adorno:

> the very mark of the modern experience of the world is that precisely such identity is impossible, and that the primacy of the subject is an illusion, that subject and outside world can never find such ultimate identity or atonement under present historical circumstances.[57]

Philosophy, like music, is confronted with this ultimate choice: *either* the pleasure that comes of regressing to an earlier, more 'positive' phase of cultural history, *or* the sad wisdom (Adorno's 'melancholy science') that results from perceiving how impossible it is for thought to maintain this deluded stance.

It might seem from all this that Adorno and Bloch are worlds apart in their attitude to music and music's role in the critique of existing social realities. And indeed their personal dealings were marked by a persistent habit of reserve, on Adorno's side at least, which suggests a deep measure of intellectual difference. But there is also a sense in which Bloch and Adorno were complementary thinkers, coming at the same basic problems and conflicts from opposed but not wholly incompatible points of view. In David Drew's words, 'the disillusionment Adorno pursues and cherishes so ardently belongs within the dark circle at the foot of Bloch's lighthouse, and is far removed from any modish cynicism.'[58] Indeed one can pick out many passages from Adorno that explicitly require some utopian dimension to complete and give purpose to the labours of negative thought. 'Without hope', Adorno writes, 'the idea of truth would be scarcely even thinkable, and it is the cardinal untruth, having recognised existence to be bad, to present it as truth simply because it has been recognised.'[59] This sentence could well have been taken from one of Bloch's meditations on the false positivity of present, self-evident fact, the way that our perceptions are hemmed in and distorted by the belief that what exists is the sole reality available to thought.

This underlying kinship is yet more evident when Adorno appeals to Kant's articulation of the faculties – of reason in its pure and practical forms with aesthetic judgment – to bring out their reciprocal involvement one with another. The passage needs quoting at length, since it is couched in that highly aphoristic but rigorously consequent style that Adorno adopted in order to head off the temptation of premature systematising thought.

> Is not indeed the simplest perception shaped by fear of the thing perceived, or desire for it? It is true that the objective meaning of knowledge has, with the objectification of the world, become

progressively detached from the underlying impulses; it is equally true that knowledge breaks down where its effort of objectification remains under the sway of desire. But if the impulses are not at once preserved and surpassed in the thought which has escaped their sway, then there will be no knowledge at all, and the thought that murders the wish that fathered it will be overtaken by the revenge of stupidity ... [This] leads directly to a depreciation of the synthetic apperception which, according to Kant, cannot be divorced from 'reproduction in imagination', from recollection.[60]

This is why aesthetic judgement plays such a crucial role in the Kantian theory of knowledge and perception. For it is, as we have seen, by way of the aesthetic that concepts join up with sensuous intuitions, thus providing a bridge between *a priori* knowledge and experience of the phenomenal world. And Adorno, like de Man, finds this union achieved not in a moment of self-present punctual grasp, but through a sequence of unstable and shifting relations where subject and object can never perfectly coincide. Thus when Kant speaks of the 'productive imagination', he connects it always with this temporal dimension where thought comes up against the limits of its static concepts and categories. This is the point, in de Man's reading, where Kantian critique takes on a distinctly allegorical aspect, a meaning that is deferred through the various figures, tropes and analogical examples to which Kant resorts in the course of his argument. And for Adorno likewise, there can be no moment of 'synthetic apperception' – no means of reconciling concepts with sensuous intuitions – that doesn't involve some appeal to desire, imagination and the future as a realm of as-yet unrealised possibility.

So it is wrong to assume that Bloch and Adorno are straightforwardly antagonistic thinkers, the one espousing a redemptive metaphysics of hope and secular salvation, the other renouncing all such beliefs in a grim determination not to be deceived by tokens of false promise. Among the many passages of Adorno that belie this reading, one in particular – from the closing paragraph of *Minima Moralia* – stands out for its clear statement of the need for negative thinking not to lose sight of its positive, utopian counterpart.

The only philosophy which can be responsibly practised in the face of despair is the attempt to contemplate all things as they would appear from the standpoint of redemption ... Perspectives must be fashioned that displace and estrange the world, reveal it to be, with its rifts and crevices, as indigent and distorted as it will appear one day in the messianic light.[61]

While the passage alludes more overtly to Benjamin, it also opens the way – as David Drew remarks – to a reading of Adorno's and Bloch's work that would treat them as paradoxically kindred thinkers, engaged in the same redemptive enterprise, though starting out from very different premises. For on Bloch's side also, any hope of attaining an authentically utopian perspective is dependent on thought's having first made the passage through a 'labour of the negative', an undeceiving process that leaves us the more acutely aware of our present, limited powers of perception. Thus

nobody has as yet heard Mozart, Beethoven or Bach as they are really calling, designating and teaching ... this objective-indeterminate element in music is the (temporary) defect of its qualities.[62]

If Adorno's negativity cannot in the end do without a countervailing impulse of hope, then equally it is the case that Bloch's utopian outlook would collapse into mere facile optimism were it not for this chastening awareness of the obstacles – the pressures of social and historical circum-stance – that stand in its path.

The same applies to de Man's practice of deconstructive reading, on the face of it a wholly negative practice, in so far as it works to undo or to problematise everything we commonly take for granted about language, experience and the nature of human understanding. Music is important for de Man because it has served as a source of that potent aesthetic ideology which locates the redemptive capacity of art in its promise of transcending the conflict between sensuous and intellectual realms of experience. But in fact, de Man argues, this promise has always turned out to be delusory, not least in those thinkers (like Rousseau) who have expressly treated music as a 'natural' language of emotions, a language that is (or that ought to be) untouched by the decadent, corrupting influence of latter-day civilised life.[63] Thus Rousseau praises the Italian music of his time for its unforced, spontaneous character, the fact that it remains close to those sources of vitality and warmth that issue directly in melody and the singing line. And he attacks contemporary French composers like Rameau for their practice of elaborate harmonisation and their use of an 'advanced' contrapuntal style which leads them to lose touch with those same elemental passions and desires. Melody is good because it belongs to that stage of human existence when the passions can still find authentic voice and there is no need, as yet, for the resort to mere artifice and stylised convention. Harmony is bad because it goes along with all those other concomitants of modern 'civilised' life – social inequality, delegated power, civil and political institutions, distinctions of class or rank on an unjust, arbitrary basis – which Rousseau denounces in the 'advanced' democracies of his day.

So his treatment of music is precisely analogous to Rousseau's thinking on matters of ethical, social and political concern. 'Man was born free, but is everywhere in chains', the freedom identified with a lost state of natural grace which has long since been overtaken by these melancholy symptoms of latter-day decline. And this also applies to language, since speech had its origin (so Rousseau asserts) in the same elemental passions and desires which produced spontaneous melody. In this original condition, language was a kind of primitive speech-song which expressed human sentiments simply and directly without any detour through arbitrary signs and conventions. For there was, as yet, no need for people to disguise and dissimulate their meaning, to adopt such forms of linguistic subterfuge by way of exerting power over others. To speak was necessarily to mean what one said, since language gave access to the speaker's innermost thoughts and sentiments, in a context of ideally reciprocal exchange where no advantage could possibly accrue from lies, hypocrisy or pretence. But here again progress has taken its toll by requiring a different, more sophisticated kind of language, one that is able to articulate abstract ideas, and to convey them not, as was once the case, through an intimate face-to-face communion of souls, but through forms of elaborated social code devoid of authentic meaning. Thus language, like music, registers the impact of a civilising process which in truth is nothing of the kind; a process that alienates man from nature, language from the expression of genuine feeling, and society from those ties of communal trust and understanding which alone provide the basis – so Rousseau believes – for a state of harmonious coexistence.

De Man's main argument is that Rousseau is too canny, too rhetorically self-aware to be wholly taken in by this seductive myth of origins. That is, he may *declare* quite explicitly that language is authentic only where it approximates to a kind of pre-articulate speech-song; that culture supervenes upon nature as a kind of progressive catastrophe, a history of absolute loss and decline; and that only by returning to a pure state of nature can humankind escape from this sorry predicament. But what emerges in the course of de Man's reading is a subtext of unsettling rhetorical implications, passages where Rousseau is constrained to state just the opposite of his overt or express intentions. Thus language turns out to be strictly inconceivable except on the basis of arbitrary signs, codes and socialised conventions which cannot have existed in that first, happy state. And Rousseau's argument again comes up against the limits of intelligibility when he tries to give substance to the claim that human beings once enjoyed a 'natural' form of organic communal life, at a time when culture had not yet obtruded its alien codes and customs. For there is simply no conceiving of society except in terms of a differential system that must always to some extent – even in 'primitive' cultures – rest upon distinctions of class, gender, kinship and other such socially-imposed categories. Rousseau is in this sense a proto-structuralist *malgré lui*, obliged to acknowledge – implicitly at least – that language and society can only exist in separation from the state of nature, or only in so far as they exhibit all the signs of cultural organisation. Any 'language' that lacked the identifying marks of structural relationship and difference would in fact not be language at all, but merely a string of pre-articulate sounds with some possible emotive significance. And likewise, any 'culture' or 'society' that hadn't yet developed to the stage of hierarchical structures, kinship-systems and so forth, would for that very reason elude all possible terms of description or analysis.

Now de Man's point is that Rousseau himself deconstructs the Rousseauist myth of origins, or – more precisely – that his text provides all the requisite materials for its own deconstructive reading. It is the mainstream *interpreters* who, with their confident knowledge of his meaning and intentions, read with an eye only to those passages or levels of explicit statement that serve to confirm their stubborn preconceptions. In so doing, they are blinded to rhetorical complexities which in fact – so de Man argues – can be seen to undo that naive mystique of origins, presence and naturalised meaning that supposedly lies at the heart of Rousseau's philosophy. And it is here that the instance of music plays a crucial role in de Man's argument. For it is usually taken as read by the commentators that Rousseau's thinking on this topic follows the familiar pattern; that he associates authentic musical expression with a language of strongly emotive and sensuous appeal that speaks directly to the heart by virtue of precisely those qualities. From which it follows that music must enter upon the road to decadence as soon as it acquires the 'civilised' graces of harmony, counterpoint, elaborated structure and all the other signs of its present, unnatural condition. And indeed Rousseau says just that in a number of passages that leave little room for a contrary or deconstructive reading. But he also says the following (as cited by de Man):

> In a harmonic system, a given sound is nothing by natural right. It is neither tonic, nor dominant, harmonic or fundamental. All these properties exist as relationships only and since the entire system can vary from bass to treble, each sound changes in rank and place as the system changes in degree.[64]

Nor does this apply to one system only – the 'harmonic' – as opposed to some other, more natural language of music that would operate in terms of melody alone, and thus escape the bad necessity imposed by the decadent turn toward harmony. For Rousseau is equally clear on the point that melody without harmony is unthinkable; that there is always an implicit harmonic dimension to even the simplest melodic idea, since otherwise we would hear it as simply a series of disconnected notes, lacking any sense of cadence or musical shape. Thus Rousseau is brought round *by the logic of his own argument* to concede that music is not, after all, a natural language of the emotions, a language whose meaning coincides at every point with the nature of its humanly-expressive sound material. Rather, it is a 'system' of tonal relationships that belongs entirely to the history of musical styles, genres, forms and conventions, and which cannot be grasped except in terms of the structural properties that make such a system possible. Rousseau very often states just the opposite, but his statements are just as often undone by the clear implications of his own more consequent thinking.

For de Man, this ambivalence in Rousseau's philosophy of music is an index to the tensions that emerge everywhere in his writing. In each case there is a conflict between Rousseau's desire to discover some authentic, natural point of origin beyond the bad effects of civilised life, and his forced recognition that no such discovery is possible; that language, art and society were *always already* caught up in that process of decline, no matter how far one tries to push back toward a lost age of communal innocence and grace. And this conflict is nowhere more evident (so de Man argues) than in Rousseau's reflections on the phenomenology of musical perception.

> On the one hand, music is condemned to exist always as a moment, as a persistently frustrated intent toward meaning; on the other hand, this very frustration prevents it from remaining within the moment. Musical signs are unable to coincide: their dynamics are always oriented toward the future of their repetition, never toward the consonance of their simultaneity. Even the potential harmony of the single sound, *à l'unisson*, has to spread itself out into a pattern of successive repetition; considered as a musical sign, the sound is in fact the melody of its potential repetition.[65]

Music thus serves as the single most striking instance of de

Man's general thesis: that whenever Rousseau seeks to articulate his philosophy of nature and origins, he must always have recourse to a language that implicitly calls such thinking into question. 'Music is the diachronic version of the pattern of non-coincidence within the moment.'[66] For this pattern is repeated in language itself, where meaning can never be consistently reduced to an order of pure, self-present, univocal sense.

What then emerges in the reading of Rousseau's texts is an *allegory* of music's failure to achieve that wished-for natural state, since neither in music itself nor in the language that purportedly emulates music can any such condition be realised. As we have seen, de Man thinks of allegory primarily in terms of its demystifying power, its capacity to keep us always in mind of the gap that opens up between nature and language, phenomenal cognition and linguistic meaning. Music has very often served the purposes of aesthetic ideology by maintaining the delusory promise of a language that would finally transcend this condition, overcoming the ontological gulf between signs and sensuous intuitions. But this promise has just as often gone along with a deeply conservative mystique that assimilates music to the world of natural processes and forms, and which thus cuts it off from any intelligible relationship to history, politics and cultural change. And indeed, this argument finds ample confirmation in subsequent versions of the Rousseauist myth, where often the theme of a return to nature takes on a decidedly conservative toning. It is then used – by ideologues like Burke – not to criticise some existing state of society, but to argue that such criticism is pointless and misguided, since national cultures evolve through a process of 'organic' growth and development which cannot be influenced (except for the worse) by any mere spirit of reformist zeal. This shift in the political currency of Rousseauist ideas is very evident in the later writings of Coleridge, and thereafter in a line of conservative culture-critics whose chief modern spokesman is T S Eliot.[67] And one major source of such thinking – as de Man makes clear – is that mode of aesthetic ideology which identifies language in its highest, most expressive forms with a

principle of nature that can then be extended to organicist ⎤
metaphors of history and social evolution. 'What we call ⎮
ideology is precisely the confusion of linguistic with natural ⎯
reality, of reference with phenomenalism.' From which it ⎮
follows, according to de Man, that ⎦

> more than any other mode of enquiry ... the linguistics of
> literariness is a powerful and indispensable tool in the
> unmasking of ideological aberrations, as well as a determining
> factor in accounting for their occurrence.[68]

We can now begin to see why Bloch insists so strongly that
music is not a 'natural' art-form, at least in any sense that
could justify the notion that its meaning derives from its
phenomenal or sensory-acoustic nature. Hence his opposi- ⎮
tion to Schopenhauer's aesthetic, where music takes
precedence over the other arts on account of its supposedly
inhabiting a realm of primeval, undifferentiated Will, a
realm where mere intellect has no place and we experience
nature as a flux of inchoate desires, instincts and sensations.
Hence also his rejection of the opposite fallacy, that which
equates the expressive power of music with the laws of
mathematical proportion and harmony.

> Whereas music as a mood remains buried within the soul and
> seems the most chthonian of the arts, so-called *musica* ⎮
> *mathematica* becomes wholly Uranian and steps off into ⎮
> heaven.[69]

For Bloch, as indeed for de Man, music is allegorical
through and through, since its significance can never be
grasped once and for all in an act of fulfilled, self-present
perception. Otherwise, as he remarks, 'music would never
have gone beyond descending fifths'. Just as melody unfolds
through a temporal process, a sequence of intervals whose
character is essentially mobile or propulsive, so musical ⎮
works take on their significance through time, in a history of ⎮
successive re-encounters whose meaning can never be
exhausted. 'Any number of human tensions are added to the
tension of the fifth to create a more complicated cadence and
thus the history of music'.[70] Bloch goes on to elaborate this

point in a passage that resembles some of de Man's formulations, transposed into a language of explicitly utopian character.

> Melody's most remarkable attribute – the fact that in each of its notes, the immediate following one is latently audible – lies in human anticipation and hence in expression, which is now above all a humanized expression.[71]

And this can only come about, Bloch argues, in so far as music (or our thinking about music) breaks with the kind of regressive appeal exerted by the spell of nature.

These beliefs were put to the test in Bloch's collaboration with Otto Klemperer on a 1929 Vienna production of *The Flying Dutchman*. This caused a great scandal at the time and was later to mark them both down as cultural bolsheviks and enemies of National Socialism.[72] The production followed closely on performances of *Mahagonny* and *The Threepenny Opera*, and it made extensive use of Brechtian techniques to undermine the sanctified aura of Wagnerian music-drama. Bloch's contribution was a programmatic essay – 'The Rescue of Wagner through Surrealistic Penny Dreadfuls' – which argued for the vitalising power of popular culture, the intimations of a better world that could be glimpsed even in 'debased' modern forms like the comic strip, sentimental romance, advertisements and adventure stories.[73] The reactions were predictable: it seemed, as David Drew nicely comments, that 'Bayreuth was about to be stormed by Peachum and his beggars'. But what lay behind this staging of the *Dutchman* was a practical experiment in redemptive hermeneutics, a version of Bloch's own ambivalent responses to Wagner. The hold of tradition could only be broken through a new kind of listening, one that denied itself the pleasures of a passive abandonment to nature's spell, and which understood music as the active prefiguring of forces and tensions beyond the grasp of any merely 'authentic' performing style. It is a theme that Bloch takes up in his essay 'Paradoxes and the Pastorale in Wagner's Music'. Where Wagner transcends the Schopenhauerian ethos, it is by virtue of his momentarily escaping the realm of blind passion or instinctual Will, and transforming this atavistic impulse into a music pregnant with future possibilities. At such moments,

> Wagner gives resonance its full due, like a vibration *ante rem* which continues to give out figured sound *in re*, not to say *post re datam*; a sound-figure through which it takes up objects of nature and seeks through art to raise them to a higher power.

This might seem utterly remote from what we learn of the Klemperer production, with its aim of 'rescuing' Wagner from the Wagner-cult by exposing his music to all manner of parody and down-market pastiche. But in fact there is a similar principle at work: namely, the belief that present conditions block and distort our ways of perceiving, so that for now at least the only way forward is to deconstruct the values, mythologies and forms of sanctified false consciousness that pass themselves off as 'natural' habits of response. It is here that Bloch's philosophy makes common cause with that strain of rigorously negative thinking espoused by theorists like Adorno and de Man. To keep faith with music's utopian potential may require an effort of demystification that appears superficially far removed from any hopeful or affirmative standpoint. But it is precisely this undeceiving 'labour of the negative' – this testing of hope through a hard-won knowledge of everything that presently conspires against it – which marks the difference between Bloch's way of thinking and other, more naive utopian creeds. Again, it is Adorno who provides the most fitting commentary when he writes that 'in the end hope, wrested from reality by negating it, is the only form in which truth appears'.[75]

Notes

[1] Fredric Jameson, *The Political Unconscious: narrative as a socially symbolic act*, Methuen 1981.
[2] See especially Louis Althusser, *For Marx* (trans. Ben Brewster), Allen Lane 1969.

[3] Marx, letter to Alfred Ruge, collected in Siegfried Kröner (ed), *Die Frühschriften*, Alfred Kröner, Stuttgart, 1979, p 171. Cited by Bloch in *The Principle Of Hope* (trans. Neville Plaice, Stephen Plaice & Paul Knight), Blackwell 1987, Vol 1, pp 155-6.

[4] Fredric Jameson, *Marxism And Form*, Princeton University Press 1971, pp 116-59.

[5] *The Principle Of Hope, op cit*.

[6] Bloch, *Essays in the Philosophy of Music* (trans. Peter Palmer), Cambridge University Press 1985.

[7] *The Principle Of Hope, op cit*, p 1064.

[8] Theodor Adorno, 'Bach Defended Against his Devotees', in *Prisms*, (trans. S. and S. Weber), Neville Spearman 1967.

[9] The Principle of Hope, *op cit*, p 1064.

[10] *Ibid*, p 1065.

[11] Arthur Schopenhauer, *The World As Will And Representation*, Vols I and II, Dover, New York 1958. See also Schopenhauer, *Parerga And Paralipomena: short philosophical essays*, Oxford University Press 1974.

[12] See for instance Bryan Magee, *The Philosophy Of Schopenhauer*, Oxford University Press, 1983

[13] *Essays in the Philosophy of Music, op cit*, p 127.

[14] *Ibid*, p 228.

[15] See Jacques Derrida, 'White Mythology: metaphor in the text of philosophy', in *Margins Of Philosophy* (trans. Alan Bass), University of Chicago Press 1982, pp 207-71.

[16] *Essays in the Philosophy of Music, op cit*, pp 130-1.

[17] Wayne Hudson, *The Marxist Philosophy of Ernst Bloch*, Macmillan 1982.

[18] *Essays in the Philosophy of Music, op cit*, p 120.

[19] Bloch, *Experimentum Mundi*, Suhrkamp Verlag, Frankfurt 1975.

[20] Friedrich Nietzsche, *The Birth of Tragedy* and *The Case of Wagner* (trans. Walter Kaufmann), Vintage Books, New York 1967.

[21] On the relationship between music, myth and ideology in Nietzsche, see especially Paul de Man, *Allegories Of Reading*, Yale University Press, New Haven, 1979, pp 79-102, and Michael Sprinker, *Imaginary Relations: aesthetics and ideology in the theory of historical materialism*, Verso 1987.

[22] See Immanuel Kant, *Critique Of Pure Reason* (trans. F Max Müller), Macmillan, New York 1922, p 116.

[23] On the relation between Kantian aesthetics and epistemology, see Paul de Man, 'Phenomenality and Materiality in Kant', in Gary Shapiro and Alan Sica (eds), *Hermeneutics: questions and prospects*, University of Massachusetts Press, Amherst 1984, pp 121-44.

[24] See Paul de Man, 'The Rhetoric of Blindness: Jacques Derrida's reading of Rousseau', in *Blindness And Insight: essays in the rhetoric of contemporary criticism*, Methuen 1983, pp 102-42.

[25] Cited by de Man in his essay 'The Rhetoric of Temporality', in *Blindness And Insight, op cit*, pp 187-228, p 195.

[26] *Ibid*, p 195.

[27] *Ibid*, p 188.

[28] *Ibid*, 206.

[29] See especially the essays collected in de Man, *The Resistance To Theory*, University of Minnesota Press 1986.

[30] *Allegories Of Reading, op cit*, p 156.

[31] De Man, 'Aesthetic Formalization: Kleist's *Uber das Marionetten-theater*', in *The Rhetoric Of Romanticism*, Columbia University Press 1984, pp 264-5.

[32] *Imaginary Relations, op cit*.

[33] *Ibid*, p 62.

[34] *Ibid*, p 68.

[35] *Essays on the Philosophy of Music, op cit*, p 220.

[36] *Ibid*, p 222.

[37] *Ibid*, p 200.

[38] See Arnold Schoenberg, 'Brahms the Progressive', in *Style And Idea* (trans. Dika Newlin), Faber 1975.

[39] Thus Schoenberg: 'even those who have so far believed in me will not want to acknowledge the necessary nature of this development ... I am being forced in this direction ... I am obeying an inner compulsion which is stronger than any upbringing' (cited by Charles Rosen, *Schoenberg*, Fontana 1975, p 15). Rosen's comments on this passage are worth quoting at length in the present context of argument. 'In his justification, Schoenberg brings forward the classic dichotomy of nature and civilization ... In this notorious pair, the rights are traditionally on the side of nature – and, indeed, Schoenberg's critics were to accuse him of violating the natural laws of music, of substituting a purely artificial system for one that [accorded with] the laws of physics ... If the dichotomy can so easily be stood on its head, it should lead us to be suspicious of the opposition. A great deal of nonsense has been written about the relation of music to the laws of acoustics ... but the irresistible force of history – Schoenberg's "inner compulsion" – ought not to inspire any greater confidence' (Rosen, p 15). These remarks have an obvious bearing on music's role as a privileged source of those organicist models and metaphors that characterise aesthetic ideology.

[40] On this and related questions, see Jacques Attali, *Noise: the political economy of music* (trans. Brian Massumi), Manchester University Press 1985; Alan Durant, *Conditions of Music*, Macmillan 1984; Joseph Kerman, *Musicology*, Fontana 1985; Richard Leppert, *Music and Image: domesticity, ideology and socio-cultural formation in Eighteenth-century England*, Cambridge University Press 1988; Richard Leppert and Susan McClary (eds), *Music And Society: the politics of composition, performance and reception*, Cambridge University Press 1988; Susan McClary, 'Pitches, Expression, Ideology: an exercise in mediation', *Enclitic*, Vol VII, 1983, pp 76-86; Richard Norton, *Tonality In Western Culture*, University of Pennsylvania Press 1984; Kingsley Price (ed), *On Criticizing Music: five philosophical perspectives*, Johns Hopkins University Press 1981; John Shepperd *et al* (eds), *Whose Music?: a sociology of musical languages*, Latimer 1978, and Rose Rosengard Subotnik, 'The Role of Ideology in the Study of Western Music', *Journal of Musicology*, Vol II, 1983, pp 1-12.

346   *Music and the Politics of Culture*

[41] *Essays on the Philosophy of Music, op cit*, p 108.

[42] Walter Benjamin, 'Theses on the Philosophy of History', in *Illuminations* (trans. Harry Zohn), Fontana 1970, pp 255-66; p 263.

[43] *Ibid*, p 257.

[44] *Essays on the Philosophy of Music, op cit*, p 35.

[45] 'Phenomenality and Materiality in Kant', *op cit*, and 'The Epistemology of Metaphor', in *Critical Inqiry*, Vol V, 1978, pp 13-30.

[46] For Kant's warning against the confusions created by uncontrolled figural language, see especially Section 59 of the *Critique Of Judgment* (trans. J C Meredith), Oxford University Press 1978. As de Man points out, Kant's language here is itself replete with metaphors, analogies and question-begging tropes which must at least throw doubt on philosophy's power to regulate its own discourse.

[47] 'The Rhetoric of Temporality', *op cit*, p 207.

[48] *Essays on the Philosophy of Music,* p 108.

[49] *Ibid*, p 129.

[50] *Ibid*, p 108.

[51] *Ibid*, p 169.

[52] *Ibid*, p 185.

[53] See especially Adorno, *Negative Dialectics*, (trans. E B Ashton) Routledge and Kegan Paul 1973; *Aesthetic Theory* (trans. C Lenhardt) Routledge 1984 and *Philosophy Of Modern Music* (trans. Anne G Mitchell and Wesley V Blomster), Sheed and Ward 1973.

[54] *Philosophy Of Modern Music, op cit*, p 69.

[55] Max Weber, *The Rational And Social Foundations Of Music* (trans. Don Martindale, Johannes Riedel and Gertrude Neuwirth), University of Illinois Press 1958.

[56] Cited by Adorno, *Minima Moralia* (trans. E F N Jephcott), New Left Books 1974, p 16.

[57] *Marxism And Form, op cit*, p 42.

[58] David Drew, Introduction to *Essays on the Philosophy of Music, op cit*, p xlii.

[59] *Minima Moralia, op cit*, p 98.

[60] *Ibid*, p 122.

[61] *Ibid*, p 247.

[62] *Essays on the Philosophy of Music*, p 207-8.

[63] 'The Rhetoric of Blindness', *op cit*, pp 102-41. De Man provides his own translation of passages from Rousseau, *Essai sur l'origine des langues*, Bibliothèque du Graphe, 1817.

[64] Rousseau, *op cit*, p 536; cited in 'The Rhetoric of Blindness', *op cit*, p 128.

[65] *Ibid*, p 129.

[66] *Ibid*, p 129.

[67] See especially T S Eliot, *Notes Towards The Definition Of Culture*, Faber 1948.

[68] *The Resistance To Theory, op cit*, p 11.

[69] *Essays on the Philosophy of Music*, p 210.

[70] *Ibid*, p 200.

[71] *Ibid*, p 200.

[72] On the background to this event and on Bloch's association with Klemperer, see Peter Heyworth, *Otto Klemperer: his life and times*, Vol I, Cambridge University Press 1983.

[73] These themes are also taken up in *The Principle Of Hope, op cit*, especially the section of Vol. I entitled 'Wishful Images in the Mirror: display, fairytale, travel, film, theatre', pp 337-447.

[74] *Essays on the Philosophy of Music*, p 181.

[75] *Minima Moralia*, op cit, p 98.

Notes On Contributors

Malcolm Barry is Director of Continuing Education at Goldsmiths' College, University of London. His research interests lie in two related fields: policy studies as applied to continuing education and the arts, and cultural politics with particular reference to contemporary music. He has published numerous essays and reviews, and is now planning a book on the work of Heinrich Schenker, the Austrian music theorist.

Alan Durant lectures in the Department of English Studies at the University of Strathclyde. He is the author of *Ezra Pound: Identity in crisis* and *Conditions of Music*, a book whose arguments are further developed in his essay for the present volume. He has also coedited *The Linguistics Of Writing*, and is currently at work on a book that examines the future of literary studies from a linguistic and inter-disciplinary standpoint.

Paul Harrington works in the Industrial Relations Division of the Civil Service. He grew up in the Cardiff dockside area and studied at Essex University. Since then he has written and produced a number of plays, including *Soliloquy And Aria* (1981), a monodrama with music about the death of Sylvia Plath, and *Intimate Confessions* (1984), an account of Wordsworth's revolutionary career as 'ardour recollected in complacency'.

Ken Hirschkop is a Teaching Fellow in English at the University of Southampton. He is currently at work on a book about the Soviet philosopher and literary theorist

Mikhail Bakhtin. He has contributed essays to various journals including *New Left Review, Poetics Today, Critical Inquiry* and *News From Nowhere*.

Meirion Hughes was educated at University College, Cardiff, where he took a degree in History and English. His subsequent research was concerned mainly with the seventeenth-century English Republican movement. He is a lecturer at Uxbridge College and is presently engaged (with Robert Stradling) on a substantial project to analyse the cultural origins and political projection of the 'English Musical Renaissance'.

David Matthews is a composer, writer and occasional broadcaster. He is the author of *Michael Tippett: An introduction* (Faber, 1980) and of numerous essays on contemporary music. His recent compositions include a work for Jill Gomez and the Bournemouth Sinfonietta, performed during the 1988 Promenade Concert season.

Wilfrid Mellers was Professor of Music at the University of York until his retirement in 1981. He has also taught at Cambridge, Birmingham and on a regular visiting basis at the University of Pittsburgh. He is a 'fairly prolific' composer with a bias toward music with literary and theatrical associations. His 16 books to date range from works on François Couperin, Bach and Beethoven to shorter studies of the Beatles, Bob Dylan, jazz and pop. His most recent is *The Masks of Orpheus*, a comparative account of versions of the Orpheus myth.

Christopher Norris is Professor of English at the University of Wales, Cardiff College. His books include a study of William Empson (1978) and six recent works on aspects of philosophy and literary theory. His volume *Jacques Derrida* appeared in the Fontana 'Modern Masters' series in 1987, followed by a study of Paul de Man and the politics of criticism. He has also edited essay-collections on Shostakovich, George Orwell and post-structuralist theory. His writings on music have appeared in various journals over the past ten years.

Lionel Pike is Senior Lecturer in Music and College Organist at Royal Holloway and Bedford New College (University of London). He is the author of *Beethoven, Sibelius and 'the profound logic'* (Athlone Press, 1978), and of studies in Renaissance and twentieth-century music. At present he is working on a book about the style and structure of late Renaissance compositions.

Claire Polin is Professor of Music at Rutgers University, New Jersey, where she teaches music history, theory and composition. Among her various awards and prizes was a Leverhulme Fellowship which enabled her to work from 1968-69 at the University of Wales, Aberystwyth. Her recordings include several works of her own and performances of music by Leonard Bernstein and others. Her book *Music of the Ancient Near East* was published by Vantage Press in 1954 and reprinted in 1975. She has also written numerous articles on ethnomusicology, early Welsh music, American psalmody and other topics.

Robert Stradling is Senior Lecturer in History at the University of Wales, Cardiff College. He is an established authority on the history of Spain, principally in the Early Modern period. His second book in that field, *Philip IV and the Government of Spain*, was published in 1988 by Cambridge University Press. His essays include contributions to *Shostakovich: the man and his music* and *Inside The Myth: George Orwell*, both published by Lawrence and Wishart.

Alastair Williams spent some years as a freelance orchestral musician in London before taking up his current position as a research student at Magdalen College, Oxford. His major interests are in postwar music, critical theory (especially the Frankfurt School), and the relation between these fields. He has written about issues in literary theory and cultural studies as well as pursuing his more specialised musical researches.

Nicholas Williams is a writer and musicologist who has also worked in music publishing.

Index